SPATIAL ECONOMIC THEORY

$$F_P$$

Edited by Robert D. Dean, William H. Leahy, and David L. McKee

SPATIAL

ECONOMIC

THEORY

THE FREE PRESS, NEW YORK · Collier–Macmillan Limited, London

Contents

Contents

Preface

In recent years, a small but growing number of enonomists in this country as well as other parts of the world have become increasingly interested in the study of spatial economics. No doubt part of this increased interest has been fostered by the realization that the way in which economic activity is spatially distributed has a significant bearing on the development problems of our urban and regional economies. Still another important reason for this attention is the growing awareness among economists that a comprehensive economic theory should consider both time and space dimensions.

The increasing importance attached to the analysis of spatial patterns of economic activity makes it imperative that more students and teachers of economics become exposed to the literature on this topic. Accordingly, we have put together a collection of the more important articles written on the subject of spatial economics since 1940. These articles, it should be added, focus attention on the theoretical aspects of the study of spatial economic activity — articles with an empirical bent have been purposefully excluded from this collection. It should also be noted that in order to have a book of manageable length, it was not possible to include in this collection all of the significant contributions in recent years. Moreover, it was felt necessary to include two articles that were written prior to World War II. The article by Harold Hotelling on spatial competition was included because it has given rise to ideas and concepts that continue to cause considerable debate among spatial economic theorists. Similarly, the article by Frank Fetter on market areas also lies outside the thirty-year period, but inasmuch as it provides the basis for the subsequent extension and development of the concept of market areas by other writers, we felt it to be a valuable addition to this volume.

The plan for this volume is simple. The introduction to the book consists of two articles, one by Edgar M. Hoover and the other by Leon Moses, which provide a general overview of the subject of spatial economics. Part I, "Least Cost Theory," deals with the role transport and operating costs play in the location of economic activities — particularly industrial activities. Part II, "Locational Interdependence, (Spatial Competition)," considers the location pattern of firms when they are faced with competition from other firms for markets. Part III, "Market Area Analysis," focuses attention on the determinants of the size and shape of the market area for a firm or industry; Part IV, "Locational Equilibrium Analysis," is concerned with optimal location patterns of industrial and agricultural firms as well as households. Part V, "General Equilibrium Theory," deals with the spatial interdependence of firms and households in a multi-location economy. Emphasis is placed on the production, trade, and pricing relationships that will establish competitive equilibrium among spatially separated markets. The concluding article, written by Edwin von Böventer, provides a synthesis of the leading theories on spatial economic structure. Von Böventer's article is also important because it identifies the economic principles that determine the spatial structure of an economy and shows the way in which various economic factors are interrelated spatially.

Although the selections have been placed under five conventional divisions of spatial economic theory, it should be pointed out that many of the articles cut across the subject matter of several or of all the sections. It was felt, however, that this was a small price for the reader to pay in order to obtain a basic understanding of the major theoretical issues in spatial economics.

Because of the practical limitations on the length of a book of this nature, the authors decided not to include in this volume that segment of the theory dealing with the spatial ordering of cities and regions. The literature on this subject is quite voluminous and will be given special attention in our forthcoming book, entitled *Urban Economics: Theory, Development, and Planning*. Edwin von Böventer's article, however, does provide a useful overview of the contributions by August Losch and Walter Christaller, two of the pioneers in this branch of spatial economic theory. Also excluded from this volume are the highly abstract regional interaction models of the Walrasian type and the multi-sector, multiplier and regional growth models. These general equilibrium models will be dealt with in the third volume of this series, entitled *The Theory and Practice of Regional Economics*.

The preparation of this book required the cooperation of many people. We are deeply grateful to the authors and the publishers for their kind permission to reprint the articles appearing herein. A special note of thanks also goes to Professor Edgar M. Hoover of the University of Pittsburgh and Melvin

Greenhut of Texas A & M University for their helpful comments and suggestions. Finally, we should like to thank Mrs. Carol Toncar and Mrs. Edith Keeling for their invaluable help in handling correspondence and preparing the selections for printing.

R.D.D.
W.H.L.
D.L.McK.

SPATIAL ECONOMIC THEORY

INTRODUCTION

The Partial Equilibrium Approach

Spatial economics deals with *what* is *where*, and *why*. The "what" refers to every type of economic entity, i.e., production establishments, other kinds of businesses, households, and public and private institutions. "Where" refers basically to location in relation to other economic activity, i.e., to questions of proximity, concentration, dispersion, and similarity or disparity of spatial patterns. The "where" can be defined in broad terms such as regions or metropolitan areas, or in microgeographic terms such as zones, neighborhoods, or sites. The "why' refers to explanations within the somewhat elastic limits of the economist's competence.

Location theory describes this kind of analysis when the emphasis is upon alternative locations for specified kinds of activities, such as industry. *Regional analysis* is concerned with groupings of interrelated economic activities in proximity, within specified areas or types of areas; and the *theory of interregional trade* refers to the economic relationships between such areas.

DECISION UNITS AND THEIR INTERDEPENDENCE

The explanations provided by spatial economic theory are ultimately in terms of the economic motivation and behavior of individual decision units and the ways in which their decisions react upon each other. A decision unit in this context can be, say, a business enterprise, a household, a public institution, or a labor union local. Here, as elsewhere in economic theorizing, simplifying assumptions about motivation are used — for example, the assumption that a business firm will prefer locations that provide higher rates of return to the investments of its owners, or the assumption that households will prefer locations with higher and more dependable levels of real income.

Location theory views a decision unit (most often a business establishment or a household) as weighing the desirability of alternative locations. The unit, wherever located, needs to obtain certain "inputs" (e.g., labor services, materials, electric energy, police protection, information) and needs to dispose of certain "outputs"

Reprinted with permission of the publisher from International Encyclopedia of the Social Sciences, David L. Sills, ed., 15: pp. 95–100. Copyright © 1968 by Crowell Collier and Macmillan, Inc.

(e.g., goods produced in a factory, labor services of members of a household, services provided by a hospital). The unit functions as a converter of inputs into outputs within technical limits described by its "production function" (for example, a shoe factory as such can convert various alternative combinations of leather, plastics, labor, energy, and so on into various alternative combinations of shoes and by-products). Finally, the unit derives from its activity a residual "return" which is the measure of satisfaction of its objectives.

From the standpoint of a particular decision unit, with a production function that gives it a limited range of alternative ways of combining inputs and producing outputs, some locations are better than others. Thus, the terms on which outputs can be disposed of will depend on access to established markets for such outputs; labor and other service inputs of the types required will be available on more favorable terms in some places than in others; land for cultivation or building will be available in different qualities and at different prices in various locations.

The process by which the decision unit weighs all these location factors and makes a choice of location and production technology is describable, as first clearly pointed out by Predöhl (1928), in terms of marginal substitutions. Such analysis is not peculiar to location economics but is part and parcel of the more general body of economic theory of rational firm and household behavior. The distinctive task of spatial economics is to identify and account for the development of systematic spatial configurations of advantage for economic activities, as they arise out of the interaction of different decision units upon one another in ways strongly conditioned by distance. There is an analogy here to the work of the physicist who identifies systematic spatial patterns of the microstructure of matter (e.g., in molecules, atoms, or crystals) and explains them in terms of the interaction of attractive and repulsive forces between units.

Some of the more important ways in which decision units interact in a systematic spatial way can be cited. For example, sellers of a product compete for markets; users of a material compete for the source of supply; firms in a labor market compete for labor; economic activities in a city compete for space. Such interrelationships appear as forces of mutual repulsion or dispersion between the competing units. At the same time, when one unit supplies a good or service to another, either or both will have an interest in proximity for the sake of reducing transport cost and inconvenience. And many kinds of production and exchange are subject to important economies of scale, calling for some degree of spatial concentration. Suppliers of complementary products and services find themselves attracted to the same markets, and buyers of jointly produced goods or services find themselves attracted to the same sources. Here we have forces of mutual attraction or agglomeration. Both the repulsive and the attractive forces can apply either as between like decision units (e.g., similar households, or firms in the same industry) or as between unlike units that are complementary or competitive (e.g., a seller and a buyer of a product, a household and an employer, or a supermarket chain and a bank both thinking of buying the same parcel of urban land).

A general equilibrium theory of spatial economic relations takes cognizance simultaneously of all the important types of spatial interdependence of firms, households, and other decision units. A partial equilibrium theory focuses on just one or a few selected relationships, which can then be explored with greater attention to realistic detail, while other elements are taken as given. Thus, by making the necessary simplifying assumptions, we can focus on, say, the way in which complexes of metals industries locate in response to given market, raw material, and technological situations; the allocations of land in an urban central business district; the patterns of residence adopted by people employed in an industrial area; the development of reciprocal trade between two regions; or the choice of a good site for a new surburban shopping center.

The remainder of this article describes some of the various lines of partial equilibrium spatial analysis that have been most extensively developed by economic theorists. In each case the point of departure is the simplest case, in which all but a very few variables are ignored. Some indication is given of the ways in which this type of analysis can gradually approach reality by successive relaxations of the initial simplifying assumptions.

TRANSPORT ORIENTATION

"Transport orientation" refers to one of the classic cases of location determination under highly simplified assumptions. It was first set forth by the engineer Wilhelm Launhardt in 1885, further developed by the economist Alfred Weber (1909), and later elaborated by Tord Palander (1935) and others. It is assumed the producer's revenues from the sale of output are determined by the cost of transport to one specified market; that the cost of each transported input is similarly determined by cost of transport from one specified source; and that not other considerations of location preference exist: All costs and prices are assumed to be constant, irrespective of the scale of output.

Under these assumptions, the optimum location is simply the location for which the combined costs of procuring and assembling inputs and delivering outputs is least per unit of output. The principal use of the analysis is in evaluating the effects on location of (1) the relative weight and relative transportability of an industry's materials and products and (2) the patterns of variation in transport cost—the existence of route networks and of nodes thereon, the cost or service differentials reflecting length or direction of haul, volume or size of shipments, mode of transport, or other factors. All these considerations can be weighed as determinants of the type of transport orientation of a specified kind of production; that is, whether production is likely to be optimally located at the market, at a source of material, or at some intermediate point, such as a junction of routes, of modes of transport, or of rate zones.

If the various inputs are required in fixed proportions, as assumed by Weber and others, the optimum production location will also be the point of minimum total transport costs of inputs and outputs; but as Leon Moses (1958) has shown, this need not be the case if the mix of inputs can be varied in response to spatial differences in their relative unit costs.

SPATIAL COMPETITION FOR MARKETS

One of the most drastic simplifications in Weber's basic transport orientation case is that all prices and costs are independent of quantities produced and sold. Relaxing this highly artificial assumption makes it possible to analyze the various ways in which producers compete for markets and the ways in which location patterns are affected by economies of scale and geographic concentration.

If the amount of output that a producer can sell in any one market without lowering his price is limited, he is likely to find it advantageous to sell in more than one market, and perhaps in a whole range of markets constituting his *market area*. Thus, one kind of situation in which producers in different locations interact through competition for markets is that in which each supplies a market area wherein he can deliver the product at a lower price than his competitor can. One branch of spatial economic analysis considers the way in which the size and shape of contiguous market areas are determined for producers whose locations are taken as fixed. The key factors here are (1) the difference between the f.o.b. (before transport cost is added) prices at the producer's locations; (2) the way in which transport costs are related to length of haul; (3) whether or not the same tariff for transportation applies to all producers. If, for example, one producer must ship at a higher tariff because his product is less compactly packed, more perishable, or shipped in smaller lots than that of his competitor, he will be under an added disadvantage at markets at longer distances, and his market area may be entirely surrounded by that of his rival who ships at a lower tariff.

The laws of market areas, first set forth in systematic form by Frank A. Fetter (1924) and subsequently elaborated by others, permit useful insights into some of the ways in which the structure of transport costs influences the location of producers in relation to their markets and the extent to which a reduction of either production costs or transport rates may enlarge the market that can be economically served from a given production location. An enterprise facing a choice among locations can use these principles under some circumstances in estimating the relative advantages, in terms of the market area and net sales revenues, of alternative locations.

In its most simplified form, market-area theory assumes that market areas are discrete because (1) the products from competing centers are highly interchangeable rather than differentiated, (2) transport costs rise continuously with distance, and (3) the output of a producer sells at a uniform f.o.b. price plus freight, rather than under a discriminatory delivered-price system involving freight absorption by the seller. This combination of conditions is rather uncommon in practice and is perhaps most closely approached in the case of the sales territories of the several separated branches of a given firm that seeks to minimize total delivery expense.

But where different firms are competing for markets and are selling somewhat differentiated products, the market areas of different production centers often overlap to a high degree. To some extent this reflects the fact that transport charges do not always rise continuously with added distance but stay constant over substantial ranges of added length of haul. More important is the fact that sellers can and do discriminate among buyers according to the buyer's location, most often by partial or complete absorption of the added transport cost of sales to the more distant markets. Full freight absorption means selling at a uniform delivered price to all markets and tends, of course, to produce a very great degree of market-area overlap and cross-hauling of products. This and a great variety of other systems of setting prices in space, such as basing-point systems, have been documented and analyzed in great detail by many writers in terms of (1) theoretical rationale from the standpoint of the seller's interest; (2) historical origins and evolution; and (3) conformity with norms of "workable competition" and with the public interest in efficient location and allocation of resources.

MARKET AREAS AND SUPPLY AREAS

The types of market-area analysis just discussed apply essentially to products that are produced at fewer points than those at which they are consumed or bought. For certain products, however—mainly agricultural ones—the characteristic situation is that of widely dispersed producers selling to a relatively small number of consuming or collecting centers. This is the inverse of the characteristic market-area situation. Accordingly, the various simplified and complex types of market-area analysis have their counterparts in the field of supply-area analysis. The most familiar examples of rather discrete supply areas are urban milksheds. The effects of various transport rate patterns and pricing policies of buyers have been worked out, in fairly close analogy to the effects of transport rate patterns and pricing policies of sellers in the market-area analysis discussed above.

Many situations in the real world are composite, with a single seller or production point serving several markets while at the same time a market is supplied by several sellers at different locations. This is particularly likely to occur where transport costs of the product in question are small relative to either (1) other considerations of production location, such as labor costs, or (2) qualitative differences between the brands of rival producers.

COMPETITION FOR SPACE

Another classic approach to spatial analysis, pioneered by Thünen, focuses upon the competition between producers for space on which to operate and upon the role of land rent as the price and allocator of space. This approach is the main root of those branches of spatial analysis which, under the broad rubric of "land utilization theory," address themselves to the question of how to use a specified area rather than where to locate a specified kind of activity.

This line of analysis uniquely points up the dual economic role that space plays—it provides *utility* as a necessary and generally scarce production input, and it causes *disutility* by imposing costs of transport or communication to bridge distances.

In the simplest case, the choice of location for the producer is assumed to rest on just two factors: the net price per unit received for his output and the price he has to pay (per acre) for the use of land, i.e., rent. The net prices realized for outputs are assumed to depend only on transport costs to a single specified market. All other location factors (such as cost of transported inputs or labor) are ignored.

The factor of access to market thus acts centripetally on producers, while the balancing centrifugal force is the higher rent resulting from competitive bidding for the space nearer the market. Each industry or kind of land use, depending on its technical production characteristics and the transportability of its output, strikes its own compromise between nearness to market and cheap land; and the equilibrium pattern of land uses is envisaged, in the simplest such case, as a systematic series of concentric ring-shaped zones, each devoted to a particular use.

Given the net price receivable for outputs at a specified location, the individual producer's profit possibilities will be greater the lower is the rent charged for the land. In general, his production function will allow considerable substitution between land and other production factors (e.g., more or less intensive cultivation of a crop, or high-rise versus lower buildings in a city). The higher the rent, the more "intensive" is the most efficient way of producing the specified product at that location. There is a maximum rent that the producer can afford to pay to occupy that specificed location. The pattern of such maximum, or ceiling, rents tolerated by a specified land use at a series of different locations is described by a "rent gradient" (along one line) or a "rent surface" (over a whole area).

A rent gradient or surface rises to a peak at the point of best access to market (e.g., a town where produce from the surrounding countryside is consumed, or the heart of the central business district in the case of many types of urban commercial land uses). The gradients or surfaces corresponding to different land uses have different heights and slopes. Competition in the real estate market, together with the incentive for owners of land to realize maximum returns, implies that each land use will tend to pre-empt those areas for which its rent surface is the highest one.

This theoretical approach is most applicable to situations in which the main factors affecting the choice of location for a variety of competing uses are (1) rents and (2) some other spatial differential that is common to all the principal alternative uses and is related systematically and continuously to distance—e.g., market access, in the illustrations cited. In practice, this applies to extensive extractive land uses like agriculture and forestry and (on a much more local scale) the main classes of urban land use within a city or metropolitan area.

With this general type of analysis it is possible to derive useful insights, for planning or prognosis, into the shifts in land-use patterns likely to result from changes in demand for products, technological and transport changes, and land-use controls. Some of the more obvious variations on the simplest case have been developed by

Thünen and succeeding generations of theorists; they include, for example, the existence of cheaper transport along certain routes, variations in the desirability of land other than those due to access to markets, labor cost differentials, economies of scale, multi-crop farming systems and other land-use combinations, trade barriers, and imperfections in the real estate market.

COMPETITION FOR LABOR

Many important and interesting questions of spatial economics relate to the spatial interaction between people and jobs. Labor is an essential input of all productive activities, and variations in the cost and availability of manpower influence the choice of location for many activities. At the same time, location theory includes the analysis of the locational behavior of the household as a decision unit with labor services for sale and with certain environmental preferences and other "input requirements." Commuting and migration are two ways in which the labor supply adapts itself to job location.

One of the oldest components of the theory of labor cost differentials rests on the proposition that living costs are lower in predominantly agricultural areas, so that a lower money wage in such areas is consistent with the equality of real wages, which is a condition for equilibrium under full labor mobility. "Equalizing differences" in money wages between areas are defined by Ohlin (1933) as those which simply reflect differences in the cost of living. In the more advanced countries, however, locally produced foodstuffs account for a smaller part of the consumer budget, and interregional differences in consumer prices within the country are narrower. Moreover, the cost of living as measured by statistical indexes omits some important considerations, such as amenity and style of life, that enter into choice of residence.

A second well-established component of the theory explicitly involves demographic behavior (fertility, mortality, and migration). Since various economic and social impediments to labor mobility exist, labor tends to be abundant and cheap where natural increase outruns the growth of labor demand. Further insight here calls for evaluation of the complex ways in which fertility and mortality are influenced by income level and the local pattern of economic opportunities, and also for more detailed analysis of the determinants of spatial mobility. The selectivity of migration plays a vital role here: mobility depends to such an extent on the age, family status, financial resources, education, and other characteristics of the individual that the pattern of manpower characteristics in areas of high unemployment and heavy out-migration contrasts sharply with the pattern in flourishing areas with heavy in-migration.

Certain important locational effects arise from the fact that (since most adults are members of households) labor is often a jointly supplied service. Specifically, labor markets highly specialized in activities employing mainly men are likely to have a surplus of female "complementary" labor which may be attractive to a quite different range of industries.

Still another principal component of the theory of labor cost differentials involves the factors of size, diversity, and productivity in a labor market. This is mentioned in the next section, in the discussion of local external economies.

AGGLOMERATION

Among the most important questions to which spatial economic theory is addressed is the degree to which a particular economic activity, or a complex of closely related activities, is concentrated in a small number of locations. The term "agglomeration" refers in a broad sense to such concentration.

Perhaps the simplest basis for spatial concentration is economies of scale for the individual production unit, such as a steel works or oil refinery. If large units are much more efficient than small ones, one large unit can serve a number of market locations more cheaply than a number of small decentralized units can, even though the total delivery cost is greater. (Similarly, the economies of concentration in a single large plant can outweigh extra costs of material assembly involved in drawing materials from a larger range of sources of supply.) In the case where scale economies and access to markets are the principal locational factors, production units will be larger when markets are more concentrated and when transport is cheap. Some degree of spatial concentration through scale economies underlies the class of situations discussed earlier in regard to spatial competition for markets, in which individual producers sell to many markets and can adopt discriminatory systems of delivered prices.

The agglomeration of a single activity by virtue of internal economies of scale, as just described, often has important indirect agglomerative effects by providing external economies to related activities. For example, fully equipped commercial testing laboratories can operate economically only where they can command a sizable volume of business; and firms using such services can save time and money by locating in a center where such service is available. Similarly, the sheer volume of demand for interregional transport (freight and passenger) to and from a large metropolitan area provides the basis for much more efficient, varied, and flexible transport services than a smaller center can support; and this advantage in transport service is an attraction to a wide range of transport-using activities.

Scale economies within individual units, specialization (division of labor among production units), and close contact among units are the elements in an external-economies type of agglomeration. Where there is a large concentration of activities in proximity, more and more particular operations, processes, or services can be undertaken on an efficient scale by separate units that serve other units in the area. In smaller areas, such specialized activities are either absent altogether or have to be provided within the firms that use them—at higher costs, because they are on a relatively smaller-scale basis. To return to the initial example of testing services for industrial products or materials, in a major industrial center various fully equipped and efficient commercial laboratories are available to provide quick service, while in a distant small town the manufacturer needing such testing service has to choose among (1) providing it himself on a small and less efficient scale, (2) having it done at a distance by a commercial facility, with costly delay and inconvenience, or (3) doing without it.

From the standpoint of the user of specialized goods and services, there are three advantages of quick access to a large source of supply—cheapness, variety and flexibility. First, the specialized producers or providers of services who exist in large agglomerations can provide their goods or services at lower cost because of their own scale economies. Second, more different grades and varieties are available at any one time, which is an important attraction to the buyer who needs to make selective comparisons (the shopper for fashionable clothes, the theatergoer, the employer who needs unusual types of labor, the manufacturer who needs highly specialized technical assistance on production or sales-promotion problems). Third, access to a large source of supply gives greater assurance of ability to meet rapidly changing and unforeseen needs and reduces the penalty arising from instability of requirements. Costly delays and inventory requirements are lessened when a firm's sudden need for additional labor, repair services, or materials is so small relative to local supplies that the firm can count on its need being met.

Agglomeration via external economies is manifest both on a large interregional distance scale (urban versus nonurban areas) and on a microgeographic intraregional scale (downtown versus outlying areas of a city or even smaller specialized areas within a city, such as shopping districts, garment districts, financial districts, or automobile rows). The distance scale depends partly on the urgency of the need for close personal contact and proximity among the units involved, and partly on the extent to which advantages of spatial concentration are offset by various disadvantages of crowding, such as high cost of space, traffic congestion, noise, and pollution.

The role of external economies in agglomeration and urbanization has been particularly well described by Florence (1948) and Lichtenberg (1960). Its importance as a field of analysis is rapidly increasing because of the increasingly urban and interdependent character of economic activities and the emergence of distinctively urban economic and social problems of the first magnitude; the increasing importance of activities that are related to others through transmission of information requiring quick, close, and detailed contact; and the increasing awareness of the important role that the industrial structure of a region plays in determining its opportunities for growth and adjustment to changing conditions.

BIBLIOGRAPHY

ALONSO, WILLIAM 1964 *Location and Land Use: Toward a General Theory of Land Rent.* Cambridge, Mass.: Harvard Univ. Press.

BERRY, BRIAN J. L.; and PRED, ALLAN 1961 *Central Place Studies: A Bibliography of Theory and Applications.* Bibliography Series, No. 1. Philadelphia: Regional Science Research Institute. Reprinted in 1965, with additions through 1964.

CHISHOLM, MICHAEL 1962 *Rural Settlement and Land Use: An Essay in Location.* London: Hutchinson University Library.

FETTER, FRANK A. 1924 The Economic Law of Market Areas. *Quarterly Journal of Economics* 39:520–529.

FLORENCE, P. SARGANT 1948 *Investment, Location, and Size of Plant: A Realistic Inquiry Into the Structure of British and American Industries.* Cambridge Univ. Press.

GREENHUT, MELVIN L. 1963 *Microeconomics and the Space Economy: The Effectiveness of an Oligopolistic Market Economy.* Chicago: Foresman.

HOOVER, EDGAR M. 1948 *The Location of Economic Activity.* New York: McGraw-Hill.

ISARD, WALTER 1956 *Location and Space-economy: A General Theory Relating to Industrial Location, Market Areas, Trade and Urban Structure.* Cambridge, Mass.: Technology Press of M.I.T.; New York: Wiley.

ISARD, WALTER et al. 1960 *Methods of Regional Analysis: An Introduction to Regional Science.* New York: Wiley; Cambridge, Mass.: M.I.T. Press.

LICHTENBERG, ROBERT M. 1960 *One-tenth of a Nation: National Forces in the Economic Growth of the New York Region.* Cambridge, Mass.: Harvard Univ. Press.

LÖSCH, AUGUST (1940) 1954 *The Economics of Location.* New Haven: Yale Univ. Press. First published as *Die räumliche Ordnung der Wirtschaft.*

MEYER, J. R. 1963 Regional Economics: A Survey. *American Economic Review* 53: 19–54.

MOSES, LEON N. 1958 Location and the Theory of Production. *Quarterly Journal of Economics* 72:259–272. [Section 4 of this volume].

NORTH, DOUGLASS C. 1955 Location Theory and Regional Economic Growth. *Journal of Political Economy* 63: 243–258.

NOURSE, HUGH O. 1967 Regional Economics. Unpublished manuscript.

OHLIN, BERTIL (1933) 1957 *Interregional and International Trade.* Harvard Economic Studies, Vol. 39. Cambridge, Mass.: Harvard Univ. Press.

PALANDER, TORD 1935 *Beiträge zur Standortstheorie.* Uppsala (Sweden): Almqvist & Wiksell.

PONSARD, CLAUDE 1958 *Histoire des théories économiques spatiales.* Rennes (France): Colin.

PREDÖHL, ANDREAS 1928 The Theory of Location in Its Relation to General Economics. *Journal of Political Economy* 36:371–390.

WEBER, ALFRED (1909) 1957 *Theory of the Location of Industries.* Univ. of Chicago Press; Cambridge Univ. Press. First published as *Über den Standort der Industrien.* Teil 1: Reine Theorie des Standorts.

2

The General Equilibrium Approach

Central to most general equilibrium models of location is a system of equations that emphasizes the interdependence of regions due to linkages between economic activities. Thus, in such models an exogenous change in demand for a commodity in one region may affect interregional trade and the spatial distribution of consumption, production, etc., of all commodities in all regions. These models represent a distinct departure from tradition in location theory. Problems in this field were first investigated formally by Weber (1909) and other European scholars who were contemporaries of Walras. Their analyses drew, however, most heavily on the partial equilibrium logic of Marshall. Their theoretical formulations did not lend themselves to consideration of mutual-interdependence issues and tended to obscure the relationship of location theory to branches of economic theory, particularly interregional trade theory, that dealt with general equilibrium problems.

Mutual-interdependence models of location and regional inter-action are of two varieties: (1) highly abstract formulations that extend Walras' reasoning to spatial phenomena; (2) models that are more restrictive in their assumptions and less general in their intent but which lend themselves to empirical application. The latter will be dealt with at greater length here. Not all of the more operational techniques, however, will be reviewed. The approach of some of them is so highly aggregative that they cannot deal adequately with factors affecting the geographic distribution of production, trade, and optimum location of investment in new capacity for individual industries. For this reason, multisector multiplier and regional growth models, while important tools of regional and interregional analysis, will not be discussed (But see Chipman 1951; Isard et al. 1960; Borts 1960). Moreover, the results of some of the aggregative formulations — economic base analysis is an example — can be derived from those that are reviewed below (Andrews 1958).

This article will concentrate on two types of models: those that employ input–output techniques and those that employ linear pro-gramming. The most important difference between the two is that the former rule out optimization by fixing geographic patterns of

Reprinted with permission of the publisher from International Encyclopedia of the Social Sciences, *David L. Sills, ed., 15: pp. 100–108. Copyright © 1968 by Crowell Collier and Macmillan, Inc.*

production and/or trade. Efforts by scholars to develop techniques that determine relative, as well as absolute, patterns of production and trade and that are concerned with the optimum use of resources led to the application of linear programming to spatial analysis.

We shall begin by considering a group of input–output models. First, the derivation of trade balances for regions is dealt with. Second, the linkages between regions or nations involved in the usual input–output system are described. Third, several full-scale regional input–output techniques that are theoretically capable of analyzing the effects of trade linkages between many regions are considered. A group of linear programming models is then reviewed.

INPUT–OUTPUT TECHNIQUES

Derivation of trade balances

Data on trade between regions of a country are not usually available, and estimates of such trade are thought to be less reliable than estimates of regional output and final demand. Given information on output and final demand and a matrix of technical coefficients, individual industry balances of trade for a region with respect to all other regions can be derived. Let $_g x_j$ be output of industry j in region g and $_g c_j$ be total consumption of the output of industry j in region g; then $_g e_j$, the net trade balance of industry j in region g with respect to all other areas, is

$$_g e_j = {}_g x_j - {}_g c_j.$$

A positive e indicates a net export balance, a negative e a net import balance. An over-all trade balance for the region is obtained by summing the e's for all industries in the region.

Total consumption, c above, is the sum of final demands, y, and intermediate or interindustry demands. The latter are derived by multiplying the known regional outputs by technical coefficients of production, that is,

$$_g c_i = \sum_{j=1}^{n} {}_g a_{ij} \, {}_g x_j + {}_g y_i.$$

The technical coefficient $_g a_{ij}$ is the amount of the output of industry i required to produce a unit of the output of industry j in region g.

There are difficulties in deriving commodity trade balances by the above technique. Coefficients of production vary between regions as a result of differences in methods of production, differences in prices, which affect the coefficients because they are in dollar terms, differences in the product mix of industries, etc. Yet, since *regional* input–output coefficients are not usually known, *national* coefficients are often employed, with resulting errors in the estimates of inter- mediate demands. It is also difficult to obtain information on con- sumption by the final demand sectors, particularly investment and government.

Import and export balances for individual industries have some- times been derived as a first step in studies whose object is to deter- mine the industries that might be encouraged to locate or expand in a region. Although the size of the import balance, or regional excess demand for the output of an industry, is only one element in such an analysis—costs of producing and transporting the inputs and outputs of an industry are also considered—it is viewed as parti- cularly important. This outlook reflects a belief that narrowing regional differentials in factor prices and production costs are lead- ing to an increased market orientation of nonprimary industry. Some studies, unfortunately, appear to settle the issue of a region's com- parative advantage by a ranking of industries in terms of the size of regional excess demand. Virtue is found in those patterns of invest- ment that contribute most to self-sufficiency, an approach that partakes of regional mercantilism.

Locational analyses based on balances of trade employ general equilibrium techniques to only a very limited degree. After the initial input–output calculations are made, an industry-by-industry approach is adopted. In general such analyses do not take into account in a systematic way the manner in which the introduction of new capacity for any one industry will affect the costs of production of all other industries in a region. Changes in outputs that are induced by cost changes are, therefore, not taken into account. Also neglected are the constraints that may exist on expansion. While factors of production are more mobile for regions of a country than they are internationally, regional supply functions for some factors may be inelastic unless there is substantial unemployment. If factor supplies and other things impose constraints on industry expansion, a pattern of investment should be selected that minimizes or maximizes some meaningful economic variable. Such an objective requires a general equilibrium system of an optimizing character. Several systems of this type are discussed below.

Trade linkages in national models

As was indicated above, balance of trade studies begin with known outputs. The main objective of most inter-industry studies is, however, to determine outputs, and the objective of regional input–output systems is to determine what effects a change, say, in final demand, in one or more regions will have on all others. The simplest approach to the latter issue is that adopted in national input–output analyses. These are in effect two-region systems, one region being the nation under study and the other the rest of the world. In such models we are given the technical coefficients of production of the region or nation, $_ga_{ij}$, for $i, j = 1, 2, \ldots, n$ industries; the final demands, $_gy_i$, of all exogenous sectors other than foreign trade; and a set of imports, $_gm_j$, and exports, $_ge_j$. In matrix notation these are represented by $_gA$, $_gY$, $_gM$, and $_gE$. Imports are arranged in two categories, competing and noncompeting goods, the latter being those for which there are no counter-parts in the region under study. Imports of these goods are entered in an exogenous import row and have no effect on regional output. Output of each of the industries in the nation or region, g, being studied is found by solving the following set of simultaneous equations:

$$_gX = [I - {_gA}]^{-1}[_gY + (_gE - {_gM})].$$

Here $_gX$ is the $n \times 1$ vector of outputs in region g. $[I - {_gA}]^{-1}$ is the inverse of $[I - {_gA}]$, the $n \times n$ identity matrix minus the $n \times n$ matrix of technical coefficients; $_gY$ is the $n \times 1$ vector of final demands $(_gE - {_gM})$ is the $n \times 1$ vector of the differences between imports and exports for each of the competing-goods industries. Negative values for these differences are precluded. Thus, if the imports of any good exceed the sum of exports and all other final demands, a zero value is assigned to the final demand for the good. Effectively, it is treated as a non-competing good.

In the above approach imports and exports are not explained within the model. There are, for example, no functions relating region g's imports of all goods to its income. Since regional linkages are external to the system, it is not possible to determine the effects on region g of such things as an exogenous increase in demand for a nontraded good in the rest of the world. We shall now consider a variety of regional input–output techniques that can determine the effects of such changes.

The Leontief intranational model

In its most general form Leontief's intranational model (see Research Project . . . 1953) involves a complex hierarchy of goods and regions. The place of any particular good within the hierarchy depends upon the degree of spatial aggregation required to obtain a balance, or equality, between regional production and consumption. An empirical application of the model employs the simpler hierarchy traditional to international trade theory, that of traded and non-traded goods, although they are referred to as national and local goods. National goods are those for which a balance between production and consumption can be struck only at the national level. Local goods are those for which there is a balance between production and consumption for each region into which the nation is divided for purposes of the study. The outline of the model's structure presented below is in terms of this simpler hierarchy.

Assume there are n industries, the first h being national and the remaining $n-h$ local. There are r regions. A national bill of final demand, Y, for all goods, a national matrix of technical coefficients, A, and a set of locational constants, ${}_g\beta_d$, for the *national goods* are given. The locational constant ${}_g\beta_d$ indicates the proportion of total output of a national good, d, produced by region g. These constants may be determined from past data on the geographic distribution of production. By definition, the locational constants for each national good sum to unity.

Total outputs of both national and local goods are determined by solving

$$X = [I-A]^{-1}Y.$$

A regional allocation of total output of each national good is then obtained by applying the locational constants as follows:

$$
{}_g x_d = {}_g\beta_d\, x_d, \quad
\begin{aligned}
&d = 1,2,\ldots,h, \text{ national industries;}\\
&g = 1,2,\ldots,r, \text{ regions.}
\end{aligned}
$$

In this expression ${}_g x_d$ represents the amount of national good d that is produced in region g and x_d represents the total output of national good d. Since the locational constants for each national good sum to unity, we are assured that the above procedure precisely allocates total output of each national good to the regions.

Derivation of regional outputs of nontraded goods is somewhat more involved. For this purpose it is convenient to think of the national matrix of technical coefficients as having been arranged so that all national-goods industries appear first. The coefficients are then in four meaningful blocks:

$$
\begin{bmatrix} A_1 & A_2 \\ A_3 & A_4 \end{bmatrix} \equiv
\begin{bmatrix} \{a_{df}\} & \{a_{dl}\} \\ \{a_{ld}\} & \{a_{lq}\} \end{bmatrix},
\quad
\begin{aligned}
&d,f = 1,2,\ldots,h, \text{ national industries;}\\
&l,q = h+1, h+2,\ldots,n, \text{ local industries.}
\end{aligned}
$$

Technical coefficients in the $\{a_{df}\}$ or A_1 block pertain to the requirements of national-goods industries for the outputs of other national-goods industries per unit of their output; coefficients in the $\{a_{dl}\}$ or A_3 block describe the requirements of local-goods industries for the outputs of national-goods industries per unit of the former's outputs, etc.

Regional outputs of local goods are determined as follows:

$$X = [I - A_4]^{-1} [A_3 \, _gX_d + _gY_l], \quad \begin{array}{l} g = 1, 2, \ldots, r \\ d = 1, 2, \ldots, h \\ l = h + 1, \ldots, n. \end{array}$$

Here $[I - A_4]^{-1}$ is the inverse of the block of coefficients that pertain to the requirements of local-goods industries for the outputs of local-goods industries; $A_3 \, _gX_d$ gives the intermediate requirements of local-goods industries in region g for production of the already determined regional outputs of national goods; $_gY_l$ is the final demand for local goods in region g.

The intranational model being considered determines all outputs. It also determines individual commodity and, therefore, aggregate trade balances for each region with respect to all others. Balances of trade between individual pairs of regions remain unknown. This is one of the senses in which the model is intranational rather than interregional. It is part of the logic of the system that the effect on a particular region of a change in final demand for national goods is the same regardless of the region in which the change takes place. Similarly, the effect on any given region of a change in final demand for local goods is the same regardless of the region (if other than itself) in which the change takes place.

The hierarchy of goods and regions, whether of a simple or complex variety, assumed by the intranational model is difficult to establish in reality. The empirical application of the system finally settled upon a definition of goods and regions that "minimized" departures from strict production–consumption balance for the entire group of industries designated as local (see Isard 1953) . . . .

Interregional models

To describe an interregional input–output system, we assume a closed economy divided into $b, g = 1, 2, \ldots, r$ regions and producing $i, j = 1, 2, \ldots, n$ goods. Technical coefficients, $_ga_{ij}$, are given for each region and may differ between them. For each region there is also given a set of trade or supply coefficients, $_{bg}t_i$, for every good, showing the relative regional composition of that region's purchases of every commodity. Thus, the coefficient $_{34}t_2 = .40$ indicates that for every dollar spent on the output of industry 2 by the sectors of region 4, 40 cents' worth is purchased in region 3. Each region's trade coefficients for each commodity add to unity: $\Sigma_{b=1}^{r}\,_{bg}t_i = 1$, $i = 1, 2, \ldots, n$. Regional final demands, $_gy_i$, are given.

From the trade and technical coefficients a new set of coefficients is derived, which describes the interregional and interindustry structure of every region:

$$A \equiv \{_{bg}a_{ij}\} = \{_{bg}t_i\,_ga_{ij}\}, \qquad \begin{array}{l} i,j = 1, 2, \ldots, n; \\ b, g = 1, 2, \ldots, r. \end{array}$$

Hereafter A will be described as the interregional input–output matrix. Consider one element of this $nr \times nr$ matrix, say, $_{34}a_{12} = .20$. The coefficient indicates that for each dollar's worth of commodity 2 produced in region 4, 20 cents' worth of commodity 1 is purchased from region 3. Since the trade coefficients for each good in a region add to unity, the sum of all a's in any column of the interregional input–output matrix yields a technical coefficient for the relevant region and industry: $\Sigma_{b=1}^{r}\,_{bg}a_{ij} = \,_ga_{ij}$.

In interregional systems, outputs of an area are determined by the amounts that the endogenous sectors of an area *ship* on final demand account rather than the amounts that its exogenous sectors consume. Shipments on final demand account, $_by_j^*$, are determined from the usual final demands and the trade coefficients:

$$_by_j^* = \sum_{g=1}^{r} \,_{bg}t_j\,_gy_j, \qquad j = 1, 2, \ldots, n.$$

Regional outputs of all goods are then obtained in the usual way, namely,

$$X = [I - A]^{-1}Y^*.$$

Here X and Y^* are the vectors, respectively, of regional outputs and of shipments on final demand account, and $[I - A]^{-1}$ is the inverse of the interregional input–output matrix. The system yields balances of trade for individual commodities and for the aggregate of all commodities between pairs of regions or for a single region with respect to all others.

The intranational model described above determines all outputs by fixing the *relative regional outputs* of national goods and the trading patterns of a class of goods, i.e., those designated as local. Interregional input–output systems allow relative, as well as absolute, levels of regional output of all goods to vary but *fix relative trading patterns of all goods* in one way or another. The model developed by Isard (1951) has a set of trade coefficients for every industry in every region. The models of Chenery and Clark (1959) and of Moses (1955), on the other hand, have a single set of trade coefficients for all sectors within a region — the assumption employed in the above description of an interregional input–output system. There are, however, differences between the latter two models.

Chenery and Clark assume that any region is more efficient than any other region in supplying its requirements of all goods that it actually produces. Each area, then, fully utilizes existing capacity before resorting to imports. Unless a capacity constraint is encountered, trade coefficients must therefore be zero or one. If such a constraint is encountered, trade coefficients will take on intermediate values, but they then cannot be stable. Moreover, this approach can be used only for a two-region system, since it has no mechanism for assigning the imports of a region to a number of different areas.

The theory of spatial competition of traditional location analysis provides the basis for the determination and stability of the coefficients employed by Moses and, with some adaptation, Isard. Thus, assume that each industry produces a single homogeneous product, so that the output of a given industry from one region is a perfect substitute in production or consumption for the output of the same industry from any other region. Each industry in each region is assumed to have *excess* capacity and to produce at constant cost. Regional supply functions of the factors of production are perfectly elastic at given factor prices, up to some limit representing regional endowments. Factors of production are perfectly mobile within each region, industry is perfectly competitive, and transport costs per unit of output increase continuously with distance but do not vary with the quantity shipped. In these circumstances there are perfectly defined market and supply areas for every site where a good is produced and consumed. Trade coefficients then reflect the aggregation of market and supply areas into regions. The world of reality departs from perfect competition, transport rate structures have many peculiarities, etc. There may, as a result, be significant differences in market and supply boundaries of different industries in a region and, therefore, intraregional differences in trade coefficients, as suggested by the Isard model.

The most questionable aspect of interregional input–output systems is their assumption of stable trading patterns. A theoretical framework can be developed, as was done above, under which trade coefficients would be stable, but it is extremely unlikely that the conditions of this framework will be met in reality. The evidence for stability that has been presented is not convincing, because all economic activity was grouped into a few gross industries and regions, with changes over time in individual market and supply areas probably balancing out (Moses 1955).

The main virtue of regional input–output models is their operational character. This is achieved at a heavy cost in terms of theoretical interest. They have no mechanism for explaining trade patterns. Aside from reductions in final demand, they have no way of explaining the disappearance of an industry from a region. Nor are they so constructed that their internal logic points to situations in which new industries will emerge in a region. The above criticism is not removed by the introduction of dynamic elements. In dynamic formulations investment in new capacity is typically related to rates of change in output of industries found in each region in the initial period. In this respect the best that has so far been done with the various input–output models is to incorporate and investigate the conclusions of separate locational and interregional trade analyses. Thus, in one study (Isard & Kuenne 1953) the ideal location of a new integrated steel plant was determined from a separate location study. The impact on the area of the mill's output was then investigated by a regional input–output analysis that involved a limited application of the trade-coefficient approach. In this approach the indirect effects that the region would have on itself because of its effects on other regions were ignored. This limited impact approach has been adopted in a number of studies (see, for example, Hirsch 1964; Moore & Peterson 1955).

Regional input–output studies have sometimes had the objective of projecting all economic activity in an area over a considerable period of time. In only one study, however, that of Berman and her co-workers (1960), has the important topic of factor redistribution, and labor migration in particular, been faced. In this study population projections derived by demographic techniques and employment projections derived by input–output analysis were made to square with one another, and it was concluded that a significant change would take place in historical migration trends.

INTERREGIONAL LINEAR PROGRAMMING MODELS

The intranational model and all of the fixed-trade interregional models treated above face a serious difficulty if a capacity constraint is encountered anywhere in the system. If the "predicted" output of even a single industry in a single region exceeds the region's capacity to produce the good, then a strict application of the model's logic requires that the final demand program be declared infeasible.

This is surely undesirable if the good is transportable and other regions have sufficient excess capacity to produce the required output. An obvious solution is to alter trading patterns, at least at the margin. In what way, however, should they be altered? If some particular region can deliver the required amounts of the good at a lower price, either because of a production or transport cost advantage, a well-formulated economic model would assign to it the task of supplying the requirements. The issue then is the following: if choice and optimization can be introduced into multiregion systems, why not eliminate the fixed, exogenously given patterns of trade and/or output entirely and formulate models that determine all outputs and trade by means of an optimizing scheme? Several techniques for doing this, all of them of a programming variety, are presented below. Their connections with the theory of interregional trade are very clear. They encompass much of what is valuable in traditional location theory but, because of their general equilibrium character, also go beyond it.

The first model to be considered involves cost minimization and is related to the well-known transportation problem of linear programming. It builds directly on a study by Henderson (1958). The existence of intermediate inputs for current production is ignored at first, and attention is focused on a number of final products. The following notation is employed:

$i = 1, 2, \ldots, n$, final consumption products;

$b, g = 1, 2, \ldots, r$, regions;

$e = 1, 2, \ldots, m$, primary factors of production;

$_b w_e$ = price of a unit of primary factor e in region b;

$_b a_{ei}$ = quantity of primary factor e required to produce a unit of good i in region b;

$_b k_i$ = capacity, or maximum rate of output, of plant and equipment producing good i in region b;

$h = 1, 2, \ldots, z$, routes or modes of transportation connecting each pair of regions, the routes between regions being entirely independent of one another.

$_{bg}^{h} s_i$ = shipment of commodity i from region b to region g by route or mode h;

$_{bg}^{h} K$ = capacity or maximum quantity of all goods that can be transported by route h between regions b and g, it being assumed that all goods are identical in their use of transport capacity;

$_{bg}^{h} t_c$ = quantity of primary factor e required to transport a unit of *any* commodity from region b to region g by route h;

$_b D_c$ = endowment of primary factor e in region b;

$_b y_i$ = final demand for commodity i in region b.

It should be noted that factors of production are perfectly mobile within regions, regional factor supply functions are perfectly elastic up to the limit imposed by endowment, and demand functions are perfectly inelastic with respect to both income and price. The assumption that goods are identical in their use of transport capacity and primary inputs for transport is employed to keep an involved notational scheme from becoming even more complicated.

The problem is to determine a regional allocation of output and trade in all goods that satisfies the fixed demands at minimum total cost, subject to the constraints on capacities and factor endowments. The system is written as follows: minimize

$$C = \sum_{b=1}^{r} \sum_{b=g=1}^{r} \sum_{e=1}^{m} \sum_{i=1}^{n} \sum_{h=1}^{z} [{}_bw_e({}_ba_{ei} + {}_{bg}^h t_e)]{}_{bg}^h s_i, \tag{1}$$

subject to

$$\sum_{b=1}^{r} \sum_{h=1}^{z} {}_{bg}^h s_i \geq {}_g y_i, \tag{2}$$

$g = 1, 2, \ldots, r$, regions, $i = 1, 2, \ldots, n$, industries;

$$\sum_{g=1}^{r} \sum_{h=1}^{z} {}_{bg}^h s_i \leq {}_b k_i, \tag{3}$$

$b = 1, 2, \ldots, r, i = 1, 2, \ldots, n;$

$$\sum_{i=1}^{n} {}_{bg}^h s_i \leq {}_{bg}^h K_i, \tag{4}$$

$h = 1, 2, \ldots, z$, routes, $b, g = 1, 2, \ldots, r;$

$$\sum_{i=1}^{n} \sum_{g=1}^{r} \sum_{h=1}^{z} ({}_b a_{ei} + {}_{bg}^h t_e) {}_{bg}^h s_i \leq {}_b D_e, \tag{5}$$

$e = 1, 2, \ldots, m, b = 1, 2, \ldots, r.$

Equation (1) states the objective—to minimize the total cost of producing and transporting all commodities. The constraints have the following meanings: (2) total shipments of each commodity into each region must be at least great enough to satisfy final demand; (3) total shipments, this being the same as output, of each commodity by each region to all regions must be less than or equal to the maximum possible rate of output; (4) total shipments of all commodities by any route must be less than or equal to the capacity of that route; (5) total requirements of each primary factor in a region for production and transport must be less than or equal to the endowment. All shipments are nonnegative.

The introduction of intermediate inputs changes the model in only one way. The first set of constraints, equations (2) above, must be rewritten to state that the total pool of a good available in a region minus the region's intermediate demand for the good must be at least as great as its final demand for the good. A region's pool of a good is defined as total shipments into it from all other areas plus the amount of the good it produces itself minus its total exports of the good.

The minimum-cost, feasible solution is the same as would be achieved by a perfectly competitive economy. The entire system is a set of linked interregional trade problems, the linkages being due to capacities and factor endowments. If these constraints did not exist or were not encountered in a particular problem, total production and transport of each commodity would be assigned to the least-cost region and route, i.e., would be determined by absolute advantage. The existence of binding constraints on factors and transport provides a solution based on considerations of comparative advantage. Moreover, in a multiregion system with positive transport costs, comparative advantage is defined in terms of markets to be served, as well as commodities produced.

The dual to the above minimizing problem is a maximizing problem that determines the delivered price of every good in every region and the quasi rent of each productive capacity, transport capacity, and factor endowment. Delivered price is determined by the marginal supply source. Thus, if any region's demand for a commodity is satisfied by more than one region, price in the consuming area will be equal to the unit production and transport cost of the least efficient supplying source. Capacity in every other area that supplies this region receives a quasi rent, or return above its cost. Capacities that are not fully utilized earn no such return.

The quasi rents are key variables for analysis of the location of investment in new capacity and the retirement of existing capacity. For this purpose it is convenient to think in terms of a planned economy that has set aside a given sum for investment in additional capacity. It is also convenient to assume that the cost of providing additional capacity to produce each good in each region and of providing additional capacity on each transport route is given. The task of the planning authority is to allocate investment among goods, regions, and routes in an optimal manner. Since final demands are fixed, the obvious criterion of optimality is to allocate investment so as to achieve the greatest reduction in total cost. The significance of the quasi rents can now be seen. Each is in fact the reduction in total system cost that would be realized if the associated capacity were increased sufficiently to permit an additional unit of output of transport. From the initial set of quasi rents, the changes that take place in the quasi rents as additional capacity is added, and the cost of providing each type of capacity, the given total investment can be assigned in an optimal manner. If, instead of taking the total amount of investment as given, we assume that an interest rate is given, the optimum level, as well as allocation, of investment in commodities, regions, and routes can be determined.

Input–output models were criticized above because they had no internal rules governing the emergence of productive capacity for particular goods in regions which have not previously had such capacity. The programming technique does not have this weakness, since in all cases of zero capacity some small fictitious quantity can be assigned. Unit costs of production and transport are determined for these capacities. The model will then determine in what regions, if any, new industry should be introduced.

The quasi rents for factors of production, so far ignored, have interpretations similar to those for capacity. They indicate how much total cost would be reduced if a region had enough of a particular primary factor to produce and transport an additional unit of output. Obviously the quasi rents will be zero in all cases where the optimal solution involves less than full employment for a factor. The optimal solution, therefore, indicates the areas from which mobile factors should migrate — those in which they are less than fully employed and earn zero quasi rents — and those which should attract them. As stated, there is some asymmetry in the system. It determines optimal patterns of interregional trade in goods but not optimal patterns of interregional migration. To include a set of relationships that would change the situation would be misleading, since there is at present no way of quantifying the social, as well as the economic, costs of migration.

The model that has been described determines optimal patterns of output, trade, and employment of primary factors. It determines geographic patterns of price and, when extended to include investment, optimal expansions in capacity for production and transport. It indicates the regions from which mobile factors should migrate and the regions which should attract them, if such decisions are made on the basis of economic considerations alone. With the two extensions suggested above, the results of the model reflect a network of comparative advantages that are defined in terms of production functions for goods and transport, supply prices of primary factors, propensities to consume, and the initial distribution of capacities. An empirical application of this type of model has been attempted by Moses (1960).

A second interregional linear programming model (see Lefeber 1958; Stevens 1958; Kuenne 1963) is almost the converse of the one presented above. It takes as given the prices of final goods in each region, rather than the minimum prices of primary factors of production. Instead of a perfectly inelastic demand for each good in each region, it assumes that demands are perfectly elastic and that a certain minimum quantity of each good is to be delivered to each region. The primal problem of this model maximizes the value of output of final goods, rather than minimizing the cost of satisfying a fixed set of demands. Given a set of final goods prices, it determines an optimal point on the production frontier of the entire economy.

The treatment given demand in both of these programming models is inadequate: one assumes a perfectly elastic demand for each commodity, the other a perfectly inelastic demand. Samuelson (1952), however, has suggested a programming formulation for a single-commodity multiregion spatial competition problem that involved regular supply, as well as demand, functions. In this formulation, total consumer surplus, as defined by Marshall, was maximized, subject to constraints imposed by demand and supply considerations in each region. Smith (1963) has provided an interpretation to the dual of this problem which shows that it involves the minimization of rents. Recently, Takayama and Judge (1964) have demonstrated that the Samuelson spatial competition problem is in reality a quadratic programming problem. They have suggested a method of solution that can be applied either to a single homogeneous good or to a number of goods produced and consumed in many regions. In the latter case, however, all of the goods must be for final consumption only.

BIBLIOGRAPHY

ANDREWS, RICHARD B. 1958 Comment re Criticisms of the Economic Base Theory. *Journal of the American Institute of Planners* 24:37–40.

BERMAN, BARBARA R.; CHINITZ, BENJAMIN; AND HOOVER, EDGAR M. 1960 *Projection of a Metropolis: Technical Supplement of the New York Metropolitan Region Study.* Cambridge, Mass.: Harvard Univ. Press.

BORTS, GEORGE H. 1960 The Equalization of Returns and Regional Economic Growth. *American Economic Review* 50:319–347.

CHENERY, HOLLIS B.; and CLARK, PAUL G. 1959 *Inter-industry Economics.* New York: Wiley See especially pages 308–332.

CHIPMAN, JOHN S. 1951 *The Theory of Inter-sectoral Money Flows and Income Formation.* Baltimore: Johns Hopkins Press.

HENDERSON, JAMES M. 1958 *The Efficiency of the Coal Industry: An Application of Linear Programming.* Cambridge, Mass.: Harvard Univ. Press.

HIRSCH, WERNER Z. 1964 [A General Structure for Regional Economic Analysis.] Introduction to Conference on Regional Accounts, Second, Miami Beach, Fla., 1962, *Elements of Regional Accounts: Papers.* Baltimore: Johns Hopkins Press.

ISARD, WALTER   1951   Interregional and Regional Input–Output Analysis: A Model of a Space-economy. *Review of Economics and Statistics* 33 : 318–328.

ISARD, WALTER   1953   Some Empirical Results and Problems of Regional Input–Output Analysis. Pages 116–181 in Research Project on the Structure of the American Economy, *Studies in the Structure of the American Economy: Theoretical and Empirical Explorations in Input–Output Analysis*. New York: Oxford Univ. Press.

ISARD, WALTER; and KUENNE, ROBERT E.   1953   The Impact of Steel Upon the Greater New York–Philadelphia Industrial Region. *Review of Economics and Statistics* 35 : 289–301.

ISARD, WALTER et al.   1960   *Methods of Regional Analysis: An Introduction to Regional Science*. New Yrok: Wiley; Cambridge, Mass.: The Technology Press of M.I.T. See especially pages 182–231.

KUENNE, ROBERT E.   1963   Spatial Economics. Pages 395–454 in Robert E. Kuenne, *The Theory of General Economic Equilibrium*. Princeton Univ. Press.

LEFEBER, LOUIS   1958   *Allocation in Space: Production, Transport and Industrial Location*. Amsterdam: North-Holland Publishing.

MOORE, FREDERICK T.; and PETERSON, JAMES W.   1955   Regional Analysis: An Interindustry Model of Utah. *Review of Economics and Statistics* 37 : 368–383.

MOSES, LEON N.   1955   The Stability of Interregional Trading Patterns and Input–Output Analysis. *American Economic Review* 45 : 803–832.

MOSES, LEON N.   1960   A General Equilibrium Model of Production, Interregional Trade, and Location of Industry. *Review of Economics and Statistics* 42 : 373–397.

RESEARCH PROJECT ON THE STRUCTURE OF THE AMERICAN ECONOMY   1953   *Studies in the Structure of the American Economy: Theoretical and Empirical Explorations in Input–Output Analysis*, by Wassily Leontief et al. New York: Oxford Univ. Press.

SAMUELSON, PAUL A.   1952   Spatial Price Equilibrium and Linear Programming. *American Economic Review* 42 : 283–303 [Selection 18 of this volume].

SMITH, VERNON L.   1963   Minimization of Economic Rent in Spatial Price Equilibrium. *Review of Economic Studies* 30 : 24–31.

STEVENS, BENJAMIN H.   1958   An Interregional Linear Programming Model. *Journal of Regional Science* 1 : 60–98.

TAKAYAMA, T.; and JUDGE, G. G.   1964   Equilibrium Among Spatially Separated Markets: A Reformulation. *Econometrica* 32 : 510–524 [Selection 19 of this volume].

WEBER, ALFRED   (1909) 1957   *Theory of the Location of Industries*. Univ. of Chicago Press; Cambridge Univ. Press. First published as *Über den Standort der Industrien. Teil 1: Reine Theorie des Standorts*.

PART I   LEAST COST THEORY

3

Distance Inputs
and the Space Economy:
The Locational Equilibrium
of the Firm

TRANSPORT-ORIENTED EQUILIBRIUM
UNDER SIMPLIFIED CONDITIONS

We propose ... to concentrate upon one of the basic units of economic analysis, the individual firm,[1] and to examine the conditions for its locational equilibrium. Concomitantly we wish to demonstrate generally and concretely the utility of the concept of distance inputs in determining the firm's geographical position. This concept will enable us to fuse much of traditional (Weberian) locational doctrine and modern production theory. It is hoped that at the same time certain difficulties which have for a long time confronted location theorists will be resolved.

At the start we want to stress the various levels of abstraction at which locational inquiry is possible. We do this in order to avoid that criticism which has been directed at Weber but which has failed to appreciate that the interpretation and significance of the Weberian doctrine is different for each of these levels.[2] We distinguish between at least four levels of inquiry:

1. For the small, individual producer who has a negligible influence upon prices (with the exception of the price of his own product), the locus of consumption, the supply costs and sources of factors, transport rates, agglomeration economies, and other locational variables;

1. For simplicity's sake we shall speak of a firm as consisting of one or more plants operating at one and only one site, and of a producer as managing one and only one firm. There is no logical difficulty in extending the analysis to enterprises which operate plants spatially separated, whether these plants correspond to the same or different stages of production. However, one must then consider distance inputs within the enterprise and consequently the analysis becomes more complex.

2. A systematic presentation and refutation (in many respects, valid) of these criticisms is found in E. Niederhauser, "Die Standortstheorie Alfred Webers," *Staatswissenschaftliche Studien*, XIV (Weinfelden, 1944).

The article is Part II of a two-part study. Reprinted by permission of the publishers from The Quarterly Journal of Economics, 65 (Cambridge, Mass.: Harvard University Press, 1951), pp. 373–97. Copyright 1951 by the President and Fellows of Harvard College.

2. For the small or large producer who does influence these variables;

3. For an industry as a whole or for a group of producers who form a meaningful aggregate for analysis because they are homogeneous with respect to certain characteristics, or because, though heterogeneous, they complement each other;[3]

4. For a regional or world economy (where general analysis must account for the determination of values for all possible locational variables).

We shall confine ourselves chiefly to the first level. However, it should be emphasized that the accepted dualism in location theory — viz., a Thünen type of analysis for the agricultural sphere, a Weberian schema for the industrial sector — and the opposition to incorporating these two models into one general framework totters once we recognize these levels of inquiry. The von Thünen school confines itself to an aggregative analysis. Its problem is the distribution of agricultural production over a given region. It assumes away any problems of location for the individual producer by assigning to him a fixed location — an infinite immobility. The Weberian school, on the other hand, is primarily concerned with the locational problem of an individual firm which produces a given product. True, the Weberian doctrine frequently shifts to aggregative analysis when it considers agglomeration economies, the various economic strata of society, and the like. But this type of aggregative analysis explicitly avoids the problem of the efficient spatial distribution, both qualitative and quantitative, of the various types of industrial production over a given region. Thus, the von Thünen and Weberian schools have carved out for themselves separate, non-overlapping areas of inquiry. In real life, of course, this clear-cut line of demarcation in locational decisions disappears. No agricultural producer is perfectly immobile; he quite frequently does consider changing location. Accordingly, the von Thünen scheme is insufficient for explaining such an agriculturalist's decision. Analysis on the individual level is also required. On the other hand, the Weberian dogma is totally inadequate for the overall regional type of industrial planning which has been undertaken in the last decade or two by international, national, and regional authorities.

---

3. Chamberlin has pointed out the limitations of the group concept for analyzing substitution effects among the products of individual firms (*The Theory of Monopolistic Competition* [Cambridge, Mass., 1933], especially pp. 103–4), and has particularly criticized the industry in this respect. See his "Product Heterogeneity and Public Policy," *Papers and Proceedings of the American Economic Association*, Vol. XL (May 1950), pp. 85–92; and "Competition, Monopoly and Economic Growth," unpublished manuscript. Our industry or group of firms, however, is conceived in terms of similar techniques of production, or inputs, or in terms of a set of external economies achieved by agglomeration of similar or dissimilar lines of production.

The von Thünen methodology can be of great service here. The task ahead is thus to conduct analysis at each level of inquiry, and to fuse the results into one comprehensive locational framework.[4]

Following the lines of the mathematical theory of production, we conceive the set of possible locations for the firm as implicitly stated by the transformation function,

$$f(y_1, y_2 \ldots y_n) = 0 \tag{1}$$

where $y_1 \ldots y_n$ represent quantities of various commodities. Commodities in this context embrace both inputs (including distance inputs) and outputs. Positive amounts of inputs are thus considered as negative amounts of corresponding commodities.

The first order equilibrium conditions for the firm desiring to maximize its profits subject to the above transformation function and a set of constant prices are given by:

$$\frac{f_i}{f_j} = \frac{p_i}{p_j}, \tag{2}$$

where p_i represents the price of the ith commodity. The second order conditions concerning stability imply that in general the transformation curve for any two commodities, given a consistent set of other commodities, is concave to the origin.[5]

In terms of distance inputs, these conditions are fulfilled by the Weberian solution for transport orientation which utilizes the familiar locational triangle. We demonstrate. In Figure 1, let M_1 and M_2 be the sources of two raw materials, eleven distance units apart, and respectively twelve and ten distance units from C, the place of consumption for a good whose production requires only these two raw materials. Like Weber, we assume that all labor and other services are available in the correct quantities everywhere on our plain at uniform costs. Accordingly, we can posit that none of the quantities of the inputs and outputs embraced by our transformation function changes as we move production from site to site on the plain except those of distance inputs. We then have only three variables to consider, namely, distance inputs in obtaining the raw material from M_1,

4. Compare O. Engländer, "Kritisches und Positives zu einer allgemeinen reinen Lehre vom Standort," *Zeitschrift für Volkswirtschaft und Sozialpolitik*, Neue Folge, Vol. V (1926), pp. 475–79.

5. For fuller statement of the theory of production, see, among others, E. Schneider, *Theorie der Produktion* (Vienna, 1934); S. Carlson, *A Study on the Pure Theory of Production* (London, 1939); J. R. Hicks, *Value and Capital* (Oxford, 1939), Mathematical Appendix; J. L. Mosak, *General Equilibrium Theory in International Trade* (Bloomington, Indiana, 1944), chap. V; and P. A. Samuelson, *Foundations of Economic Analysis* (Cambridge, Mass., 1947), chap. iv.

distance inputs in obtaining the raw material from M_2, and distance inputs in getting the product to C. Henceforth, we will speak merely of distance inputs from M_1, distance inputs from M_2 and distance inputs to C. Since Weber also postulates that the amounts of raw materials required per ton product are invariable with any shift of location, we can simplify the problem by using as weight units the amounts of the raw materials from M_1 and M_2 respectively required per ton of product; and with respect to distance inputs to C, one ton of product. With weight units so defined, distance inputs can be simply measured: the number of distance inputs from M_1 corresponds to the distance from M_1, etc. The variables become the actual distances.

Following customary procedure in illustrating graphically the equilibrium conditions between the quantities of any two commodities in our transformation function,[6] we assume a consistent set of quantities for all commodities but two. Assigning a value, let us say eight units, to the variable distance inputs to C, we obtain the arc TS in Figure 1 which is the resulting locus of consistent production sites within the locational triangle CM_1M_2.[7] This locus of sites can be expressed in terms of quantities of the distance inputs from M_1 and distance inputs from M_2 (since by definition these quantities

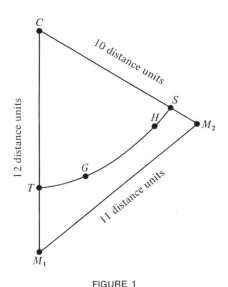

FIGURE 1

6. As in K. E. Boulding, *Economic Analysis* (New York, 1948), chap. 31.

7. When one of the required materials is immobile, we have as Weber indicated, production at the source of that material. No locational problem exists. The distance input from that source is zero and the distance inputs from sources of other materials and to the place of consumption are rigidly determined and are invariable.

are equated numerically to actual distances from M_1 and M_2 respectively). Hence, this locus yields for these two variables the transformation curve TS of Figure 2, which is convex to origin Q.[8] Since these variables are inputs, and thus by definition negative commodities, the convexity of TS to origin Q is equivalent to concavity of the transformation curve to an origin from which positive quantities of the two commodities are measured.

Following Weber, we first postulate that transport facilities of the same character radiate in all directions from all points in the plain and that transport rates are proportional to weight and distance. Since the transport rate is the price of a distance input, we can establish the relevant price ratios and construct price-ratio (or iso-outlay) lines once we know the quantities of each raw material from M_1 and two tons of the raw material from M are required per ton of product. Suppose three tons of the raw material from M_1 and two tons of the raw material from M_2 are required per ton of product. Each price-ratio line would have the same slope as lines AB and CD in Figure 2. Point J, the point of tangency of the transformation curve and price-ratio line CD, would represent the partial equilibrium set of quantities of our two variable distance inputs and thus would determine the site of production under our set of postulates. Of all points lying on the transformation curve TS, representing various combinations of these two distance inputs, J lies on the lowest price-ratio line and thus reflects a lesser outlay on transport than any other point. The first and second-order equilibrium conditions are fulfilled at point J for the quantities of this pair of distance inputs.

If different quantities of raw materials were required per ton of product, say four tons from source M_2 and three tons from source M_1, the price-ratio lines would have a different slope, namely that of line EF. The quantities of the distance inputs corresponding to point K would determine the equilibrium site.

In each case, however, we have only a partial locational solution, one that depends on the assumption that the site of production is

8. Our transformation curve is represented entirely by the stretch TS, since we do not consider points outside the locational triangle lying on the extensions of arc TS in Fig. 1. If we were to do this, we would be covering unnecessary distance. This would be inconsistent with our model as elaborated so far just as to employ five units of labor when four will suffice, given the wage, is inconsistent with the traditional statement of the transformation function. However, realistic situations with complicated institutional wage structures may involve the latter theoretical inconsistency. And as we shall see later, when there are limited transport facilities, or when discriminatory transport rates nullify the distance principle and make the cost between two termini less than that between an intermediate point and one of the termini, or when other conditions obtain, it is quite possible for an entrepreneur to choose a location involving unnecessary distance in the transformation sense.

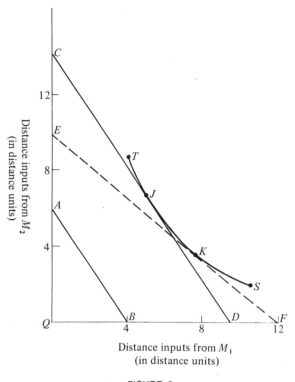

FIGURE 2

eight distance units from C. We must also allow variation in the quantity of distance inputs to C. If we do this, then we know from our transformation function that the transformation curve between the quantities of the distance inputs from M_1 and distance inputs from M_2 will change. Likewise, the respective partial equilibrium points. We would continue to vary the number of distance inputs to C, so long as the partial spatial equilibrium point for the two distance inputs from M_1 and M_2 did not correspond at the same time: (1) to a point of partial equilibrium for the two variables, distance inputs to C and distance inputs from M_1 (i.e., to a point of tangency between the transformation curve for quantities of these two inputs and the relevant price-ratio line) for the above or any other preliminary partial equilibrium quantity of distance inputs from M_2; and (2) to a point of partial equilibrium for the two variables distance inputs to C and distance inputs from M_2, for the above or any other preliminary partial equilibrium quantity of distance inputs from M_1. In brief, the first and second order conditions must be fulfilled for each of the three pairs of variables possible in our assumed situation. When such is the case we have an overall spatial equilibrium point which corresponds to Weber's transport optimal location or the location of minimum transport cost.

TRANSPORT-ORIENTED EQUILIBRIUM WITH REALISTIC RATE STRUCTURES

Hitherto, we have treated a very simplified model. We now relax one by one our unrealistic assumptions about the number of raw materials entering production and about the nature of transport facilities and the rate structure.

First, if we consider a production process utilizing three or more raw materials, each indispensable, mobile, and obtainable at an only source which does not coincide with the source of another, we are forced to pose the substitution question somewhat differently. Ordinarily we would hold constant the quantities of all inputs and outputs but two and observe the technical substitution relations between these two. However, if we were to assign a consistent set of quantities to two or more distance inputs, we would thereby unequivocally determine within the locational figure the site of production and the quantities of all other distance inputs; no substitution problem could arise.[9] To permit substitution among distance inputs, we need only set a total amount to be expended on all distance inputs but two. In this way we can obtain a locus of points consistent with any meaningful transport cost restraint and so attack the problem of finding the point representing the correct combination of the relevant

9. For example, if in considering location within the quadrilateral $CM_1M_2M_3$ we assign quantities to the distance inputs from M_1 and M_2, let us say RM_1 and RM_2

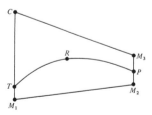

respectively, necessarily the site of production must be at R to be consistent with these quantities, and the quantities of the other inputs are uniquely determined, being measured by RC and RM_3. This situation resembles one where we examine the substitution relations between two factors, the quantity of each one for technical reasons bearing a fixed relationship to the quantity of another factor in a given basket of commodities. In effect there is no possibility of substitution.

pair of distance inputs.[10] The geographic rigidity resulting from setting constant the quantities of two distance inputs is avoided.

Second, we recognize that transport facilities do not radiate in all directions from all points. Rather they connect a finite number of points within any locational polygon with all or some of the corners of that polygon. Thus, to the individual firm not contemplating the construction of its own transport facilities, for any quantity of distance inputs to C, there may be relatively few, if any, sites to consider. In Figure 1, points T, G, H, and S may be the only ones having transport connections with the corners of the locational triangle. Accordingly, the transformation curve of Figure 2 would degenerate into four points. However, if we connect these points by dashed lines, as for example we connect the points B, E, F, D, and C in Figure 3, we can still state equilibrium conditions which resemble the conditions that apply when the transformation curve is a continuous function. In general, when viewed from Q as origin to the left of the partial equilibrium point, the arithmetic slope of the price-ratio line must be less than that of the dashed transformation "line," and to the right, the arithmetic slope of the former line must exceed that of the latter.[11] This point would then in the customary case lie on the lowest price-ratio line. Point D in Figure 3 would fulfill these conditions and would thus be a partial equilibrium point, if the price-ratio lines of Figure 3 did not have "tails" (which will be discussed below).

10. In the quadrilateral of the previous footnote, let us concentrate upon the technical substitution relations between the quantities of the two variables distance inputs to C and distance inputs from M_3. If in order to simplify our presentation we assume that transport cost is proportional to weight and distance and that equal weights or raw materials from sources M_1 and M_2 are required, we can indicate the locus of possible production sites by an elliptical curve, on which at any point the sum of miles from M_1 and miles from M_2, and thus the amount expended on transport of raw materials from M_1 and M_2 is constant. Assume a transport cost restraint on these two raw materials consistent with the elliptical curve TRP. This locus of points representing various combinations of the quantities of the variables distance inputs to C and distance inputs from M_3 would yield a transformation curve of the order of $TJKS$ in Fig. 2 if the quantity of one of the inputs is plotted horizontally, that of the other vertically, from origin Q.

11. When distance inputs from M_1 and distance inputs from M_2 are viewed as negative quantities of commodities r and s respectively, and the graphical solution is approached from an origin from which positive quantities of these commodities are measured. And in mathematical terms, we have: to the left of the partial equilibrium point, $p_r/p_s > -(\Delta y_s/\Delta y_{rr})$; and to the right of the partial equilibrium point, $p_r/p_s < -(\Delta \hat{y}_s/\Delta y_r)$, where Δy_r and Δy_s are finite changes in the quantities of the commodities, r and s when one moves from the partial equilibrium point to a point representing the next possible site of production in the relevant direction along arc TS, and p_r and p_s are respectively the prices of the distance inputs from M_1 and M_2, or, with the units adopted earlier, the transport charges per unit distance on the raw materials from M_1 and M_2 required for the production of a unit of output.

However, when we recognize that a transformation "line" may consist of only a finite number of points, twin partial solutions may be possible for any pair of distance

Of still greater moment is the relaxation of our assumption that transport rates are proportional to distance, an assumption which is only valid for areas where primitive transport mechanisms still operate. In areas girded by modern transport media which require large overhead expenditures and incur many costs and offer many services (especially terminal), which are unrelated to the distance covered in a given shipment, typically, tariff per distance unit or zone falls abruptly from the first to the second zone and considerably less abruptly between each succeeding zone (or set of zones) and the one after. Tariff structures are graduated, rates being less than proportional to distance.[12]

One can best demonstrate the significance of typical modern rate structures for the spatial equilibrium of the firm by constructing appropriate price-ratio lines or iso-outlay lines. We utilize the standard maximum first class rates on freight shipments prescribed by the United States Interstate Commerce Commission for railroads operating in the Eastern Territory.[13] On the basis of two short tons of raw material from source M_2 and one ton from source M_1 we have constructed on Figure 3 price-ratio or iso-outlay "lines" corresponding to outlays of $24.00, $26.40 and $30.00.[14]

Three characteristics of these iso-outlay lines are important to note. First, in effect they are not lines, but a series of rectangles and squares which have been blacked in. These rectangles and squares border each other or are connected by dashed lines. This particular form of iso-outlay line results from the zonal character of the rate structure. For example, the rate for a shipment of a given weight is the same for all distances 40 miles or less but greater than 35 miles. Hence, if we consider two shipments of different goods and weights,

inputs. This will occur if the slope of the price-ratio line is the same as that of the dashed line connecting two consecutive points of the transformation "line," each of which lies on the lowest of the price ratio lines which course through points of the transformation "line." This introduces a certain degree of indeterminacy into the overall solution. But this indeterminacy is not a major consideration in view of the analysis to come. The reader can easily restate the graphic and mathematical conditions for a twin solution.

Also see Samuelson, *op. cit.*, pp. 70–74 for a treatment of discontinuities in the production function.

12. For further details, see E. M. Hoover, *The Location of Economic Activity* (New York, 1948), chaps. 2–4.

13. As published in I.C.C. Docket 15879 Appendix E and as given in *The Freight Traffic Red Book* (New York, 1945), pp. 1194–95 in the column Appendix E under Eastern Class Rates.

14. Along each axis of Figure 3 we measure mileage from the respective source and also cost of transporting over the different distances the amounts of raw materials required per ton of output. The $30.00 line for example shows the various combinations of the quantities of the distance inputs from M_1 and distance inputs from M_2, which would occasion a total transport outlay on these two inputs of $30.00 per ton of product.

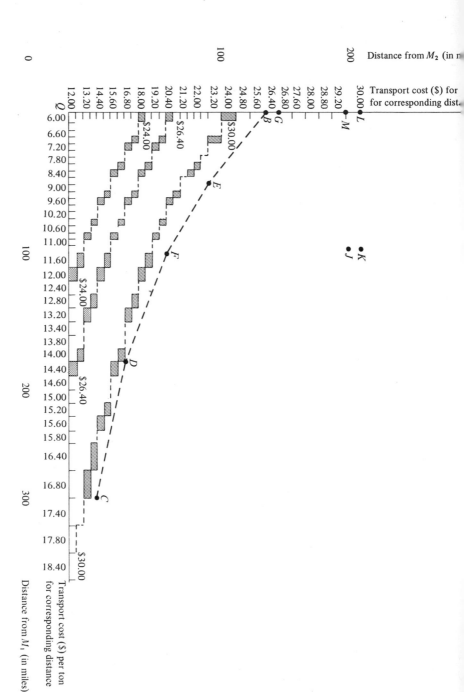

FIGURE 3

we find that total cost of these shipments will not vary for any combination of distances for these two shipments which can be represented by a point lying within a square (such as square *A* of Figure 3) which is bounded on two sides by two 40-mile lines and on the other two sides by two lines approaching the limit of 35 miles. Thus the producer may have considerable leeway in choosing a rational location and may select a site which compels him to traverse "unnecessary distance" (in terms of the minimum quantities hypothesized in the transformation function) without increasing his costs.[15]

Second, because the rate structure is graduated, the iso-outlay lines tend to be convex to origin *Q*, as in Figure 3. This has significant implications. Customarily, price-ratio or iso-outlay lines are taken to be straight or concave to the origin. One then obtains a unique, stable solution that involves quantities of both inputs, when, as is usually the case, the transformation curve is convex to the origin from which positive quantities of inputs are measured. If both the transformation "line" and iso-outlay "line" are irregularly convex to the origin, particularly if the latter is more convex than the former, as it may well be with modern rate structures, then the equilibrium point is likely to be an "end" point, that is, a realistic point on one of the ends of the transformation "line" and one which also may correspond to a corner of the locational polygon. The equilibrium point always is an "end" point in the case where the locational polygon collapses to a line, that is, where there is only one raw material used in the production process.[16]

Third, the likelihood of an "end" point solution is considerably increased by the fact that modern rate structures call for a relatively large increment in shipping charges from the zero (i.e., not shipping at all) to the first zone and relatively small increment for any other two successive zones. For example, on the horizontal scale of Figure 3 transport cost for one tone of the raw material from M_1 rises \$6.00 if one decides to ship one mile instead of zero miles, but rises only 20 cents if one decides to ship six miles instead of five. As a result price-ratio or iso-outlay lines have "tails" on both ends. Our \$30.00 and \$26.40 lines have respectively the vertical stretches *LM* and *BG* as tails on

15. Such a minor degree of indeterminacy also appears with respect to the quantities of other factor inputs employed when these inputs are sold in lot quantities which are not divisible, as where the services of a machine are rented by the month. The analysis is not seriously qualified, even though the typical mathematical solution implies unique amounts of inputs.

16. In this case, the transformation "line" is a straight line or consists of a number of realistic points lying on a straight line. Location will be at the raw material source if there is weight-loss in the production process and no addition of ubiquities, and at the place of consumption if there is no weight-loss in the processing of the raw material and if weight-contributing ubiquities are used. Compare Alfred Weber, *Über den Standort der Industrien* (Tübingen, 1909), pp. 62–63; and Dean, *op. cit.*, pp. 17–18.

the left.[17] Their tails on the right (horizontal stretches) are not shown in Figure 3 since they extend beyond the limits of the diagram.

In Figure 3 we have constructed the transformation line, *BEFDC*. Point *B* corresponds to the source of M_1; it represents zero quantity of distance inputs from M_1. At point *D* the usual equilibrium conditions are satisfied, since to the left of *D* the arithmetic slope of the iso-outlay line ($30.00) is less than that of the transformation line, and to the right of *D*, the arithmetic slope of the former exceeds that of the latter. However, *D* is only a relative minimum transport cost point. Only in contrast to the points in its own neighborhood does it represent the most desirable combination of distance inputs. End point *B*, lying on the tail *GB*, is still more desirable, for it falls on the $26.40 iso-outlay line, not on the $30.00 one. In the given situation and for this pair of distance inputs, *B* represents the position of stable equilibrium.

Thus, our technique clearly demonstrates the strategy of locating at corners of the locational polygon, given modern transport rate structures.[18] It is consistent with the emphasis that Palander, Hoover, and others[19] have given to such location, and the minor importance they have attached to locations intermediate between raw material sources and market centers. It implies that the individual producer must not be content with an equilibrium position arrived at by the usual substitution operations conceived in modern production theory,[20] but must compare the spatial equilibrium so obtained with each possible relative minimum transport cost position which corresponds to a zero amount of one of the distance inputs.[21]

17. In the case of our $30.00 line, a decision not to ship the raw material from M_1 at all instead of to ship it to a point within five miles permits a saving of $6.00, or allows the movement of the raw material from source M_2 over an additional 90 miles without increasing transport cost. Thus, the tail *LM*.

18. In situations where neither one raw material nor the market is dominant (in Weber's sense) so that locational polygons are meaningful constructs, it should not be inferred that relative minimum points will never exist at corners of these polygons unless there is a large initial increment followed by relatively small increments in the rate structure. Palander (*op. cit.*, pp. 314–16) has demonstrated that relative minima may occur at corners of polygons, when a tariff structure mildly graduated from beginning to end is in vogue. However, the advantage of corner location is generally not so pronounced with such a structure.

19. Palander, *op. cit.*, pp. 198–99, 330–33; Hoover, *op. cit.*, pp. 52–57; and B. Ohlin, *Interregional and International Trade* (Cambridge, Mass., 1933), pp. 185–202.

20. Thus the mathematical theory of production, as extended above to encompass distance inputs, although extremely valuable for its general statement, loses much of its force when one attempts to incorporate into his analysis such realistic complexities as modern transport rate structures.

21. Making this comparison is not so difficult as might appear. When any distance input is assigned a zero value, the quantities of the other distance inputs are uniquely determined. Thus the producer need only calculate the total transport cost for each corner of his locational polygon and for whatever relative minimum cost points (in the usual case, only one) may be determined through spatial substitution within the locational polygon.

We pause to consider a significant aspect of our technique. One of the most devastating shortcomings of the Weberian model has been its inability to encompass realistic transport rate structures less than proportional to distance. Weber proposed to take account of such rate structures by using fictitious distances. Distances should not be stated in their geographic length, but in proportion to the decreasing rate scale.[22] In general the longer the distance, the more it should be shortened for geometrical analysis. Bortkiewicz early showed that such a procedure is inconsistent with the construction of a locational polygon.[23] For how can we know how much to shorten the distance of any corner of the locational polygon from the given site of production and thus be able to calculate the relative distances between the various corners of the locational polygon until the actual location of the production site is determined; whilst on the other hand the very location of the production site is dependent upon the relative distances between the various corners of the locational polygon?

It is just this Weberian dilemma that our present technique cuts through. We need not speak of fictitious distances nor are we bound to a geometrical technique applicable only to situations where rates are proportional to distance.[24] Further, our technique brings out the critical importance of terminal and loading charges which the Weberian analysis essentially sidesteps.

Returning to the main thread of the argument, we find it also possible to account for the effects of breaks in transport routes, which characteristically occur at transport junctions where the direction of movement has to be changed, or where the shipment has to be unloaded and reloaded onto another transport medium or system, or where another scale of transport charges becomes effective, and so forth. To passover such breaks entails sudden large increments in transport cost, whether due to switching, loading or other charges. Industry often locates at such breaks in order to avoid these large increments. This is borne out by Figure 4. Here we assume a break in a given transport route 100 miles from each of the two sources M_1 and M_2. Along each axis is measured the cost of transporting over various distances the amount of raw material from the respective source which is required to produce one ton of finished product.

22. Weber, *op. cit.*, pp. 43–44.

23. L. von Bortkiewicz, "Eine geometrische Fundierung der Lehre vom Standort der Industrien," *Archiv für Sozialwissenschaft und Sozialpolitik,* Vol. XXX (1910), pp. 769–71. On this point Niederhauser's defence of Weber (*op. cit.*, pp. 173–75) is not convincing.

24. We should mention that when the transport rate structure is not proportional to weight, it is perfectly admissible, though we do not do so, to make adjustments as Weber does (*op. cit.*, pp. 44–46). A rate per ton-mile greater than normal for a given good, whatever the reason, implies an "ideal" weight greater than actual; a rate below normal implies an "ideal" weight less than actual.

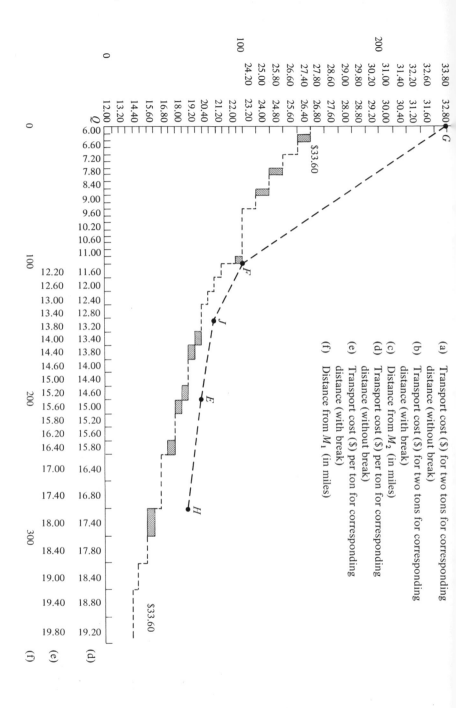

(a)   Transport cost ($) for two tons for corresponding distance (without break)
(b)   Transport cost ($) for two tons for corresponding distance (with break)
(c)   Distance from M_2 (in miles)
(d)   Transport cost ($) per ton for corresponding distance (without break)
(e)   Transport cost ($) per ton for corresponding distance (with break)
(f)   Distance from M_1 (in miles)

FIGURE 4

46

If there were no break in the transport route we would have a cost scale along each axis similar to that on Figure 3. But a break does exist and to pass over it involves an added cost of 50 cents per ton of raw material from M_2 and 60 cents per ton of raw material from M_1. Accordingly we have added another scale (the outer one) of transport charges for various distances along each axis after the hundred-mile mark. At point F, the graphic position of the break, the raw materials can be assembled from both sources M_1 and M_2 without either one bearing the added expense of passing over the break. The total transport cost is \$33.60 and we have constructed the iso-outlay line of \$33.60.[25] We also have inscribed a transformation "line" *GFJEH*. If no break existed, the equilibrium point would be G where the transformation "line" would meet the tail end of the iso-outlay line of \$32.80. But because there is a break, which necessitates additional transport expense, G lies on the tail end of an iso-outlay line of \$33.80. Point F, which satisfies the equilibrium conditions when quantities of both inputs are used, lies on the iso-outlay line of \$33.60. It is the preferred position.

One can handle many other transport rate irregularities by adjusting the vertical and horizontal scales and by constructing alternative ones.[26] It is sufficient to say that it is possible to encompass

25. In constructing this iso-outlay "line" we have assumed that to reach points other than the break itself one of the raw materials must pass over the break. Obviously the other must travel less than one hundred miles in this case since the line goes through the break itself and since we have taken it to be regular in its course. Complications, however, can arise when different assumptions are made.

26. As when different ton-mile rates apply to different commodities—whether because one is more bulky than the other, more valuable, more fragile or perishable, more difficult to handle, closer to the stage of finished product, better able to bear a high transport charge, etc. Or, in cases where different rates are set for different directions of movement, because one is uphill and the other downhill, because one encounters other more severe topographical obstacles, because one bears a greater volume of traffic, because greater speeds are attainable in one direction, etc. Or, where different types of transport facilities are used in any one journey or are available for reaching the various possible production sites. Or, when various types of import and export duties, or special levies or transport expenses are incurred at points along a given route.

It should also be mentioned that eccentricities in transport rate structures which run counter to transport cost as a monotonically increasing function of distance are reflected in eccentricities of iso-outlay lines. For example, the historically important practice in the United States of levying a smaller total charge for movement between two nodal termini served by two or more competing railways than for movement between one of these termini and an intermediate point or between two intermediate points on one of the alternative routes causes the iso-outlay lines to criss-cross. If, for instance, the raw material from M_2 could be moved from its source, a terminal, to another terminal 210 miles distant on a special rate, then point K in Fig. 3, which may represent a combination of the corresponding distance inputs and the distance inputs which correspond to a 100 mile movement of the raw material from M_1, would lie on a lower iso-outlay line than point J. Obviously such eccentricity enhances the attraction of terminal sites, particularly when these sites are raw material sources or consumption

in our locational equilibrium analysis for the firm the complexities of existing transport rate structures which reflect the inequalities from site to site of transport resources and facilities, whether man-made or geographically imposed. Thus, using the concept of distance inputs, we have been able to fuse much traditional (Weberian) locational doctrine on transport orientation and modern production theory for the firm, thereby in a sense extending both.

It is vital that we appreciate the general applicability of the concept of distance inputs. In terms of distance inputs we can express the locational adjustments of each transport-oriented production process. Take for example the iron and steel industry. The United States Steel Corporation recently announced plans to construct two million tons of steel capacity immediately below Trenton for serving the eastern seaboard market centering around New York City with steel produced from Venezuelan ore. Of the suitable waterfront sites, this was probably the closest to New York City. In choosing a site at Trenton rather than one farther from the market but closer to coal, the corporation substituted distance inputs from the coal source for distance inputs to the market. Considering, first, the possible combinations of quantities of these two distance inputs, given the quantity of distance inputs from Cerro Bolivar, Venezuela, which for practical purposes remains constant for all Middle Atlantic seaboard points, and second, considering the quantities of coal and scrap that might be used per ton steel, and the ton-mile transport charges on these items, and as a consequence the significantly higher price of a distance input to the market than of a distance input from the coal source—one can easily portray the Trenton site as the point of locational equilibrium in the given situation.[27]

For other transport-oriented industries, too, rational locational decisions can be expressed in terms of a correct combination of distance inputs. To be sure, a comparative cost calculation might

---

places. As a consequence, a commodity may travel an unnecessary distance, that is, to a site lying outside the locational polygon. Similarly, when back hauls and round-about hauls take place because of the rigidities of the transport net, especially in water and water-rail transport.

27. In making this statement we also consider variation in the quantity of distance inputs from Cerro Bolivar, for the given requirement of ore per ton steel. A meaningful larger quantity of this input would involve an inland location which in view of the significant cost of transshipment to rail and of the geography of ore, coal and market sites would not be an overall locational equilibrium point when translated into the relevant sets of transformation and iso-outlay "lines." Neither would a location in the Southern Atlantic seaboard, which would involve a smaller quantity of this input.

See in this connection, W. Isard and J. Cumberland, "New England as a Possible location for an Integrated Iron and Steel Works," *Economic Geography*, Vol. 26 (October 1950), pp. 245–59.

be a more direct and less awkward way of explaining the logic of each specific locational decision. Expressing decisions in terms of a *common* concept of distance inputs, however, permits us to carry over conclusions from one location study to another. Furthermore, and much more significant, such a procedure greatly facilitates the tasks of describing and understanding the operation of a space-economy, of interpreting empirical findings such as those of Zipf and Stewart, and of envisaging and planning an optimum joint geographic distribution of industry.[28]

Another critical point needs to be discussed. Given existing transport rate structures, the advantage of locating at terminal points and corners of the locational polygon is in many cases marked. Small changes in the prices of distance inputs resulting from small changes in raw material requirements per unit product or in the transport rate structures very likely may not result in a shift of the locational equilibrium position. That is, there very likely may not be any substitution of one set of distance inputs for another. Thus, in spatial production analysis emphasis on fine adjustments to price changes, as is implied for example in Hicksian production theory,[29] may not be warranted. On the other hand the input-output technique based on constant production coefficients has considerable validity. The criticism of this technique for its partial exclusion of substitution among inputs[30] loses much of its force in locational analysis, where small substitutions among distance inputs are not too frequent, and where large substitutions are easily discernible, and adjusted for.

SUBSTITUTION BETWEEN OUTLAYS AND REVENUES AND OTHER FORMS OF ORIENTATION

Heretofore, we have examined the conditions for spatial equilibrium of transport-oriented production processes, postulating that differentials among sites in every cost item and revenue[31] except transport either do not exist or are insignificant. But what if, as in

28. Compare T. C. Koopmans, "The Optimum Geographical Distribution of Population and Industry in the United States," unpublished memorandum of the Cowles Commission for Research in Economics.

29. Hicks, *op. cit.*, chap. vi.

30. As in the discussion papers on "Input–Output Analysis and its Use in Peace and War Economies," *Papers and Proceedings of the American Economic Association*, Vol. 39 (May 1949) pp. 226–40.

31. We consider differentials in revenue since a firm may consider several production locations, which may be gateway points to different markets, where different prices for the firm's product or products obtain.

the case of aluminum, differentials in some of these costs or revenues do exist and are marked?

To incorporate such differentials into general locational analysis for the firm, it is necessary to think in terms of substitution between outlays and revenues. It is not sufficient here to speak of substitution between the commodities encompassed by our transformation function, for it is the variation from site to site in the prices of these inputs and outputs which induce locational shifts. For example, Weber discusses the phenomenon of labor-orientation, where a firm does not locate at the transport optimum point representing the best combination of distance inputs, but rather at a cheap labor point. When these two points are not identical, the firm thereby consumes more distance inputs and increases its transport outlays while it simultaneously holds constant (or even increases) its labor inputs but reduces its labor outlays, *ceteris paribus*. We do not have substitution between distance inputs and labor inputs, but rather between transport outlays and labor outlays.

It is possible to develop elaborate conceptual schemes to treat substitutions between outlays and revenues. Weber made extensive use of such concepts as the critical isodapane[32] when speaking of labor orientation. One can think of critical isodapanes with respect to other types of orientation,[33] which theoretically are of the same order as labor orientation, though in reality less significant. Or one can construct diagrams of substitution lines for each pair of outlays, or for each pair of groups of outlays, or for each set of a revenue and an outlay, or for each set of a group of revenues and a group of outlays or for each pair of revenues, or for each pair of groups of revenues and with the appropriate iso-outlay lines or iso-revenue-less-outlay lines, or iso-revenue lines demonstrate the various substitution operations that may be performed in attaining the optimum location for the firm.[34] We refrain, however, from doing this. For,

32. An isodapane is a curve connecting points representing locations involving the same increases of transport cost over the cost incurred at the transport optimum point. The critical isodapane for any cheap labor site is the one which represents an additional transport outlay equivalent to the saving in labor outlay at the cheap labor site. If the site lies anywhere within the area bounded by the critical isodapane, it will attract the production process under consideration (Weber, *op. cit.*, pp. 102–04).

33. As Predöhl does in "The Theory of Location in its Relation to General Economics," *Journal of Political Economy*, Vol. 36 (June 1928), pp. 386–87.

34. As a typical case, one may treat graphically substitution between transport outlays and labor outlays. To every realistic point on the transformation "line" for a pair of distance inputs we can assign not only a necessary transport outlay as given by the iso-outlay line which passes through it, but also a labor outlay. Thus if we take the realistic points G, F, J, E and H on the transformation line in Fig. 4, and assume that labor outlay per ton of product is $20.00 at each of the sites represented by these points, except the cheap labor site represented by J, where it is only $16.00, we can

aside from the variation associated with increase in transport cost with greater distance from a given reference point, variations in the prices of inputs and outputs do not proceed with regularity over space. For example, cheap labor points may occur in unpredictable fashion; the geographic tax pattern may be extremely haphazard. Thus, at this stage, where we are concerned with the development of equilibrium analysis for the firm as an integral part of a general theory of space-economy which is independent of any particular cultural, institutional or geographic frame of reference, there is little value in attempting to treat elaborately substitution between outlays and revenues. Rather, where a particular process is not transport-oriented, i.e., where transport cost differentials among sites

depict the respective transport and labor outlays incurred at these sites by corresponding points on Fig. 5. In this figure, labor outlays and transport outlays are measured along the vertical and horizontal axes, respectively.

Also, on this figure we have plotted the points L, M, N and R which represent other cheap labor sites. These additional positions do not have corresponding realistic points on the transformation "line" of Fig. 4. But in the light of all possible variations in all distance inputs (distance inputs from M_1, from M_2 and to C), they correspond to realistic points on relevant transformation lines when the quantity of the distance input to C is different from that assumed in Fig. 4. When, of two or more points incurring the same labor outlay, we consider only the one which involves the least transport outlay, and when we connect these points in order according to transport outlay, we obtain the line $FJLMNR$ which may be called an "outlay-substitution" line. It presents the meaningful substitution possibilities between transport and labor outlays, just as the transformation line does for two inputs. We also construct a new set of iso-outlay (transport plus labor outlay) lines which are straight and obviously have a negative slope of unity when the same scale is used along both axes.

Of all points on the "outlay-substitution" line, J lies on the lowest iso-outlay line. It indicates location at a cheap labor site and a substitution of transport outlays for labor outlays.

The reader, if he cares to, may state formal conditions for equilibrium with respect to these two outlays. He may also extend his statement of conditions in order to consider other possible substitutions between outlays and revenues, such as when differentials among sites exist with respect to rent outlays, prices of raw materials, tax outlays, revenues from sale of products, and so forth. The statement becomes elaborate especially since some of the segments of "outlay-substitution" lines and other substitution lines which would have to be treated would have positive slopes in contrast with the negative ones depicted above, and since sites frequently may differ with respect to more than two outlays and revenues. We do not present such a statement here, because, as indicated in the text, it would only have very limited significance for general spatial theory.

Incidentally, the approach illustrated by the above figure does away with the unnecessarily complex Weberian technique for determining whether or not an operation will be labor-oriented, and if so, to which cheap labor site. According to Weber one must construct the critical isodapane for each cheap labor site, consider only those sites which fall within their critical isodapanes, and select that site which in terms of "ideal" distance lies farthest from its critical isodapane. Using the above graphic technique, one needs to observe whether or not any points representing cheap labor sites lie on lower iso-outlay lines than the point representing the transport optimum site, and if so, select that site represented by the point lying on the lowest iso-outlay line. Also, when adjustment is made for transport savings from the use of replacement deposits, the Weberian technique is unnecessarily complex.

are not the dominant ones, it is best in ascertaining the maximum profit location merely to recognize that substitutions do take place among outlays and revenues and to focus attention upon the more important substitutions. To be specific, the indirect shift of textile capacity from New England to the cheap labor point of Puerto Rico involved a substitution of transport outlays for labor outlays. The cheap labor point, however, was in no way *generally* related to a distance factor. It could have existed elsewhere. This arbitrariness emasculates any attempt at stating general formal equilibrium conditions regarding this substitution in analyzing the spatial equilibrium of this case.[35]

Still another important matter which deserves explicit mention is the relation between the location of a firm and its scale of operations; this relation is contained within our general transformation function for the firm. Heretofore we have been implicitly assuming that total output is given. But as we let output change, the substitution possibilities between any pair of inputs may also change. For example, for a given scale of operations, the substitution relations between the different distance inputs and outlays and revenues may dictate a location at a concentrated source of a raw material. However, with a larger scale of operations it may be feasible to adopt a somewhat different method of production—but one implicit in our transformation function—whereby the raw material is partly processed at its source, as in benefication of ore, and then shipped in purer form and thus at lower transport expense per unit of output to the market where production is completed. Such a change in output involves, in addition to numerous other substitutions, substitution of distance inputs from the source of the raw material for distance inputs to the market, and a locational shift of part of the production process. Or, it may be that with a larger scale of operation it becomes feasible to construct a new transport facility in order to shift production operations to a cheap labor site. In Figure 5 we have: substitution between revenues and outlays, as is implied in the variation of output; substitution between outlays, specifically transport outlays for labor outlays; and relative to the increased scale of operations, substitution between distance inputs as well as between other inputs. And so forth. In short, scale of operations is one of the important factors which affect location.[36]

35. To be sure, when our interest narrows down to a particular region, which at a given time does possess a singular cultural and geographic pattern of resources, costs, and prices, it may then turn out to be worthwhile to advance formal equilibrium conditions for substitutions between outlays and revenues.

36. Note, again, that locational shifts involved with change in scale of operations and in the substitutions of one outlay for another may very likely be of the type which require abrupt and frequently sizeable spatial jumps. At each site under consideration,

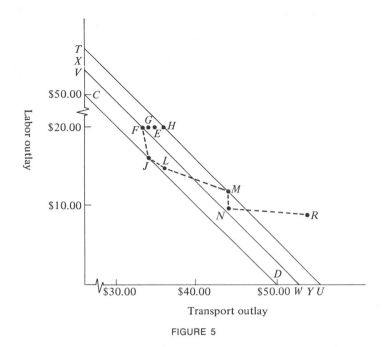

FIGURE 5

EQUILIBRIUM WITH AREAL MARKETS AND MATERIAL SOURCES

We now can relax another simplifying postulate, namely, that all markets and raw material sources are points. Incidentally, for a long time, location theorists treated separately the problems of production for a one-point consumption place and production for a market area.[37] Using the concept of distance inputs, we shall briefly

coefficients of production with regard to distance inputs may usually with good reason be taken as fixed. Small variations in the prices of these inputs may often have no effect upon location. When they do, locational shifts are frequently marked, and are often associated with shifts in technique of production. These conditions make the use of the input-output technique of analysis more feasible for spatial problems.

37. Launhardt, who presented the first significant treatment of industrial location theory, distinguished between the partial problem of determining the site of production within or at the corners of a locational polygon, where the corners represented raw material sources and a one-point consumption place ("Dei Bestimmung des zweckmassigsten Standortes einer gewerblichen Anlage," *Zeitschrift des Vereines Deutscher Ingenieure*, Bd. 26 March 1882), and the partial problem of supplying a consuming area from a given point of production (*Mathematische Begründung der Volkswirthschaftslehre*, Leipzig, 1885, Pt. III). Although he handled both problems comprehensively for his time, he made no attempt to put them together. Weber, in his analysis, treated only the first of these problems. Engländer, perhaps the first to recognize that these two problems are fundamentally one and the same (in his caustic criticism of Weber, "Kritisches und Positives..." *op. cit.*), nevertheless did not adequately synthesize them in this and his other works. The later writings of Palander, Hoover and Lösch are much more satisfactory in this respect.

demonstrate how the former may be viewed as a special case of the latter.

Because of space limitations, we shall treat only a few types of situations involving spatial spread of consumers and of raw material sources. For the moment assume that raw material sources are points. If consumers come to a particular site and make their purchases there, or arrange transportation from that site on the item purchased, then to the producer of this item, that site is the market. For that individual producer, whom for the present we take to be an isolated monopolist in the Chamberlain sense,[38] our spatial equilibrium analysis need not be extended. From the standpoint of society, however, when consumers are actively responsible for the transportation of the item, another set of distance inputs may be involved. If the consumers are other producers farther along in the stage of manufacture, then this transportation appears as distance inputs on raw material from a point source in these producers' calculations; and again no extension of our analysis is required. On the other hand, if consumers are households, we are not thus far able to account for the distance inputs for which they are actively responsible.[39] However, once we make the assumption, usually considered legitimate for economic analysis, that tastes and space preferences are known, and thus demand schedules and the spatial pattern of population about any given pattern of focal points, we necessarily "explain" the total quantity of distance inputs for which household consumers are actively responsible.

Consider situations, where, in contrast, the producer is actively responsible for transporting his products to the places of use, where each consumer is charged a price equal to a quoted price at a focal point plus transport cost to his place, and where the producer arranges the distribution of his product from that focal point. If the consumer is an industrial producer, he has in effect made the decision to contract for the distance inputs involved in delivery from the focal point to the place of use by having chosen to locate where he is rather than at a site closer to the focal point. He incurs the expense of these distance inputs indirectly by paying a higher

38. See Chamberlin, *The Theory of Monopolistic Competition, op. cit.*, p. 74; and particularly Chamberlin's unpublished manuscript, "Competition, Monopoly and Economic Growth."

39. To do so would take us into the realms of sociology and social psychology. For to explain the spatial distribution of household consumers around focal points — for example, the population spread around any given metropolitan core — requires knowledge of the process by which tastes are molded and, in particular, understanding of the space preferences of consumers. Human ecology promises eventually to provide such an understanding. (See Bogue, *op. cit.*; McKenzie, *op. cit.*; and A. Hawley, *Human Ecology*, [New York, 1950]).

delivered price. From society's standpoint, we may still consider the transport cost on the product paid by the first producer as outlays by the second producer on distance inputs required to obtain one of his raw materials. Once again our analysis needs no extension. If the consumer is a household, and we take his tastes, space preference and thus demand schedules as given, we necessarily "explain" the distance inputs involved in the delivery of the product from the focal point. The consumer's willingness to pay the delivered price signifies his willingness to incur the costs of these distance inputs. When the household is unwilling to incur these costs and when the industrial consumer finds it expedient to avoid distance inputs in obtaining the product which he uses as a raw material, then the market for the producer of this product reduces to a point. Production for a one-point market is thus a special case of production for a market area, continuous or discontinuous.

Where the individual producer distributes his products from several focal points, we have to treat not one category of distance inputs in reaching the market, but several sub-categories. We proceed in the same manner as when we increase the number of raw materials required in the production process, and thus the number of distance inputs apropos the assembly of raw materials. Analysis of any concrete situation becomes more complicated, but the technique remains the same.

Alternative geographic pricing arrangements—such as uniform and zonal price systems—can likewise be broken down into relations which can be attacked for each firm in terms of substitution between distance inputs and between various outlays and revenues. Similarly, geographic price discrimination.

When we go beyond the first level of inquiry as stated [at the beginning of this article], or more explicitly, when we deal with individual producers who are not isolated monopolists, then various complications and indeterminacies appear. The nature of some of these is well brought out in the literature on spatial competitions along a line.[40] Such competition is but a special simplified case of market area competition but has considerable counterpart in reality where there are a limited number of modern transport lines serving a given area. Here, however, we shall not develop spatial analysis for firms which are not isolated monopolists.

Finally, we can handle in somewhat parallel fashion situations where raw material sources are not points but are areas, as is

40. The reader is referred in particular to Launhardt, *op. cit.*, E. Chamberlin, *The Theory of Monopolistic Competition* (Cambridge, 1948), 6th ed., Appendix C, and to the writings of Hotelling, Zeuthen, Palander, Lerner and Singer, Smithies, Ackley, Schneider and Möller, all cited in Chamberlin's bibliography.

particularly striking in production processes utilizing agricultural products. If a specific raw material obtained from many suppliers is collected at a focal point, to simplify analysis it is best to conceive of each supplier as being responsible for the distance inputs required in moving his product to the focal point. This, even though the consuming firm may purchase at the place of production of each one of these suppliers.[41] If the consuming firm is located at this focal point, with reference to its operations no distance inputs are required for the assembly of this raw material. If the firm is not located at the focal point, then it is responsible for the distance inputs in moving the raw material from that focal point only. If there is more than one focal point, then we must consider in our substitution analysis distance inputs from each focal point. Clearly, point sources of raw materials can be viewed as a special case of areal sources or supply areas, occurring where all suppliers happen to be concentrated at one or a few particular focal points, as frequently is the case with ore mining. The quantity of distance inputs involved in the assembly of a raw material at a focal point is then zero.

CONCLUSIONS

We have sketchily presented empirical findings of Zipf, Stewart, and others which point up the direct and indirect relations of diverse variables to the distance factor—such as the rank-size rule for cities, the linear statistical relations (logarithmic scales) between the P_1P_2/D factor and each of a number of variables; the linear statistical relations (logarithmic scales) between potential of population or demographic energy and each of a number of variables. These extensive empirical findings call for a systematic study of the roll of distance in the functioning in an economy. We have chosen to follow a theoretical approach.

To help understand the time-space continuum of society we develop the concept of distance inputs. We define a distance input as the movement of a unit weight over a unit distance. In the growth of a simple nucleus of population distance inputs early become basic elements. They permit the increased productivity which accrues from (1) postponing and mitigating agglomeration diseconomies and the forces of diminishing returns and (2) exploiting the unequal distribution of natural resources. These same basic forces

41. We are tacitly assuming that the difference between price at the focal point and price at the place of production is equal to the cost of transport. When pricing arrangements are made otherwise, we must consider substitution not only between distance inputs, but in addition between outlays and revenues.

operate in our modern world-economy with its complex hierarchy of cities and spatial distributions of population.

There are interesting parallels between capital inputs and distance inputs. Both can be thought of as derived and as indicating roundaboutness in the production process. Corresponding to the former we have such concepts as time extent (period) of investment, time discount, and time preference; to the latter, spatial extent of production, space discount and space preference. Space preference, in the usual case, is positive, and may be thought of as a psychological or biological force which manifests itself in the social nature of man, in his propensity for intricate forms and patterns of herd existence.

The transport rate is the price of a distance input. Its determination may be accounted for by a conventional demand and supply analysis for distance inputs. A fall in the price of a distance input induces a spatial lengthening of production and may be associated (as is historically the case) with both a scale and a substitution effect.

We visualize a distance input as a service, of which there can be no stocks. For distance inputs are simultaneously rendered by combinations of other services. One need not, however, attempt to insert distance inputs in the traditional classifications of production factors and services. More important is a recognition of their role.

Turning to the individual firm as a basic unit of economic analysis, we find that its locational problem can be conceived as implicitly stated by a transformation function and that its spatial equilibrium can be viewed in terms of first and second order conditions when distance inputs are treated explicitly. The Weberian solution for transport-oriented production processes can be alternatively presented with the use of the techniques of modern production theory. Locational triangles reduce to transformation lines between distance inputs. Relative transport rate structures (including "ideal weight" adjustments) are reflected in price-ratio or iso-outlay lines. At the same time, with these techniques which emphasize substitution among distance inputs, we can incorporate more of reality into locational analysis. Particularly, we can handle the graduated feature of modern transport rate structures with their sudden marked changes and irregularities without confronting the inconsistencies which have plagued Weberian students. The character of these rate structures, especially the large charge for shipment to any point within the first zone, as well as the limited number of transport routes, brings out the strategy of locating at an end point, that is, at a corner of the locational polygon rather than at an intermediate point within the figure. The strong attraction of breaks in transport routes is also clearly depicted.

When major differentials among sites in various cost and revenue items do exist, especially when a process is not transport-oriented, it is also necessary to think in terms of substitutions among outlays and revenues, as in the case of labor orientation. However, for developing a general theory of space-economy, it is not feasible to elaborate upon these substitutions, since the cost and revenue differentials underlying them are generally in no way related to the distance factor.

Lastly, market areas for products and supply areas of raw materials can be expressed in terms of distance inputs. Our technique embraces both point and areal location analysis.

In closing, we wish to reiterate that with the concept of distance inputs we are able to extend modern production theory to cover the spatial equilibrium of the firm, and that at the same time we are able to go considerably beyond traditional Weberian location doctrine. More important, the concept of distance inputs is a common, operational one. In terms of it, the spatial pattern of each line of economic activity can be expressed. Thus it facilitates the construction of a general theory to explain the intricately woven fabric of our space-economy.

4

Location and the Theory
of Production

This paper deals with the theory of the firm in a spatial setting. The paper is motivated by a belief that modern location theory still assumes a linear production function and in this respect has not progressed beyond Alfred Weber's original formulation of the location problem.[1] My objective is to place the theory of location within the main body of economic theory. More specifically, I wish to make the theory of location an integral part of the theory of production and to investigate the implications of factor substitution for the locational equilibrium of the firm. My main conclusion is that profit maximization requires a proper adjustment of output, input combination, location, and price. Moreover, the optimizing values of these three variables can be determined with analytical tools derived directly from traditional economic theory. There is no need for much of the esoteric paraphernalia sometimes employed by location specialists.

Most of the theory will be developed for the simple case of a firm which employs two transportable inputs to produce a single product that is sold in a single market point. Figure 1 depicts the locational problem. M_1 and M_2 are the sites of the two materials and C is the market point. The distances M_1M_2, M_1C, and M_2C are known. The latter two distances will be referred to respectively as "a" and "b". The values of the included angles are also known, though we will be concerned only with the angle θ. Before enumerating the remainder of the notation it should be mentioned that the geometry is incidental to the concepts that emerge.

NOTATION:

P_1, the price of the first input at its source
P_2, the price of the second input at its source
r_1, the transport rate on the first input

1. *Alfred Weber's Theory of The Location of Industries*, trans. C. J. Freidrich (The University of Chicago Press, 1929).

While assuming responsibility for any errors, the author wishes to express his gratitude to James M. Henderson, Marie McCarthy, Alan Strout, and Mary Sullivan for their helpful suggestions.
Reprinted by permission of the publishers from The Quarterly Journal of Economics, 72 *(Cambridge, Mass.: Harvard University Press, 1958), pp. 259–72. Copyright 1958 by the President and Fellows of Harvard College.*

r_2, the transport rate on the second input

s_1, the distance from M_1 to the locus of production of the final product

s_2, the distance from M_2 to the locus of production of the final product

P'_1, the price of the first input *delivered* to the locus of production of the product

P'_2, the price of the second input *delivered* to the locus of production of the final product

I assume that inputs are sold f.o.b. Their delivered prices are, therefore, equal to price at the source plus full freight. If inputs are sold according to some other geographical pricing technique, delivered prices may be greater or less than f.o.b. prices, but this will not invalidate our analysis.

At the outset we deal with a partial equilibrium problem in which the distance that the final product must be shipped is held constant. Thus, an arc is described in Figure 1 from C which cuts the triangle at

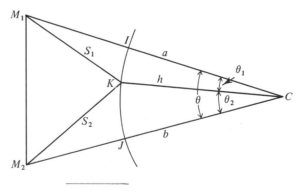

FIGURE 1

I and J. This arc is a segment of the circle with center at C and radius h. All points along the arc are a fixed distance from C and – initially – are the only ones which are considered as possible locations for the plant. With transportation cost on the final product fixed, we can concentrate on the problem of factor substitution as affected by variations in transportation expenditure. We do this by focusing attention on the ratio of delivered prices along the arc. In other words, each small move along the arc from I towards J increases the distance which the first raw material must be shipped, decreases the distance which the second raw material must be shipped, and alters the ratio of delivered prices.

In order to achieve a more rigorous statement of the problem, the angle θ is treated as being composed of two angles, θ_1, and θ_2. θ_1 is permitted to take on all values between zero and θ. θ_1, being assigned some value, θ_2 is equal to θ minus θ_1. It is the variation in the angle θ_1 which defines the moving point that is the locus of production. For example, if θ_1 is equal to θ, then J is being considered as the production site. Suppose a value is assigned to the angle θ_1 which defines the point K on the arc. Join the points M_1 and M_2 with K. By the law of cosines, the distances from the two material sites to K can be determined:

$$s_1 = \sqrt{a^2 + h^2 - 2ah \cos \theta_1} \tag{1}$$

$$s_2 = \sqrt{b^2 + h^2 - 2bh \cos (\theta - \theta_1)} \tag{2}$$

The letters a, b, and h in the above equations represent the known distances M_1C, M_2C, and KC, respectively.

Since base prices and transportation rates are known, and since we have assumed that the materials are sold on an f.o.b. basis, the prices of the two materials delivered to K can also be determined.

$$P_1' = P_1 + r_1 \sqrt{a^2 + h^2 - 2ah \cos \theta_1} \tag{3}$$

$$= P_1 + r_1 s_1$$

$$P_2' = P_2 + r_2 \sqrt{b^2 + h^2 - 2bh \cos (\theta - \theta_1)} \tag{4}$$

$$= P_2 + r_2 s_2$$

We may also form a ratio between equations three and four:

$$\frac{P_1'}{P_2'} = \frac{P_1 + r_1 s_1}{P_2 + r_2 s_2}$$

What is this ratio? *It is the constant slope of the system of iso-outlay lines when production takes place at K.* There is no ambiguity concerning these iso-outlay lines. Each point along the arc IJ is characterized by a definite ratio of delivered prices on the two inputs. This ratio defines the slope of the system of iso-outlay lines at that point.

Two iso-outlay lines are shown in Figure 2. Both represent the same total expenditure — taking into account base prices, and transportation — on the two material inputs. However, AB is one of the system of iso-outlay lines associated with production at I whereas DE is one of the system of iso-outlay lines associated with production at J. In the figure, emphasis is given to those portions of the two lines which make up the line AFE. The reason for the emphasis is that up to

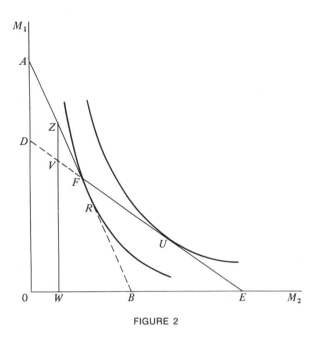

FIGURE 2

the point F, outlay line AB (and hence, location at I) offers the possibility of purchasing the same amount of one input, say M_1, as outlay line DE (representing location at J) but more of the other input. For example, consider the points V and Z, both involving the same expenditure. V lies on the iso-outlay line corresponding to location at I while Z lies on the iso-outlay line corresponding to location at J. The figure indicates that if the firm locates at I it will be able to purchase the same quantity of M_2 as it could if it located at J, but that it can acquire a greater amount of M_1 (equal to VZ) with total expenditure the same. To the right of point F the situation is reversed. Location at J permits the same quantity of M_1 to be purchased as at I but more of M_2, expenditure given. In any particular case, the isoquants determine the relative profitability of locating at J or at I.

Suppose the firm decides to expend upon production an amount which corresponds to the iso-outlay lines of Figure 2. In this case — questions of demand elasticity aside — the profits of the firm would be greater if it located at J rather than at I since the same total expenditure yields a higher output at the former. Two points of tangency, R and U, are shown in the figure. R is a tangency point produced by an isoquant and that portion of the outlay line AB which lies below F. Clearly, the firm is better off if it locates at J and uses the combination of inputs associated with the tangency point U since the latter lies on a higher isoquant than R.

Up to now only two locations along the arc IJ have been considered, and therefore, only two differently sloped iso-outlay lines appear in Figure 2. If each of the infinite number of points along the arc IJ is treated as a possible location, then the discontinuous line AFE becomes a smooth curve. The reason for this is that each point along the arc has a unique ratio of delivered prices. We will call this smooth curve the locational iso-outlay curve. *Each point along this curve corresponds to a particular location along the arc IJ, and shows the one combination of factors which the firm would purchase at that particular location, given the dollar expenditure, transport rates, and base prices of the inputs.* It must be emphasized that if continuous spatial substitution is possible (i.e., all points along the arc IJ may become the site of production), then there is only one combination of inputs which is optimal for each location. All other combinations are of the same sort as those depicted by R and V in Figure 2. In other words, the locational iso-outlay curve represents the results of an optimization process. Uneconomic combinations of inputs do not appear in it. Which combinations of inputs are uneconomic for each location can be decided without reference to the production function. The relevant factors are distance relations, the spatial structure of transport costs, and the prices of inputs at their sources.

The nature of the locational iso-outlay curve can be brought out still more clearly by analogy with the familiar case of production with variable input prices. Consider a producer, who, by varying the manner in which he apportions a given expenditure on two inputs, can reduce the price of one but only at the expense of an increase in the price of the other. The firm seeking a location along the arc IJ is in a similar position. It can reduce the *delivered* price of M_1 by selecting a location along the arc closer to the source of this input, but only at the expense of an increase in the delivered price of M_2. As an aside we may also mention that if each point along the arc IJ has its own ratio of delivered prices, then each point also has its own total cost curve. All of these cost curves together form what we may call the "locational planning curve," to draw another analogy from traditional theory.

Figure 2 considers only one level of expenditure. If different levels of expenditure are considered, then a system of locational iso-outlay curves will be generated. The dashed curves of Figure 3 depict such a system. All of these curves pertain to locations along the arc IJ of Figure 1, but each represents a different level of expenditure upon the inputs. The solid curves of the diagram are isoquants. The slope of the line KL defines a point along the arc IJ of Figure 1.

Suppose the firm wished to deliver a fixed number of units of the product to the market, for example 1000. As in traditional theory,

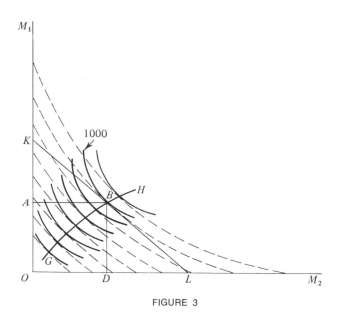

FIGURE 3

optimality is characterized by the tangency condition, i.e., at *B* in Figure 3. *However, the point B represents not only a particular combination of inputs — as in traditional theory — but also a particular location along the arc IJ.* The firm chooses that location at which the ratio of delivered prices is equal to the slope of the 1000 unit isoquant. In this location the firm will use *OA* units of M_1 and *OD* units of M_2. The marginal rate of outlay substitution will be equal to the marginal rate of input substitution. In other words, within the dimensions of the problem as so far formulated, the optimum location along the arc *IJ* of Figure 1 is the point at which total expenditure is a minimum. At this location the factors will be combined in such a way that the ratio of their marginal productivities is equal to the ratio of their delivered prices. It would be purely by chance if total transportation costs were a minimum at this point. The conclusion anticipates the brief survey of literature found in the final pages of this paper.

   In analyzing the location problem of an individual firm, Weber, Hoover, and Isard begin by assuming that there are no geographic variations in the prices or qualities of inputs at alternative sources.[2] From this assumption they derive two conclusions: (1) that there are no geographic differentials in production costs, and hence, that (2) the optimum location is the point of minimum transportation costs. However, the two conclusions do not follow from the aforementioned assumption alone. They also involve an additional one, namely,

   2. Specific footnote references to the works of these authors follow.

that the production function is linear. There are no alternative sources for inputs in the example with which we have been working. However, we have permitted factor substitution and therefore have altered the conditions for optimality in location. This difference is not the only one which emerges.

A number of points of tangency between locational iso-outlay lines and isoquants is shown in Figure 3. These points trace an expansion path, labelled *GBH*. It differs from the expansion path of traditional theory in that each point along its length refers to a location (along the arc *IJ* in the present case) as well as a level of output and a combination of inputs. This expansion path brings an interesting point to light, and one which, to the author's knowledge, is not made clear in previous works on the theory of location. *If the production function is not homogeneous of the first degree there is no single optimum location along the arc IJ. The optimum location varies with the level of output.* Moreover, if continuous spatial, as well as factor, substitution is possible there will be a different optimum for every level of output. This being so, demand considerations should be introduced into the analysis. However, before doing so, there are two additional points that require consideration.

First, as we have drawn the iso-outlay lines and isoquants in Figure 3, there is a single point of tangency for each output or each level of expenditure. There is no *a priori* reason for this condition. In actuality, there may be more than one point of tangency, i.e., alternative locations may exist which are equally good for producing a given output or expending a given amount upon production.

Second, we have drawn the curves of Figure 3 so that the tangency points are equilibrium points. There does not appear to be any reason why this must be so. The isoquants can be tangent to the outlay lines from below. Whether they are or not will depend in any particular case on the production function, base prices of materials, transportation rates on materials, and their geographic position relative to one another. We are still considering the partial problem of location along the arc *IJ* of Figure 1. In this case, if the isoquants are tangent to the outlay lines from below, the firm would locate either at *I* or *J*. In order to bring out a somewhat different point, let us postulate that transportation costs on the final product are negligible, and that the firm is free to locate anywhere in the locational triangle of Figure 1. In this case, if the inputs are substitutable in the extreme — by which we mean that the product can be produced entirely with one or the other of them — then the firm will locate at the source of one of the inputs and use none of the other. If the inputs are not substitutable in the extreme, the firm will be drawn close to the source of one of them, and use relatively more of it than the other.

Above, it was stated that demand considerations should be introduced into the analysis. In order to save space this issue will be treated in conjunction with a number of other factors so far ignored. First, regional variations in the money price of a given input will be introduced. Second, the effect of transportation cost incurred in shipping the product to the market will be taken into account. As to the latter, the reader will recall that up to this time we have been wholly concerned with substitution between inputs, transportation on the product being held constant. Now we wish to allow this latter distance to vary. In effect, we will analyze a problem which is equivalent to allowing the arc of Figure 1 to shift either closer or farther away from the point of consumption.

For these purposes a still more simplified locational figure will be employed, the straight line.[3] We assume a productive process that requires two inputs, a single localized raw material, M, and labor. Labor is available both at the site of the raw material and at the market for the product, C. However, its money price is lower at the latter. The quality of the labor at the two places is identical. The price differentials implicit in the problem give rise to the V-shaped iso-outlay lines of Figure 4. The more steeply sloped portions of these lines represent combinations of inputs which can be purchased for a given expenditure if the firm locates at M. The more gently sloped

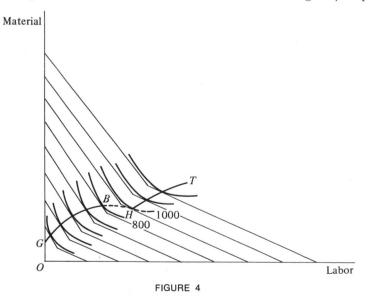

FIGURE 4

3. Since the locational figure is so simple there is no need for a figure.

portion of each outlay line shows the combination of inputs which can be purchased for the same expenditure if the firm locates at C. The difference in slope arises from the fact that at M the price of the raw material is lower than at C, while the price of labor is higher than at C. Thus, for a given expenditure, more of the material and less labor can be acquired if the firm locates at M. The reverse is true at C.

A system of isoquants and the expansion line formed by their points of tangency with the locational iso-outlay lines are shown in Figure 4. Each point of tangency[4] indicates two things: the best location for producing a given output;[5] the best combination of inputs for producing that output at that location. According to the expansion line, GBHT, location at the raw material site, M, is a superior location for outputs up to 800 units, whereas location at the market site, C, is superior for outputs of 1000 or more units. This result is brought out more clearly in Figure 5, which contains two total cost curves.[6] TC_m is the total cost curve the firm would have if it

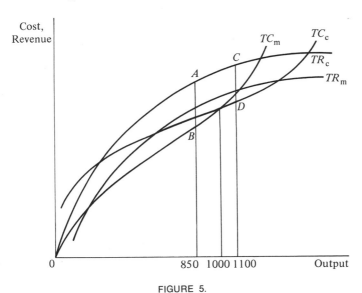

FIGURE 5.

4. In order to keep the diagram simple only one equilibrium location and combination of inputs is shown for each output. There is no reason why it is not possible to have a condition of double tangency for some outputs. This condition would mean that the two locations are equally good for producing the outputs in question. The cost of distributing the product would then become the crucial factor in determining the optimum location.

5. Optimality in location is indicated by the portion of a given locational iso-outlay line where tangency with an isoquant occurs.

6. These curves are two of the family of such cost curves (comprising the locational planning curve) that we would have to consider if all points between the raw material site and the consumption point were treated as possible locations.

located at the site of the raw material. TC_c is the total cost curve the firm would have if it located at the market. The figure also depicts two total revenue curves. These curves will help us to appraise the effect of transportation cost on the product.

TR_c is the total revenue curve for a monopolistically competitive firm as it exists in the market. (We do not present it, but the argument can readily be formulated for the purely competitive case.) TR_m is the same total revenue curve reduced by the amount of transportation cost the firm would incur on each output in shipping this output to the market. In other words, if the firm locates at the site of the raw material, it will not realize the price the product sells for in the market but rather this price less the per unit transportation charge. The curve TR_m is derived by multiplying the prices net of transportation costs by the corresponding outputs.[7]

From the figure, we see that if transportation cost on the product were zero (and TR_m therefore identical to TR_c), the firm would maximize its profits (AB) by locating at the site of the raw material and producing 850 units. However, as we have drawn the total revenue curves, transportation cost on the final product is not zero. The firm maximizes its profits (CD) by locating at the market and producing 1100 units. It should be understood that a shift in the demand relation from which the total revenue curves are derived could alter both the optimum output and location. Thus, the optimum location is seen finally to depend on the following factors: base prices on inputs; transportation rates on inputs and on the final product; the geographic position of materials and markets; the production function; the demand function. We consider these the primary factors, but they do not comprise a complete list. For example, selling costs can influence the demand function and therefore influence location.

As stated earlier, the main objective of this paper is to make the theory of location an integral part of the theory of the firm. Since this is not the first such effort, I will now briefly indicate the similarities and differences between the present paper and several others.

In 1928 Andreas Predöhl commented that the problems of location had been barely touched upon in systematic theories of economics and that these theories must be applicable to the problem of location: "... they must contain the undeveloped principles of location."[8] In his view, the problem of location was the problem of combining

---

7. One could just as easily proceed by thinking of price as being set at the place of production and then reducing the quantity demanded on the basis of transportation charges added to this price.

8. Andreas Predöhl, "The Theory of Location in its Relation to General Economics," *The Journal of Political Economy*, XXXVI (1928), 371–90.

the means of production by different technical methods and therefore should be amenable to analysis by the principles of substitution.

There is little in Predöhl's paper with which the present author disagrees. Rather, my criticism is that he contented himself with a bare statement of the problem. He failed to develop and explain the mechanism through which factor substitution works when transportation costs are introduced into the theory of production; nor did he develop the substitution relation between transport expenditures for gathering raw materials and those for shipping the product to the market. Nevertheless, the present paper may be viewed as an effort to make explicit, propositions which are implicit in Predöhl's paper and to investigate their implications Walter Isard's recent volume may be similarly viewed.[9]

Professor Isard works out some elaborate substitution problems in his study. However, I do not believe he has achieved a generalization of location theory. Rather, he has presented us with a novel and rigorous formulation of Weber's theory of transport and other orientation, which is location under the assumption of a linear production function. In one place, Isard almost states this as his objective. He claims that the concept of a transport unit — defined as the movement of a unit weight over a unit distance — " . . . will enable us to fuse much of traditional Weberian location doctrine and modern production theory."[10] Weberian location doctrine is concerned almost entirely with the case of constant coefficients of production whereas the theory of production focuses interest on cases in which inputs are substitutable.

The term "substitution" occurs frequently in Isard's volume but the concept is employed in the context of one, or a combination, of the following situations:

1. Substitution between transport expenditures on various mobile inputs, the weights of each of them require per unit of output held constant;

2. Substitution between transport outlays for mobile inputs and outlays for some immobile input such as labor, the weights of the mobile inputs as well as the quantity of labor required per unit of output held constant;

3. Substitution between transport outlays for gathering mobile inputs and outlays for immobile inputs on the one hand, and transport outlays for shipping a unit of the product to market on the other,

9. Walter Isard, *Location and Space Economy* (New York: jointly by the Technology Press of Massachusetts Institute of Technology and John Wiley and Sons, 1956).

10. *Ibid.*, p. 91.

with the weights or quantities of the inputs required per unit of product held constant.

Isard's adherence to the assumption of a linear production function leads him to the conclusion that, for the case in which there are no alternative sources of inputs or no regional variations in their base prices, there is a single best location and this occurs where transportation costs on the inputs — those on the product held constant — are a minimum. I have indicated that his result is a special case. If inputs are substitutable, there is no single optimum location. The optimum location then depends on the scale of operations and other things mentioned earlier.

Isard is, of course, not unaware of the importance of scale economies. However, they are brought explicitly into the analysis only after a location has been decided upon. Thus, in discussing market and supply areas, he employs Professor Hoover's concept of a margin line. This line shows how delivered price at the edge of a market varies as the extent of the market, and hence output, varies, the geographic position of the firm being fixed.

Much the same approach is found in Hoover's first volume on location.[11] Constant costs are relied upon in determining the optimum location. The usual U-shaped cost curve is brought into the analysis only after the firm has been located. However, Hoover appears to be disturbed by an apparent conflict between reality and theoretical conclusions based on Weberian location doctrine. Reality presents numerous instances in which firms in a given industry have different orientations. Weberian location doctrine favors the conclusion that there is a single best location for each type of activity. In order to bring the theory into closer accord with reality, Hoover introduces such things as variations in the quality of a given input at alternative sources, differences in transport rate gradients in different directions, etc. He uses these differences to derive zones of orientation.[12] Some of these zones are characterized by orientation to market, some by orientation to one or another raw material. Variations in the quality of inputs and peculiarities in transport rate structures are undoubtedly important in explaining realistic location patterns. However, it is equally important to introduce factor substitution. Hoover does recognize this in his later volume.[13]

The theory of the location of economic activity studies individual economic units, as well as groups of interrelated units and regional economies. The present paper has been concerned with the former.

11. Edgar M. Hoover, Jr., *Location Theory and the Shoe and Leather Industries.*
12. *Ibid.*, pp. 48–51.
13. Edgar M. Hoover, Jr., *The Location of Economic Activity*, pp. 44–46.

Its object has been to make the theory of location, as applied to the individual firm, an integral part of the general theory of production. Towards this end, we have given emphasis to the inseparability of three problems: the optimum output; the optimum combination of inputs; the optimum location. The approach developed in the present paper facilitates analysis of the spatial aspects of many problems traditionally considered in theory: i.e., the implications for location of variable input prices, of discrimination between markets, etc. The idea of a break in the expansion line—developed in Figure 4— may shed light on the establishment of branch plants.

Finally, the paper contains an implicit warning against a narrow technological approach to location, such as is practised by some of the largest engineering consulting firms. This engineering approach tends to restrict, to an unwarranted extent, the range of possible types of locations which individual plants may consider. It may also delimit too severely the range of possible types of industries which underdeveloped areas are advised to consider in their development plans. We are not suggesting that it is feasible or even necessary to work with continuous factor substitution in solving practical location problems. However, it does seem that it would at least be worthwhile to investigate the possibility of producing according to alternative linear production functions.

5

A Theoretical Framework for Geographical Studies of Industrial Location

One of the most important requirements in geographical research today is a sound theoretical basis for studies in economic geography. The belief that economic activity can be explained as a response to the physical environment is no longer regarded as an adequate interpretation of the spatial arrangement of economic phenomena, but an alternative set of principles with a firm foundation of economics has not yet gained general acceptance. The basis which is needed is what William Warntz has described as "macro analysis," the aim of which is to develop "concepts at a more meaningful level of abstraction so as to make possible the understanding of the whole economic system and to provide a conceptual framework into which to put the micro-descriptions."[1]

The need for some such theoretical base is particularly urgent in industrial geography. Much empirical research remains to be done in the field of industrial location, and an understanding of the factors influencing the siting of factories is becoming increasingly important in national and regional planning. Any attempt to explain the location of a particular industry or the industrial geography of a particular region or to solve local or regional employment problems requires some knowledge of how locations are arrived at in general. Geographers are well aware of the factors which influence industrial location, but they seem less certain of precisely how these operate and how the relative importance of particular causal factors can be assessed in any specific case.

Industrial geography is concerned with the description and interpretation of the real world rather than with the derivation of abstract theory. Consequently, the student of industrial location has to go to the work of economists such as Hoover, Lösch, Isard, and Greenhut for a thorough grounding in location theory. But much of this work is aimed at bringing the space dimension into conventional economic

1. W. Warntz, Progress in Economic Geography, *in* P. James, Ed.: *New Viewpoints in Geography* (Washington, 1959), p. 55.

The author is grateful to Mr. E. M. Rawstron, Reader in Economic Geography at Queen Mary College, University of London, for reading this paper in draft, and for a number of helpful suggestions.

Reprinted by permission of the publishers from Economic Geography, *42 (April 1966), pp. 95–113.*

theory rather than providing a background from which to embark upon empirical studies of industrial geography. If the geographer seeks a theoretical basis for his examination of the real world, he will only achieve it by adapting or reformulating existing location theory for his own particular purposes.

To provide the background he needs, the industrial geographer must examine the location problem afresh—he must return to first principles. This study is an attempt to approach industrial location in elementary theoretical terms by constructing a series of simple models to demonstrate the influence of various factors on the location of plants and industries. The approach developed here embodies contributions of various other writers whose work is already well known to the geographer, but some of the means of analysis and illustration employed here may be less familiar. The aim is to provide a theoretical background from which a more realistic way of looking at location problems in the real world may emerge.

FIRST PRINCIPLES

In setting up a factory a businessman has to make a number of decisions, one of which is where to put the plant. On the assumption that he is in business to make money, he will, other things being equal, choose the location at which he can make maximum profits. The locational decision is not, of course, taken in isolation, but is related to other considerations such as scale of operations, combination of factors of production, and market conditions. The maximum profits location may be different combinations of factors, and demand may vary with the choice of location. The interrelation of all these factors makes the analysis of location an extremely complex matter, but by making certain simplifying assumptions the problem may be reduced to elementary terms.

In any industry, costs vary from place to place in accordance with variations in the cost of the necessary factors of production and in the cost of marketing. The total revenue obtainable also varies from place to place according to variations in demand and price. The most profitable location will clearly be where total revenue exceeds total costs by the greatest amount. The effect of spatial variations in cost and price are illustrated in Figure 1, which indicates the sort of conditions which exist, in a far more complicated form, in any industry in the real world. The spatial cost/price situations as shown here represent the simplest possible conditions, and are based on the assumption that cost and price are fixed and cannot be altered by the individual firm by, say, large-scale production, changes of technique

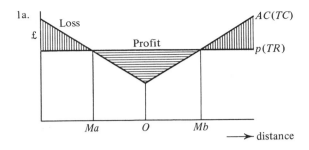

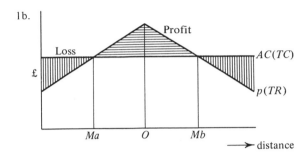

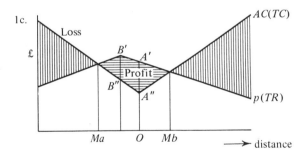

FIGURE 1 Optimum location and spatial margins to profitability in different cost/price situations.

or factor combination, and entrepreneurial skill. For simplicity of presentation it is also assumed that output is constant in space, and that variations in demand, if they exist, are reflected in variations from place to place in price. Cost and price (£) are plotted on the y axis, and distance on the x axis.

The effect of variation in cost and price on location can best be seen by assuming one to be variable and the other constant. In Figure 1a costs are variable in space while demand is constant and the price obtainable (p) is the same everywhere. The average cost per unit of production at any point is indicated by the appropriate value on the line AC, which rises in both directions from point O. This line may be termed the *space cost curve* (not to be confused with the cost curve of conventional economic theory), and is the basic analytical tool in the more detailed discussion which follows. O represents the point of minimum costs and Ma and Mb the points where the average cost is just equal to the price obtainable. The vertical distance between p and AC where price is above average cost (i.e., between Ma and Mb) indicates the average profit on each unit of production. As it is assumed that output does not vary from place to place, the spatial average cost/price situation indicated in Figure 1a also holds good for the total situation, with the appropriate adjustment of values of the y axis.[2] Average cost thus becomes total cost (TC) and the price line shows total revenue (TR), all values having simply been multiplied by a constant representing total output. The vertical distance between $AC(TC)$ and $p(TR)$, where the revenue line is above the cost line, now represents total profits, so O becomes the point of maximum profits, or the optimum location.

But Figure 1a shows more than simply the derivation of optimum location in a given cost/price situation. It also indicates limits to the area in which profitable operation is possible. These spatial limits, or *margins*, to profitability[3] are indicated by Ma and Mb, which correspond with the points where $TC = TR$, i.e., where firms can just break even. Beyond the margin, where costs exceed revenue, firms can only operate at a loss, the size of the loss being indicated by the vertical distance between TC and TR.

Figure 1b represents the reverse of the situation illustrated in Figure 1a, with costs assumed to be the same everywhere but with spatial variations in price. These price variations reflect variations in demand, p being highest where demand is greatest. Again O is the location where average profit per unit of output is greatest, and Ma and Mb are the break-even points. As with Figure 1a this diagram can be taken to represent the total situation, as output is assumed constant and cannot respond to spatial variations in demand. AC thus becomes TC, and p becomes TR. O is now the point of maximum profits—the

---

2. If this assumption of constant demand had not been made, the point of least average cost need not have been the point of least total cost ($TC = AC \times$ output), and the line of total revenue would not have remained horizontal. This would have complicated the diagrammatic representation without any compensating advantages in realism or clarity.

3. The concept of spatial margins to profitability is developed in E. M. Rawstron: Three Principles of Industrial Location, *Trans. and Papers, Institute of Brit. Geogrs.*, No. 27, 1958, pp. 135–142. Much of the thought underlying the discussion of margins in the present study is derived from Rawstron's writing and teaching.

location at which TR exceeds TC by the greatest possible amount—and Ma and Mb represent the margin to profitability beyond which a loss would occur. This is, of course, only one possible way of representing a situation with spatial variation in demand; alternatively, price could have been held constant and output allowed to vary, with the possibility of economies of scale introduced. But the simple situation illustrated in Figure 1b is sufficient to show that the concepts of optimum and marginal locations apply in just the same way as in a situation in which demand is constant.

In reality, of course, both cost and demand (as reflected in price in this simplified presentation) are likely to vary from place to place. This sort of situation is shown in Figure 1c, where the average cost rises away from point A, and where price is reduced away from B as demand falls off. Again the assumption of constant output enables TC to be substituted for AC and TR for p. An examination of the vertical distance between TR and TC now shows that the maximum profit point is A, where costs are lowest. Profit here ($A' - A''$) is greater than at the point of highest price, or greatest demand ($B' - B''$), and the manufacturer seeking maximum profits will therefore choose the least cost location despite the lower total revenue obtainable there. The reverse situation with maximum profits at the high price (i.e., demand) location, could be illustrated simply by altering the gradients of the price and cost lines.

From the foregoing analysis it is possible to state the fundamental principle underlying industrial location in any cost/price situation. Spatial variations in total cost and total revenue impose limits to the area in which any industry can be undertaken at a profit. Within this area the amount of possible profit is likely to vary, and unless maximum profits are sought, the individual manufacturer is free to locate anywhere. It is further evident from Figure 1 that the steeper the gradient of the cost or price lines (i.e., the greater the spatial variation), the more localized the industry is likely to be, and the shallower the gradient, the more dispersed will be the distribution pattern.

Further generalization would be possible from a more detailed analysis of the relationship between cost and price lines in Figure 1, but the value of this is restricted by the simplifying assumptions which have been made. It is now necessary to introduce some of the complications which exist in the real world and to consider the implications of changes in the spatial cost/price situation through time. This can be done within the analytical framework set up in this section, but before proceeding it is necessary to examine certain alternative approaches briefly in order to establish the most suitable theoretical model.

THE LEAST COST AND MARKET AREA APPROACHES

Until about ten years ago the various attempts on the part of economists to develop a theory of industrial location could be divided fairly rigidly into two types. These may be termed the "least cost" and the "market area" approaches.[4]

The least cost approach arises largely from the work of Alfred Weber,[5] and is directed toward the determination of the least cost location. It assumes that costs vary from place to place, largely in accordance with transport costs, and that a market exists at a particular point. Demand is assumed constant or unlimited, and cannot be influenced by the action of individual firms. The situation envisaged is, in fact, similar to that depicted above in Figure 1a.

The market area approach, the best-known exponent of which was August Lösch,[6] is based on conditions of monopolistic competition, as opposed to the perfect competition existing in the least cost theory. Costs are assumed constant in space and the market widely scattered. Producers seek the location giving them greatest profit by attempting to control the largest possible market area, thus maximizing sales and total revenue. Within their market area they will have a monopoly position. Away from the point of production the delivered price to consumers rises with transport costs, and the boundary of the market area is reached when the price becomes so high that consumers buy from an alternative source. If the manufacturer maintains a uniform price, he will not normally sell beyond the point where the cost of distribution absorbs his profit.

Melvin Greenhut has attempted to fuse these two approaches, and Walter Isard[7] has developed a general theory based on the principle of substitution. However, the acceptance of spatial variations in demand as well as cost makes the formulation of a theory of plant location an extremely complex matter, particularly when it is recognized that each firm influences and is affected by the locational decisions of other firms. In attempting to demonstrate in simple graphical terms how locational decisions are governed and freedom of choice restricted, it is clearly necessary to simplify the complex situation which exists in the real world. This can most readily be done by assuming either costs or demand conditions constant in space.

4. For a full comparison between the two approaches, see M. Greenhut, *Plant Location in Theory and Practice* (Chapel Hill, 1956), pp. 3–100 and 253–272.

5. A. Weber, *Theory of the Location of Industries* (1909), trans. by C. J. Friedrich (Chicago, 1929).

6. See A. Lösch, *The Economics of Location* (New Haven, 1954).

7. W. Isard, *Location and Space Economy* (Cambridge, Mass., 1956).

The approach adopted here is fundamentally the least cost approach, with demand and price held constant. In attempting to formulate a way of looking at location problems which has practical application in empirical research, the least cost approach has certain advantages. The most important of these from the geographical point of view is that it enables the effect of the location of spatially variable supplies of materials and labor to be considered, which is impossible under Löschian assumptions of a uniform plain with scattered population. Despite the value of the concept of market areas, its application to the interpretation of industrial patterns in a country like Britain, or in the more heavily industrialized parts of the United States, is strictly limited. Some industries, like brewing and grain milling, may comprise a series of individual plants surrounded by their own market area, but most leading industries in Britain, for example, are concentrated in particular localities and serve a national or world market. Few firms making cotton yarn, clothing, machine tools, or motor cars would claim to have their own market area with some degree of local monopoly.

Under the conditions operating in an advanced industrial economy with a high degree of geographical specialization, the least cost approach to the search for the most profitable location, therefore, seems the most realistic one. However, in theoretical analysis the simplifying assumption of constant demand conditions must always be borne in mind, and the possibility of spatial variations in the size of the potential market must always be considered in the interpretation of specific cases.

SPATIAL VARIATIONS IN COSTS: SOME GENERAL CONSIDERATIONS

Before attempting to develop a simple model to illustrate the effect of spatial variations in costs on locational decisions, it is necessary to consider in general terms how costs come to vary from place to place. In order to produce a given quantity of any goods, the manufacturer must assemble at one point the necessary amount of the four factors of production—land, labor, capital (including materials and machines), and enterprise. The cost of each of these is likely to vary from place to place. In considering the cost of factors of production it is useful to distinguish between basic cost and locational cost. The basic cost is the sum which must be paid irrespective of location, e.g., the cost of a raw material at source, or the cost of labor at its cheapest point. The locational cost is the additional expenditure incurred in bringing the factor to the place where is it needed (i.e., the factory), which varies according to where the factory is situated. Just as each factor of production has its basic and locational cost, so these two elements can be distinguished in the total cost of any firm or industry. This is illustrated in Figure 2, an adaptation of Figure 1a. It is obvious that the least cost (maximum profit) location will be where total locational costs (the sum of the locational cost of all factors) is at a minimum, for each factor's basic cost is, of course, constant in space.

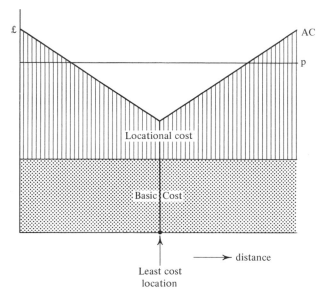

FIGURE 2   The distinction between basic and locational cost.

It is unnecessary to describe in detail how the cost of the various factors of production differs from place to place.[8] Some brief comments may be helpful, however, in explaining what is included in the cost of each factor. The cost of land includes any particular physical attributes of the site, such as flatness or the presence of a stream for water power. A level site or a water-power site can be created anywhere providing the financial inducement is great enough, but if they occur naturally costs will be reduced. The cost of labor varies from place to place according to wage rates and efficiency; labor costs may be less with highly paid and highly efficient workers than with cheap but unskilled labor, but this is not necessarily always

8. This is considered in detail elsewhere, the most useful discussion being in Greenhut, *op. cit.*, Part Two (pp. 103–177). See also E. M. Hoover, *The Location of Economic Activity* (New York, 1948), Part One (pp. 15–141); and R. C. Estall and R. O. Buchanan, *Industrial Activity and Economic Geography* (London, 1961), Chapters 2, 3, and 4 (pp. 24–101).

the case. In areas of labor shortage additional costs may be incurred in providing welfare facilities, bonus schemes, etc., in order to attract labor. The capital item may for the purposes of location analysis be separated into financial capital, equipment, and materials (including power). Financial capital for certain types of enterprise may be more easily (i.e., cheaply) obtained in some places than in others—in the Industrial Revolution in Britain, for example, capital to back new inventions in textile machinery was generally more forthcoming in existing textile manufacturing towns. The cost of machinery, materials, and power varies from place to place largely in accordance with transport costs. To what extent the cost of managerial skill varies from place to place it is difficult to say, but it could be argued that the same skill would cost more in an area with an unattractive environment than in a pleasant town with many social attractions. A comparison between southeastern England and parts of the northern industrial areas may be relevant in this respect, greater inducements being needed to attract skilled management north.

In order to evaluate the influence of individual factors of production in any specific locational study, it is necessary to know not only how their costs vary from place to place, but also their relative importance in the cost structure of the industry in question. The cost structure will, of course, be an average figure for the industry as a whole, as it will differ for each firm according to location and combination of factors. As a general rule, the factor or factors making up a relatively large share of total cost and showing relatively large spatial cost variations are likely to have the greatest influence on variations in total cost and thus on location. A small component of total costs may have an important influence on location if its cost varies from place to place to a much greater extent than that of other factors. A factor which is ubiquitous in space, and therefore has no locational cost, will not influence location, no matter how high a proportion of total cost it comprises.[9]

A SIMPLE LOCATIONAL MODEL

The ground has now been prepared for a more detailed examination of the way in which industrial location is influenced by spatial variations in costs. This can be done with the help of a simple hypothetical model, which can be used to illustrate how the space cost curve introduced above can be derived in practice, and how optimum

9. For further discussion of these points, and for illustrative examples, see Rawstron, *op. cit.*, pp. 136–140.

location and spatial margins arise. The model can also be adapted to illustrate the effect of certain influences on industrial location which have not yet been considered.

Assume that an imaginary manufacturing industry exists and that for production it requires land, a certain amount of labor, and a given quantity of a single raw material. It sells its products to a dispersed market. Assume that the material is found at point A, the labor is concentrated at B, and the center of the market is at C.[10] Assume further that to manufacture and market each unit of product, a firm requires £40 worth of materials, £30 worth of labor (both these figures representing basic cost at source, i.e., at A and B respectively), and £10 worth of land (which is the same price anywhere), and that sales costs are £20 at a location at the center of the market. The *basic* cost structure of the industry, per unit of production is shown in Table 1.

TABLE 1

ITEM	COST (£)
Land (ubiquitous)	10
Marketing (at C)	20
Labor (from B)	30
Material (from A)	40
Total	100

Locational cost must now be considered. Assume for the sake of simplicity that the cost of transporting £40 worth of material increases proportional to distance at £1 per mile, that labor costs rise £1 per mile away from B (perhaps additional wages have to be paid to attract workers from their home town), and that the average cost of marketing one unit increases by £1 per mile the farther away from the center of the market (C) the factory is established. Land costs are assumed constant in space, so no locational costs arise. If it is also assumed that points A, B, and C are in a certain situation in relation to one another (say, equidistant from each other and 30 miles apart), then cost isopleths can be constructed and a space cost curve can be derived graphically.[11]

10. The assumption of a dispersed market with the cost of marketing rising from a central point is a convenient device for overcoming the Weberian assumption of a punctiform market without having to introduce the concept of market areas.

11. The assumptions that A, B, and C are equidistant from each other and that the cost of the necessary quantity of labor, materials, and marketing all vary spatially to the same degree (£1 per mile), have been made in order to simplify graphical presentation. The assumption that the cost of transportation is proportional to distance is also unrealistic, and has been made for the same reason. None of these simplifying devices invalidate conclusions drawn from the model.

Before proceeding further it is necessary to state certain fundamental simplifying assumptions which underlie this analysis. Any model which attempted to take into account all variables likely to have a bearing on locational choice would be very complex indeed, and in order to reduce the location problem to its basic essentials, some causal factors must be eliminated or held constant. Such an approach is perfectly valid as long as the extent of the simplification adopted is made clear, so that the limitations of any conclusions drawn can be fully understood. The assumptions which have been made throughout this and the following section (for reasons which should be self-evident) are as follows:

1. All producers are in business to make a profit (but not necessarily maximum profit), and choose their location with this in mind.

2. They are all aware of the spatial variations in costs and profits which exist in their industry.

3. Sources of factors of production are fixed, supply is unlimited, and substitution between factors is impossible.

4. Demand and price are constant in space.

In deriving a space cost curve applicable to an entire industry (i.e., to every firm) it is also necessary to assume that returns to scale are constant so that no firm can take advantage of economies of scale, that firms do not influence each other's location and no advantages are to be derived from agglomeration, that all entrepreneurs are equally skillful, and that no location is subsidized. These assumptions will later be relaxed in turn to show the locational effect of the various considerations involved. It is also necessary to emphasize that this is a static analysis at one point in time, and that price, costs, combinations of factors, and techniques cannot be changed. Some dynamic aspects of industrial location will be considered in the next section.

The spatial cost situation in the hypothetical case outlined above is illustrated in Figure 3. Here a series of concentric circles have been drawn about points A, B, and C at five mile intervals (the thin lines) each circle indicating an increase of £5 in the cost of the necessary material, labor, and marketing. From this the total cost per unit of production at any point can be worked out, and a series of isopleths joining points of equal cost can be derived (the thick lines).

Figure 3a shows that costs rise away from a point O. Because of the particular values chosen for the combination of factors and their cost variations, this is exactly in the middle of the triangle formed by points A, B, and C. The solution of the problem of least cost site within a so-called "locational triangle" has been attempted in a

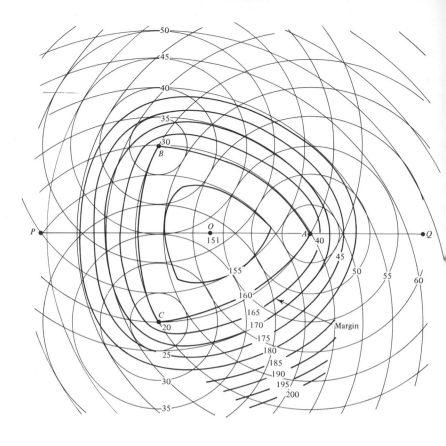

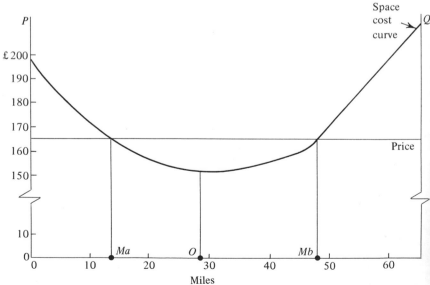

FIGURE 3 A simple locational model illustrating the derivation of cost isopleths and a space cost curve.

number of ways. Weber regarded each corner as exerting a force pulling the least cost location toward it and showed how the point could be found by geometry and by Varignon's mechanical model.[12] Isard approaches it as a substitution problem, analyzed through his *transformation lines*.[13] But the derivation of cost isopleths seems the most direct and realistic method, and it has the important advantage of also revealing the spatial margin to profitability when price is introduced into the analysis.

This is illustrated in Figure 3a. Assume that for each article produced a price of £165 is obtainable. The £165 cost isopleth thus becomes the margin—inside the line a profit can be made, outside it firms will operate at a loss. Profitable operation is possible at the source of material (*A*), at the least cost labor point (*B*), and at the center of the market (*C*), but there are other more advantageous sites nearer to *O*. In Figure 3b a space cost curve for the situation under review has been derived simply by taking a cross-section through Figure 3a along the line *PQ*. The introduction of a price line shows the area of profitability between *Ma* and *Mb*. At the optimum location costs are minimized at £151 per unit of production, giving a (maximum) profit of £14. At this point the basic cost, as everywhere, is £100, while the locational cost is, of course, £51.

It must be emphasized that although in this simple model the optimum location is within the triangle ABC, this need not be the case. In practice the least cost location is very often at the source or least cost point of one factor of production. It can easily be shown (for example, by Varignon's mechanical model) that if the pull exerted by one corner of the triangle is greater than that exerted by the other two corners together, least cost location will be at that corner. In terms of the present model the force exerted by each corner is equivalent to the gradient of the space cost curve of its own factor, which in each case is £1 per mile. Expressed another way, the pull is equal to the cost of the required quantity of the factor in question at source multiplied by the percentage increase in cost per unit of distance. This is illustrated by Table 2.

TABLE 2

ITEM	COST OF REQUIRED QUANTITY AT SOURCE (a)	PERCENTAGE COST INCREASE PER MILE (b)	LOCATIONAL PULL (a × b)	GRADIENT OF SPACE COST CURVE (£'s/mile)
Land	10	nil	nil	nil
Marketing (*C*)	20	5.0	100	1
Labor (*B*)	30	3.3	100	1
Material (*A*)	40	2.5	100	1

12. Weber, *op. cit.*, pp. 53–58 and 227–239.
13. Isard, *op. cit.*, pp. 95–104 and 119–125.

No pull is exerted by land, with no cost variation, but the forces exerted by A, B, and C are equal; therefore, the least cost location is centrally placed between these points. If, however, £100 worth of material had been needed, with its cost still increasing by 2.5 percent per mile, $a \times b$ for point A would have been 250 (more than twice that at B and C) and least cost location would have been at A. Similarly, if the cost of moving £40 worth of material had increased to, say, 6 percent per mile, the pull (240) would again have been dominant.

The model worked out in Figure 3 illustrates the value of the concept of cost isopleths. This idea appears to have originated with Alfred Weber's *isodapanes* — lines joining places of equal transport costs — and was extended by (in particular) Palander and Hoover.[14] It is undoubtedly one of the most valuable analytical tools yet devised for the study of industrial location in theory and in practice. The construction of maps of "cost contours" should commend itself to the geographer as an application of a familiar technique, though in practice the lack of complete statistical data limits its use in empirical research. If sufficient material were available, it would no doubt reveal different patterns of contours for different industries, varying from the steep mountain and valley topography of an industry with large spatial cost variations to the almost level plain of the "footloose" industry with a wide range of locational choice.

The derivation of space cost curves — sections through the contour map — is a logical extension of the idea of cost isopleths. Again, the shape of the curves will differ from industry to industry. A line showing a number of v-shaped depressions (like sections of steep-sided valleys) separated by more elevated areas would indicate a series of separate low-cost locations, perhaps coinciding with isolated towns in a rural area. A single broad depression bounded by areas of higher costs might represent a more extensive area with cost advantages, coinciding with a regional concentration of industry. Information on the likely form of cost isopleth maps and the gradient of space cost curves is of fundamental importance in both the interpretation of existing industrial location patterns and the formulation of plans for the future.

VARIATIONS IN THE SIMPLE MODEL

Having shown how optimum location and the spatial margins to profitability are derived from a set of cost isopleths and a space cost curve in a simple set of circumstances, it is now possible to introduce

14. T. Palander, *Beitrage zur Standortstheorie* (Uppsala, 1935); and E. Hoover, *Location Theory and the Shoe and Leather Industries* (Cambridge, Mass., 1937).

some of the complications of the real world which were earlier assumed not to exist. These are differences in entrepreneurial skill, subsidy of certain location, and the effect of external economies arising from agglomeration. The element of chance and the purely personal factor in locational decisions must also be considered.

Entrepreneurial Skill

In practice, the degree of skill possessed by businessmen will vary from one to another, and this will influence freedom of locational choice. With entrepreneurial skill as a variable, there is, in effect, a separate spatial cost situation for each firm, with wide margins for the highly efficient entrepreneur and only a narrow range of choice around the most profitable location for the less efficient firm.

This can be illustrated simply by using the space cost curve derived in Figure 3. Assume that this represents the average situation in the industry as a whole (AC in Figure 4). Within the industry the firm S has a management which through its high efficiency can produce at a cost 10 percent below the average. The space cost curve for this firm (ACS) shows that a profit is possible anywhere between MSa and MSb—wider limits than for the average firm (Ma–Mb). Similarly, if firm T has less efficient management and operates

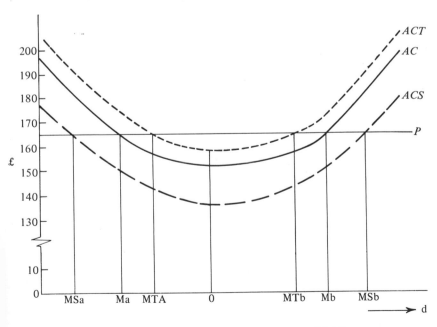

FIGURE 4   The effect of differences in entrepreneurial skill.

at 5 percent above the industry's average cost its cost curve (*ACT*) will indicate only a small area where a profit can be made (*MT*a–*MT*b).

In theory, the limiting cases would be where management is so efficient that a profit could be made in any location, or where a firm was so inefficient that it could not remain in business anywhere. However, the former situation is far less likely to happen in practice than the latter: there are spatial limits beyond which even the most efficient entrepreneur is unlikely to succeed.

The fact that certain industrial pioneers were highly skilled entrepreneurs helps to explain why the initial location of certain industries appears to have been determined by fortuitous circumstances. The location of the Morris motor works at Oxford, the founder's home town, is a case in point, and other examples readily come to mind. But these men operated within wide spatial margins created by their personal enterprise, and freedom of choice as to precise location was therefore relatively great. An observation by Lösch is relevant in this context: "Imitating entrepreneurs easily forget that this range [of locational choice] is more restricted for them than for their abler pioneers. A location that may yield the latter some profit, though not the greatest possible, may result in losses to the former."[15]

Subsidy

Firms can operate in relatively high-cost locations if they are subsidized. A subsidy, in effect, reduces costs, thus increasing the profit obtainable at the point in question if it is within the margin, or changing a loss to a profit if the location is beyond the margin.

This can be illustrated by using the space cost curve for our hypothetical industry. Assume that for social reasons, perhaps high unemployment, it is felt necessary to attract the industry to the area *E–F* outside the normal margin (Figure 5). This can be made a profitable location by providing a subsidy sufficient to bring the cost curve below the price line between *E* and *F*. If, for example, a subsidy of £20 per unit of production were offered, a new section of the cost curve (*E'–F'*) would operate between *E* and *F*, offering an average profit ranging from about £2.10s. at *E* to £10 at *F*. This artificially created situation could, then, attract new industrial development.

The effect of increased taxation at a certain point, perhaps imposed to restrict industrial expansion in a congested location, can be illustrated in a similar way. Assume that it was considered

15. Lösch, *op. cit.*, p. 16 (note 1).

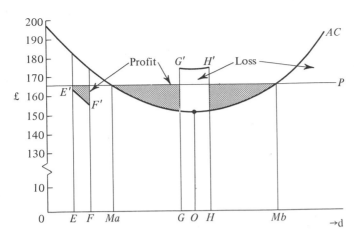

FIGURE 5   The effect of a subsidy beyond the margin and of a tax imposed in an advantageous location.

necessary to restrict new industrial growth in the area *G–H* round the optimum location. The imposition of a tax which had the effect of increasing cost per unit of output by £20 would raise the cost curve to *G'–H'*, making the area no longer a profitable location for new firms or branch factories.

These illustrations help to emphasize that the attraction of industry into a high-cost location by offering a subsidy, or the possible alternative of restricting industrial growth in certain areas is not a simple matter. In the case of a subsidy, the desired end will not necessarily be achieved by offering all firms and all industries the same arbitrarily chosen grant relating to, for example, the cost of their factory or machines. If plans for industrial relocation are to succeed in a predictable way the appropriate subsidy must be worked our carefully for each industry in relation to the prevailing spatial cost situation. Only if the subsidy is large enough to make the location in effect intra-marginal and competitive with other locations will the plan succeed, and this cannot necessarily be achieved by guesswork. An analysis of spatial variations in costs (and by implication profit potential) industry by industry is the essential prerequisite to the formulation of realistic plans for selective industrial redistribution, for it is only with this knowledge that the subsidy needed can be calculated with any precision.

External Economies

Like entrepreneurial skill and financial subsidy, external economies derived from the congregation of firms in the same industry can operate as cost reducing factors. These economies are derived from such things as collective marketing and research facilities and the existence of specialized ancillary trades like machine repairers or (in textiles) finishing plants. If, for example, such considerations operated at point A in our model (Figure 3) to the extent of reducing the average cost per unit at that place from £160 to £140, this would become the least cost location.

In practice, of course, the reduction in costs attributable to the existence of external economies is difficult, if not impossible, to measure. But in investigations of particular industries the possible operation of such factors must always be considered. They may distort the general cost/price situation in space and may be significant in explaining the persistence of an industry in a location which no longer seems to be advantageous from the point of view of low-cost assembly of factors of productions under present conditions.

The influence of external economies on industrial location is closely related to scale of operations. In general, the location of large firms is less likely to be determined by the operation of external economies than is the location of small firms, for large firms can create their own internal economies of scale. This helps to explain the high degree of localization of some industries with a relatively small size of plant—the manufacture of sporting guns, jewelry, and clothing in Britain, for instance. This provides just one example of the fact that in practice the locational decision cannot be examined in isolation without reference to scale, for there may be different optimum locations and margins for plants of different sizes.

Chance and Purely Personal Factors

The operation of chance and personal non-economic factors in no way inhibits the theoretical analysis of locational problems. Lösch mentioned briefly that as long as capricious choice of location costs no more than the entrepreneurial profit it is still consistent with theory,[16] though he did not elaborate the point. Greenhut, however, gives full weight to the influence of purely personal considerations, introducing to location theory the concept of "psychic income" as a measure of the non-pecuniary satisfaction that a particular choice of location might offer to the individual manufacturer.[17] Greenhut suggests that each entrepreneur will choose the location at which his total satisfaction in terms of financial and psychic income is maximized. The logical extension of this argument is that the location

16. Lösch, *op. cit.*, p. 16 (note 2).
17. Greenhut, *op. cit.*, pp. 175–176.

theorist should regard the maximization of personal satisfaction as the entrepreneur's goal rather than the maximization of financial profit, but, as Greenhut points out, this creates difficulties. To say, in effect, that man puts his factories where it pleases him is clearly an inadequate basis for a theoretical framework aimed at assisting the interpretation of business behavior. Useful though the concept of the maximization of total satisfaction may be in the explanation of particular cases, it is with the economic forces influencing locational choice that the theorist is primarily concerned.

The intention here is simply to integrate the operation of chance and personal factors into the theoretical framework developed above, based as it is on the profit motive. This is assisted by the recognition of spatial margins to profitability, for it can be stated as a general principle that within the margin freedom of choice exists, and the exact location of any plant may be determined by non-economic considerations or by pure chance.

The operation of personal factors on plant location may be illustrated with the help of Greenhut's "psychic income," and Weber's concept of forces diverting factories from the least (transport) cost location.[18] Figure 6 shows a map of isopleths of average profit per unit of output derived from Figure 3. The maximum profit (least cost) location is in the center (O), and the margin line is where profit is nil. The negative figures beyond this indicate a loss. Let X be a point within the margin which has certain personal attraction for one manufacturer—perhaps a golf course or an attractive house available. If the numbers on the isopleths in Figure 6 are now taken to refer to "units of satisfaction" and not to money (e.g., £5 profit gives 5 units of satisfaction), the situation can be analyzed theoretically in terms of psychic income. The manufacturer will site his factory at X if the psychic income obtainable there (measured in units of satisfaction) exceeds the loss of satisfaction (i.e., 9 units) resulting from getting a profit of £5 on each of his products instead of the £14 possible at O. The plant is thus diverted from the maximum profit location by personal factors offering higher total satisfaction. If the psychic income at X is 9, then, in Weberian parlance, X would be exactly on the "critical isodapane," for the 5 isopleth indicates a loss of 9 units of satisfaction by moving from maximum profit location. In these circumstances the businessman would be indifferent as to whether he locates at O or X. If X ($=9$) had been beyond the critical cost isopleth, then the least cost location would still have been preferred despite the non-economic attraction of the alternative site.

18. This is the basis of Weber's analysis of agglomeration economies and the effect of a cheap labor location See Weber, *op. cit.*, pp. 102–104.

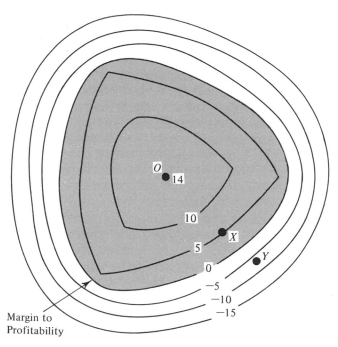

FIGURE 6   An illustration of the operation of personal, non-economic factors.

In theory, of course, there is no reason why a manufacturer may not operate outside the margin, at a loss, if he maximizes his satisfaction by so doing. A firm at Y in Figure 6 might be in this position, if his psychic income was, say, 25 units, or greater than the sum of the pecuniary satisfaction he is foregoing by not being at O (14 units) and the loss of satisfaction incurred by producing at a loss of £8 (8 units).

It could be argued that a philanthropist running a factory to provide work in an isolated location is in this position, but this kind of situation can best be explained as subsidizing an extra-marginal location. It is conceivable that an individual might derive satisfaction in certain other circumstances from operating a factory at a loss, but the interpretation of such behavior would hardly come within the sphere of location theory.

SOME DYNAMIC ASPECTS OF INDUSTRIAL LOCATION

The analysis of the previous sections was confined to one point in time. It is only under this condition that the least cost or maximum profit site and the spatial limits to profitability can be regarded as having a definite location, for their position is constantly changing through time with changes in the spatial cost/price situation. As Lösch put it: "Dynamically there is no best location, because we cannot know the future."[19] In practice, a manufacturer is unlikely to go to great lengths to find the most profitable location, because he knows that it will not always be in the same place. He is more likely simply to ensure that his location is within the margin in the long run, relying on his efficiency and enterprise to build up profits.

At this point it is worth stressing that the present distribution of an industry, or its distribution at some point in the past, represents but a single stage in a long process of evolution. The interpretation of distribution patterns as they are found in the real world requires an understanding of the evolutionary process. A theoretical background is just as important in this context as in static investigation of industrial location. The theoretical framework developed above can easily be adapted to illustrate the effect of changes in price, costs, techniques, and combination of factors of production, introducing further realism into the simple basic model. This kind of analysis may assist in the interpretation of locational change in reality, where something more than merely a description of the evolutionary process is required.

Changes in Price

The effect of a change in price can be illustrated easily by returning to the model developed in the previous sections. In Figure 7 the

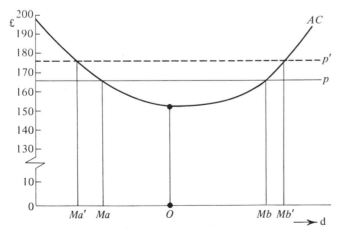

FIGURE 7   The effect of a change in price.

19. Lösch, *op. cit.*, p. 16 (footnote 3).

original space cost curve is shown, together with the price line (*p*) at £165. If the price is raised by £10, a new price line (*p'*) can be drawn at £175. This of course changes the position of the spatial margin, the area in which a profit can be made being extended to *Ma'* and *Mb'*. A reduction in price would have the opposite effect, narrowing the area in which the industry can be undertaken successfully. But as long as the change in price is uniform in space, the position of the optimum location will remain unchanged.

Changes in Cost

A uniform change in cost has exactly the same effect as a change in price. If, for example, £10 is added to the cost of each unit of production irrespective of location, a new cost curve (*AC'*) can be drawn above the original curve (*AC*), as shown in Figure 8. The new

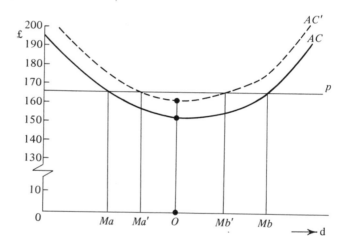

FIGURE 8   The effect of a change in average cost.

positions of the spatial margin (*Ma'* and *Mb'*) indicate a contraction of the area in which a profit can be made. A reduction in costs results in a widening of the margin. As in the case of a uniform change in price, the optimum location remains the same.

The effect of changes in costs which are not uniform in space and of changes in the cost of individual factors of production can best be examined in the context of changes in technique and in factor combination, for this enables the fundamental reason for the changes in cost to be introduced into the analysis.

Changes in Factor Costs, Techniques, and Combination of Factors

Changes in the cost of individual factors of production, in techniques, and in the combination of factors influence industrial location through their effect on cost structure and on the spatial cost/price situation. This could be illustrated with further adaptations of the model which has been used already, but it is more convenient to use a slightly different framework. Assume that an industry exists using two factors of production, the basic cost of each being £10 per unit of output. Let the source or least cost point of these factors be A

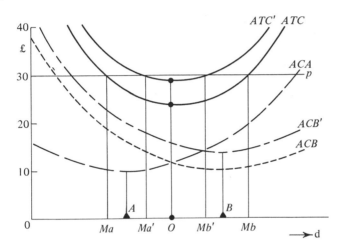

FIGURE 9   A change in the basic cost of one factor of production.

and B respectively (Figure 9). The cost of the factors rises away from A and B, the space cost curves having identical shallow "U" shapes.[20] A curve for total cost per unit (ATC) can be derived from the two factor cost curves (ACA and ACB), and when a price line at £30 is introduced the limits of the area of profitability can be indicated by Ma–Mb. Optimum or least cost location is at O.

20. This assumption of a "U" shaped space cost curve, which may be realistic when related to average total cost (as in Figure 3b), is not realistic when the cost of individual factors is considered. Transport costs are the main determinants of spatial cost variations for most factors, and freight rates tend to fall off with increasing distance. (For further details on this point, see Hoover: The Location of Economic Activity, pp. 15–26, and Isard, *op. cit.*, pp. 104–112.) The "U" shaped cost curve has been adopted in this model simply as a device for ensuring that optimum location lies initially between the sources of the two factors, so that their relative pull under different circumstances can be considered. The same situation could, of course, be created under more realistic conditions, but the model would be too complex for the present purpose.

The first case to be examined is a change in cost structure result-ing from a uniform increase in the basic cost of one factor. Assume that the cost of factor B at source is increased by 50 per cent (perhaps the result of a rise in the cost of extraction of a mineral), resulting in an increase of £5 in the cost of each unit of output. The new cost curve for factor B is ACB', and the average total cost curve becomes ATC'. The spatial margin contracts to $Ma'-Mb'$, but the position of the optimum location remains the same. The effect is thus the same as in the cases of the uniform change in price or cost considered above.

The effect of a change in the locational cost of one factor is illustrated in Figure 10. Assume that the cost of moving factor B

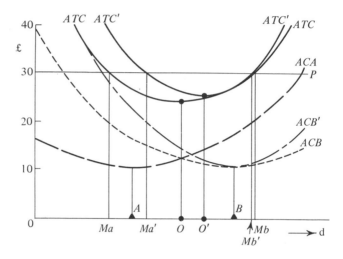

FIGURE 10   A change in the locational cost of one factor of production.

from its source doubles as a result of a change in freight rates. The new cost curve ACB' is drawn, and from it a new average total cost curve ATC'. The result of this is not only a contraction in the margin (from $Ma-Mb$ to $Ma'-Mb'$) but also a shift in optimum location to O'. The least cost point has moved toward the source of factor B, in response to its increase in locational cost.

The two cases examined in Figures 9 and 10 reveal an important distinction between the effect on location of changes in basic costs and locational costs, which can be stated as a general principle. A change in the basic cost of a factor of production will, other things (including price) remaining the same, lead to a change in the spatial margin to profitability, but will leave optimum location unaltered, whereas a change in locational cost is likely to affect the position of both the margins and the optimum location.

In many instances in the real world a simultaneous change in both basic and locational cost may take place. In Figure 11 the quantity of factor *B* required in the productive process is halved, perhaps by an improvement in technique. As a result basic and locational costs are both halved, giving a new cost curve (*ACB'*) below the old one. *ATC'* becomes the new average total cost curve, which indicates a widening of the margin, and there is a shift in the optimum location toward the source of factor *A*, the locational pull of which has been strengthened.

A final example indicates the result of the replacement of a factor with considerable locational cost by one which is ubiquitous. This may

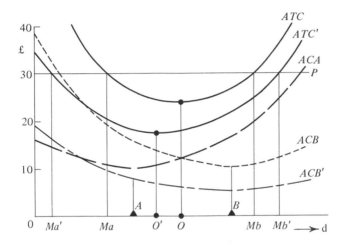

FIGURE 11   A change in both basic and locational cost of one factor of production.

arise from technical innovation, such as the introduction of electricity as an alternative to steam power based on coal as a source of motive power in industry. In Figure 12 let factor *B* be coal, the cost of which increases away from its source. The use of electricity is introduced, the cost involved being, say, £13 per unit of output irrespective of location. The cost "curve" for electricity is therefore a horizontal line (*ACE*). The figure of £13 has been chosen to introduce a complication, namely that the cost of coal at source (£10) is cheaper than electricity, and that between the points *R* and *S* (perhaps representing the coal-field) it is in fact cheaper to continue to use coal than to change to electricity. The new cost curve for "power" as opposed to either electricity or coal would therefore follow electricity's horizontal line as far as *R* but then dip down to follow the coal curve to *S*. This is also reflected in the new total cost curve (*ATC'*), which corresponds with

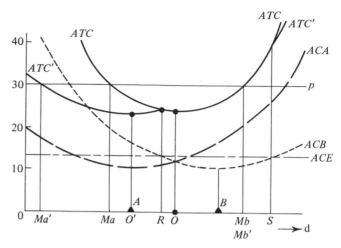

FIGURE 12 The replacement of a spatially variable factor of production by one which is ubiquitous.

the original curve (ATC) between R and S. The general effect of the introduction of electricity is, however, to reduce costs over a large area, resulting in a widening of the margin. But the margin is extended in only one direction; on the coalfield the original cost situation still obtains, and the margin remains unaltered. The introduction of electricity results in a shift of the optimum location to the source of factor A under the conditions postulated in this simple model.

Many other situations could be illustrated in the way those considered above have been. Increasing realism could be introduced, with more complex situations illustrated by three-dimensional diagrams if necessary. However, these four cases are sufficient to show that locational changes may be analyzed in the same way as a static situation, with space cost curves indicating optimum and marginal locations as the basic tools.

CONCLUSION

The approach to industrial location outlined and illustrated here has been expressed in abstract theoretical terms. The models which have been introduced are extremely simple, with many of the complexities of the real world assumed not to exist. As has been emphasized a number of times, it is only by simplifying that the location problem can be reduced to fundamentals. As each of the simplifying assumptions is relaxed the situation more closely resembles reality, but it also becomes steadily more complex. For example, it is easy to visualize the difficulty of analyzing the sort of situations considered above if the assumption of constant demand were relaxed and potential sales varied from place to place as well as costs and could be influenced by the action of individual firms.

How far is the theoretical approach demonstrated here of value in the interpretation of the real world? It is highly unlikely that in reality the student of industrial location can construct precise sets of cost isopleths and space cost curves. This may be possible for a single factor of production, but the absence of statistics may make it impossible for total costs. However, the same is true of the economist's average cost, marginal cost, and marginal revenue curves and so on, but this does not prevent suggestions as to their likely form from being used in the interpretation of business behavior in the real world.

The value of theoretical analysis in the field of economics has been suitably expressed by R. B. McNee:

> Economics has attained great intellectual heights in the building of abstract models, though these models have not always been tested in the real world. Perhaps many of them are not testable. Nevertheless, these models are of great value in interpreting, if not predicting, economic behavior in the real world. As guiding hypotheses, they are superior to anything else thus far developed in the social sciences.[21]

It is precisely in this light that the present study, or any similar work of a theoretical nature, should be viewed. In any industry at any time a spatial cost/price situation similar to, though far more complex than, those illustrated here actually exists, and even the most incomplete statistical data may give a clue to the nature of this situation in the case being studied. A point of departure for realistic interpretation may thus be established.

What is offered here is an *approach* to industrial location rather than a set of formulae or laws which can provide the immediate solution to particular cases. What is offered is simply a way of thinking around practical locational problems, based on deductive knowledge of the nature of locational problems in general. If the application of such an approach does no more than indicate in the broadest possible way how far the location of a particular industry is restricted, and how this restriction is imposed, it may at least provide some insight into the reasons behind industrial patterns which have so far only been explained in terms of an undifferentiated list of "favorable factors." In addition, it may provide some guidance to planners concerned with regional employment problems and the redistribution of industry, if only by helping to reveal something of the nature and complexity of the situations which they face.

21. R. B. McNee, "The Changing Relationships of Economics and Economic Geography," *Econ. Geog.*, 35 (1959), p. 191.

PART II

LOCATIONAL INTER-DEPENDENCE (SPATIAL COMPETITION)

Stability in Competition

After the work of the late Professor F. Y. Edgeworth one may doubt that anything further can be said on the theory of competition among a small number of entrepreneurs. However, one important feature of actual business seems until recently to have escaped scrutiny. This is the fact that of all the purchasers of a commodity, some buy from one seller, some from another, in spite of moderate differences of price. If the purveyor of an article gradually increases his price while his rivals keep theirs fixed, the diminution in volume of his sales will in general take place continuously rather than in the abrupt way which has tacitly been assumed.

A profound difference in the nature of the stability of a competitive situation results from this fact. We shall examine it with the help of some simple mathematics. The form of the solution will serve also to bring out a number of aspects of a competitive situation whose importance warrants more attention than they have received. Among these features, all illustrated by the same simple case, we find (1) the existence of incomes not properly belonging to any of the categories usually discussed, but resulting from the discontinuity in the increase in the number of sellers with the demand; (2) a socially uneconomical system of prices, leading to needless shipment of goods and kindred deviations from optimum activities; (3) an undue tendency for competitors to imitate each other in quality of goods, in location, and in other essential ways.

Piero Sraffa has discussed[1] the neglected fact that a market is commonly subdivided into regions within each of which one seller is in a quasi-monopolistic position. The consequences of this phenomenon are here considered further. In passing we remark that the asymmetry between supply and demand, between buyer and seller, which Professor Sraffa emphasizes is due to the condition that the seller sets the price and the buyers the quantities they will buy. This condition in turn results from the large number of the buyers of a particular commodity as compared with the sellers. Where, as in new oil-fields and in agricultural villages, a few buyers set prices at

1. "The Laws of Returns Under Competitive Conditions," *Economic Journal*, XXXVI (December 1926), pp. 535–550, especially pp. 544 ff.

Presented before the American Mathematical Society at New York, April 6, 1928, and subsequently revised. Reprinted from the Economic Journal, *39 (March 1929), pp. 41–57, by permission of the Royal Economic Society and the author.*

which they will take all that is offered and exert themselves to induce producers to sell, the situation is reversed. If in the following pages the words "buy" and "sell" be everywhere interchanged, the argument remains equally valid, though applicable to a different class of businesses.

Extensive and difficult applications of the Calculus of Variations in economics have recently been made, sometimes to problems of competition among a small number of entrepreneurs.[2] For this and other reasons a re-examination of stability and related questions, using only elementary mathematics, seems timely.

Duopoly, the condition in which there are two competing merchants, was treated by A. Cournot in 1838.[3] His book went apparently without comment or review for forty-five years until Walras produced his *Théorie Mathématique de la Richesse Sociale*, and Bertrand published a caustic review of both works.[4] Bertrand's criticisms were modified and extended by Edgeworth in his treatment of duopoly in the *Giornale degli Economisti* for 1897,[5] in his criticism of Amoroso,[6] and elsewhere. Indeed all writers since Cournot, except Sraffa and Amoroso,[7] seem to hold that even apart from the likelihood of combination there is an essential instability in duopoly. Now it is true that such competition lacks complete stability; but we shall see that in a very general class of cases the independent actions of two competitors not in collusion lead to a type of equilibrium much less fragile than in the examples of Cournot, Edgeworth and Amoroso. The solution which we shall obtain can break down only in case of an express or tacit understanding which converts the supposed competitors into something like a monopoly, or in case of a price war aimed at eliminating one of them altogether.

Cournot's example was of two proprietors of mineral springs equally available to the market and producing, without cost, mineral water of identical quality. The demand is elastic, and the price is determined by the total amount put on the market. If the respective

2. For references to the work of C. F. Roos and G. C. Evans on this subject see the paper by Dr. Roos, "A Dynamical Theory of Economics," in the *Journal of Political Economy*, XXXV (1927), or that in the *Transactions of the American Mathematical Society*, XXX (1928), p. 360. There is also an application of the Calculus of Variations to depreciation by Dr. Roos in the *Bulletin of the American Mathematical Society*, XXXIV (1928), p. 218.

3. *Recherches sur les Principes Mathématiques de la Théorie des Richesses*. Paris (Hachette). Chapter VII. English translation by N. T. Bacon, with introduction and bibliography by Irving Fisher (New York, Macmillan, 1897 and 1927).

4. *Journal des Savants* (1883), pp. 499–508.

5. Republished in English in Edgeworth's *Papers Relating to Political Economy* (London, Macmillan, 1925), I, pp. 116–26.

6. *Economic Journal*, XXXII (1922), pp. 400–7.

7. *Lezioni di Economia Mathematica* (Bologna, Zanichelli, 1921).

quantities produced are q_1 and q_2 the price p will be given by a function

$$p = f(q_1 + q_2). \tag{1}$$

The profits of the proprietors are respectively

$$\pi_1 = q_1 f(q_1 + q_2) \tag{2}$$

and

$$\pi_2 = q_2 f(q_1 + q_2).$$

The first proprietor adjusts q_1 so that, when q_2 has its current value, his own profit will be as great as possible. This value of q_1 may be obtained by differentiating π_1, putting

$$f(q_1 + q_2) + q_1 f(q_1 + q_2) = 0. \tag{3}$$

In like manner the second proprietor adjusts q_2 so that

$$f(q_1 + q_2) + q_2 f(q_1 + q_2) = 0. \tag{4}$$

There can be no equilibrium unless these equations are satisfied simultaneously. Together they determine a definite (and equal) pair of values of q_1 and q_2. Cournot showed graphically how, if a different pair of q's should obtain, each competitor in turn would readjust his production so as to approach as a limit the value given by the solution of the simultaneous equations. He concluded that the actual state of affairs will be given by the common solution, and proceeded to generalize to the case of n competitors.

Against this conclusion Bertrand brought an "objection péremptoire." The solution does not represent equilibrium, for either proprietor can by a slight reduction in price take away all his opponent's business and nearly double his own profits. The other will respond with a still lower price. Only by the use of the quantities as independent variables instead of the prices is the fallacy concealed.

Bertrand's objection was amplified by Edgeworth, who maintained that in the more general case of two monopolists controlling commodities having correlated demand, even though not identical, there is no determinate solution. Edgeworth gave a variety of examples, but nowhere took account of the stabilizing effect of masses of consumers placed so as to have a natural preference for one seller or the other. In all his illustrations of competition one merchant can take away his rival's entire business by undercutting his price ever so slightly. Thus discontinuities appear, though a discontinuity, like a vacuum, is abhorred by nature. More typical of real situations is the case in which the quantity sold by each merchant is a continuous function of two variables, his own price and his competitor's. Quite commonly a tiny increase in price by one seller will send only a few customers to the other.

I

The feature of actual business to which, like Professor Sraffa, we draw attention, and which does not seem to have been generally taken account of in economic theory, is the existence with reference to each seller of groups of buyers who will deal with him instead of with his competitors in spite of a difference in price. If a seller increases his price too far he will gradually lose business to his rivals, but he does not lose all his trade instantly when he raises his price only a trifle. Many customers will still prefer to trade with him because they live nearer to his store than to the others, or because they have less freight to pay from his warehouse to their own, or because his mode of doing business is more to their liking, or because he sells other articles which they desire, or because he is a relative or a fellow Elk or Baptist, or on account of some difference in service or quality, or for a combination of reasons. Such circles of customers may be said to make every entrepreneur a monopolist within a limited class and region—and there is no monopoly which is not confined to a limited class and region. The difference between the Standard Oil Company in its prime and the little corner grocery is quantitative rather than qualitative. Between the perfect competition and monopoly of theory lie the actual cases.

It is the gradualness in the shifting of customers from one merchant to another as their prices vary independently which is ignored in the examples worked out by Cournot, Amoroso and Edgeworth. The assumption, implicit in their work, that all buyers deal with the cheapest seller leads to a type of instability which disappears when the quantity sold by each is considered as a continuous function of the differences in price. The use of such a continuous function does, to be sure, seem to violate the doctrine that in one market there can at one time be only one price. But this doctrine is only valid when the commodity in question is absolutely standardised in all respects and when the "market" is a point, without length, breadth or thickness. It is, in fact, analogous to the physical principle that at one point in a body there can at one time be only one temperature. This principle does not prevent different temperatures from existing in different parts of a body at the same time. If it were supposed that any temperature difference, however slight, necessitates a sudden transfer of all the heat in the warmer portion of the body to the colder portion—a transfer which by the same principle would immediately be reversed—then we should have a thermal instability somewhat resembling the instability of the cases of duopoly which have been discussed. To take another physical analogy, the earth is often in astronomical calculations considered as a point, and with substantially accurate results. But the precesion of the equinoxes becomes explicable only when account is taken of the ellipsoidal bulge of the earth. So in the theory of value a market is usually considered as a point in which only one price can obtain; but for some purposes it is better to consider a market as an extended region.

Consider the following illustration. The buyers of a commodity will be supposed uniformly distributed along a line of length l, which

FIGURE 1   Market of length $l = 35$. In this example $a = 4, b = 1, x = 14, y = 16$.

may be Main Street in a town or a transcontinental railroad. At distances a and b respectively from the two ends of this line are the places of business of A and B (Figure 1). Each buyer transports his purchases home at a cost c per unit distance. Without effect upon the generality of our conclusions we shall suppose that the cost of production to A and B is zero, and that unit quantity of the commodity is consumed in each unit of time in each unit of length of line. The demand is thus at the extreme of inelasticity. No customer has any preference for either seller except on the ground of price plus transportation cost. In general there will be many causes leading particular classes of buyers to prefer one seller to another, but the ensemble of such consideration is here symbolized by transportation cost. Denote A's price by p_1, B's by p_2, and let q_1 and q_2 be the respective quantities solid.

Now B's price may be higher than A's, but if B is to sell anything at all he must not let his price exceed A's by more than the cost of transportation from A's place of business to his own. In fact he will keep his price p_2 somewhat below the figure $p_1 - c(l - a - b)$ at which A's goods can be brought to him. Thus he will obtain all the business in the segment of length b at the right of Figure 1, and in addition will sell to all the customers in a segment of length y depending on the difference of prices and lying between himself and A. Likewise A will, if he sells anything, sell to all the buyers in the strips of length a at the left and of length x to the right of A, where x diminishes as $p_1 - p_2$ increases.

The point of division between the regions served by the two entrepreneurs is determined by the condition that at this place it is a matter of indifference whether one buys from A or from B. Equating the delivered prices we have

$$p_1 + cx = p_2 + cy. \tag{5}$$

Another equation between x and y $^\sigma$

$$a+x+y+b=l. \tag{6}$$

Solving we find

$$x = \tfrac{1}{2}\left(l-a-b+\frac{p_2-p_1}{c}\right), \tag{7}$$

$$y = \tfrac{1}{2}\left(l-a-b+\frac{p_1-p_2}{c}\right),$$

so that the profits are

$$\pi_1 = p_1 q_1 = p_1(a+x) = \tfrac{1}{2}(l+a-b)p_1 - \frac{p_1^2}{2c} + \frac{p_1 p_2}{2c}, \tag{8}$$

and

$$\pi_2 = p_2 q_2 = p_2(b+y) = \tfrac{1}{2}(l-a+b)p_2 - \frac{p_2^2}{2c} + \frac{p_1 p_2}{2c}.$$

If p_1 and p_2 be taken as rectangular co-ordinates, each of the last equations represents a family of hyperbolas having identical asymptotes, one hyperbola for each value of π_1 or π_2. Some of these curves are shown in Figure 2, where (as also in Figure 1) we have taken $l = 35, a = 4, b = 1, c = 1$.

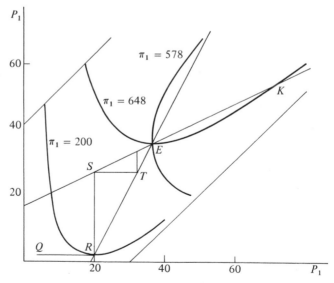

FIGURE 2   Conditions of competition for the market of Figure 1. The co-ordinates represent the prices at A's and B's shops for the same article. The straight lines through E are the two lines of maximum profit. On one of the curves through E, A's profit is everywhere 648; on the other, B's is 573. The lower curve is the locus on which A's profit is 200.

Each competitor adjusts his price so that, with the existing value of the other price, his own profit will be a maximum. This gives the equations

$$\frac{\partial \pi_1}{\partial p_1} = \tfrac{1}{2}(l + a - b) - \frac{p_1}{c} + \frac{p_2}{2c} = 0, \tag{9}$$

$$\frac{\partial \pi_2}{\partial p_2} = \tfrac{1}{2}(l - a + b) + \frac{p_1}{2c} - \frac{p_2}{c} = 0,$$

from which we obtain

$$p_1 = c\left(l + \frac{a-b}{3}\right), \tag{10}$$

$$p_2 = c\left(l - \frac{a-b}{3}\right);$$

and

$$q_1 = a + x = \tfrac{1}{2}\left(l + \frac{a-b}{3}\right),$$

$$q_2 = b + y = \tfrac{1}{2}\left(l - \frac{a-b}{3}\right).$$

The conditions $\partial^2\pi_1/\partial p_1{}^2 < 0$ and $\partial^2\pi_2/\partial p_2{}^2 < 0$, sufficient for a maximum of each of the functions π_1 and π_2, are obviously satisfied.

If the two prices are originally the co-ordinates of the point Q in Figure 2, and if A is the more alert business man of the two, he will change his price so as to make his profit a maximum. This is represented graphically by a horizontal motion to the point R on the line $\partial\pi_1/\partial p_1 = 0$. This line has the property that every point on it represents a greater profit for A than any other point having the same ordinate. But presently B discovers that his profits can be increased by a vertical motion to the point S on his own line of maximum profit. A now moves horizontally to T. Thus there is a gradual approach to the point E at the intersection of the two lines; its co-ordinates are given by the values of p_1 and p_2 found above. At E there is equilibrium, since neither merchant can now increase his profit by changing his price. The same result is reached if instead of Q the starting point is any on the figure.[8]

8. The solution given above is subject to the limitation that the difference between the prices must not exceed the cost of transportation from A to B. This means that E must lie between the lines $p_1 - p_2 = \pm c(l - a - b)$ on which the hyperbolic arcs shown in Figure 2 terminate. It is easy to find values of the constants for which this condition is not satisfied (for example, $l = 20$, $a = 11$, $b = 8$, $c = 1$). In such a case the equilibrium point will not be E and the expressions for the p's, q's and π's will be different; but there is no essential difference either in the stability of the system or in the essential validity of the subsequent remarks. A's locus of maximum profit no longer coincides with the

Now it is true that prices other than the co-ordinates of the equilibrium point may obtain for a considerable time. Even at this point one merchant may sacrifice his immediate income to raise his price, driving away customers, in the hope that his rival will do likewise and thus increase both profits. Indeed if A moves to the right from E in Figure 2 he may reasonably expect that B will go up to his line of maximum profit. This will make A's profit larger than at E, provided the representing point has not gone so far to the right as K. Without this proviso, A's position will be improved (and so will B's as compared with E) if only B will sufficiently increase p_2. In fact, since the demand is inelastic, we may imagine the two alleged competitors to be amicably exploiting the consumers without limit by raising their prices. The increases need not be agreed upon in advance but may proceed by alternate steps, each seller in turn making his price higher than the other's, but not high enough to drive away all business. Thus without a formal agreement the rivals may succeed in making themselves virtually a monopoly. Something of a tacit understanding will exist that prices are to be maintained above the level immediately profitable in order to keep profits high in the long run.

But understandings between competitors are notoriously fragile. Let one of these business men, say B, find himself suddenly in need of cash. Immediately at hand he will have a resource: Let him lower his price a little, increasing his sales. His profits will be larger until A decides to stop sacrificing business and lowers his price to the point of maximum profit. B will now be likely to go further in an attempt to recoup, and so the system will decend to the equilibrium position E. Here neither competitor will have any incentive to lower his price further, since the increased business obtainable would fail to compensate him.

Indeed the difficulties of maintaining a price-fixing agreement have often been remarked. Not only may the short-sighted cupidity of one party send the whole system crashing through price-cutting; the very fear of a price cut will bring on a cut. Moreover, a price agreement cannot be made once for all; where conditions of cost or of demand are changing the price needs constant revision. The result is a constant jarring, an always obvious conflict of interests. As a child's

---

line $\partial\pi_1/\partial p_1 = 0$, but consists of the portion of this line above its intersection with $p_1 - p_2 = c(l-a-b)$, and of the latter line below this point. Likewise B's locus of maximum profit consists of the part of the line $\partial\pi_2/\partial p_2 = 0$ to the right of its intersection with $p_2 - p_1 = c(l-a-b)$, together with the part of the last line to the left of this point. These two loci intersect at the point whose co-ordinates are, for $a > b$,

$$p_1 = c(3l-3a-b), \ p_2 = 2c(l-a),$$

and the type of stability is the same as before.

pile of blocks falls to its equilibrium position when the table on which it stands is moved, so a movement of economic conditions tends to upset quasi-monopolistic schemes for staying above the point E. For two independent merchants to come to an agreement of any sort is notoriously difficult, but when the agreement must be made all over again at frequent intervals, when each has an incentive for breaking it, and when it is frowned upon by public opinion and must be secret and perhaps illegal, then the pact is not likely to be very durable. The difficulties are, of course, more marked if the competitors are more numerous, but they decidedly are present when there are only two.

The details of the interaction of the prices and sales will, of course, vary widely in different cases. Much will depend upon such market conditions as the degree of secrecy which can be maintained, the degree of possible discrimination among customers, the force of habit and character as affecting the reliance which each competitor feels he can put in the promises of the other, the frequency with which it is feasible to change a price or a rate of production, the relative value to the entrepreneur of immediate and remote profits, and so on. But always there is an insecurity at any point other than the point E which represents equilibrium. Without some agreement, express or tacit, the value of p_1 will be less than or equal to the abscissa of K in Figure 2 and in the absence of a willingness on the part of one of the competitors to forego immediate profits in order to maintain prices, the prices will become the co-ordinates of E.

One important item should be noticed. The prices may be maintained in a somewhat insecure way *above* their equilibrium values but will never remain *below* them. For if either A or B has a price which is less than that satisfying the simultaneous equations it will pay him *at once* to raise it. This is evident from Figure 2. Strikingly in contrast with the situation pictured by Bertrand, where prices were forever being cut below their calculated values, the stabilizing effect of the intermediate customers who shift their purchases gradually with changing prices makes itself felt in the existence of a pair of minimum prices. For a prudent investor the difference is all-important.

It is, of course, possible that A, feeling stronger than his opponent and desiring to get rid of him once and for all, may reduce his price so far that B will give up the struggle and retire from the business. But during the continuance of this sort of price war A's income will be curtailed more than B's. In any case its possibility does not affect the argument that there is stability, since stability is by definition merely the tendency to return after *small* displacements. A box standing on end is in stable equilibrium, even though it can be tipped over.

II

Having found a solution and acquired some confidence in it, we push the analysis further and draw a number of inferences regarding a competitive situation.

When the values of the p's and q's obtained [in equations (6) through (10)] are substituted in the previously found expressions for the profits we have

$$\pi_1 = \frac{c}{2}\left(l + \frac{a-b}{3}\right)^2, \pi_2 = \frac{c}{2}\left(l - \frac{a-b}{3}\right)^2.$$

The profits as well as the prices depend directly upon c, the unit cost of transportation. These particular merchants would do well, instead of organizing improvement clubs and booster associations to better the roads, to make transportation as difficult as possible. Still better would be their situation if they could obtain a protective tariff to hinder the transportation of their commodity between them. Of course they will not want to impede the transportation of the supplies which come to them; the object of each is merely to attain something approaching a monopoly.

Another observation on the situation is that incomes exist which do not fall strictly within any of the commonly recognized categories. The quantities π_1 and π_2 just determined may be classified as monopoly profits, but only if we are ready to extend the term "monopoly" to include such cases as have been considered, involving the most outright competition for the marginal customer but without discrimination in his favor, and with no sort of open or tacit agreement between the sellers. These profits certainly do not consist of wages, interest or rent, since we have assumed no cost of production. This condition of no cost is not essential to the existence of such profits. If a constant cost of production per unit had been introduced into the calculations above, it would simply have been added to the prices without affecting the profits. Fixed overhead charges are to be subtracted from π_1 and π_2, but may leave a substantial residuum. These gains are not compensation for risk, since they represent a minimum return. They do not belong to the generalized type of "rent," which consists of the advantage of a producer over the marginal producer, since each makes a profit, and since, moreover, we may suppose a and b equal so as to make the situation symmetrical. Indeed π_1 and π_2 represent a special though common sort of profit which results from the fact that the number of sellers is finite. If there are three or more sellers, income of this kind will still exist, but as the number increases it will decline, to be replaced by generalized "rent" for the better-placed producers and poverty for the less fortunate. The number of sellers may be thought of as increasing as a result of a gradual increase in the number of buyers. Profits of the type we have described will exist at all stages of growth excepting those at which a new seller is just entering the field.

As a further problem, suppose that A's location has been fixed but that B is free to choose his place of business. Where will he set up shop? Evidently he will choose b so as to make

$$\pi_2 = \frac{c}{2}\left(l + \frac{b-a}{3}\right)^2$$

as large as possible. This value of b cannot be found by differentiation, as the value thus determined exceeds l and, besides, yields a minimum for π_2 instead of a maximum. But for all smaller values of b, and so for all values of b within the conditions of the problem, π_2 increases with b. Consequently B will seek to make b as large as possible. This means that he will come just as close to A as other conditions permit. Naturally, if A is not exactly in the centre of the line, B will choose the side of A towards the more extensive section of the market, making b greater than a.[9]

This gravitation of B towards A increases B's profit at the expense of A. Indeed, as appears from [equations (6) through (10], if b increases so that B approaches A, both q_2 and p_2 increase while q_1 and p_1 diminish. From B's standpoint the sharper competition with A due to proximity is offset by the greater body of buyers with whom he has an advantage. But the danger that the system will be overturned by the elimination of one competitor is increased. The intermediate segment of the market acts as a cushion as well as a bone of contention; when it disappears we have Cournot's case, and Bertrand's objection applies. Or, returning to the analogy of the box in stable equilibrium though standing on end, the approach of B to A corresponds to a diminution in size of the end of the box.

It has become common for real-estate subdividers in the United States to impose restrictions which tend more or less to fix the

9. The conclusion that B will tend to gravitate *infinitesimally* close to A requires a slight modification in the particular case before us, but not in general. In [note 8] it was seen that when A and B are sufficiently close together, the analytic expressions for the prices, and consequently the profits, are different. By a simple algebraic calculation which will not here be reproduced it is found that B's profits π_2 will increase as B moves from the centre towards A, only if the distance between them is more than four-fifths of the distance from A to the centre. If B approaches more closely his profit is given by $\pi_2 = bc(3l - a - 3b)$, and diminishes with increasing b. This optimum distance from A is, however, an adventitious feature of our problem resulting from a discontinuity which is necessary for simplicity. In general we should consider q_1 and q_2 as continuous functions of p_1 and p_2, instead of supposing, as here, that as $p_2 - p_1$ falls below a certain limit, a great mass of buyers shift suddenly from B to A.

character of future businesses in particular locations. Now we find
from the calculations above that the total profits of A and B amount
to

$$\pi_1 + \pi_2 = c\left[l^2 + \left(\frac{a-b}{3} \right)^2 \right]. \tag{11}$$

Thus a landlord or realtor who can determine the location of future
stores, expecting to absorb their profits in the sales value of the land,
has a motive for making the situation as unsymmetrical as possible;
for, the more the lack of symmetry, the greater is $(a-b)^2$, which appears in the expression above for $\pi_1 + \pi_2$.

Our example has also an application to the question of capitalism
versus socialism, and contributes an argument to the socialist side. Let
us consider the efficiency of our pair of merchants in serving the
public by calculating the total of transportation charges paid by
consumers. These charges for the strip of length a amount to $c \int_0^a t\, dt$,
or $\frac{1}{2}ca^2$. Altogether the sum is

$$\frac{1}{2}c(a^2 + b^2 + x^2 + y^2). \tag{12}$$

Now if the places of business are both fixed, the quantities a, b
and $x+y$ are all determined. The minimum total cost for transportation will be achieved if, for the given value of $x+y$, the expression $x^2 +
y^2$ is a minimum. This will be the case if x and y are equal.

But x and y will not be equal unless the prices p_1 and p_2 are equal,
and under competition this is not likely to be the case. If we bar the
improbable case of A and B having taken up symmetrical positions
on the line, the prices which will result from each seeking his own gain
have been seen to be different. If the segment a in which A has a
clear advantage is greater than b, then A's price will be greater than
B's. Consequently some buyers will ship their purchases from B's
store, though they are closer to A's, and socially it would be more
economical for them to buy from A. If the stores were conducted for
public service rather than for profit their prices would be identical
in spite of the asymmetry of demand.

If the stores be thought of as movable, the wastefulness of private
profit-seeking management becomes even more striking. There are
now four variables, a, b, x and y, instead of two. Their sum is the fixed
length l, and to minimize the social cost of transportation found above
we must make the sum of their squares as small as possible. As before
the variables must be equal. This requires A and B to occupy sym
metrical positions at the quartiles of the market. But instead of doing
so they crowd together as closely as possible. Even if A, the first in

the field, should settle at one of these points, we have seen that B upon his arrival will not go to the other, but will fix upon a location between A and the centre and as near A as possible.[10] Thus some customers will have to transport their goods a distance of more than $\frac{1}{2}l$, whereas with two stores run in the public interest no shipment should be for a greater distance than $\frac{1}{4}l$.

If a third seller C appears, his desire for as large a market as possible will prompt him likewise to take up a position close to A or B, but not between them. By an argument similar to that just used, it may be shown that regard only for the public interest would require A, B and C each to occupy one of the points at distances one-sixth, one-half and five-sixths of the way from one end of the line to the other. As more and more sellers of the same commodity arise, the tendency is not to become distributed in the socially optimum manner but to cluster unduly.

The importance and variety of such agglomerative tendencies become apparent when it is remembered that distance, as we have used it for illustration, is only a figurative term for a great congeries of qualities. Instead of sellers of an identical commodity separated geographically we might have considered two competing cider merchants side by side, one selling a sweeter liquid than the other. If the consumers of cider be thought of as varying by infinitesimal degrees in the sourness they desire, we have much the same situation as before. The measure of sourness now replaces distance, while instead of transportation costs there are the degrees of disutility resulting from a consumer getting cider more or less different from what he wants. The foregoing considerations apply, particularly the conclusion that competing sellers tend to become too much alike.

The mathematical analysis thus leads to an observation of wide generality. Buyers are confronted everywhere with an excessive sameness. When a new merchant or manufacturer sets up shop he must not produce something exactly like what is already on the market or he will risk a price war of the type discussed by Bertrand in connection with Cournot's mineral springs. But there is an incentive to make the new product very much like the old, applying some slight change which will seem an improvement to as many buyers as possible without even going far in this direction. The tremendous standardization of our furniture, our houses, our clothing, our automobiles and our education are due in part to the economies of large-scale production, in part to fashion and imitation. But over and above these forces is the effect we have been discussing, the tendency to make only slight deviations in order to have for the new

10. With the unimportant qualification mentioned in footnote 8.

commodity as many buyers of the old as possible, to get, so to speak, *between* one's competitors and a mass of customers.

So general is this tendency that it appears in the most diverse fields of competitive activity, even quite apart from what is called economic life. In politics it is strikingly exemplified. The competition for votes between the Republican and Democratic parties does not lead to a clear drawing of issues, an adoption of two strongly contrasted positions between which the voter may choose. Instead, each party strives to make its platform as much like the other's as possible. Any radical departure would lose many votes, even though it might lead to stronger commendation of the party by some who would vote for it anyhow. Each candidate "pussyfoots," replies ambiguously to questions, refuses to take a definite stand in any controversy for fear of losing votes. Real differences, if they ever exist, fade gradually with time though the issues may be as important as ever. The Democratic party, once opposed to protective tariffs, moves gradually to a position almost, but not quite, identical with that of the Republicans. It need have no fear of fanatical free-traders, since they will still prefer it to the Republican party, and its advocacy of a continued high tariff will bring it the money and votes of some intermediate groups.

The reasoning, of course, requires modification when applied to the varied conditions of actual life. Our example might have been more complicated. Instead of a uniform distribution of customers along a line we might have assumed a varying density, but with no essential change in conclusions. Instead of a linear market we might suppose the buyers spread out on a plane. Then the customers from one region will patronize A, those from another B. The boundary between the two regions is the locus of points for which the difference of transportation costs from the two shops equals the difference of prices, *i.e.* for which the delivered price is the same whether the goods are bought from A or from B. If transportation is in straight lines (perhaps by aeroplane) at a cost proportional to the distance, the boundary will be a hyperbola, since a hyperbola is the locus of points such that the difference of distances from the foci is constant. If there are three or more sellers, their regions will be separated from each other by arcs of hyperbolas. If the transportation is not in straight lines, or if its cost is given by such a complicated function as a railroad freight schedule, the boundaries will be of another kind; but we might generalize the term hyperbola (as is done in the differential geometry of curved surfaces) to include these curves also.

The number of dimensions of our picture is increased to three or more when we represent geometrically such characters as sweetness of cider, and instead of transportation costs consider more generally the decrement of utility resulting from the actual commodity being in a different place and condition than the buyer would prefer. Each homogeneous commodity or service or entrepreneur in a competing system can be thought of as a point serving a region separated from other such regions by portions of generalized hyperboloids. The density of demand in this space is in general not uniform, and is restricted to a finite region. It is not necessary that each point representing a service or commodity shall be under the control of a different entrepreneur from every other. On the other hand, everyone who sells an article in different places or who sells different articles in the same place may be said to control the prices at several points of the symbolic space. The mutual gravitation will now take the form of a tendency of the outermost entrepreneurs to approach the cluster.

Two further modifications are important. One arises when it is possible to discriminate among customers, or to sell goods at a delivered price instead of a fixed price at store or factory plus transportation. In such cases, even without an agreement between sellers, a monopoly profit can be collected from some consumers while fierce competition is favoring others. This seems to have been the condition in the cement industry about which a controversy raged a few years ago, and was certainly involved in the railroad rebate scandals.

The other important modification has to do with the elasticity of demand. The problem of the two merchants on a linear market might be varied by supposing that each consumer buys an amount of the commodity in question which depends on the delivered price. If one tries a particular demand function the mathematical complications will now be considerable, but for the most general problems elasticity must be assumed. The difficulty as to whether prices or quantities should be used as independent variables can now be cleared up. This question has troubled many readers of Cournot. The answer is that either set of variables may be used; that the q's may be expressed in terms of the p's, and the p's in terms of the q's. This was not possible in Cournot's example of duopoly, nor heretofore in ours. The sum of our q's was constrained to have the fixed value l, so that they could not be independent, but when the demand is made elastic the constraint vanishes.

With elastic demand the observations we have made on the solution will still for the most part be qualitatively true; but the tendency for B to establish his business excessively close to A will be less marked. The increment in B's sales to his more remote customers when he moves nearer them may be more than compensation to him for abandoning some of his nearer business to A. In this case B will definitely and apart from extraneous circumstances choose a location at some distance from A. But he will not go as far from A as the public welfare would require. The tempting intermediate market will still have an influence.

In the more general problem in which the commodities purveyed differ in many dimensions the situation is the same. The elasticity of demand of particular groups does mitigate the tendency to excessive similarity of competing commodities, but not enough. It leads some factories to make cheap shoes for the poor and others to make expensive shoes for the rich, but all the shoes are too much alike. Our cities become uneconomically large and the business districts within them are too concentrated. Methodist and Presbyterian churches are too much alike; cider is too homogeneous.

7

Optimum Location in Spatial Competition

INTRODUCTORY

The purpose of this paper is to take some further steps in the direction of generalizing the theory of spatial competition. The very fact that Professor Harold Hotelling's pioneer article[1] explained so successfully the close similarity of the Republican and Democratic platforms in 1928 indicates that something more was needed in 1936. It was probably true to say in 1928 that by moving to the center of electoral opinion neither party risked losing its peripheral support. The situation at the present time requires no elaboration; suffice it to say that neither party feels itself free to compete with the other for the undecided vote at the center, in full confidence that it will retain its support from the extremes of political opinion. Leaving the political analogy, Hotelling's assumption of completely inelastic demand means that neither competitor makes sacrifices at the ends of the market when he invades his rival's territory; thus there is no check on the two competitors' moving together. Actually, elastic demands do impose such a check and do account for the fact that equilibrium is frequently established, with the competitors free to move but spatially separated. I do not dispute Hotelling's conclusion that there is a tendency for two competitors to cluster nearer to the center than to the quartiles of a linear market; I suggest, however, that it is important to analyze not only the forces that tend to bring them together but also those that keep them apart. An important step in this direction was made by A. P. Lerner and H. W. Singer,[2] who modified Hotelling's assumption of complete inelasticity by postulating that demand was inelastic over a price range extending from zero to a finite upper limit. However, it seems desirable to go further and assume an elastic demand function at every point of the market. This I shall do in this paper, to the modest extent of assuming an identical linear demand function at every point of a linear market.

1. "Stability in Competition," *Economic Journal* (March 1929), p. 41. [Reprinted as Selection 6 of this volume.]
2. "Some Notes on Duopoly and Spatial Competition," *Journal of Political Economy* (April 1937), p. 145.

Reprinted from The Journal of Political Economy, *49 (June 1941), pp. 423–39, by permission of* The University of Chicago Press and the author.

Hotelling and Lerner and Singer have confined themselves substantially[3] to the extreme competitive assumption that each competitor fixes his price and location, assuming that the price and location of his rival remain unaffected by his action. In this paper I shall consider, in addition, cases where each competitor makes his adjustments expecting reactions from his rival.

Finally, a considerable part of this paper will be concerned with the effects of the magnitude of the freight rates[4] and the changes in marginal costs for one or both producers.

The analysis of these problems can be carried out rigorously only by mathematical methods. Although the methods are elementary, their application is complicated.[5] For this reason and also for the reason that the mathematics do not bring out clearly the economic principles involved, I have attempted to present the whole argument in purely verbal form and to indicate in an appendix the general mathematical methods.[6]

Considerations of space suggest that the discussion should be confined to cases where the producers are free to shift their locations at will. However, some indication of the solution of fixed-location problem[7] in its relation to freight rates will be given in footnotes.

Assumptions

We have now to formulate two sets of assumptions—the structural assumptions which limit the problem as a whole and the assumptions as to the character of the competition.

The structural assumptions are as follows:

1. There is a linear market bounded at both ends.

2. At every point of the market there can be only one price, and there

3. Lerner and Singer do modify this assumption in cases where one competitor attempts to cut out his rival entirely. I shall deal with this point later.

4. Hotelling's simple result (*op. cit.*, p. 50), that profits depend directly on freight rates, is true only in the special-demand situation he has examined. Lerner and Singer's treatment of freight rates (*op. cit.*) depend on the setup of their particular problem, and no general principles are developed. I know of no treatment of the problem of changes in marginal costs.

5. G. H. Orcutt of the University of Michigan has constructed a mechanical model for solving this problem with a greater degree of generality than is possible by analytic methods. The principle of the machine is to represent, for each competitor, price, quantity per unit distance, and distance by voltage drops along linear resistance wires. The resistance wires are included in an electric circuit such that the product of these three voltages, i.e., total profits, can be read off a voltmeter. The machine is operated by varying price and distance for each competitor, in accordance with the assumptions of the problem, until a simultaneous maximum is achieved.

6. The need to return to Marshallian orthodoxy in this problem has been impressed on me equally by Lerner and Singer's geometry and by my own algebra.

7. For a discussion of equilibrium in the fixed-location problem see Erich Schneider, "Bermerkungen zu einer Theorie der Raümwirtschaft," *Econometrica* (January 1935), p. 79. Schneider does not deal with the freght-rate problem.

are identical linear demand functions relating price to quantity sold per unit of time at that point. Thus, the total amount sold at any point is supplied by the competitor charging the lower delivered price at that point.

3. There are two competitors, A and B, having single locations. We can, without loss of generality, assume that A is located to the left of B.

4. The competitors are subject to constant marginal costs. Except where we are considering the effects of (small) changes in the costs of one or both competitors, marginal costs for both competitors will be assumed equal and zero. Fixed costs will be ignored throughout.

5. There is a uniform freight rate per unit of distance for both competitors, which is independent of distance and of the price and quantity of the goods transported.

6. Each competitor will sell on an f.o.b. mill basis.[8] That is, he will fix a mill-price to prevail at the point where he is located, and his delivered price will be computed by adding to the mill-price the freight cost from his mill to the point of delivery.

7. Each competitor is free to move his location instantaneously and without cost.[9]

8. Each competitor will attempt to fix his mill-price and his location so as to maximize his instantaneous rate of profits in respect of his total sales.

9. The relation of demand conditions is such that, in all the cases under examination, there are sales at every point of the market.[10]

8. I am restricting this paper to f.o.b. mill selling entirely for reasons of space. The analysis of the case where each producer attempts to maximize his expected profits at every point of his sections of the market is very similar to the f.o.b. case. Whereas in the f.o.b. case delivered price, by definition, exceeds mill-price by the full amount of freight costs from the mill to the point of delivery, in this case, given the linear demand conditions we have assumed, delivered price will be equal to mill-price *plus* half the freight costs from the mill to the point of delivery. Thus, since in both cases we have a linear relation between mill-prices and delivered prices, the qualitative results of the argument will be the same.

9. Although these assumptions are quite unrealistic in many cases, I feel — and I take it that Lerner and Singer also feel — that they are useful for demonstrating clearly certain fundamental economic tendencies that have a wider application than merely to the problem at present in hand. I need only refer once more to Hotelling's brilliant analogies and to the use made by Chamberlin (*Theory of Monopolistic Competition* [Harvard University Press, 1933]) of the theory of spatial competition to illustrate the theory of product differentiation.

10. This assumption avoids the necessity of considering the possibility of locational indeterminateness. This question has been adequately dealt with by Lerner and Singer (*op. cit.*, p. 150).

The setup described by the above assumptions can be illustrated by Figure 1. *CD* represents the linear market of length *l*, and *A* and *B* the positions of producers A and B, respectively. *AM* and *BN* are their respective mill-prices, denoted by p_1 and p_2. The lines *MP* and *MR* show delivered prices for A, while *NR* and *NQ* show delivered

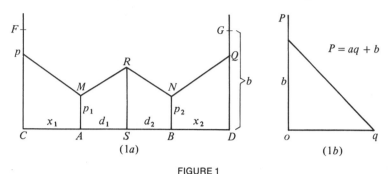

FIGURE 1

prices for B. The slopes of these delivered-price lines will depend on the freight rate. It is evident that A will not be able to sell to the right of *S*, or B to the left of it. The vertical lines *CF* and *DG* are drawn for reference, of height *b* being the price intercept of the demand curve—shown in Figure 1b, which is assumed to be of the form $p = aq + b$,[11] where *p* denotes the delivered price charge at any point in the market and *q* the quantity sold at that point, and $a < 0, b > 0$. The distances *AC* and *BD* of the competitors from their respective ends of the market are denoted by x_1 and x_2, respectively, while their distances from *S* are denoted by d_1 and d_2. It is worth emphasizing that x_1 and x_2 are within the complete control of the competitors, whereas d_1 and d_2 depend on the mutual interactions of their price policy and their location policy. We shall term the regions *AC* and *BD* the "hinterlands" of A and B, while *AB* will be called their "competitive region."

Our next problem is to consider the conjectural hypotheses made by the competitors as to each other's behavior. In contrast to the nonspatial problem of imperfect competition, each competitor's policy will depend on his estimate of his rival's reactions in respect both of price and of location. We shall be concerned with the following three cases.

1. Each competitor in making an adjustment assumes that his rival will set a price equal to his own and will adopt a location symmetrical with his own. By this is meant that A in fixing his location

11. Although in our present problem price is the independent variable, the demand function is written in this form for the sake of convenience in the mathematical analysis.

will assume that B will fix his location so as to make $BD = AC$ in Figure 1. Our analysis will show that if the competitors behave in this way the equilibrium position they will achieve will be the same as if they had acted jointly as a monopolist. Thus, for want of a better term, I shall describe this situation as "full quasi-co-operation."

2. Each competitor assumes that his rival will have the same price reactions as above but will keep his location unchanged. This situation may be termed "quasi-co-operative as to prices and competitive as to locations."

3. Lastly,[12] we have the case which is substantially that examined by Hotelling and Lerner and Singer, where each competitor assumed that both the price and the location of his rival will be fixed independently of his own. That is, there is competition both as to prices and as to location. This we may term "full competition." However, I shall not assume, as Lerner and Singer do originally,[13] that this assumption holds where one competitor adopts a price and location policy designed to cut his rival out of the market entirely; such credulity as this implies is fantastic — as Lerner and Singer realize. Nor shall I consider their amendment[14] — that a competitor adopts such a price and location, not with the hopes of cutting his rival out entirely, but with the strategic purpose of forcing him into a disadvantageous location. It seems to me that such action is virtually a declaration of economic war which is likely to be reciprocated and that the competitors will try to achieve *Lebensräume* satisfactory to both before resorting to policies of extermination. However, we shall see that in some conditions no such equilibrium is possible — and in those cases the possibilities of economic warfare must be considered.

The three cases proposed for examination are, of course, extreme, and in general the situation would be somewhere between quasi-co-operation and full competition. I have elsewhere[15] used generalized methods of formulating the problem so as to cover such intermediate cases, but in the present problem the complexity involved is too great to make that procedure worth while. Examination of the extreme cases indicates, at any rate, the qualitative results for the intermediate cases.[16]

12. Considerations of symmetry would seem to suggest that we should consider also competition as to prices and quasi-co-operation as to location. However, since such a situation seems of little importance, it is omitted for the sake of brevity.

13. *Op. cit.*, p. 151.

14. *Ibid.*, p. 161.

15. A. Smithies, "Equilibrium in Monopolistic Competition," *Quarterly Journal of Economics* (November 1940), p. 95; and A. Smithies and L. J. Savage, "A Dynamic Problem in Duopoly," *Econometrica* (April 1940), p. 130.

16. The foregoing statement of the problem has ignored (for the sake of simplicity) the possibility that a competitor expects his rival to react to a price or location change by adjusting, respectively, his location or price.

VERBAL ARGUMENT

The attempt to solve our problem by purely verbal argument will involve little more than an appeal to informed common sense, but it seems worth while to make it in order to establish some general principles which will help to indicate the solution to problems that are too complex to be treated by rigorous methods. Our first problem is to determine the equilibrium position under our various competitive hypotheses. However, it seems pedagogically helpful to begin with a discussion of the (well-known) equilibrium position of a monopolist in the type of market and subject to the cost and f.o.b. selling conditions we have postulated for competitors. Second, we shall consider the dependence of equilibrium on the level of freight rates and, third, determine the effects of changes in marginal costs for one or both competitors.

Conditions for Equilibrium

Monopolist A monopolist will be free from the asymmetry of having a hinterland on one side of him and a competitive region on the other. His markets on both sides of his mill will be equally exploitable. Assuming the monopolist has one plant, then, if he had no freight to consider, it would be indifferent to him where he located, and he would charge a price of $b/2$ at every point in the market in order to maximize his profits. Now, how will the existence of a freight rate affect him? It will mean, first, that he is unable to charge a uniform price at every point and, second, that he must decide how much of the freight to absorb himself and how much to "pass on" to consumers. Both of these exigencies will adversely affect his profits, so that his third problem is to locate himself at the point where their burden is minimized. It requires no argument to answer the third question; obviously, the monopolist will locate at the center of the market. Turning to the second question, the imposition of a freight rate is precisely analogous to the imposition of an excise tax per unit of commodity, uniform at every point of the market but, for any one point, linearly dependent on its distance from the mill of the producer. Now, for the cost and demand conditions assumed it is well known that a monopolist will absorb part of the tax himself and will pass some on to consumers in the form of a higher price. These considerations apply to the present case, and when the requirement of f.o.b. selling is introduced it can be adduced that at his mill (located at the center he will charge a price which is less than $b/2$ by a determinate amount which is less than the cost of transporting a unit of commodity over half the length of the market, while at the ends of the market he will charge a price which is greater than $b/2$ by another such amount).

If a monopolist should have two plants instead of one,[17] the considerations of the foregoing paragraph make it evident that in order to maximize profits he will locate one plant at each quartile of the market, and in respect of each plant he will behave, in respect of its own half of the market, in the same way as the monopolist with the single plant behaved in respect to the whole market.

Full quasi-co-operation   The essential difference between two competitors and a two-plant monopolist is that each competitor strives to occupy more than half the market, whereas the monopolist aims at maximizing profits in each half of the market. Successful invasion on the part of one competitor involves both enlarging his hinterland and occupying a greater fraction of the competitive region. The essential limitation on such incursions is that every move to add new territory is accompanied by less successful exploitation of the original hinterland (because of the higher freight charges involved).

Now, in this case of full quasi-co-operation we are, in effect, postulating that there are no profits to be gained from invasion—for each competitor assumes that any price he sets and any location he adopts will be identically met by his rival. Then, no matter what he does, neither competitor can expect to occupy more than half the market. Hence, he will not be prepared to make any sacrifices in his hinterland, and his efforts will be directed to exploiting half the market so as to maximize profits. It is evident that in this case the mutual actions of both competitors will result in an equilibrium position that is identical with that of the two-plant monopolist.

Quasi-co-operation as to prices; competition as to locations   In this case each competitor believes to an equal degree that he has one effective strategy for increasing his territory—namely, moving closer to the center while expecting that his rival will not change his location but will meet price competiton. We can thus expect (except in the limiting cases to be dealt with) that equilibrium will be achieved with each competitor at an equal distance from the centre of the market and closer to it than the quartiles. Although each competitor will be disappointed in his hopes for territorial expansion, neither will retire toward the quartile position because he believes that any gains he may make in his hinterland will be more than offset by losses to his rival, whom he does not expect to retreat.

Although we have excluded competitive price-cutting from this case, the (equal) equilibrium mill-prices for the competitors will be lower than in Case B. This is due to the fact that average freight

17. I am not here concerned with the interesting theoretical problem of the optimum number of plants for a monopolist. I merely assume that the optimum number is two.

charges to the hinterland of each producer will be higher than if he were situated at his quartile, and in order to maximize his profits he will charge a price lower than $b/2$ by an amount greater than that in Case A.[18]

Full competition Here each producer thinks he can increase his territory both by moving toward the center and by price-cutting. And, what is more, he believes that these strategies are not independent of each other in their effectiveness. Price-cutting increases the advantages of territorial advance and vice versa.[19] and, as before, he has to make hinterland sacrifices in respect of both strategies. Again equilibrium will be achieved, with equal prices and equal territories, closer to the center than to the quartiles. The prospects of gain from price-cutting and of loss from price-raising will result in a lower equilibrium price than in Case B, while the complementary relationship of price-cutting and locational advance will mean that the latter policy will be carried further than in Case C and equilibrium will be established closer to the center of the market.

In the light of our analysis we can now see the implications of Hotelling's assumption of zero elasticity of demand. This means that a producer by altering his position does not affect his position in the hinterland, since he can always pass on to the consumer his entire freight charges without affecting profits. Thus, there are no restraints to territorial advance, so that the competitors, if both are free to move, will inevitably both move to the center of the market.

Dependence on Freight Rates

The argument of the preceding paragraphs has clearly indicated that the relation of freight charges to demand conditions is of

18. In discussing the process of adjustment in this and the following case, I am implicitly assuming that the starting-point of each competitor is farther from the center of the market than his ultimate equilibrium position. This is not necessary; the equilibrium position is independent of the starting-points. Suppose (in Figure 1) B is located as a monopolist at the center. Then A, assuming B will remain there, will locate at the optimum position between C and B. Producer B will then find it profitable, to some extent, to sacrifice some of the competitive region in order the more effectively to exploit his hinterland. This retirement of B will encourage further advance of A, and so on. The process of adjustment will involve successive advances by A and successive strategic retirements by B, until each reaches his equilibrium position. It is also evident from this example that if B is originally located at the center we have lost no generality by assuming that A locates to the left of B. Also, once A has located to the left of B, B will move to his right; and A will have no inducement to move to the right of B, since the greater segment of the market lies to the left of B, where A already is.

19. This proposition can be proved mathematically. It is to be noted that this complementary relationship also obtains in Case C, but since in that case price-cutting is not undertaken, the relation in that case will be inoperative in inducing the competitors to move nearer the center than they otherwise would.

critical importance in the quantitative determination of equilibrium. In our present problem our special assumptions make it possible to say that the critical relation is the ratio of the cost of transporting a unit of commodity the whole length of the market to the price intercept of the demand curve, i.e., b. For brevity, I shall denote this ratio by s. Our present purpose, then, is to supplement the discription of the four equilibrium positions we have determined by considering specifically their dependence on s.

Cases A and B (two-plant monopoly and full quasi-cooperation) In these cases we have seen that the equilibrium location is uniquely determined — at the quartiles. The magnitude of s is therefore relevant only in so far as it affects the equilibrium price and profits. We have already seen that if the freight rate approaches zero the equilibrium price will $b/2$, and as freight rate increases it will be profitable for the producers to absorb some of the increase in the form of a lower mill-price. Hence, the greater the value of s, the smaller will be the equilibrium mill-price. Also, it follows from general principles that profits will decrease as s increases.

It remains to determine the conditions under which the whole market will be supplied. Clearly, s can have a value in excess of which it will be unprofitable for each producer to supply the outlying parts of his market. This critical value of s is determined by finding the value for s for which the delivered price both at the ends and at the center of the market is b; and sales at these points, consequently, are zero. A simple calculation shows that this is the case if $s = 8/3$, and at that point the equilibrium mill-price $p = p_1 = p_2 = b/3$.

Cases C and D In both these cases it follows from our previous arguments that hinterland sacrifices will be greater and prospective gains from territorial expansion toward the center will be less, the greater the value of s. This suggests, first, that s may be sufficiently high to force the competitors to establish equilibrium at the quartiles and, second, that s may be sufficiently low for the hinterland deterrents to be inoperative, so that the competitors will both move to the center.

Such is the case. If we determine the conditions under which the competitors are charging a price b and selling zero quantity at the ends of the market, we find that they will be located at the quartiles and will also be charging price b and selling zero quantity at the center. The necessary and sufficient conditions are again $s = 8/3$, and again we have $p = b/3$. Hence we can say that in the cases examined, for $s = 8/3$, the equilibrium price and location of the competitors is independent of the nature of the competition.

Let us next consider the effect of low values of s. We have seen that the tendency to move toward the center of the market is stronger in Case D than in Case C, so that we should expect the minimum value of s necessary to keep the competitors apart to be greater in the latter case than in the former. Our calculations confirm this inference; we find that d_1 and d_2 in Figure 1 will be zero if $s = 4/7$ in Case C, and $8/11$ in Case D. The corresponding prices are $3b/7$ and $3b/11$, respectively. If s is less than $4/7$ in the one case and $8/11$ in the other, the competitors will still move to the center and remain there in their efforts to maximize profits, although a maximum in the mathematical sense will not have been attained.

Hotelling[20] recognizes the instability of this situation; and this implies that in his case the stability in competition depends on the difficulties of shifting location, which may be overcome in the long run. Equilibrium at the center would be stable only if one assumes that each competitor sells only in his own hinterland and does not attempt to invade the hinterland of his rival. I prefer to say that the forces of competition that eliminate the competitive region also destroy the inviolability of the hinterlands, and that once the competitors have come together they compete as duopolists in the entire market; and that the whole question must then be reopened and examined from the point of view of the theory of duopoly in a nonspatial market, which theory can be applied to the present case with but trivial modifications and upon which I shall not attempt to embark here.

Our next problem is the somewhat more complicated one of determining the general relations between s and the equilibrium price and profits. We have seen that forces of competition drive the competitors nearer to the center of the market than in the case of full quasi-co-operation, in futile endeavors to increase their territory; and the deterrent to these activities is the magnitude of s with which they are faced. In this case it is by no means clear that maximum profits are associated with the lowest possible freight rates or that, as freight rates increase, equilibrium mill-prices decrease. In fact, for Case D, we have already seen that where $s = 8/3$ the mill-price is greater than where $s = 8/11$. One is led to believe that there are values of s between these extremes which will maximize prices and profits, respectively. In other words, up to a certain level freight rates will serve to protect the competitors from their own self-destructive instincts. (This point may be readily apprehended by imagining the extreme case of an insuperable wall erected at the center of the market. This would undoubtedly increase profits for both producers, since they would then be forced to act as monopolists.) Our previous argument has shown that in Case C the competitors need less protection against themselves than in Case D. This suggests that the optimum value of s is lower in Case C than in Case D. The effect of higher

20. *Op. cit.*, p. 52.

freight rates is to make the behavior of the competitors more monopolistic; this has the effect initially of increasing both prices and profits. But in the cases under examination the rise of prices under the influence of increasing freight rates will persist longer than the rise of profits—appreciably longer in Case D and inappreciably longer in Case C. Eventually, however, the competitors will find it profitable to absorb part of the increase of freight rates by charging lower mill-prices.

The results of this argument can now be summarized by giving the results of the numerical calculations in Table 1.[21]

TABLE 1

SITUATION	S	PRICES (b multiplied by)	PROFITS ($b^2 l$ multiplied by)	LOCATION $x_1 = x_2$ (l multiplied by)
Case C:				
Equilibrium at the center	4/7(0.57)	3/7(0.43)	9/98(0.092)	1/2(0.50)
Maximum profits	0.72	0.44	0.094	0.43
Maximum price	0.72	0.44	0.094	0.43
	2.00	0.37	0.072	0.27
Equilibrium at the quartiles	8/3(2.67)	1/3(0.33)	1/18(0.056)	1/4(0.25)
Case D:				
Equilibrium at the center	8/11(0.73)	3/11(0.26)	9/121(0.074)	1/2(0.50)
Maximum profits	1.00	0.33	0.084	0.39
Maximum price	1.70	0.36	0.077	0.29
	2.00	0.36	0.070	0.27
Equilibrium at the quartiles	8/3(2.67)	1/3(0.33)	1/18(0.056)	1/4(0.25)

21. It is worth recording that the analysis of the section applies also to the fixed-location problem dealt with by Hotelling in the first part of his paper where locations are fixed and each competitor assumes his rival will keep his price unchanged. If the

TABLE 2

SITUATION	S	PRICES (b multiplied by)	PROFITS ($b^2 l$ multiplied by)
Zero freight rates	0.00	0.00	0.00
Maximum profits	0.50	0.375	0.110
Maximum prices	1.00	0.40	0.095
Zero quantities at the ends and center of the market	8/3(2.66)	1/3(0.33)	1/18(0.056)

freight rate is zero, it is obvious that the competitors will cut prices to zero on these assumptions. Also, if we assume that the fixed locations are at the quartiles, the situation where the whole market is only just being supplied will be identical with the cases already examined; namely, we shall have $s = 8/3$ and $p = b/3$. In the same way as before, freight rates up to a certain level will protect competitors against the destructive effects of price competition; up to that level a rise of freight rates will increase profits, while prices will continue to rise somewhat longer. Table 2, analogous to Table 1, summarizes the numerical results.

Changes in Marginal Costs

In this section we shall consider the effects on the equilibrium situation of (*a*) a small change in marginal costs equal for both producers (i.e., we shall consider the effects of marginal costs rising above the zero level that we have hitherto assumed) and (*b*) a small increase in the level of marginal costs for one producer alone. We shall also, as before, consider the case of the monopolist for the sake of comparison.

(*a*) This case offers no difficulty; the general reasoning from nonspatial markets indicates that in all the cases examined, including the monopolist, it will be profitable to pass on part, but only part, of the increased costs to the consumer in the shape of higher prices. In Cases A and B, where equilibrium is established at the quartiles, this rise of price will have no effect on location. In cases C and D, where the equilibrium positions of the competitors are, in general, closer to the center than to the quartiles, they will find it profitable to move back toward the quartiles in order to reduce the incidence of higher prices on sales in their hinterlands, which constitute the greater part of their respective markets. In fact, if marginal costs rise sufficiently we shall have a case analogous to that examined in the last section, where the competitors will not move from the quartiles, no matter what competitive assumptions are made.

(*b*) This case is more complicated, and we must consider the various cases separately.

Case A: If the costs rise for one plant of a monopolist, it will be profitable for him to raise the price charged in that plant, but it will also be profitable for him to use his low-cost plant to supply more than half the market. Further, as we have seen, it is profitable for him to locate each plant at the center of the part of the market that it supplies. Hence, the monopolist will move his high-cost plant nearer to its end of the market than to the quartile and his low-cost plant nearer the center. This readjustment will also involve reducing the mill-price charged by the latter plant.

Case B: The case of full quasi-co-operation is now somewhat different from that of the monopolist. For the small rise of marginal costs for one competitor is assumed not to alter either producer's expectation that he will continue to supply half the market. The competitors will continue to locate the quartiles. Producer A, whose marginal costs have risen, will raise his price in order to charge the monopoly price appropriate to his new cost situation for half the market, while producer B, whose costs have not changed, will continue to charge his old price. Although A will be disappointed with the results and B will be pleasantly surprised, we are still entitled to regard the situation as one of equilibrium. However, this equilibrium will contain the germs of instability. Depending on the size of the rise of A's marginal costs, B's joy and A's consternation will tend to make them revise their assumptions in the direction of B's expecting A to charge a higher price than his own and vice versa. Our analysis must, therefore, be confined strictly to small changes of marginal costs.

Cases C and D: In both these cases A, whose marginal costs have risen, will charge a higher mill-price and move back toward his quartile. A's retreat will improve B's position in the competitive region. This opens up to B the possibilities of charging higher prices and of moving toward the center, except that the more he moves toward the center, the less profitable will it be for him to charge a higher price. In fact, it may be profitable for him to charge a lower price, depending on the extent of his move. What he actually does is to depend on the freight rate or, more accurately, on s. The smaller the value of s, the greater will be the tendency for him to move toward the center and charge lower prices, while for larger values of s he will move less toward the center and will raise his price. The critical values of s are approximately 0.65 in Case C and 1.70 in Case D.

This concludes the verbal argument. It should be pointed out that in this type of argument it is impossible to do justice to the essential character of the adjustment as one of mutual determination, and in this respect the arguments of this part sin more than once.

MATHEMATICAL APPENDIX

In this appendix I shall merely indicate the general methods used to reach the conclusions arrived at by verbal argument in the preceding section.[22]

We shall make use of the following symbols. Geometrical references are to Figure 1. Let l = the length of the market; r the freight rate per unit of distance; x_1 and x_2 the distances of A from D and B from C, respectively; d_1 and d_2 the distances from S of A and B, respectively; p_1 and p_2 their mill-prices; and c_1 and c_2 their marginal costs.

The variables within the control of the competitors are p_1 and x_1 for A and p_2 and x_2 for B. The quantities d_1 and d_2 are dependent variables and may be expressed in terms of the four independent

---

22. A detailed presentation of the mathematical argument is available in mimeographed form on application to the author.

variables. Then letting π_1 and π_2 be the profits of A and B, respectively, we may write

$$\pi_1 = \pi_1(p_1, x_1, p_2, x_2, r, c_1, l),$$

$$\pi_2 = \pi_2(p_2, x_2, p_1, x_1, r, c_2, l).$$

The producers aim at maximizing not their actual profits but their expected profits. Expected profits for A may be obtained from these functions by substituting for p_2 and x_2 the values that A expects these variables to take on as the result of his own action. Thus, in Case A he will expect $p_1 = p_2$ and $x_1 = x_2$, while in Case B he will expect $p_1 = p_2$ and x_2 to remain unchanged by his action. In Case C he will expect both p_2 and x_2 to remain unaffected by his action.

Now, for A and B simultaneously to maximize their expected profits, the following conditions are necessary:

$$\frac{\partial \pi_1}{\partial x_1} = \frac{\partial \pi_2}{\partial p_1} = \frac{\partial \pi_2}{\partial x_2} = \frac{\partial \pi_2}{\partial p_2} = 0.$$

In order to obtain manageable solutions to these four equations, it was necessary to assume $c_1 = c_2$ and to assume a linear demand function at every point of the market. The solutions then express the optimum values of $p_1, p_2, x_1, x_2; \pi_1$ and π_2 as functions of $r, l,$ and c.

By investigating the behavior of these functions with respect to r the results given in Table 1 can be obtained. The results given in Table 2 are obtained by imposing the restriction $x_1 = x_2 = l/4$.

The effects of a change in marginal costs for both producers are found by determining the effects of a small change in c, while the effects of a change in the marginal costs of one producer are found by taking as our starting-point $c_1 = c_2$ and determining the effects of a small change in c_1, c_2 remaining unchanged.

A Dissenting View
of Duopoly and Spatial
Competition

The process of competitive product-differentiation has a three-fold foundation. A firm in competition aspires to maximum profits by seeking an efficient combination of three economic variables: adjustments over *space*, and changes in both *quality* and *price* of product. Unlike price analysis, however, the theory of location or of quality under conditions of imperfect competition has never been a *cause célèbre*.[1] Significantly, too, over the years economists have suffered

1. Except for two articles written on the subject several decades ago, spatial competition, in the present context, cannot be said to have attracted to date more attention than has been afforded to it by the occasional deferential references to Professor Hotelling's views on "centre-clustering", in "Stability in Competition," *Economic Journal* (March 1929) [Selection 6 of this volume]. See in this connection A. P. Lerner and H. W. Singer, "Some Notes on Duopoly and Spatial Competition," *Journal of Political Economy* (April 1937); A. Smithies, "Optimum Location in Spatial Competition," *Journal of Political Economy* (June 1941) [Selection 7 of this volume]; and E. H. Chamberlin, *The Theory of Monopolistic Competition*, eighth edition (Cambridge, Mass., 1962), pp. 260–65. For spatial theory in political science, where the notion of centre-clustering again features prominently, see D. E. Stokes, "Spatial Models of Party Organization," *American Political Science Review* (June 1963).

For some background literature, however, the reader may also wish to consult E. Schneider, "Bemerkungen zu einer Theorie der Raumwirtschaft," *Econometrica* (January, 1935); W. Lewis, "Competition in Retail Trade," *Economica* (November 1945); E. M. Hoover, *The Location of Economic Activity* (New York, 1948); S. Enke, "Equilibrium among Spatially Separated Markets," *Econometrica* (January 1951) [Selection 17 of this volume]; P. A. Samuelson, "Spatial Price Equilibrium and Linear Programming," *American Economic Review* (June 1952) [Selection 18 of this volume]; A. Loesch, *The Econimics of Location* (New Haven, 1954); Stefan Valavanis, "Loesch on Location," *American Economic Review* (September 1955); W. Isard, *Location and Space-Economy* (New York, 1956); M. L. Greenhut, *Plant Location in Theory and Practice* (Chapel Hill, 1956) and *Microeconomics and the Space Economy* (Chicago, 1963); E. W. Smykay and others, *Physical Distribution Management* (New York, 1961); V. L. Smith, "Minimization of Economic Rent in Spatial Price Equilibrium," *Review of Economic Studies* (February 1963); E. S. Mills and M. R. Lav, "A Model of Market Areas with Free Entry," *Journal of Political Economy* (June 1964) [Selection 12 of the volume]: and T. Takayama and G. G. Judge, "Equilibrium among Spatially Separated Markets: A Reformulation," *Econometrica* (October 1964) [Selection 19 of this volume].

An earlier version of this paper was presented to Lord Robbins' Seminar at the London School of Economics in 1964. The author has profited from the Seminar's attention and suggestions. Professor R. G. D. Allen's comments, on a different occasion, have also been helpful.

Reprinted from Economica, *May 1965, pp. 140–60, by permission of the London School of Economics and Political Science and the author.*

a growing tendency to regard the concepts of "price competition" and "competition" as synonymous. As a result, the term "spatial competition" is gradually disappearing from our vocabulary, though sporadically one still encounters it in the classroom and in print. But if this anomaly persists, an undesirable imbalance in micro-economic theory may become entrenched. A change in emphasis, therefore, is mandatory. Accordingly, my primary concern in this essay is to stimulate thought and discussion on so deserving a topic, chiefly by presenting the reader with a fresh pattern of analysis. The new analytical apparatus, leading to some interesting conclusions, is introduced below in a manner also suitable for the study of competition in quality.

We open the discussion with a quotation from Professor Chamberlin's summary endorsement of the prevailing views on spatial competition between two sellers. The reference is a convenient one. It contains both a clear statement of, and a typically faithful attachment to, a veteran thesis, in turn the principal target against which this article is directed:

> The fundamental question is whether sellers (of the same commodity) will tend to concentrate at one point or to disperse over the area so as to give a maximum of convenience to the buyers. Let us begin by assuming the buyers to be uniformly distributed; and the problem will be simplified (without affecting the nature of the conclusions) by considering them as distributed along a line instead of over an area. *It has been shown by Professor Hotelling that, where buyers are distributed along such a line, and where there are but two sellers, these latter will, contrary to expectations, locate as close to each other as possible, instead of at the quartile points of the line where convenience to the buyers would be a maximum....* The final equilibrium point may, in fact, be defined with precision. It would be located at the centre of the line, since, if it were elsewhere, the seller whose market were smaller would move to the other side of his rival, and such moves would continue until both were established at the mid-point. *This is a conclusion of great importance.*[2]

An operational mechanism capable of questioning the significance of the Hotelling thesis on duopoly, and establishing an alternative formulation of the equilibrium process, is set forth here. The analytical background required for this purpose is developed ... first; it is then put into use, ... and a concise statement of the proposed

---

2. *Op. cit.*, p. 260, my italics. Chamberlin goes on next to disagree with the Hotelling thesis under conditions of triopoly. Where three sellers make up the market, he argues in favour of definitive dispersion, contesting Hotelling's explicit belief that centre-clustering recurs. Neither solution, however, is satisfactory because, under their particular assumptions, fluctuations between the two extremes are most likely to occur. This is recognized by R. G. Lipsey, *An Introduction to Positive Economics* (1963), pp. 252–6. Unfortunately, Lipsey's analysis is in agreement with the accepted view, questioned in this essay, that clustering at the centre is inevitable in a duopolistic market.

thesis is presented. We shall thus be enabled to demonstrate in a novel manner why competition over space between duopolists may well discourage centre-clustering — and produce instead results shown to favor community convenience, even where we have product standardization. . . .

Basically, I dispense with the customary assumption of a linear market, or "highway" restriction; and, generalizing the interpretation of the competitive plane, conclude that centre-clustering cannot be said to imply a stable location equilibrium. The various other assumptions employed also contribute to a more realistic setting, and allow us to discount best the allegedly inherent tendency in spatial competition for contestants to cluster at the centre. This is particularly so with the negatively-sloping demand curve postulated here, an approach in distinct contrast to Professor Hotelling's addiction to an infinitely inelastic flow of demand. Briefly, the familiar argument that maximization of each competitor's "hinterland" is the firm's main objective, leading to general equilibrium at the centre, will prove untenable. Equally problematic will emerge Professor Smithies' variation of the same argument, or that equilibrium at the centre is stable "if one assumes that each competitor sells only in his own hinterland and does not attempt to invade the hinterland of his rival".[3] As it is not difficult for the reader, however, to familiarize himself with the limited literature, I prefer not to expatiate on it in this article. Finally, the method in this study is abstract rather than empirical. Field-work and further research, along the new lines suggested below, are required to test the significance of our purely theoretical contribution.

ASSUMPTIONS

1. We imagine any delimited *area* populated by evenly scattered and perfectly (i.e. linearly) mobile consumer units.

2. Consumers behave consistently, enjoy adequate knowledge, and minimize travelling distance (transport costs) subject to some *minimum sensible* constraint of indifference. Quite simply, the principle put forth is that some positive minimum, however small or large, exists for the consumer where the difference in distance between patronizing one store rather than the other can be axiomatized as inconsequential, and thus too weak a criterion for practical choice or revealed preference. The consumer's postulated apathy toward applying the traditional economic calculus "to the letter" beyond a

---

3. Smithies, *loc. cit.*, p. 434.

given stage may be conveniently interpreted as the effect of discontinuities in utility functions.[4]

3. Consumers within what I define below as the "doubtful area," or region of uncertainty, are subject to a "fashion effect." Further, the probability of mass imitation is said to rise the greater that area. The likelihood of serious inventory difficulties, as we show below, prescribes the adoption of this assumption, insofar as an even division at all times of the total market between the two sellers is ruled out. Nor would an even division of the total clientele in the *long run* be a consolation. It is essential, we see, to cover against the eventuality of an explicit economic need to have a steady stream of customers over a shorter period of time.

4. Consumers as a whole optimally frequent a seller only where the latter is "best" located. In spatial competition a store's better proximity to the consumer is the equivalent of a price-cut in price competition.

5. Transport costs vary in direct proportion to travelling distance; or, more generally, distance is measured in terms of cost of transport.

6. We have only two firms. They sell at common prices an identical commodity whose price elasticity of demand is negative and finite, and whose income elasticity of demand is positive and finite.

7. Prices and everything else but location "remain equal"; firms vary sales only by varying their location, and are symmetrically mobile along a given axis. Symmetry, to begin with, is introduced in order to avoid an otherwise serious diagrammatical predicament. More basically, of course, symmetry is essential because only such a process of adjustment allows for full maximization of profits, *as long as both firms are taken to be mobile*. Asymmetrical reciprocation is of necessity inferior to symmetrical reactions to the moves of one's competitor. As will become clear from the new pattern of analysis, asymmetrical adjustment is tantamount to near-instantaneous symmetrical clustering at the centre, where a smaller total market

4. For example, to put it differently, let a consumer have to travel ten miles to go to one store, or ten miles but one step, as it were, to go to the other. Next, let the *difference* in distance travelled be measured along the x-axis, and consumer disutility along the y-axis. Our postulate explains that an upward-sloping disutility curve results, cutting the x-axis at some *positive* interval, equal to the prevailing *minimum sensible* (or one step in this case), where this *minimum* remains permanently constrained away from nought. The attraction of the new principle, it will be seen, lies primarily in its ability to "humanize" the analysis considerably. Inasmuch as knowledge is normally imperfect, we have formalized, in essence, the reasonable notion that checking a pile of, say, pennies to establish whether one possesses 10,000 or 9,999 coins is confirmed nonsense for most human beings. In addition, we understand that random factors outside the system will also qualify the *minimum sensible*. Lastly, it is necessary to note here that our model will continue to function smoothly as long as the *minimum sensible* is *any* positive number, and even if the *minimum* under consideration should ever become an exceedingly small number.

obtains, and inventory difficulties, together with the doubtful area, generally reach a maximum. Nor does the suspension of symmetry, however, alter the conclusions of this study. Such a move, on the other hand, would amount to a blemish in the economics of our model—except where one of the two firms, the new entrant, is free to seek a spatial optimum on the assumption that the other is permanently assigned to a fixed location. Thus, in sole harmony with the analytic style of previous models, we recognize as feasible the ability of both firms to readjust their locations freely. In this respect the device of the highly mobile "ice-cream stand" proves an excellent windfall. But the reader may also note that an efficient decision-making unit normally makes it its business nowadays to enjoy a constant flow of adequate knowledge about pending moves of competitors.

8. Profits and sales are linearly related, and marginal revenue is equated to constant marginal cost (the latter long-term for simplicity). Buyers alone bear the cost of transport.

9. With no external economies, and under conditions of market homogeneity, no groups of consumers need by wooed differentially, and product standardization is complete.

10. Sellers maximize profits considering both a maximum share of the market, and maximum total sales for the industry. I elaborate briefly on this assumption because it is central to the development of the general argument. Any competitive firm, as we know, has three ways open to it for increasing its sales and profits: (*a*) securing a larger share of a given market; (*b*) maintaining that share, and endeavoring to enlarge instead the market in the aggregate in order to increase total sales; or (*c*) aiming at some combination of both. To reach a solution of centre-clustering, therefore, the analysis would have to be based, among other things, on the unnecessarily restrictive assumption that total sales are always fixed—and the two competing firms then said to be intent on enlarging their share of a given, non-expandable, market in order to increase profits. Such an approach, however, is unrealistic because total sales, and hence the firms' profits, vary significantly depending upon the locations chosen by the two firms. Indeed, there will always be some locations which minimize transport costs for the community as a whole, and thus make possible increases in total sales for the industry by exploiting released purchasing power. Hence, the income elasticity of demand is given due attention here.[5]

5. It is not difficult to perceive that, given a clustered equilibrium anywhere on the plane, by removing one of the two stores to any other (dispersed) position we are necessarily lowering the average distance travelled for the community as a whole. We [will]. . . discuss this basic principle, and show that *minimum* average transport costs are reached through optimal dispersion. In fact, tracing the implications of this obvious

THE "DOUBTFUL AREA"

The "Minimum Sensible" and the Hyperbolic Boundaries

We let the larger of the two circles, or the discontinuous lines forming a rectangle, in Figure 1, denote some delimited space defining the extent of the market or town under consideration. Ignoring the *minimum sensible*, or allowing it for the moment to be zero, if we consider a consumer located, say, at (X_b, Y_b) it is clear that

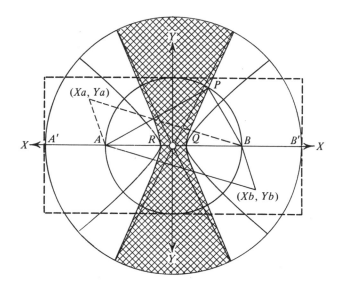

FIGURE 1

he would choose in favor of store B. He travels least to get to B, and gets standard service there. Similarly (X_a, Y_a) prefers store A. Hence, the reasonable conjecture that consumer units located to the right of the ($\pm$) y axis are likely to prefer B; just as consumer units located to the left thereof must prefer A. Only those consumers remain undecided who live on the y-axis. Clearly, too, this division obtains regardless of the particular (symmetrical) locations assumed by the two firms.

As soon as we introduce into the picture the *minimum sensible*, however, or constrain it away from nought, the pattern of the distribution of patronage becomes much less obvious. We gather at once

---

deduction, we conclude that maximum disposable income for the community must be maximally conducive to maximum profits and sales. Yet both in Chamberlin (*op. cit.*, p. 260) and in Smithies (*loc. cit.*, p. 432) concern over the distance travelled by the community is incidental. Neither author has appreciated sufficiently the significance of the "gravitational" properties of the average distance minima.

that A and B will be be inclined to locate themselves anywhere at random. The central question we thus pose is: If the two stores are assumed to move symmetrically along a given axis, what direction will spatial competition between them take, and what are the main welfare implications?

We take as given the location of two stores A and B (where $OQ = a$, and $OB = t$), distance $2t$ apart, so that we have $A(-t, 0)$ and $B(t, 0)$. Next, we assume $2a$ to be the *minimum sensible*, or the consumer's critical difference of distances for preference between A and B (i.e., if $BP - AP > 2a$, consumer at P goes to store A; if $AP - BP > 2a$, he goes to store B; and if $AP - BP \leq 2a$, there is no preference). It then follows that the locus of points P dividing the no-preference region from the preference region will be given by a fixed hyperbola — in turn, a result of unique significance for the kinetics of our model. Essentially, the discovery means that some area of uncertainty or indifference must exist, descriptively called "doubtful", and that *at any given time its form and extent depend upon the actual degree of dispersion undertaken by the two sellers.* Better still, we understand that the boundaries of this area are defined throughout by sets of confocal hyperbolae whose behavior is governed consistently by the spatial adjustment of the two foci (or two sellers) in the system. Considering Figure 1, therefore, our no-preference region is defined by the expression, $PA - PB = 2a$, which immediately gives (where $t > a$) the pure hyperbola:[6]

$$[x^2/a^2 - y^2/(t^2 - a^2)] = 1, \text{ with asymptotes } y = \pm \sqrt{(t^2 - a^2)/a^2}x.$$

Hence, we have the mechanism yielding our shaded or doubtful area, pictured as a "hyperbolic fan," and engulfing the set of all those consumer units said to be indifferent between patronizing either one

---

6. Where $PA^2 = (t+x)^2 + y^2$; $PB^2 = (t-x)^2 + y^2$; and $PA^2 - PB^2 = 4tx$, our *no-preference* region is defined by: $|PA - PB| = 2a$. We then have

$$PA^2 = PB^2 \pm 4aPB + 4a^2$$
$$PA^2 - PB^2 - 4a^2 = \pm 4aPB$$
$$(PA^2 - PB^2 - 4a^2)^2 = 16a^2 PB^2$$
$$(4tx - 4a^2)^2 = 16a^2[(t-x)^2 + y^2]$$
$$(t^2 x^2 - 2a^2 tx + a^4) = a^2(t^2 - 2tx + x^2 + y^2)$$
$$(t^2 - a^2)x^2 - a^2 y^2 = a^2(t^2 - a^2),$$

thus giving the *pure hyperbola* $[x^2/a^2 - y^2/(t^2 - a^2)] = 1$.

The reader will note that it has been found necessary, mostly for achieving clarity of exposition, to simplify matters and take in this model the *minimum sensible* as a fixed positive number regardless of distance travelled, and identical for all consumers. Relaxation of this postulate, whether in the direction of introducing (*a*) a uniformly or otherwise varying relationship to distance travelled by the consumer; and/or (*b*) varying evaluations *per capita*, and in turn independent of distance travelled, would

of the two stores. Hence, too, we have the asymptotic properties of the system, which define the "beam" or particular "opening" assumed at any one time by the doubtful area.[7] The spatial adjustment of the two competing firms is necessarily causal, therefore, and accounts for the behavior of all possible "duets" of hyperbolae in the map.

The Basic Kinetic Concept

In order to clarify the significance of what has been introduced so far, we continue with the suggestion that the parameters a and t can be changed in a variety of interesting ways. Naturally, we assume here a fixed (consumers' pattern of discrimination), with t (the distance separating the two sellers) increasing as the two stores move apart.[8] Where such a relationship obtains, the slope of the asymptotes, $\pm\sqrt{[(t^2 - a^2)/a^2]}$ rises inevitably: thus indicating that the system of asymptotes, and hence the doubtful area, closes up via progressive store-dispersion, and *vice versa*. The construction is fundamental. It

---

seriously complicate the analysis — to little, if any, advantage. Although the implications of the model would persist, the distinction between our two contrasting regions would no longer be as clear-cut. For example, let us take the *minimum sensible* as a number independent of distance travelled, but varying *per capita*. We could then go on and consider the straightforward supposition that the lower bound of some random variable ν' has a probability density over the population, and denote by ν the expected (or true average) lower bound. For an estimate of ν, and equally simply, we might then use the sample mean (or median, mode, etc.):

$$\bar{\nu} = \frac{i = 1 \sum^{n} \nu'i}{n}, \ [\nu'i]i = 1, \ldots n$$

applying a set of n random observations on ν'. Indeed, our estimator would become yet more efficient in various ways, such as by stratifying the population (say be distance from centre, possibly sub-divided into concentric circles), and using the stratified mean as our estimate of ν. Whatever our results, however, we would always find it most perplexing to present them diagrammatically. For the distinction between the doubtful area and the rest of uncertainty would really lie outside it, and *vice versa*. It has been found best, therefore, to introduce the principle of the *minimum sensible* as was done above, and thus convey the message of the study both simply and more effectively.

7. Given any degree of store dispersion, our doubtful area consists of the *whole* shaded segment lying between the branches of the appropriate two quadratics, and *not* only of that encompassed by the two straight line asymptotes from the origin, O, to the relevant two curves. The properties of hyperbolae disallow tangents, as points of tangency with straight lines through the centre are reached invariably at infinity. This is important. The reader is reminded further that confocal hyperbolae consider the distance between two foci as regarded from any (third) point on and along them. We know that in Figure 1 the difference between distances AP and BP is necessarily constant for any point P on the hyperbola in question. This simple mathematical property is the cornerstone of the mechanics of our model.

8. Two other cases would be: (1) a and t increase in proportion, with $t = \lambda a$, where λ is fixed. Then $y = \pm\sqrt{(\lambda^2 - 1)}x$ gives the relevant sets of asymptotes, with slopes fixed as $\pm\sqrt{(\lambda^2 - 1)}$. A system of hyperbolae of fixed asymptotes and of a generally steep nature emerges, therefore, as the two firms disperse progressively, cutting the

endows our competitive plane with a set of hyperbolae, always through fixed R and Q, becoming *flatter* (steeper asymptotes) as *t rises*, or as the two firms disperse. Conversely, it confirms that *through progressive falls in the value of t the doubtful area opens up until it reaches its maximum with centre-clustering, or where the two foci degenerate to one focal point.*

With *one* focal point, the entire region which society occupies becomes doubtful. As the two foci close in toward the centre, the increasingly more curved branches of the new hyperbolae which emerge reveal the actual pattern pursued by the spreading uncertainty. It is essential, however, to understand that the entire area becomes doubtful at an even earlier stage. This is because *complete* uncertainty is also generated where we have *insufficient* dispersion. Clearly, given the *minimum sensible* preference constraint, $2a$ (or RQ), it follows that as soon as the two foci come to lie exactly on positions R and Q respectively, the whole region emerges as totally doubtful. The branches of the "hyperbolic fan" are again perfectly collapsed along (featured asymptotic to) the x-axis: and the difference in distance between patronizing either one of the two sellers becomes equal to, or less than, the *minimum sensible* for every consumer in the market.

Conversely, the farther away from the centre, the more the doubtful area is being eliminated, and the better each store is assured of gaining its maximum share, or one-half, of the market. For any consumer the difference in distance between going to A or to B is thus accentuated, a conclusion again dictated by the system's asymptotic properties. In the limit (i.e., extreme bi-polar outskirts of the town with respect to the x-axis), the doubtful area is reduced to its minimum. As the consumer has been assumed indifferent between the two sellers if the difference in distance in patronizing either one should be equal to, or less than, $2a$ (or RQ), consumer choice automatically proves easier where the two firms disperse. The difference between going to either firm becomes more pronounced in this matter alone. At some extreme outskirt positions A' and B', therefore, we expect the doubtful area to reach its minimum. Represented geometrically, that minimum is given by a rectangle. The region of uncertainty is then encompassed by two confocal hyperbolae emerging through R and Q, with A' and B' as their focal points, and their branches asymptotic to straight vertical lines through R and Q, respectively.

x-axis at increasingly greater intervals (and *not* passing only through fixed R and Q). It should be as though "stretching" the map would "straighten" all hyperbolae, whilst letting it shrink would cause the opposite to occur. (2) t fixed (stores in given positions) and a increases (increasing lack of discrimination by consumers). We then have a system of confocal hyperbolae for boundary regions, such that all curves move outwards with flatter asymptotes as a increases.

Of course, we may or may not want to assume that consumers live on the ($\pm$) y-axis.

Individual and Aggregate Uncertainty

We conclude this section with the explanation that we choose to understand by the shaded area a region of uncertainty not only on the basis of *individual* consumer uncertainty of choice, but, in addition, in terms of *aggregate* consumer uncertainty of choice. This surface is taken to quantify uncertainty, from the viewpoint of the two stores, as far as everyone enveloped by it is concerned. Uncertainty continues to persist, in short, notwithstanding the possible contention that if taken as a whole (and, therefore, if believed to involve large enough numbers of consumers) the no-preference region might divide evenly (split automatically into one-half for each) between the two stores in question. Anticipating the arguments presented in the following sections, at least two reasons come to mind why we may consider it as singularly unlikely that the said probability distribution must follow, or that it ever should apply in this context.

First, marketing experience of revealed preference patterns could be invoked, and would probably confirm, that where some initial wave of customers choose, at random or otherwise, to patronize any one store in particular, the possibility arises that a *fashion* or *imitation effect* then comes into operation, and patronage quickly snowballs. Worse yet, however, even if the equal division were at all likely to occur, it might well extend over an uneconomic time-period, or one causing serious inventory anomalies to the firms. This is discussed later. An equal division of the total clientele between the two stores in the *long run* cannot be of much use to the firm with an interest in enjoying a steady stream of customers over a shorter period of time. And there are many examples of such cases in the real world. I am prompted to underline, therefore, the possibility of sudden and random mass "walk-outs" in some *one* direction—as long as the doubtful area remains large. Hence, I postulate a pivotal rôle for the uncertainty-per-individual factor, and later emphasize the serious concern which this factor creates in the aggregate for the two sellers. The economist's intuition, in fact, would seem to suggest (the existing "standardization" assumption notwithstanding) that our doubtful area probably breeds such band-wagon phenomena; and that the latter become, in turn, the rule rather than the exception the larger that area of uncertainty.

Second, again invoking market experience, it appears no less useful to suggest that even where the equal division takes place in a manner satisfying our foregoing reservations, the result may still prove inadequate. For the two sellers, as I postulate further, are not interested only arithmetically in some given share of the market — or regardless, that is, of their clientele's composition per unit-time and unit-space. They display instead a marked preference for serving consistently the same, or some very moderately varying, mix of the total consumer force to which they cater. Inasmuch, therefore, as each new (and, at best, only remotely equal) division of the market between the two contestants consists necessarily of a different set of customers, the result will always prove disagreeable to our firms. Both psychological and technical considerations are relevant here, and especially where product maintenance or servicing is concerned. Hence, our twofold assumption remains throughout that (a) the doubtful area portrays the uncertainty obtaining with respect both to individual consumers taken separately and/or all consumers taken as a whole; and, by implication, that (b) the two firms are anxious to keep that area at some optimum minimum, as we will see later.

THE AVERAGE DISTANCE MINIMA AND NEW ENTRY

From the discussion in the preceding pages it cannot reasonably be deduced that the two firms will enjoy any real advantage by moving off to the extreme outskirts of the x-axis. This observation holds even though we may have shown that the doubtful area can be reduced progressively to its rectangular minimum in this manner. Bi-polarity will generally prove uneconomical, and dispersion may be expected to cease, therefore, at some earlier stage, as will be shown in the remainder of the study.

Average Distance Minima

We begin with the essential observation that some symmetrical positions, duly dispersed (rather than clustered at the centre, or at R and Q), do exist, fixed at approximately A and B in our main diagram, *where average distance travelled is at a minimum.* This important constraint is certainly obvious to the eye, but not as easy to prove mathematically. Its validity was established formally with the Monte Carlo method of random simulation — and irrespective, of course, of the *minimum sensible.* The exercise was performed on the London University "Mercury" computer, and confirmed the notion that for any market area some *dispersed* symmetrical positions will always minimize average distance travelled. A value of approximately 0.4 times the radius was obtained for each semi-circular market. In the alternative case of a rectangular market area, and one consisting of two square regions, minimum average distance travelled occurs at approximately the centre of each regional square.

It will be of interest to the reader to trace this useful conclusion in another way. Taking first the case of a circular market area, we let S be the average distance walked, evaluated for a quadrant of a circle or radius r, over a uniform distribution of population. We thus write:

$$S = \int_0^r \int_0^{r^2-y^2} \sqrt{(x-m)^2 + y^2}(dxdy).$$

And we then solve for the minimum by putting $\partial S/\partial m = 0$:

$$-\tfrac{1}{2}\{r\sqrt{r^2 + (r-m)^2} + (r-m)^2 \log [\sqrt{r^2/(r^2-m^2)} + r/(r-m)]$$

$$- r\sqrt{(r^2 m^2)} - m^2 \log [\sqrt{r^2/m^2 + 1} + r/m]\} = 0.$$

Using Newton's Approximation, the value which satisfies this equation is $m \cong 0.42 \times r$.

Further, in the case of a rectangular market area, we consider the top right-hand quarter of a rectangle (Figure 2), and consider next moving from the centre of line EF, b, to b'. It follows that Area

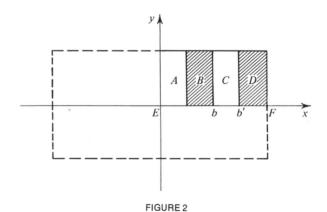

FIGURE 2

C is indifferent about the move. Area B loses as much as Area D gains, and *vice versa*: i.e. $(B+D)$ is indifferent about the move. If, and only if, b is the mid-point for a move of any magnitude in either direction will there be an Area A which suffers a net loss. If b' is to the right of b, A will be to the left, and *vice versa*. Hence, b, the mid-point, is the optimal point.

Given, therefore, the existence of our average distance minima, we shall be led to infer below that the two stores do not disperse maximally. Bi-polarity emerges almost as disadvantageous as centre-clustering—

although average distance travelled is at its maximum with centre-clustering.[9] But this decisive consideration figures more prominently in the next section, where the two sellers end up efficiently located under the gravitational pull of the two average distance minima.

New Entry

Extreme symmetrical dispersion, however, is always undesirable on a further argument. The explanation which follows holds not-withstanding (*a*) the consideration that *two* nuclei of maximum satis-faction for the "neighbouring lucky few" (as opposed to one nucleus in the case of centre-clustering) are created through *any* dispersed positions; and/or (*b*) the possible claim that as long as they each retain half of a (smaller) market, the two sellers may just as well disregard the implications of a poorly served consumer force. The overriding argument here is obvious: namely, that the probability of new entry is also maximized where dispersion is allowed to approach its maxi-mum. For the likelihood of some store *C* entering the market cannot be negligible where a huge spatial gap is encouraged between the two firms. (The same consideration pertains to the clustered position, due to the exaggerated "spatial availability" that such a location also implies.) Therefore, even though the doubtful area can be reduced to

9. Extreme dispersion is less undesirable than centre-clustering. For any area the average distance travelled by the consumer will be greater where the two firms are clustered rather than maximally dispersed. Our diagram is self-explanatory, where any given market area is imagined to be inhabited by a series of, say, concentric "population rings", each *n* distance apart and populated identically. If the two firms cluster at the centre, the entire diagram, illustrating any one such "ring", becomes

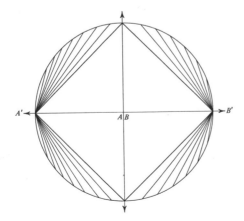

completely covered with straight lines from the circle's periphery to the centre, de-picting accordingly total distance travelled as per the population ring in question. On the other hand, it is equally clear that extreme dispersion is responsible for the rectangular portion "saved", or left intact in the diagram.

its minimum by persistent symmetrical dispersion, we already anticipate with reasonable certainty that the competing duopolists will tend to settle in the vicinity of the two average distance minima. The argument is finalized in the section which follows.

CENTRE-CLUSTERING VS. DISPERSION

We have now developed the various principles essential for the operation of our model. We begin, therefore, this section with a brief analytical statement of the proposed thesis. As different results obtain, however, depending upon whether or not we introduce inventory costs into the picture, the first half of the section is divided into two parts, the first excluding and the second including these costs. The sub-section including inventory costs should be understood as providing a supplement mainly to 2(i), 2(iii), 3(i) and 3(iii), below. Together with considerations relating to the average distance minima and new entry, the inventory-costs argument contributes heavily to the defense of the thesis against centre-clustering. Also, in both of these two broad parts we deal in terms of three relevant cases: government control, collusion and competition. In each case we list briefly the sets of factors conducive to centre-clustering, dispersion and bipolarity. The section ends with a descriptive (mathematical) presentation of the solution mechanism. Equilibrium, we find, is generally reached at some dispersed positions, such as A and B in Figure 1, rather than at the centre. An explicit solution, however, is not advanced. Specific results will naturally vary widely depending upon the particular properties ascribed to the chosen constraints on the firms' utility functions.[10]

A.   The Analysis: Inventory Costs Excluded

1.   Government Control   Locations can be easily dictated in whatever fashion the authorities see fit. As such, therefore, this case is of no especial interest.

2. Collusion

CENTRE-CLUSTERING   (i) The solution of centre-clustering may be sought through disregard of (*a*) the total-sales-for-industry com-

---

10. The actual shape of the market is also relevant here. For instance, a "tall" rectangular market (height much greater than width) would hardly induce the same degree of store dispersion as a "long" rectangular market (width much greater than height). Such matters, however, are not explored here. Together with a set of comprehensive quantitative tests, they would provide ample material for a further study. (See conclusion.)

ponent of profit-maximization; and (*b*) the notion, even where shares are fixed, that the complete uncertainty implied by maximization of each firm's hinterland can be disadvantageous, inasmuch as centre-clustering always drives the doubtful area to an automatic maximum.[11]

DISPERSION   (ii) Where shares are *fixed* (and whatever the division undertaken there can be no adverse effects to the model), dispersion is naturally pursued to increase total sales for the industry. The average distance minima will be approached, therefore, subject to (*a*) the income elasticity of demand; (*b*) the price elasticity of demand; and (*c*) the possible higher frequency of patronage.[12] (iii) Dispersion up to, and possibly beyond, the average distance minima will also be initiated on the basis of evaluating the behavior of the consumer force enveloped by the doubtful area. The firms then consider (*a*) the "fashion effect" — where unfavorable mass imitation will be more likely the greater the area of indifference; and/or (*b*) the same-mix-of-clientele consideration. For psychological or technical reasons, and depending largely upon the type of product sold, a firm may be interested in the same share of a given body of customers, but also in an extended market. (iv) Further, the probability of new entry is highest with centre-clustering as "spatial availability" for new sellers is thereby maximized, both topographically and by way of the consequent bad service (highest transport costs for the community). Hence, an additional tendency to disperse exists, always subject to the consideration that extreme dispersion, or bi-polarity, can also be disadvantageous. (v) The final incentive to reject centre-clustering and proceed to disperse is twofold, and will come through (*a*) the realization that centre-clustering becomes conspicuously open to possible anti-trust sanctions since it maximizes public inconvenience [the same would apply to extreme dispersion in 2(iii)]; and (*b*) the apprehension that certain costs (rents, etc.) are usually highest in the immediate vicinity of the "city centre," whilst prices offered to the consumer might have to be reduced to compensate for the rise in average distance travelled.

BI-POLARITY   (vi) Extreme dispersion is rendered possible by 2(i), 2(iii), 2(v)*b*; but is incompatible with 2(ii), 2(iv), 2(v)*a*.

11. Far from being a theoretical caprice, our *minimum sensible* threshold is a fundamental concept. Elegantly reflecting the functional rationality of human beings (or, alternatively, formalizing consumer "irrationality"), it warns that the maximization of each firm's hinterland can be a very undesirable practice. For better or worse, in short, men are not robots in this theoretical construction.

12. The observation implies that total *visits* to the stores reach a maximum in the vicinity of the average distance minima. For we suspect that one does not normally get into the "habit" of travelling many miles to reach, of all things, a store. Whereas if a store is least inconveniently located the probability that the average custumer will develop a *taste* for maximum visits naturally becomes greater.

3.   Competition

CENTRE-CLUSTERING   (i) Equilibrium at the centre is again unsatisfactory because it carries no guarantee of the maximization of profits. A possible, but improbable, maximization of each firm's *share* of the market is coupled with an unwise disregard of the total-sales consideration. In addition, the highly dangerous maximization of the doubtful area persists of necessity.

DISPERSION   (ii) The possibility is always present that profits may increase through increasing total sales for the industry. The realized degree of dispersion, however, depends upon whether profits would be greater through (*a*) higher total sales [with the three relevant variables accordingly operative, above 2(ii)], accompanied by a *possible* decline in the share, than they would be (*b*) by accepting whatever share obtains and forgoing the greater total of industry sales. (iii) The clustered position holds our doubtful area at its maximum, and a further tendency to disperse will depend, therefore, upon the extent of pressure coming from the two relevant variables here, as in 2(iii). (iv) Considerations of new entry will be the same as above, 2(iv). (v) Finally, dispersion may occur in order (*a*) to avoid maximal inconvenience to the public, and thus various possibly undesirable consequences of government intervention; and (*b*) to keep low certain costs such as rents, as in 2(v).

BI-POLARITY   (iv) Extreme dispersion is rendered possible by 3(i), 3(iii) and 3(v)*b*; but is incompatible with 3(ii), 3(iv), 3(v)*a*.

B.   The Analysis: Inventory Costs Included

The inventory-costs argument, here set forth briefly, is vital. It affords several interesting considerations relating to the significance of the extent of the doubtful area. Inventory costs constitute the most important reason, perhaps, why the firms will be interested in keeping the doubtful area to some optimum low level.

1.   Government Control   Intervention could keep costs to a minimum by specifying which half of the consumer force enclosed in the area of uncertainty should continue to buy from one firm or the other.

2.   Collusion   The cartel, on the other hand, cannot specify which individuals are to buy from which firm. Thus if, beyond the inventory period, fewer than half buy from one firm, the problem arises that although the costs of *total* inventory remain constant, the firms are faced with the cost of moving goods between themselves. We then perceive (i) a *centripetal* force, viz. the closer together the two firms, the lower the cost of transport between them; (ii) a *centrifugal* force, viz. the closer together the two firms, the larger the doubt ful area: and the greater, therefore, the possibilities of sales switching outside the inventory period — and hence the greater the probability of given quantities of goods having to be sent from one firm to the other. Lastly, (iii) we bear in mind that total sales may become lower (income effects, etc.) as the two firms move outward and beyond the average distance minima.

It thus follows that as the consideration in (i) exceeds the considerations in (ii) and (iii), the two firms locate closer together than in the original (non-inventory) optimal positions, and conversely.

3. Competition   As the firms do not co-operate, consideration 2(i) above is excluded. We write, therefore: (i) if, beyond the inventory period, fewer than half the total clientele in the doubtful area buy from one firm — and although over the "year" each firm may expect with confidence its maximum share, or half of the total — an outward movement of the two firms reduces their inventory costs. (ii) Again, however, an outward movement beyond the average distance minima may lower total sales and profits.

Thus if (i) is more significant than (ii), some outward movement, and one possibly persisting even beyond the optimal locations required socially, will yield the true equilibrium; whereas if, on the other hand, (i) is equal to or less than (ii), the two firms may well locate precisely at the two average distance minima, respectively.

C.   The Analysis: Circular Distribution of Equilibria

In this final part of the section we begin with the solution of our problem in two-dimensional diagrammatical form, and conclude with a very brief, but more general, algebraic statement. The latter formulation will include the three variables which have been found to be the main relevant factors (doubtful area, average distance travelled by the community, and new entry). The reader can easily add more detail, however, on the basis of the simple framework which has been set out in this article.

1. The Geometric Representation   To start with, we visualize a situation where the two firms taken to be, say, maximally apart at A' and B' respectively (in Figure 1), proceed to discriminate in favor of positions closer to the two average distance minima. Both firms choose to operate on the basis of some "swap" rate between magnitudes relating to the doubtful area, the average distance travelled by consumers, and considerations of new entry. Each alternative position is evaluated in terms of the different degrees of utility which it is thought to yield. Clearly, by moving away from the extreme outskirt positions and toward A and B (by assumption at no extra cost), profits and sales are bound to be increasing. More people have to travel less, the doubtful area increases insignificantly at first, and the threat of new entry is reduced. Approaching, therefore, the two average distance minima, an optimal limit is to be sought, and a determinate solution found. It will lie where the two sellers best balance the threat of new entry with the position of having the greatest number of well-served customers (i.e. customers required to travel least), and also with the largest increase in the doubtful area which they see fit to tolerate. There, of course, profits reach their maximum. If for any reason, however, calculations prove to be erroneous, and the two firms overshoot the (spatial) optima, the tendency to converge unduly toward the centre can soon be corrected. Progressive dispersal "backwards" will then continue until profits are restored to their maximum.

Restating the matter from the opposite starting-point, in order to express the solution in diagrammatic form, let C and D (in Figure 3)

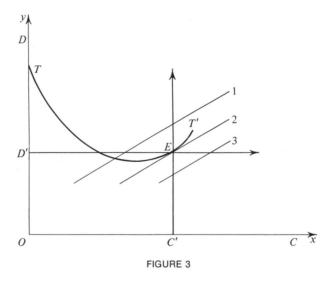

FIGURE 3

stand for the certainty (*not* doubtful) area and for the average distance travelled by consumers, respectively. Thus the object of the firms is to maximize the internally-constrained function U where $U = U(C, \dot{D})$ with $\partial U/\partial C = 0$, $\partial U/\partial D = 0$, and where

$$\partial^2 U/\partial C^2 < 0 \quad \begin{vmatrix} \partial^2 U/\partial C & \partial U/\partial C\partial D \\ \partial U/\partial C\partial D & \partial^2 U/\partial D \end{vmatrix} > 0.$$

Upward-rising indifference curves emerge where C and D are measured on the x-axis and y-axis, respectively, and where these two variables are functions of the analogous positions of the two firms on the x-axis. Utility is expressed along the invisible (third) axis looking straight into one's eye as one looks at the origin, O. It is equally clear that for any symmetrical locations of the two firms some area of certainty (which may be zero) obtains together with some average distance (which cannot be zero) travelled by the consumers. But we know that as the two focal points disperse along the x-axis, and away from the centre, the certainty area automatically increases; whereas, on the contrary, the average distance travelled by consumers begins to fall. We know, too, that this distance reaches its minimum at some positions A and B (in Figure 1), beyond which points it tends to rise. Hence, we have our TT' curve, which illustrates this simple relationship between C and D, and affords the relevant tangential solution, E, with the self-explanatory co-ordinates OC' and OD'. It is noteworthy, next, that equilibrium E lies to the right of the minimum point on the TT' curve, thus indicating that segment AB (and, therefore, any other relatively more "clustered" position) is incompatible with the equilibrium solution.

Two (symmetrical) equilibrium locations are implied, therefore well away from the maximally doubtful centre, and converging toward the segregated positions which community convenience requires, or the well-known points A and B (in Figure 1). The gravitational pull of these quartile points cannot but be decisive. Of course, actual locations assumed would probably vary with each duopoly case, as utility is maximized by the two firms in accordance with a subjectively given pattern of evaluating the pertinent variables. It should be clear, too, that as the market is not linear, but defined instead by any given area (circular or other), there will be many possible alternative (pairs of) equilibria to the ones in fact attained by any one realized process of competitive behavior. Each point on every such pair invariably will be a symmetric "reflection" of the other. Also, all pairs would lie on the small circle in Figure 1, with radius approximately OB. Orientation and length, respectively, of the radius-axis will depend upon the direction of competition over space, and the particular weights assigned by the duopolists to the several variables under consideration. Further, any one pair of these possible equilibria will be found to lie always on the same one set (duet) of confocal curves. Finally, as was implied earlier, the location segments actually contested would probably be AA' for the firm on the left of the y-axis, and BB' for its opposite.

2. The Algebraic Representation To conclude, we sketch a somewhat more general expression of the solution. Equilibrium is reached where the symmetrically mobile duopolists maximize utility in accordance with a subjectively-given pattern of weighing three pertinent variables. Writing C for the certainty area, D for the average distance travelled by consumers, and E for the probability of new entry, optimum utility obtains by maximizing the internally-constrained function $U = U(C, D, E)$ subject to the condition:

$$\partial U/\partial C = \partial U/\partial D = \partial U/\partial E = 0 \tag{1}$$

$$b < 0 \tag{2}$$

$$\begin{vmatrix} b & g \\ g & c \end{vmatrix} > 0 \tag{3}$$

$$\begin{vmatrix} b & g & f \\ g & c & e \\ f & e & d \end{vmatrix} < 0 \tag{4}$$

where b, c, d, e, f, g denote, respectively $\partial^2 U/\partial C^2$, $\partial^2 U/\partial D^2$, $\partial^2 U/\partial E^2$, $\partial^2 U/\partial C\partial D$, $\partial^2 U/\partial C\partial E$, $\partial^2 U/\partial D\partial E$.

At this point the reader will agree that it is not difficult to dispense altogether (by definition) with the case of centre-clustering. In other words, one may simply constrain the position of maximum utility to be necessarily away from the centre. Any credible reason could prompt this action — always depending, as has been said, upon the subjective views of the two units in competition. For example, a realistic constraint might be $D < D_0$, where D_0 denotes the average distance travelled if the duopolists are clustered in the "city centre". Alternatively, the existence of the *minimum sensible* may be said to imply another highly operational constraint in this connection. Thus, as in Figure 1, the location segments actually contested lie outside OR and OQ for our two respective firms.

CONCLUSION

The reader will now appreciate the limitations of the thesis of centre-clustering. For if, and only if, we are willing (*a*) to ignore the significance of varying total sales for the industry as the two firms change their locations, (*b*) to postulate price and income elasticities of demand to be zero, (*c*) to hold, in addition, that discontinuous utility functions for the consumer are a distinct impossibility, or that the concept of the *minimum sensible* is a casual embellishment, and (*d*) to axiomatize that each seller contemplates alternative locations on the assumption that the other is incapable of adjusting symmetrically, is it at all likely that the two sellers would converge toward, and ultimately cluster at, the centre. But if we reflect on what has gone before, all this adds up to a rather long list of uneasy concessions to have to make. Clearly, if the duopolists converge unduly toward the centre, each would be able, at best, to count on the possible patronage of everyone in general, and hence of no one in particular. Inadequately dispersed, neither seller can rest at all assured of enjoying one-half of the total clientele at minimum cost. Worse still, in its dual rôle of consumer and administrator, the community would probably resent articulately the "solution." The theoretical conclusion is submitted, therefore, that in the *absence* of an uneven distribution of the population (which is normally directly responsible for the clustering that we observe in the world around us), the spatial equilibrium between two sellers of the same commodity is a dispersed one. Of course, the location problem does not arise in the same light where we have product differentiation. For then a firm may well operate under the assumption that its "addicts" will always seek to patronize it.

It follows, too, that where one of the two sellers is permanently established anywhere in a given market (and where, therefore, symmetrical reciprocation does not obtain), the potential new entrant will not choose to locate of necessity as closely as possible to the original firm. Evidently, for any given market configuration it is possible to compute "expected market share," "expected sales for the industry," and "expected sales for each firm." If we then take one firm to have a fixed location in the market, we can easily obtain the optimum position of the other (mobile) firm, such that the above economic variables be maximized, and where (*a*) the dimensions of, say, a rectangular market, (*b*) the distance of the fixed firm from a given boundary of the market, and (*c*) the *minimum sensible* are parameters. The maximum is thus found by a series of calculations where the distance between the two firms is a variable. And, as one may subsequently wish to show in a more heuristic study, store dispersion shall prevail once again. Basically, however, it is the *minimum sensible* constraint on consumer utility maximization that we shall always recognize as the critical element in any dispersion solution. In fact, one might consider further that, if adequately generalized, this useful concept would enable us to rid current consumer behaviour theory of much of its ancient cumbersomeness. As such, the *minimum sensible* only serves to formalize the common secret, amongst those of us who normally glance at the world in which we live, that we are on the whole too clever to worry about petty differentials in our affairs; or, to put it differently, that most people view as an onerous burden the psychic and material cost attached to behaving like perfect economic robots. Finally, it is imperative to stress that our "hyperbolic fan" mechanism will still be operative, and its consequences felt, as we have shown in this article, even where we assign to the *minimum sensible* an exceedingly small value.

I conclude with a somewhat philosophical parenthesis. For if it can be said that the majority of "truths" in theoretical economics are generally sad creatures because, unlike the wise economist, they are afraid to die, the modest conclusion of this theoretical essay should be classed among the few joyful exceptions. I elaborate briefly.

The *raison d'être* of all sound theory, in economics as elsewhere, is threefold. (1) A theoretical apparatus helps us to understand and explain *observed* phenomena, which are either felt to be immediately relevant to some aspect of our welfare, or simply interesting and curious enough to merit, pedagogically or otherwise, our scientific attention. (2) A theoretical construction assists us to understand and predict or forecast "behavior" as yet *unobserved* or possibly altogether unrevealed. Here, too, the reasons are the same as before. (3) In the last analysis, however, all reputable theories are found to prepare the ground for the ascent of their superior successors. But this truth, whose essence is beyond dispute historically, has never been popular amongst economists. Instead, over the years, and as our science has become progressively more analytical, the historian of economics has often encountered some of the profession's chief exponents unduly lamenting the passing of various favorite systems; or, worse still, emerging with the futile impression that permanently valid new ones ("changes") have become at last squarely established. Invariably, it has been a wrong approach, yet one that has frequented theoretical economics with disquieting persistence. Recently, things have improved considerably. Almost everyone nowadays takes the view that the first two objects which I have given above are realistic. Unfortunately, the same cannot be said of the third. In so far, therefore, as I classify this theoretical essay roughly under the second sub-division, and whilst I subscribe thoroughly to the third, I may ask the sympathetic reader (whether empirically or theoretically inclined, or both) to consider himself as having just acquired a fairly reasonable task to perform.

PART III MARKET AREA ANALYSIS

The Economic Law of Market Areas

The subject of this paper may be called the law of market-district limits, or the law of market tributary territory, or, more briefly, the law of market areas. The term "law" surely should be applied sparingly and used not at all where such terms as principle, hypothesis, doctrine, or theory, may serve to describe the character of generalization attempted. The most noteworthy "economic laws," such as Gresham's Law, the law of diminishing returns, of price, of supply and demand, of population, are hardly more than general descriptive phrases to indicate problems, or at most broad explanations, which cannot well be formulated in single propositions. Few of them approximate a precise mathematical form such as do laws of physical science: the laws of gravitation, falling bodies, expansion of gases (Boyle's Law), planetary motions (Kepler's Laws), and many others. It would be extravagant to claim for "the law of market areas" the character of a physical law. But it does parallel closely in form and expression some physical laws, and while not revolutionary of fundamental economic opinions, it brings greater precision and clearness into a field of economic thought of large importance both in practice and in theory.

The problem is to get a definite idea of the extent and shape of market tributary territory as related to any given levels of market prices and of freight rates. The markets here considered are, typically, meeting-places of considerable numbers of buyers and sellers, trading under something like true competitive conditions. Of course, every market both buys and sells; but in relation to scattered buyers and consumers, the market from which they buy presents the aspect of a selling market; and to scattered small producers, the market to which they ship their produce presents the aspect of a buying market. In the one the movement of goods is centrifugal, from a market; in the other the movement is centripetal, toward a market. A manufacturing center in relation to consumers exemplifies the one; large produce exchanges in relation to the scattered producing farms exemplify the other; and middlemen's markets, such as stock exchanges and jobbing centers, present now the one now the other aspect to different groups of traders. The district including the producers who bring or send their products to a buying market may

Reprinted by permission of the publishers from The Quarterly Journal of Economics, 39 (Cambridge, Mass.: Harvard University Press, 1924), pp. 520–29. Copyright 1924 by the President and Fellows of Harvard College.

be said to be tributary to that buying market, or to be dependent upon it as an outlet for sales. Conversely, the district including the various delivery points to which the buyers from a selling market take their purchases may be said to be tributary to that selling market. It will simplify the discussion if attention is here directed mainly to the case of centrifugal (selling) markets, and the principle thus developed can then be readily adjusted to the case of centripetal markets. We confine our attention here to the problem presented in the case of uniform and standardized commodities, as individual commodities differing widely in variety and in quality may present quite different problems, such as the economic and social stratification of groups of purchasers, who may be widely scattered over non-contiguous territories, rather than geographically grouped as in the case of buyers of standard and homogeneous commodities.

If two selling markets, A and B, are geographically so situated that goods may be shipped from one to the other, obviously the prices in the two markets cannot (except accidentally and temporarily) differ by more than the amount of the freight (and incidental expenses) between the two points. If the difference exceeded that sum, the one market would destroy the other. For example, if freight is 10, then the base price in A may be 100, and that in B, at the utmost, 110; for if it were higher, the competition of A would wipe B off the map. Or, if the base price of B should be reduced below 90, it in turn would wipe A, with its base price of 100, off the map. Anywhere between these two ratios, each market could continue to exist. To the amount of the freight difference each market center has in respect to sales in its immediate neighborhood an advantage over outside competitors, the same in its effect as a protective tariff on goods coming to its very doors. Otherwise expressed, both markets can exist so long as the price difference of the two markets is less than the full freight difference. Conceivably, also, at the very limit of the difference of price, some portions of the purchases at one locality might be bought from each market, the net delivered costs to the buyers being just equal. The foregoing considerations apply to the sales at the mill door in either market and to the possibilities of cross shipments between the two markets, and this part of the subject has long been pretty well developed, or at least implied, in the case of rents, so far as they are related to distance and transportation costs between two centers, and also in the case of trade between two foreign ports.

But what as to the division of the customers and sales in the territory lying between the two markets? In the case of foreign trade by water, this question can hardly arise; as to domestic trade, scarcely a word is to be found on this subject until recently. Many vague expressions imply merely that sellers in the two markets will compete indifferently in the interjacent territory. No theoretically defined point or line, however, was indicated as necessarily resulting from given conditions of freights and prices. Possibly the first effort to attack this problem was contained in the revised edition of J. B. Clark's *Control of Trusts*.[1] Here with simple diagrams it was shown that the point on the direct line between the two markets to which each could sell, was determined by the relation between freights and base prices. But a curious hesitancy pervades the discussion, and a note of apology that this theoretical meeting-place of geographically separated competitors should be a point instead of a zone or band on indifference as to delivered prices. The authors make various concessions with a view to blurring this definiteness of market limits. This attitude of mind reflected something of the uncertainty above referred to, as to the sales territory properly tributary to respective markets. When the ablest of all our theoretical students of this problem felt thus, it is not surprising that even greater confusion of thought on these points entered into the shaping and phrasing of the anti-trust legislation that was going upon our statute books about that time. The somewhat vague thought of the time seemed to be that every seller should compete at every geographical point to ensure the public effective competition, and should be enabled to do so by whatever device of freight concessions and of price-cutting might be necessary. The present writer attempted to carry the analysis further,[2] and elaborated a number of diagrams showing the effect of various policies of price-cutting and "absorbing freight" on the range of sales from each of two markets. It was there indicated that under the normal operation of fair competition the geographical point separating two markets is definitely fixed by the relation between prices and freight rates. So far, however, these studies of market limits, it will be observed, related only to a point on a straight line between two markets, and the diagrams gave a profile view of price plus freight taken along but the one line.

There has been, so far as the writer has found, no discussion directly of the shape of the profile taken along other lines radiating from either market, or more generally of the shape of the curve dividing two market territories on a surface map, viewed from above (bird's-eye view). This problem seems to have been uncritically assumed that the line between the two districts would be a straight line (as under very rare conditions it may prove to be). Then an occasion arose where, in a case of great practical importance, this very theoretical issue was involved. The question was whether, as between two

1. First edition, 1901; revised and enlarged in 1912 by J. B. and J. M. Clark. The diagrams appeared first in the revised edition, pp. 104–112.
    2. *Economic Principles* (1915), especially in chap. 31.

producing centers where certain commodities were sold locally at different base prices, the balance of shipment between the two markets and the districts connected with them was in one direction or the other. The argument and the compilation of statistics were based essentially on what economists now denominate "the marginal principle." If regularly a surplus of shipments has to be made from one market to the other market, then the general market price in the latter must be high enough to cover the market price in the former plus the entire freight to the latter. Thus stated, the proposition has a *prima facie* color of validity, and repeatedly men of economic training have been impressed with it without appreciating how the problem is altered if inter-market shipments are made to localities other than the exact competing market itself. Along these lines elaborate statistics were collected to demonstrate the existence of a regular, or chronic, shortage in the one district that had to be supplied from the other market.

Evidently some dividing line on the map has to be assumed before any such table can be compiled, and in the case mentioned a straight line was more or less arbitrarily located and drawn nearly at right angles to the shortest line connecting the two producing market centers. In the absence of any recognized principle to suggest the theoretical location of this district boundary line, it had, as drawn, an appearance of fairness. But by what criterion could this be judged? How should a correct boundary line be fixed? What are the boundaries of each of the two districts, and how are they related to each other? The outcome of this balance sheet of shipments is quite dependent upon the line of division chosen, both as to the point at which it intersects the line of shortest distance and even more as to its shape and direction at either side of the intersection.

Obviously the location of a point of indifference in delivered costs to any buyer between two markets is determined by the combination of base prices and freight rates. This had been shown to be true of the point on a direct line between the two markets, and the same reasoning applies to any other point on the plane on either side of the axis formed by this direct line. For the freight rate from one market may exceed that from the other to any location only by the amount of the difference in base prices at the two markets. The location is on the boundary, or point of indifference, in respect to two markets when the sum of base prices and freights is exactly equal. On either side of such a point, in the direction of the two markets respectively, as the freight rates are higher or lower, the delivered cost from one market must be greater or smaller than that from the other. This is a numerical relationship of just the same kind as that in the formula of a hyperbolic curve, which is such that the difference of the distances from any point of it to two fixed points called *foci*, is the same. Railroad freights are paid to overcome distance and vary more or less proportionally to distance. A succession of such points of indifference in delivered cost would take graphically the form of a hyperbolic curve in just the measure that freight rates did vary in exact proportion to distance, and that goods could be shipped on a perfectly straight route from each market to every point in the territories considered, assuming likewise that the two base prices were alike to all buyers at the same time, as they would be under full competitive demand and supply conditions. On these conditions we get the following formulation of the general law of market areas:

The boundary line between the territories tributary to two geographically competing markets for like goods is a hyperbolic curve. At each point on this line the difference between freights from the two markets is just equal to the difference between the market prices, whereas on either side of this line the freight difference and the price difference are unequal. The relation of prices in the two markets determines the location of the boundary line: the lower the relative price the larger the tributary area.

Some of the leading characteristics of such a boundary line may be indicated as follows. At the extreme points of difference in base prices the territory tributary to the market of higher prices (B) becomes a straight line (theoretically without breadth) beginning at the market and extending in a direction away from the competing market. At this stage the other market (A) would supply all of the remaining territory, which would all but entirely surround the other market, and with the smallest increase in the base price differential between the two, would sweep the higher price-center off the map (see Figure 1).

Lowering the difference between the two base prices would (freight, or freight differences remaining the same) gradually widen the district tributary to market B, until at the other extreme of the differential scale it would reduce the market area of A to a mere line, and then eliminate A as a competitor.

When the two base prices are equal, the boundary line becomes a straight line at right angles with the shortest line connecting the two markets, and equidistant at all its points from the two markets (a hyperbolic curve with the constant difference of zero), and this is the only relationship of prices between the two markets at which the boundary between them can be a straight line (under the assumed conditions as to routes and freight rates).

With any other relationship of base prices between the two extremes, the boundary between the two tributary territories is a curve bent around the focus, or market, with the higher base price

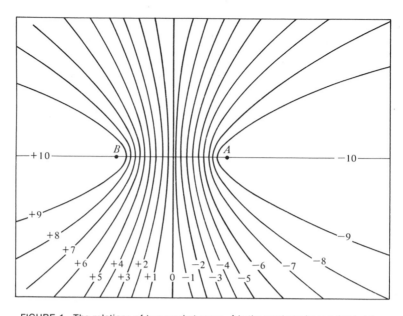

FIGURE 1   The relations of two market areas. *A* is the market whose price is taken as 100 per unit. The freight on that unit to *B*, the other market, is 10. The curves connect all points of differences of freight, by differences of one unit from plus 10 to minus 10. If in each of these markets the conditions are competitive, and consequently the rule holds of "one price in a market," a supply and demand price of 110 (the full "plus" freight from *A* to *B*) could prevail only while the supply in *B* is insufficient for, or barely sufficient for, demand in the narrow strip of territory along the line market *B* to plus 10. With a differential price of the full "plus," all the area north and south of the line *B* to plus 10 should be supplied by *A*. If the price in any of this area is less than 110 then, on the marginal principle, the f.o.b. market price at *B* should be the same for sales to all the area to the left of the curve touched by such lower price. If the output exceeds the amount demanded at price 110 by enough to supply the needs of the area delimited by the line plus 9, the "supply and demand" price must fall to 109, and so successively as supply increases at *B*. The larger demand is partly called forth by the lower price in the area already tributary, and partly is captured from the area formerly supplied by *A*. The excess of supply at any price involving less than the full "plus" of 10, should appear statistically in comparisons of production with consumption on either side of a plus curve and, except when the price differential is zero, not on either side of a vertical (north and south) line.

and with its two sides diverging in a general direction away from the focus, or market, with the lower base price.

In case both market prices change at once, either in the same or opposite directions, the effect upon the shape of the boundary curve depends not on the absolute change but on the relative change, or change in the differential between them.

Size of market territories thus may be said to be a function of the differential of market base prices, freight rates remaining constant, and *vice versa*: that is, the higher the market price in any market, relative to that in its geographical competitor, the narrower the territory that economically is tributary to it.

Increase of freight rates has the effect of removing competition to a greater distance from the market of higher prices, making possible either a larger market area at the same price difference or the retention of the same area at a higher difference. Simultaneous changes of freights and of price differences in the same direction neutralize each other.

We may now see the relation of this analysis to tabulations of statistics intended to show excess or deficiency in the districts on either side of their boundary. Such a boundary line is not fixed and independent of price, or of price differences, but varies with the difference in base prices of the two markets. As the price difference approaches the maximum—the total freight—the boundary line bends back and around the market of higher prices, leaving a smaller and smaller area tributary to that market.

In the case of buying—centripetal—markets, to which products are sent for sale from numerous decentralized producing points, the foregoing principles hold, *mutatis mutandis*. The boundary curve will change in location and in shape with changes in prices, but will be curved around the market of lower price, embracing a smaller area, and will curve away from the market of higher price. The buying market price in this case is the sum of the net amount received by the producer, and of the freights (and other costs of bringing the goods to market). Hence the higher the buying market price of a market relative to its competitor, the larger the area from which it can attract sellers to it.

The assumptions made and the abstract nature of the formula must not be forgotten or misunderstood. It is merely in the nature of a first approximation to the solution of the various practical problems that may arise. If freight rates are not plain mileage rates, but are tapering by any fixed rule, the limiting curves between markets may still be symmetrical, the differing in location from those resulting from rates on the mileage principle. Inasmuch as the actual structure of freight rates departs from the principle of strict proportionality to distance, the boundary lines will be shifted; likewise, according to other irregularities in freight, whatever be the cause, such as water transportation or topographical obstacles, making longer routes necessary. In peculiar cases geographical relations may be quite inverted. Thus the ground plan of hyperbolic curves corresponding to different base prices would be more or less obscured on the map, appearing as contour lines traced on slopes at various elevations, marked by the freight differences between the two markets; but despite great irregularities at many points the underlying pattern of the hyperbolic curves must be revealed on almost every portion of the map. This fundamental feature of constant difference having the mathematical basis of a hyperbolic curve may be said to continue still as measured by freights, but to be distorted graphically by the lack of correspondence of freights to distance. A chart so drawn as to show each place of delivery located with reference to dollars in freight instead of at its actual location on the map, shows the exact hyperbolic curves; a chart drawn on the actual map reveals the irregularities in freight. Various examples of these inductive verifications have been found, but no attempt is made here to develop this evidence.

The law of market areas, in its general theoretical form, might be deemed to be merely a corollary of the general law of demand and supply. It is, to be sure, derived deductively from this, taken in connection with the assumption that transportation costs vary with distance. But the relations shown here have been so far from merely obvious and axiomatic, that they have hitherto escaped formulation, and views contrary to them have been somewhat uncritically assumed to be true by men familiar both with the general principle of market price and with the main effects of freights upon local prices.

Various possibilities of the practical applications of the law of market areas suggest themselves. It appears to throw new light upon some pending questions of industrial prices, especially those of different geographical centers. It should be of aid toward solving the problem of public regulation of prices, both in the drafting and in the administration of laws. It may explain some puzzling cases in the working of duties on imports, showing more clearly how and why the effect of duties varies at different ports and in different parts of a country. It should be of service in the whole field of the economics of marketing, now so actively studied. However, these possibilities of practical application have not primarily concerned us here. The purpose of this brief essay is to set forth a law of market areas in its theoretical aspects, regardless of its practical applications. The formulation of such an economic law is justified on grounds of pure science if it aids in the analysis and clearer understanding of any set of economic relationships.

C. D. HYSON and W. P. HYSON

10

The Economic Law of Market Areas

A formalization of the "law of market areas" first appeared, so far as we know, in a note by Frank A. Fetter in the *Quarterly Journal of Economics*, May 1924. The law may be stated as follows:

> The boundary line between the territories tributary to two geographically competing markets for like goods is a hyperbolic curve. At each point on this line the difference between freights from the two markets is just equal to the difference between the market prices, whereas on either side of this line the freight difference and the price difference are unequal. The relation of prices in the two markets determines the location of the boundary line: the lower the relative price the larger the tributary area.[1]

This hyperbolic law assumes that the freight rate per unit distance is the same between all points in the area under consideration. We wish to point out that this is but a special case of a more general law which may be derived as follows:

Given two fixed markets A and B (see Figure 1) and external consuming points such as P to which the goods are shipped from these markets, under what conditions will it be equally advantageous to buy from either market? It is assumed that the commodity is standard, that complete knowledge of market conditions prevails, and that freight charges are equal to the distance as the crow flies from the market multiplied by the freight rate per unit distance between the market and the point in question.

Suppose the market price of this commodity at A to be P cents per unit sold, and at B to be q cents per unit sold. Suppose, furthermore, that between P and A the freight rate is r cents per unit per mile, whereas between P and B the freight rate is s cents per unit per mile. *Our specific problem is logically inevitable, for instance, if competing modes of transportation such as air and rail are contemplated.*[2]

---

1. Frank A. Fetter, "The Economic Law of Market Areas," *Quarterly Journal of Economics*, XXXVIII (May 1924), p. 525.
2. A more general problem is to assume that "local" transport costs vary with topography over the plane. For example, the freight cost in the vicinity of A is lower if A is easily accessible by river or rail. We have aimed to consider here a specific illustration where each of the freight rates per unit distance is constant.

The authors wish to express their great appreciation to Joseph Leonard Walsh, Perkins Professor of Mathematics, Harvard University, without whose kindly counsel and valuable comments this paper might never have been written. Professors Wassily Leontief and Paul Samuelson provided helpful suggestions.

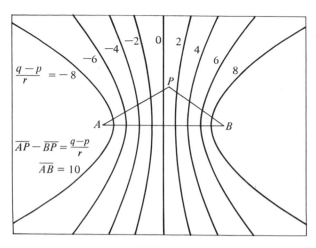

FIGURE 1

If the consumer at P buys from A, he will pay $(p+r\overline{PA})$ cents for each unit bought; that is to say, the total cost to him of one unit will be the market price increased by the freight costs. Similarly, if he buys at B he will spend $(q+s\overline{PB})$ cents for each unit purchased. When $(p+r\overline{PA}) = (q+s\overline{PB})$ the consumer will be indifferent as to which markets he patronizes.

It may be said that the boundary line between the territories tributary to markets A and B will be determined by the equation:

$$p+r\overline{PA} = q+s\overline{PB},$$

or

$$\overline{PA} - \frac{s}{r}\overline{PB} = \frac{q-p^3}{r}$$

This describes the family of indifference curves represented in Figures 1 to 4, which for simplicity we call *hypercircles*. The distinguishing mathematical feature of this family is that any one curve

3. Here we have considered the case of a consumer at P buying from producers at A and B. Suppose, however, that a producer at P wishes to determine whether to sell his product at markets located at A or B. If he sells at A, he will receive $(p-r\overline{PA})$, and if he sells at B he will receive $(q-s\overline{PB})$, where the market prices at A and B are p and q respectively. In this case the indifference curves will be determined by the equation

$$(p-r\overline{PA}) = (q-s\overline{PB})$$

or

$$\overline{PA} - \frac{s}{r}\overline{PB} = \frac{p-q}{r}$$

Except for a change in notation this is precisely the equation studied in detail in the text and illustrated in the figures.

represents the locus of all points the ratio of whose distances from two fixed circles is a constant.

Since s/r must always be a positive quantity, and $q-p/r$ may be positive or negative, the equation may be expressed in the form

$$\overline{AP} - h\overline{BP} = \pm k,$$

where $h = s/r$,
  $+ k = (q-p)/r$ when $(q-p)/r > 0$,
  $- k = (q-p)/r$ when $(q-p)/r < 0$.

These *hypercircles* comprise then half the family of curves described by the equation

$$\overline{AP} \pm h\overline{BP} = \pm k.$$

This family was first discovered by Descartes as the solution to a problem in optics, and the curves which make it up have since been called Descartes' ovals.[4]

When $s = r$ (i.e., when freight rates for AP and for BP are the same), the curve becomes one branch of a hyperbola. When $s \neq r$, and $p = q$ (i.e. when the two market prices are equal), the curve becomes a circle. When both these conditions hold (i.e., when $s = r$, and $p = q$), the curve degenerates into a straight line, the perpendicular bisector of the line joining the two markets.

It is clear from this that the size of the tributary area is determined not only by the relative prices at the two markets, but also by the ratio of the freight rates and the ratio of the freight rates and the ratio of the difference in price to the freight rates. Figures 1, 2, 3, 4 will give an idea of how any change in the factors involved will change the size of the tributary area.

Figure 1 shows the familiar family of branches of hyperbolas, in which the area tributary to market B increases as the ratio $q-p/r$ decreases, assuming that the two freight rates, r and s, remain equal. Notice that an increase in the quantity $(q-p)$ may be compensated for by an increase in r so that the size of the area will not increase, and that an increase in the freight rate, unaccompanied by a change in the price differential, will bring about a decrease in the area tributary to market B.

Figure 2 shows the shape of the tributary areas when the selling prices at the two markets are equal, but the freight rates from the two markets are unequal. As the ratio s/r decreases, the size of the area tributary to market B increases. The indifference curves have now become circles.

4. F. Gomes Teixeira, *Traité des Courbes Spéciales Remarkables* (Coimbre, 1908), Vol. I, p. 218.

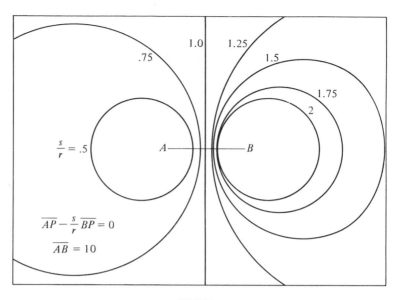

FIGURE 2

Figure 3 shows a more general situation where the quantity $q - p/r$ is given a constant value unequal to zero, and the ratio of the freight rates is allowed to vary. The curve where $s/r = 1$ is a branch of a hyperbola. As in Figure 2, a decrease in the ratio s/r will bring an increase in the area tributary to market B.

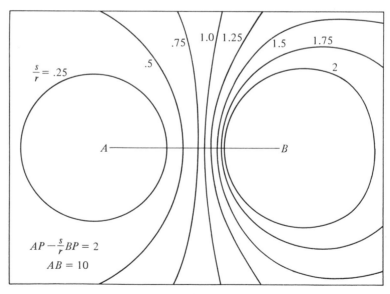

FIGURE 3

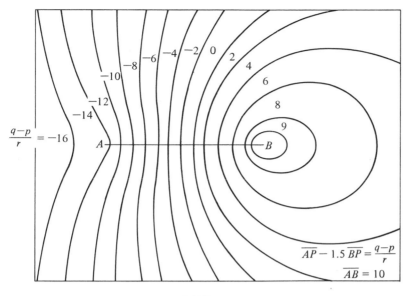

FIGURE 4

In Figure 4 the quantity $(q-p)/r$ is allowed to vary while the ratio s/r maintains a constant value greater than one. A decrease in $(q-p)/r$ will be accompanied by an increase in the size of the areas tributary to market B. If the ratio s/r should be less than one the size of the tributary area will vary in the same manner, but the shape of the indifference curves will be altered.

In summary, the economic law of market areas should be more generally stated as follows: The boundary line between the territories tributary to two geographically competing markets for like goods is a *hypercircle*. At each point on this curve the difference between freight costs from the two markets is just equal to the difference between the market prices, whereas on either side of this line the freight differences and the price differences are unequal. The ratio of the price difference to the freight rate, and the ratio of the freight rates from the two markets, determine the location of the boundary line; the higher the relative price, and the lower the relative freight rate, the larger the tributary area.

The Size and Shape of the Market Area
of a Firm

There has been increasing interest in recent years in the size and shape of the market area[1] of a firm. This concern has resulted largely from the realization that manufacturing plants sell to buyers who are scattered over an area rather than to consumers who are concentrated within a market center. The locational triangles which once played so prominent a part in theory, therefore, have given way to broader models which attempt to determine the spatial features of a firm's market. These recent models have presented conceptions of the firm's market area ranging from the hexagon to a perfect or incomplete circle.

The studies, which attempt explanation of the size and shape of the firm's market area, are closely related to others that stress the locational interdependence of firms. In analytical frameworks, these schools are, however, sharply distinguishable. The market area approach assumes fixed locations, and is, thereby, essentially an analysis of short-run phenomena. At best, it appears capable of yielding knowledge of some particular long-run equilibria in space, notwithstanding an attempt to derive a general equilibrium theory within its framework. On the other hand, the locational interdependence school hypothesizes either movable locations (without cost), or planned future locations; its framework is, inherently, designed for long-run

1. The term *market area* does not refer directly to square miles but to dollar volume of sales. Because, in spatial analysis, consumers are assumed to be evenly scattered and to have identical demands, this dollar volume of sales is made synonymous with the number of square miles of market area that is controlled by a firm. This identity will be assumed throughout the present article, except when otherwise indicated.

A distinction between two types of market areas must, also, be kept in mind. One, the entire market area, will refer to the aggregate of homogeneous consumers dispersed over an area. Two, the market area of a firm, will refer to the homogeneous consumers who advantageously buy from this firm, thus purchasing nothing from its competitors.

The author wishes to acknowledge his indebtedness to the Research Foundation of the Alabama Polytechnic Institute for a grant and for encouragement. Since this article was written, the author has become an economist with the Birmingham Office of Price Stabilization. The views mentioned in the article are not in any way associated with the philosophy or policy of the OPS.

Reprinted from the Southern Economic Journal, IXX (July 1952), pp. 37–50, by permission of the publishers and the author.

analysis; its conclusions must be considered by those who hope to deduce a general equilibrium theory, within a market area framework.

This article confines its interest largely to the market area type of analysis. It presents, in section II, a quasi-historical treatment of the more important contributions to market area analysis. This method of procedure offers a natural way of discussing changing directions of thought as well as problems and points of study that have been largely neglected. In section III, the location interdependence *framework* is examined in order to ascertain points of difference between it and the market area system, as well as limits to market area analysis. The fourth and final section presents suggestions for future analysis. In sum, this paper does not aim at a new theory; any innovation lies in classifying, tracing the development, and indicating the merits and shortcomings of the market area type of analysis of plant location and spatial equilibrium.

II

The size of a firm's market area suggests the wisdom with which its plant location has been selected. Thus, if (1) buyers are assumed to be evenly scattered and to have identical demand schedules, (2) the market is monopolistically competitive *because* firms are geographically dispersed, (3) all rivals charge a net-mill price which is marked up above their cost by the same sum, (4) the product is sold on a f.o.b. mill basis, and (5) the freight rates on the final product are the same for all sellers, the least cost producer will quote the lowest mill price and thus will capture the largest sales territory, i.e., market area. Under these assumptions, locational efficiency may be ascertained by investigating the size of the firm's market area; the larger it is, the wiser is the locational choice.

The sales price and the freight rate on the final product are the immediate determinants of a company's market territory under the f.o.b. mill system of pricing. Any decrease, in either the freight rate or sales price of a firm, widens the market area controlled by this firm; any increase narrows this area.[2] It follows that two sellers, located in different sectors, divide an entire market area equally between them, if their locations are symmetrical to the entire market area, and if they are burdened with the same freight rates, charge identical net-mill

2. Hans Ritschl, "Reine und historische Dynamik des Standortes der Erzeugungszweize," *Schmoller Jahrbuch für Gesetzgebung*, LI (1927) pp. 813–870, and see pp. 814, 815, 816, 847, 848, where Ritschl repeatedly stresses the fact that a lowering of freight rates increases the market area of a firm.

prices, and sell a homogeneous product.³ This division produces a straight line separating the markets of each producer. (See *MN*, Figure 1a, where the entire market area is assumed to be in the form of a circle.⁴)

By positing (1) heterogenous duopoly *because* firms are geographically separated, (2) an entire market area circular in form, (3)

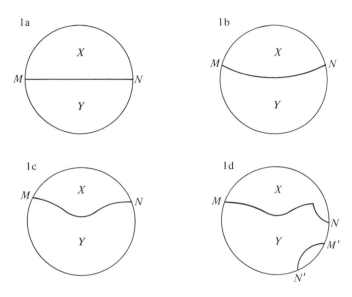

FIGURE 1

f.o.b. mill system of pricing, (4) transport costs proportional to distance, (5) net-mill prices marked up above cost by the same sum, and (6) either a higher net-mill price and/or freight rate on the finished product for one enterpriser as compared to his rival, the straight line, dividing the entire market area, gives way to a curve. This curve bends backwards towards the plant which pays the higher freight

3. Frank Fetter, "The Economic Law of Market Areas," *Quarterly Journal of Economics*, XXXIX (1924) pp. 520–529, 527. It is deserving of special mention that Fetter is accredited by many as the writer who stimulated interest in market areas. Before Fetter, John Bates Clark in his *Control of Trusts*, 1st ed., 1914, pp. 104–112, had inquired into this problem by describing the indifference line separating the market area of competitors. In fact, much earlier than this, a German writer (Launhardt) combined an analysis of cost orientations and market areas. Launhardt's lack of reputation in the United States is due principally to the fact that his book is out of print and not generally available in this country. (Wilhelm Launhardt, *Mathematische Begründung der Volkswirtschaftslehre* (1885).)

4. Each firm (*X* and *Y*) is located at a point which minimizes the transport distance over the half-circle surrounding its plant. It can be shown that this point is at a distance $4r/3\pi$ from the center of the circle, on the perpendicular bisector of the diameter of the circle.

and/or is burdened with higher costs of production.[5] (See *MN*, Figure 1b.[6]) Freight and/or production cost disadvantages narrow the market area of a firm.[7] In fact, the firm's entire market may be

5. See Erich Schneider, "Bemerkung zu einer Theorie der Raumwirtschaft," *Econometrica*, III (1935), pp. 79–101, 83–89, where these general propositions are proved by means of elementary mathematics. Thus, Z_1 and Z_2 refer to the distance from the customers to producers 1 and 2 respectively; II_1 and II_2 are the factory prices for the respective producers; F is the constant freight rate on the final product, which is assumed to be the same for both sellers. Schneider then solves for the isostante (the indifference line between the competitors).

$$II_1 + F(Z_1) = II_2 + F(Z_2) \tag{1}$$

$$Z_1 - Z_2 = \frac{II_2 - II_1}{F} \tag{2}$$

If the prices at the factories are equal, $Z_1 = Z_2$. If $II_1 \neq II_2$, an hyperbolic curve results, which bends backwards towards the factory charging the higher price.

As soon as the constant freight charges are assumed unequal (e.g., because of shipments by water, railroad, highway, or rate policies of the different carriers), the equation for the indifference line becomes

$$II_1 + F_1 Z_1 = II_2 + F_2 Z_2. \tag{3}$$

If $II_1 < II_2$, and $F_1 < F_2$, a fourth degree curve bends around producer 2. If $II_1 < II_2$, but $F_1 > F_2$, producer 2 gains control over the regions remotely situated from producer 1. If $II_1 = II_2$

$$\frac{Z_1 - F_2}{Z_2 - F_1} \tag{4}$$

The isostante, in this case, is inversely proportional to the freight rate; it, therefore, takes the form of the circle of Apollonius.

6. The curved line *MN* (Figure 1b) represents the loci of points corresponding to the mileage differential needed to offset *Y*'s assumed advantage(s). Also see Hoover, *The Location of Economic Activity*, 1st ed. (1948), p. 53.

7. It is worthy of note that when one firm suffers a freight cost or production cost disadvantage, the long-run location of each firm may not be at the points described in footnote 4. For example, if it is assumed that (1) costs of production are equal at all locations, but the freight rate on the final good is higher in one zone than the other, (2) the cost of transporting the final good is not too significant a part of delivered-to-customers cost, and (3) demand is highly inelastic, the firm in the higher rated zone gains by moving to a location near the center of the entire market area. This move increases its market area while not causing significant losses in sales to buyers situated far from the plant; further, this relocation forces the rival firm to move to a site proximate to its competitor. The actual long-run locations will be in the lower-rated zone; such sites minimize total freight costs on the final good, regardless of which method is used by the carriers in constructing rates between zones.

The location significance of American freight-rate structure may be seen also by reference to the practice of establishing rate advantages for freight moving in a particular direction. This type of system produces results similar to those described above. Firms minimize transport costs by sending more freight in the direction favored by the carrier, rather than *vice versa*.

If the curve in Figure 1b is due to production-cost differentials rather than freight-rate inequalities, firms may move near to or at the center of the market. More definite determination of their long-run locations depends upon the costs hypothesized for the several locations, the conjectural beliefs of the locators as regards their rival's plans, and other factors too numerous to examine in this article.

destroyed if its net-mill price plus freight cost (to any and all buyers) exceed those of the other firm.[8]

The boundary separating the markets of two firms may take irregular shapes when transport costs increase at variable decreasing rates over longer distances. Mathematical determination of the nature of the curve depends upon the rates of change in the prices charged by each carrier and the values assigned to the constants (the freight rate applicable to the first unit of distance of each carrier). These freight rate progressions, which may produce equal freight charges for varying distances within particular mileage brackets, as well as lower mileage charges over longer distances, could yield a curve such as that shown by the *MN* line in Figure 1c. Further, if a cheaper method of transport to parts of the entire market area is assumed to exist for one firm, a highly irregular boundary becomes possible, and an invasion of territory quite near to the plant of a competitor may occur. (See *MN* and *M'N'*, Figure 1d.)

Carriers often use "basing points" or "basing lines" in order to meet competition of rival transport agencies. This practice further distorts market areas of firms, for, when rates are reduced to certain points, the firm, which is so located as to reap this advantage, gains an expansion in its market area. The straight line that separates market areas, when net-mill prices and freight rates are equal, and competition is perfect *except* for geographical separation of firms, gives way to indentations following the outlines of carrier's "basing areas." (See *MN*, Figure 2a.) In similar manner, a wave-like type of boundary

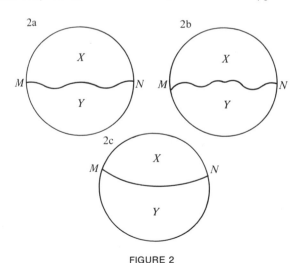

FIGURE 2

8. Fetter, *op. cit.*, pp. 522. "Both markets can exist so long as the price difference of the two markets is less than the full freight difference."

appears if one carrier uses the group rate system of generally decreasing its rates with distance though charging a constant sum for given distances along its route, while the carrier in the other sector establishes freight mileage rates which not only decrease relatively but also continuously over distance. (See *MN*, Figure 2b.)

The price policies of firms also distort market areas. Thus, where duopolists are heterogeneous *because* firms are geographically separated, and one of the sellers uses a constant net-mill price under the f.o.b. mill system of pricing, while his rival adopts an identical net-mill price for proximate buyers but reduces this net-mill price for distant buyers, the boundary separating the firms becomes a curve, even though freight rates are equal. (See *MN*, Figure 2c.) If two sellers, using the f.o.b. mill system, vary their net-mill price in such manner as to discriminate against nearer buyers in an identical way, a straight line divides the entire market area in half, assuming freight rates are equal. If both sellers use an equalizing delivered-price system (all customers pay the same delivered price regardless of location), the boundary between the sellers will be completely eliminated, *except* when marginal production costs plus weight on the final product limit the range of operations of one or both firms, and/or where contact advantages and the importance of time-of-delivery form a market ring around a factory which cannot be penetrated by a distant seller.

A sharp spatial division of markets is, similarly, precluded by the single or multiple basing-point systems of pricing, *except* when (1) the total delivered-to-customers cost of a firm is in excess of the price quoted at a given point(s), or (2) contact advantages and/or the impact of time-of-delivery create a market ring around the rival's plant. In the initial case, a seller may voluntarily give up this buying point(s) to his rival, rather than sell at a delivered price(s) which does not cover marginal costs; while, in the second case, a seller may find that he cannot invade the market area adjacent to his rival's factory, without violating the basing-point system of pricing.

Such monopolistic features, as (1) heterogeneity of products, (2) spatial price discrimination whereby both sellers quote the same delivered price to buyers within given mileage brackets, or (3) identical group-rate systems by carriers prevent the *MN* lines drawn in Figures 1 and 2 from always being sharp and distinct. A zone of transition or indifference is found when markets are less than perfectly competitive for reasons in addition to space and number of sellers. Within this zone, some buyers (assumption 1 above) or all buyers (assumptions 2 and 3 above) are indifferent to slight price differentials (assumption 1 above) or sellers (assumptions 2 and 3 above); in other words, an overlapping of market areas exists. This overlapping can be caused by freight absorption either by the buyer,[9] the seller, or the transfer agency.[10] The dotted lines in Figure 3 define a zone of indifference.

The models presented above emphasize the influence of two forces (the freight rate on the final product, and the sales price) on

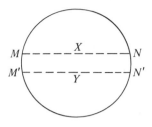

FIGURE 3

the size of firms' market areas and the shape of the boundary line. But they do not advance understanding of the cost and demand limitations on the maximum extent of a firm's market area, the necessary minimum size of its market area, the localization and/or dispersion of industry, and the number of producers in the market. One step towards an explanation of these problems was undertaken in the late 1930's by Edgar M. Hoover.[11]

In Hoover's study, emphasis was given to the slope of the "margin line" (see ST, Figure 4) the line which represents the increase in delivered prices with growing distance from the mill. Any influence

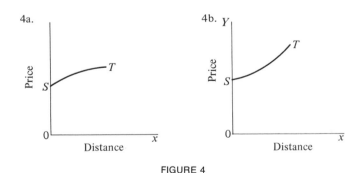

FIGURE 4

9. See Hoover, *The Location of Economic Activity, op. cit.*, pp. 58, 59, where differentiation as to product is cited as a cause of market overlapping. Also see August Lösch, *Die räumliche Ordnung der Wirtschaft*, 1944, p. 8, wherein he cites heterogeneity as a cause of overlapping. The buyer, in effect, may willingly absorb freight on the preferred product.

10. The use of freight rates which in a relative sense tend to ignore distance.

11. *Location Theory and the Shoe and Leather Industries* (1937), pp. 12–23.

tending to cause convexity upward of this line (decreasing unit cost due to increasing scale of production, and/or nonproportionality of freight rates with distance) diminishes the number of independent sources of supply, while, at the same time, promoting an extension of the firm's market area. (See *ST*, Figure 4a.) On the other hand, the steeper the slope of the margin lines, the greater are the number of different sources utilized and the smaller the market area for each.[13] Thus, as in Figure 4b, the margin line first rises slowly and then sharply, thereby indicating that though freight rates are proportional to distance, or even increase at diminishing rates with greater distance, the expansion of output (market area of the firm) causes marginal costs to rise so much as to produce a margin line which is concave upward.

Besides marginal costs and freight, Hoover considers, (1) the distribution of consumers to be significant in determining the slope of the margin line. Should there be a concentration of buyers at a given distance from the seller's plant, the steepness of the margin line would, if costs are increasing, be augmented at this point; and contrariwise. (2) The elasticities of demand of buyers who are located at given distances from the seller also affect the slope. This slope would increase with a smaller elasticity, and flatten with greater elasticity, if costs are increasing.[13]

According to Hoover's analytical pattern, it can be concluded that, if (1) heterogeneous duopoly exists *because* firms are geographically separated, (2) rivals are situated at a distance from each other, though close enough to compete at points equidistant from their

---

12. Hoover points out that returns to scale (increasing and decreasing) play a more variable role than freight rates. See *Ibid*, p. 20. And see p. 94, "So long as extension of the market lowers costs, the slope of the margin line will be less steep than that of the transport gradient. In fact it may be negative."

13. *Ibid*, p. 21. "If the demand is highly elastic, so that a great deal less is bought in such a case, then the extension of the market area may bring comparatively little increase in output and comparatively little rise in prices. . . .Elastic demand, then, is a factor tending to localize extractive industries."

While Hoover's solution of the effect of an elastic demand on the slope of the line is indisputable, there is some questioning the applications he makes for his deduction. Firms *might* localize (or shall we say, a single firm may not have enough incentive to establish a branch plant) and they would sell over a larger market area but, more probably, and according to the school of writers which stresses the location interdependence of firms (see *infra*, Section III), the existence of an elastic demand promotes dispersion.

Probably, the contradiction in theory is due to the difference in emphasis among the writers in question. The type of approach used by Hoover takes location as datum, and, accordingly, is concerned primarily with the size and shape of the firm's market area; the locational-interdependence school stresses the impact of demand on location, thereby confining its interest largely to the factor which causes firms to be attracted to or repulsed by each other. The extent and shape of the market area is of lesser interest to these writers than are the locational techniques for maximizing demand.

plants, (3) the entire market area is not being supplied by the existing sellers, (4) the freight rate on the final product is equal for each seller and proportional to distance, (5) the final product is sold on an f.o.b. mill basis, and (6) marginal costs increase with greater production, attempts by one firm to expand its market area will cause its net-mill price to rise and the boundary line to retreat and bend backwards towards this firm, Such expansion will be carried out only if the increase in sales to buyers located far from the rival establishment is sufficient to offset the loss in sales to (a) the original buyers who purchase less at the higher price, and (b) those former buyers who now purchase from the rival source. On the other hand, if marginal costs decrease with a given increase in output, the boundary line will move and bend away from the expanding firm.

While Hoover's analysis afforded valuable insight into the forces determining the number of producers, and the size of the firm's market area, the problems of minimum size, maximum size, and localization or dispersion remained largely unsolved. An endeavor in these directions was made a few years later by August Lösch, in his *Die räumliche Ordnung der Wirtschaft*.[14] Lösch sought to define further the economic region, a concept popularized by Ohlin,[15] and in the process derived his "ideal economic region."

Lösch postulates a broad homogeneous plain with uniform transport features in all directions, and with an even scatter of sufficient raw materials. Furthermore, the agricultural population is uniformly distributed over this plain, each individual having identical tastes, preferences, technical knowledge, and production opportunities; the result of these assumptions is the dotting of the plain with completely self-sufficient homesteads.[16]

Lösch begins his analysis by inquiring into the situation in which a farmer seeks to supply beer to others, in addition to himself. Though limited by freight costs, this would-be entrepreneur gains the advantages of larger scale of operations and of specialization. If the market demand is sufficient, the farmer advantageously sells over a circular area; if the demand is too small relative to costs, this would-be entrepreneur retires to his domicile.

Under the assumptions that the market is monopolistically competitive *because* firms are geographically scattered, and that the demand curve for the individual farmer exceeds his costs at some levels of output, production is immediately profitable. But in time the entrance of competitors compresses the circular area into smaller and smaller size. This decrease in sales reflects the leftward shifting of the

14. *Op. cit.* See, in particular, pp. 71–94.
15. *Interregional and International Trade*, 1935.
16. Lösch, *op. cit.*, p. 72.

demand curve, which continues until the Chamberlinean tangential point is reached.

But, the circular market areas of firms cannot remain; for, even though these ideal shapes are close enough to touch each other, perfect merging is impossible. Accordingly, profits continue and new firms enter; it is only when the circular area is reshaped in the form of a hexagon[17] that the equilibrium conditions can be satisfied.[18] The ultimate balance in spatial competition is realized only when the hexagon is so reduced in size that profits are completely eliminated.[19]

Once Lösch drops the assumption of continuous settlements, the door is reopened to other polygonic and circular conceptions of the market area. These imperfectly shaped economic areas are due to the fact that sales to one community may be insufficient to make produc-

17. Lösch depicts the hexagon as the most perfect market area shape. It has the advantage of being most akin to the circle, and, therefore, as compared to other polygons, such as the triangle and square, shipping distance is minimized, and, accordingly, demand is maximized. It has the advantage over the circle in that the number of independent producers is the largest possible, while the elimination of the empty corners maximizes the demand of the entire population. See pp. 74–77. "Zusammenfassend können wir festellen, dass das regelmässige Sechseck um so mehr die vorteilhafteste Gebeitsform wird, je grösser und abgerun deter das Gesamtgebiet, je elastischer die Nachfrage an der Gebietsgrenze und je näher die notwendige Versendungsweite der möglichen ist," p. 78.

18. Lösch's equilibrium is determined by a system of equations for which the first condition is, (1) that each producer maximizes his gains. This condition involves equality between marginal revenue and marginal cost. The next three conditions require the number of independent existences to be maximized. Thus, (2) all areas are served by at least one firm. This leads to the third condition, (3) that all extraordinary profits must disappear, for, under the competitive free-entry assumption, new rivals will eventually eliminate all rent-like incomes. This condition implies the fourth, (4) that the area served by each individual be the smallest possible; for, if the area served by it is too large, profits would exist. The fifth condition of equilibrium requires, (5) that any consumer on a boundary line be indifferent to the possible sources from which he can obtain a given commodity at minimum cost. Without this condition, the boundaries would overlap, and the points of indifference would take on zonal qualities. See Lösch, *op. cit.*, pp. 65, 66.

19. After establishing the hexagon as the ideal market or shape, Lösch views the trading area of the various products as nets of such hexagons. Depending upon the nature of the product, the respective sizes vary from very small hexagons to very large ones. By turning the nets around a common center six sectors are obtained where production centers are most frequent, and six others result where production centers are scarce. The coincidence of many of these centers minimizes the freight burdens and perforce enhances the consumer demand by enabling purchases from many local mills. This is then the reason why Lösch maintains that industry tends to agglomerate. How many self-sufficient systems come into existence depends upon the commodity having the largest necessary shipping radius. These self-sufficient regions are styled the ideal economic region. See pp. 84–90. See also Francois Perroux, "Economic Space: Theory and Applications," *Quarterly Journal of Economics*, LXIV (1950), pp. 89–104, wherein the author inquires into the economic self-sufficient region. In a negative type of approach, Perroux states that the normal economic unit is that which if it happened to disappear would make the others inadequate. "It is, therefore, not the self-sufficient unit." See pp. 103, 104.

ion feasible. Sales to a more distant community are, therefore, necessary to cover costs. But, in fact, because this more distant community may contain a large number of buyers, its inclusion within the firm's market area may bring profits.[20] Obviously, if spatial concentrations of consumers make profits possible, existing hexagonic shapes would be largely coincidental and not always minimum in size.

III

While these theories of the market area of a firm are somewhat similar to the presentations which stress the interdependence of plant location, the objectives of the two approaches are not identical. The studies that have been outlined in section II are based upon assumed locations; from this point of departure, the size and shape of firms' market areas are derived. The interdependence approach, on the other hand, seeks to find reasons for a particular location; it assumes freely movable locations and/or planned future locations; thus, it stresses the attraction of repulsion of a firm caused by the presence (existing or expected) of a rival at a specific location. These two approaches differ in analytical patterns; they are alike in emphasizing the monopolistic aspects of space.[21]

20. *Op. cit.*, pp. 82, 83, "Als wichtigsten Ergebnis aber folgt aus dem Vorhergehenden, dass bei diskontinuierlicher Besiedlung auch die mögliche Grösse der Marktgebiete und die Zahl der von ihnen umfassten Siedlungen diskontinuierlich wachst. Das weiterum ermöglicht Sondergewinne. Denn wenn beispielsweise der Absatz an 32 Siedlungen notwendig wäre, damit eine bestimmte Fabrikation sich lohnt, nach dem zu kleinen Gebiet Nr 13 mit 31 Siedlungen aber ohne Übergang gleich das unnötig grosse Gebiet 14 mit 36 Siedlungen kommt, so muss der Absatz sich eben auf 36 Siedlungen ausdehnen. Die Nachfragekurve schneidet dann die Kostenkurve, statt sir nur zu berühren — und damit enstehen Sondergewinne in dieser Branche. Solche nässigen Gewinne sind geradezu die Regel, denn es ist ein Zufall, wenn die Nachfragekurve auf ihren Sprüngen die Kostenkurve eben noch berührt."

For other discussions on Lösch's theory, see Stolper, "Book Review," *American Economic Review*, XXXIII (Sept. 1943), pp. 626–636.

Also see Walter Isard, "The General Theory of Location and Space Economy," *Quarterly Journal of Economics*, LXIII (1949), pp. 476–506, 495–502.

And see Lösch, "The Nature of Economic Regions," *Southern Economic Journal*, V (1938), pp. 71–78.

Also see Gardner Ackley, "Spatial Competition In A Discontinuous Market," *Quarterly Journal of Economics*, LVI (1942), pp. 212–230, 212, wherein the central thesis s that spatial discontinuities induce monopolistic price behavior and offer profits.

21. The writers, who are interested primarily in the spatial interdependence of irms, assume a linear market for methodological simplicity. They are not concerned, o a significant degree, with the problem of the size and shape of the market area of a irm. This school of thought, therefore, lies largely outside the scope of the present paper. Its brief mention here is for the purpose of showing the relationship between it nd the market area school, and thereby to uncover certain limitations in the market rea type of analysis described in section II.

The inquiries into the spatial interdependence of locations began with Hotelling.[22] By assuming (1) an even spatial scattering of consumers, (2) an infinitely inelastic demand for the product of an industry, (3) equal costs of procuring and processing raw materials at all locations, (4) the same freight rate on the final product at all locations, (5) a perfectly competitive market except as regards space, and (6) sale of goods on an f.o.b. mill basis, Hotelling reasoned that firms would concentrate at the mid-point of the entire market area. From this vantage point, each firm could supply buyers located at the extremities of the entire market area while not surrendering locational advantage to rivals; the fact that the transportation cost on the final product could never lessen the amount of sales made at such points accounts for this result.

Locational dispersion occurs once the demand assumption is changed to permit some elasticity in the buyer's demand for a product.[23] With this precondition, freight costs become a limiting factor to sales. By locating at the center of the entire market area, any one firm could minimize freight costs and thereby maximize sales. But once more than one firm is admitted to the conceptual picture, departure from the mid-point becomes profitable. Thus, if (1) consumers are assumed to have identical demands and to be scattered evenly over an area shaped in the form of a square, (2) the demand curve of each consumer is in the form of a straight line, negatively sloping, (3) the other assumptions listed earlier in this section are still applicable, and (4) a line is drawn horizontally from one side of the square to the opposite side, and in such way as to bisect these sides, one of two firms would locate at the first quartile point on this line, while the other firm would locate at the third quartile point. From these vantage points, each firm would monopolize half of the entire market area. Such locations are the most profitable ones, for they maximize sales by minimizing transfer costs.[24]

A spatial scattering of sellers is therefore the rule under the above assumptions.[25] But once all factors[26] influencing locational

22. H. Hotelling, "Stability in Competition," *Economic Journal*, XXXIX (1929), pp. 41–57 [Selection 6 in this volume].

23. See A. Smithies, "Optimum Location in Spatial Competition," *Journal of Political Economy*, XLIX (1941), pp. 423–439 [Selection 7 in this volume].

And similarly, if a finite limit to an inelastic demand is assumed, firms will tend to disperse. See A. P. Lerner and H. W. Singer, "Some Notes on Duopoly and Spatial Competition," *Journal of Political Economy*, XLV (1937), pp. 145–186.

24. These locations are at the same points as those which would be selected by the biplant monopolist. Such locational selections are termed "quasi monopolistic." See Smithies, *op. cit.*, p. 429. But if uncertainty exists regarding the competitor's choice of a quartile location, for example, because the duopolists have long-been extremely competitive in price and location, both firms will be found at the center of the entire market area.

25. Lösch's somewhat deficient system can be brought into play at this point; the rectangular area belonging to the sellers thus being replaced more or less perfectly, in the long run, by a group of nonprofit hexagons, as population shifts in order to maximize its consumption. See footnotes 19 and 20.

26. Space does not permit detailed examination of forces generally mentioned as determining locational interdependence. Thus, the following discussion is severely condensed. It divides locational interdependence factors into two groups, pure and imperfect.

(A) The Pure Factors include those economic forces which would create locational interdependence (and thus the possibility of concentration) in even such an economy as one where, (1) resources and population (at least in the precommercial [handicraft] economy) are evenly distributed over a homogeneous plain, (2) there are no market imperfections other than *space* and *number* of firms, and (3) rivals know that competitors will, *generally*, locate quasi-monopolistically, while competing actively in net-mill price. (The slightly *less than perfect assurance* of rivals' location policies arises only when the pure factor is itself of such type as to cause uncertainty. See A-(2), (3), and (4), this footnote.) (1) The elasticity of the demand curve is a pure factor which influences concentration or dispersion of firms. The more inelastic the demand for the product of an industry, the greater is the tendency to concentrate (see Hotelling, *op. cit.*, p. 52), and *vice versa* (see Morris Copeland, "Competing Products and Monopolistic Competition," *Quarterly Journal of Economics*, LV (1940–41), pp. 1–35, 3, 23). (2) The shape of the marginal cost curve is another pure determinant of locational interdependence. If, in a given industry, this curve is negatively sloping, throughout almost all ranges of output, and the f.o.b. mill system of pricing is followed, the effect of freight cost is to cause a large increase in net-mill price, or, in other words, the freight cost absorption in price is slight, if not, in fact, negative. (To illustrate: when marginal costs are falling, the addition of freight costs to marginal costs causes the intersection of the marginal revenue and marginal cost [freight included] curve to occur at a relatively high point on the marginal cost [freight included] curve. This rather quick intersection of the marginal values calls forth a high net-mill price.) Because the existence of freight cost causes a relatively large increase in net-mill price, sales to buyers located at the extremities of the entire market area are small or non-existent. This condition signifies a narrow market area for the firm at the center of the entire market area; it encourages all competitors to disperse, and threby to gain, lower freight costs, larger outputs, and concomitantly, lower production costs. But if marginal costs are increasing, the opposite type of conjecture is admissable. For, while firms would always gain by dispersing, *ceteris paribus*, the incentive is not quite so obvious when unit costs rise with expanding production. In this case, the relatively small increase in net-mill price on account of freight, or in other words, the large absorption of freight costs in price, signifies a relatively wide market area for the firm at the center of the entire market area. It tends to create uncertainty as regards dispersion of rivals, which, in turn, promotes concentration. (See Joan Robinson, *The Economics of Imperfect Competition* [1934], pp. 30, 32, 55, and Chapter V, for discussions suggesting the impact of freight cost on net-mill price. Also see Smithies, *op. cit.*). And, note the difference in deductive findings in this type of analysis and Hoover's discussion of margin lines; a divergence in theory which is due to (a) the present inclusion of freight cost with marginal cost, and, accordingly, an examination of its impact on net-mill price, and (b) a consideration of the conjectural hypotheses of competitors as regards their rival's locational selections. And see footnote 13. (3) The height of the freight rate is another pure determinant of locational interdependence. The lower the freight rate, the greater is the tendency to concentrate, and *vice versa*. (See Alfred Marshall, *Principles of Economics*, 8th ed. [1949], p. 273.) (4) Unequal costs (resulting from agglomerating advantages) at alternative locations is another pure factor governing localization or dispersion of industry; it tends to promote concentration at a few centers.

(B) In addition to the above determinants, certain market imperfections, such as, personal contact, uncertainty, competition from substitutable products, price policies, and unequal costs (different freight rate structures) influence concentration or dispersion of firms. Briefly, (1) where entrepreneurs believe that personal acquaintanceships

interdependence are considered, concentrations at a few production centers may be explained. The market area type of analysis disregards factors of concentration; its framework assumes that firms are never attracted to sites proximate to their rivals; thus it does not adequately explain (1) those cases where the market areas of firms are identical, nor (2) those cases where the market demand is largely concentrated at a point.

The location of and the size and shape of the market area of a firm have been drawn in market area analysis by abstracting from not only the imperfectly competitive but also the pure factors considered in the theory of locational interdependence. It follows that, with its given locations, the leading contribution of market area analysis has been confined to a short-run horizon. It is in this time period that there exists the stochastic market areas and the dynamic changes in freight rates and mill prices which are so aptly described in market area diagrams. This type of analysis has, however, not yet succeeded in developing a pictorial representation of a general spatial equilibrium, nor does it seem likely that such can be accomplished;[27] more

---

with bankers, material suppliers, and customers facilitate procurement of loans, materials, and sales, the location of rivals will be of lesser force than if such belief was nonexistent. (See M. Greenhut, "Observations of Motives to Industry Location," *Southern Economic Journal*, XVIII, pp. 225–228). (2) The less certain an entrepreneur is concerning the location policies of his rival(s), the less willing he will be to chance a location away from the center of the market area. If the firms in an industry are highly competitive in location as well as price, they will tend to concentrate. (See Smithies, *op. cit.*, pp. 429–432, and see E. Chamberlin, *The Theory of Monopolistic Competition*, 5th ed. (1936), Appendix C.) (3) The greater the rivalry from differentiated products the weaker is the expectation that competitors (homogeneous and heterogeneous) will locate quasi-monopolistically with regard to the firm in question. (4) The basing point and equalizing delivered price systems tend to discourage dispersion. (See Gardner Ackley's article on "Price Policies," which is included in the National Resources Planning Board's study, *Industrial Location and Natural Resources* (1943), and see Arthur Smithies, "Aspects of the Basing Point System," *American Economic Review*, XXXII (1942), pp. 702–726.) And (5) unequal costs (different freight rate structures) at alternative locations promotes concentration.

Obviously, we can add other factors to the list, such as, (1) uneven scatter of population, which may be caused by topographical differences, gregariousness, and, of course, the pure and imperfect forces cited above, (2) regional, and other, buyer types of prejudice and (3) the impact of time-of-delivery on sales.

27. Because they inherently disregard dynamic factors of locational interdependence (especially the pure forces of location interdependence), it seems that attempts such as Lösch's to explain a spatial general equilibrium, by ascertaining the size and shape of the firm's market area, must remain of limited value. Another type of approach is needed for this particular objective.

It is worthy of special note that Lösch's system though inapplicable to a private capitalistic economy (for reasons cited above) is patently of value in economic planning. In fact, this is the use to which Lösch eventually dedicated his theory. (See his reference to the *then* conquered areas of Soviet Russia, *op. cit.*, p. 93: "Dennoch hat eine solche einfache Landschaft etwas Bestechendes, und vor allem ist sie wahrscheinlich das Äusserste, was bei bewusster Planung heute bewältigt werden kann. Sie liegt denn auch, dem Einzelfall angepasst, der Neugliederung im Osten weithin zugrunde.")

within its capacity are pictorial representations of many kinds of particular equilibria in space.

IV

Speculations on the size and shape of firms' market areas have progressed from simple models, which analyze the boundary line separating two firms, to more ambitious studies, which attempt to describe the shape of firms' market areas as the economy moves to a long-run equilibrium. Furthermore, recent market area analyses have been concerned, somewhat, with the factors that determine the number of production centers and the degree of concentration at these places.

While these interests and emphases on underlying location factors are integral to economic thought, it is this writer's belief that additional theoretical and empirical research on two particular forces is needed. The relationship between long-run marginal cost and price, and the relationship between freight cost and price must be more clearly defined. That is, at some point, diseconomies of scale and increasing freight costs (as the market-area expands) rise sufficiently relative to the prevailing and/or expected price to warrant the establishment of a branch plant or an entirely new organization.[28] Theoretical and empirical data on these matters will further our understanding of the underlying structural pattern of economic society.[29]

28. It can be shown that when (1) marginal costs are constant, (2) the demand curve of homogeneous consumers is of the negatively sloping straight line variety, and (3) these consumers are evenly scattered, a spatial monopolist, who practises a non-discriminatory f.o.b. price system, absorbs, in his net-mill price, no less than one-third of the freight cost to the most distant buyer. Thus, attempts to expand market areas lessen the value of the markets more proximate to the seller's factory. Clearly a distance will be reached which is too remote from the plant to be included profitably within its market area.

29. The literature on the market area of a firm still lacks an emphasis on as well as a sufficiently precise measurement of maximum size. Further, market area analysis lacks a complete (all-embracing) accounting for the firm's minimum-size market area which may be at a point, polygonic, or circular in shape. Until these two problems are solved either by the market area type of analysis and/or by an entirely different type of approach, much of our theorizing on the location of branch plants and/or new establishments, and on a spatial general equilibrium must remain fairly unproductive.

12

A Model of Market Areas with Free Entry

INTRODUCTION

The purpose of this paper is to analyze a model of location within a single industry under the special assumption that space is uniform and undifferentiated in several important ways. The definitive work on this problem is that of Lösch,[1] who claimed that free entry must result in space-filling, hexagon-shaped market areas. We will show that this claim is incorrect and that a wider variety of results is consistent with Lösch's assumptions. Lösch's mistake (repeated by Valavanis[2] and by Kuenne[3]) is to *assume* that a necessary condition for industry equilibrium with profit maximization and free entry is that market areas be space-filling. This ought instead to be presented as a *theorem* and, as such, it turns out to be false.

We have chosen to analyze a special case, involving assumptions of linearity at several important steps. Our model is simple enough to permit a fairly exhaustive analysis, yet general enough to display a wide range of possible results. In addition to a detailed analysis of the conditions under which Lösch's claim is correct, our model permits us to obtain explicit results for several interesting variables such as price and costs.

In the last section of the paper we analyze the welfare problem posed by our model of location. The major question to be asked is whether free entry results in a socially efficient use of resources in production and transportation. We show that efficiency is a more complicated notion in our model than in the standard models of resource allocation, and conclude with the demonstration that, on one plausible criterion, free entry does not result in an efficient use of resources.

1. August Lösch, *The Economics of Location* (New Haven, Conn.: Yale University Press, 1954), pp. 105–14.
2. Stefan Valavanis, "Lösch on Location," *American Economic Review*, XLV (September, 1955), 637–44.
3. Robert E. Kuenne, *The Theory of General Economic Equilibrium* (Princeton, N.J.: Princeton University Press, 1963), pp. 451, 452.

The authors are indebted for a number of valuable suggestions to the members of the Political Economy Seminar at Johns Hopkins University and to the members of the Econometrics Workshop at the University of Chicago.

Reprinted from the Journal of Political Economy, (June 1964), pp. 278–88, by permission of The University of Chicago Press and the authors.

THE MODEL

We consider a single commodity that can be produced at any point in two dimensional space with the same cost function. We cannot, however, also assume that average cost at a given point is the same at each level of output, since it would then be possible to avoid all transportation costs by producing a small amount of the product at each point in space. Next to a constant average cost, the simplest assumption to make is that marginal cost is constant but less than average cost. We therefore assume that, at any point in space, the total cost of producing x units of output per unit time can be represented by[4]

$$A + kx. \tag{1}$$

We also assume that transportation cost per unit per mile is the same between every pair of points. The cost of shipping a unit a distance of u miles can therefore be represented by

$$tu. \tag{2}$$

We assume that each firm sets the f.o.b. price at its profit-maximizing level and sells at that price to all who wish to buy. In principle, any firm can discriminate by charging a higher f.o.b. price to customers close to it than to those far away. In fact, such discrimination exists, and charging the same delivered price to all customers (for example, under a basing-point policy) is an example. However, geographical discrimination requires the seller to have detailed knowledge concerning the locations of his buyers, and in many industries it is not worthwhile to collect such information. If a seller sets a fixed f.o.b. price, he need neither know nor care where his buyers live in order to find the optimum price.

We assume that potential customers ("families") are spread with a uniform density of D per square mile over an infinite plain. We ignore all problems concerned with the boundary of the industry's market area and carry out the analysis in terms of the number of firms per square mile. Each family has the same demand curve, which is linear in the delivered price and can thus be represented by

$$x_F = a - b(p + tu), \tag{3}$$

where x_F is the demand per family and p is the f.o.b. price. Each family buys from the firm closest to it.

4. This term refers to the cost of producing at a rate of x units in a plant that is optimum for that output. We assume that there are no economies of multiplant operation.

The firm's total sales can be found by integrating equation (3) over its market area and multiplying by D. Both firms and industry can be in equilibrium only when each firm's market area is the same size and shape. Further, these shapes must be regular. Irregular shapes are precluded by their inefficient transportation patterns. Any irregular market area can be replaced by a regular one of smaller area but of the same profitability, thus permitting more firms per square mile. We therefore restrict consideration to regular polygons and to the limiting form of circles. If we define u to be the shortest distance from the firm to any point on the perimeter of its market area, the total sales x of a firm with a market area of size U are

$$x = 2sD \int_0^{\pi/s} \left\{ \int_0^{U/\cos \theta} \times [a - b(p+tu)] u\, du \right\} d\theta \qquad (4a)$$

if its market area is a regular s-sided polygon, and

$$x = D \int_0^{2\pi} \times \left\{ \int_0^{U} [a - b(p+tu)] u\, du \right\} d\theta, \qquad (4b)$$

if its market area is a circle.

The firm's total profit is, of course,

$$Y = px - A - kx. \qquad (5)$$

Substituting equation (4) for x and integrating, we can express the firm's total profit as a function of p and U for any regular market area. For the triangle, square, hexagon, and circle, the results are

$$Y_T = (6DU^2) \left(\frac{a\sqrt{3}}{2} - \frac{bp\sqrt{3}}{2} - 0.7969btU \right)(p-k) - A, \qquad (6T)$$

$$Y_S = (8DU^2) \left(\frac{a}{2} - \frac{bp}{2} - 0.3848btU \right)(p-k) - A, \qquad (6S)$$

$$Y_H = (12DU^2) \left(\frac{a}{2\sqrt{3}} - \frac{bp}{2\sqrt{3}} - 0.2027btU \right)(p-k) - A, \qquad (6H)$$

$$Y_C = (2\pi DU^2) \left(\frac{a}{2} - \frac{bp}{2} - \frac{btU}{3} \right) \times (p-k) - A. \qquad (6C)$$

PROFIT MAXIMIZATION

The purpose of this section is to lay the foundation for the analysis of free entry in the following section. The major building block in the foundation is the investigation of the firm's profit-maximizing policy when its sales area is restricted to one of the four figures discussed in the previous ection. In the absence of nearby competition the firm would set the profit-maximizing price and sell to all who wished to buy at that price. It is well known and is shown below that the resulting sales area would be circular. However, the presence of competition may constrain the firm to a particular market area shape and to a particular U. It will therefore be useful for further analysis to find the profit-maximizing p for each U in each of the four market area forms and to express the resulting profit level as a function of U. Equating to zero the partials of equations (6T), (6S), (6H), and (6C) with respect to p gives

$$p_T = \frac{a}{2b} + \frac{k}{2} - 0.4601tU, \tag{7T}$$

$$p_S = \frac{a}{2b} + \frac{k}{2} - 0.3826tU, \tag{7S}$$

$$p_H = \frac{a}{2b} + \frac{k}{2} - 0.3509tU, \tag{7H}$$

and

$$p_C = \frac{a}{2b} + \frac{k}{2} - 0.3333tU, \tag{7C}$$

where the subscript designated an optimum value for the indicated market area shape. It is worth noting that, for a given U, price will be highest for the circular market area, next highest for the hexagon, next to lowest for the square and lowest for the triangle.

Eliminating p from equations (6T)–(6C) by equations (7T)–(7C), we get

$$Y_T(U) = 1.1004Dc_4U^4 + 2.3910Dc_3U^3 + 1.2990Dc_2U^2 - A, \tag{8T}$$

$$Y_S(U) = 0.5855Dc_4U^4 + 1.5304Dc_3U^3 + Dc_2U^2 - A, \tag{8S}$$

$$Y_H(U) = 0.4269Dc_4U^4 + 1.2160Dc_3U^3 + 0.8660Dc_2U^2 - A, \tag{8H}$$

$$Y_C(U) = 0.3491Dc_4U^4 + 1.0472Dc_3U^3 + 0.7854Dc_2U^2 - A, \tag{8C}$$

where

$$c_4 = bt^2, \; c_3 = -t(a - bk), \; c_2 = \frac{1}{b}(a - bk)^2$$

$a\text{-}bk > 0$ if and only if demand would be positive for a family immedi-ately adjacent to the firm when f.o.b. price was as low as marginal cost.

If that inequality did not hold no firm would ever enter the industry even as a monpoly, and it is assumed to hold in all the following analysis. We thus have

$$c_4 > 0, c_3 < 0, c_2 > 0, \text{ and } c_2 c_4 = c_3{}^2.$$

If we multiply both sides of equations (8T)–(8C) by $c_4/c_2{}^2 D$ and use the above relationship among the c's, we can express the quartics in new units $Y' = (c_4/Dc_2{}^2)Y$ and $U' = (c_3/c_4)U$. In these transformed units, the c's, D, and A appear only in the constant term, which becomes $-Ac_4/Dc_2{}^2$. Therefore, graphs of the quartics in the new units will reveal relationships among the equations that are independent of the values assigned to the parameters. Such graphs are presented in Figure 1, where $Ac_4/Dc_2{}^2 = 0.01$. Changing any parameter in the

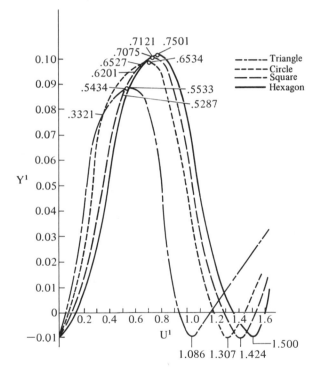

FIGURE 1

model is equivalent to sliding the horizontal axis up or down, but leaving the graphs otherwise unchanged. We can infer a number of characteristics of these graphs. Most will be useful in the further analysis, but a few are presented for completeness.

(*a*) Each quartic has exactly two distinct minima and one maximum. For each quartic, one minimum occurs at $U = 0$, at which point $Y(0) = -A$. Information on the maximum and the other minimum is summarized in Table 1. Here it is worthy of note that, if the profit-maximizing U is inserted in equations (7T)–(7C), the price is the same for each market area form

$$p = \frac{a}{2b} + \frac{k}{2} + 0.25\frac{c_3}{c_4}.$$

That is, for the most profitable U the profit-maximizing price is the same whether the firm sells in a triangular, square, hexagonal, or circular market area. The resulting profits are not, however, the

TABLE 1

	TRIANGLE	SQUARE	HEXAGON	CIRCLE
Profit-maximizing U	$-0.5434\, c_3/c_4$	$-0.6534\, c_3/c_4$	$-0.7121\, c_3/c_4$	$-0.7501\, c_3/c_4$
Maximum profit	$0.0959\,(c_2{}^2/c_4)$ $D-A$	$0.1067\,(c_2{}^2/c_4)$ $D-A$	$0.1098\,(c_2{}^2/c_4)$ $D-A$	$0.1104\,(c_2{}^2/c_4)$ $D-A$
Profit-minimizing U	$-1.0863\, c_3/c_4$	$-1.3070\, c_3/c_4$	$-1.4242\, c_3/c_4$	$-1.5000\, c_3/c_4$
Minimum profit	$-A$	$-A$	$-A$	$-A$

same. In fact, both the profit-maximizing U and the level of maximum profits increase as one moves across the above table from left to right. It follows that the firm will always choose a circular market area unless competitors constrain it to some other market-area form. The notion that firms prefer circular market areas goes back to the nineteenth century and follows from the simple observation that, if a firm finds it profitable to sell to a family u miles away in one direction, it must be profitable to sell to families u miles away in each direction.

(*b*) It follows from the results under point (*a*) and from the fact that Y goes to infinity as U goes to plus or minus infinity, that each quartic has three real positive roots and one real negative root if there exists a value of U at which the firm can break even.

(*c*) It is important for further analysis to establish points of intersection for the four quartics. These are given in Table 2. It is clear from this table that the graphs must stand in the relationship shown in Figure 1. As we move from the triangle to the square to the hexagon to the circle the graphs move upward and to the right. Furthermore it is obvious that the graph for the circle is a limiting form and that the graphs for higher-order polygons would lie "between" those for the hexagon and the circle.

TABLE 2

VALUES OF U FOR INTERSECTION WITH	TRIANGLE	SQUARE	HEXAGON	CIRCLE
Square	$\begin{cases}-0.3321\,c_3/c_4\\-1.3393\,c_3/c_4\end{cases}$		$-0.6201\,c_3/c_4$ $-1.3622\,c_3/c_4$	$-0.6527\,c_3/c_4$ $-1.3919\,c_3/c_4$
Hexagon	$\begin{cases}-0.5287\,c_3/c_4\\-1.2159\,c_3/c_4\end{cases}$	$-0.6201\,c_3/c_4$ $-1.3622\,c_3/c_4$		$-0.7075\,c_3/c_4$ $-1.4624\,c_3/c_4$
Circle	$\begin{cases}-0.5533\,c_3/c_4\\-1.2353\,c_3/c_4\end{cases}$	$-0.6527\,c_3/c_4$ $-1.3919\,c_3/c_4$	$-0.7075\,c_3/c_4$ $-1.4624\,c_3/c_4$	

(d) The graphs do not take account of non-negativity conditions on x_F and p and therefore include points that are not possible decisions for the firm. It follows from equations (7T)–(7C) that, as U increases, p decreases for each market-area form. However, as the perimeter of the market area moves out, transportation cost to the perimeter rises faster than p decreases. Therefore delivered price rises on the perimeter as U increases and the demand per family on the perimeter falls. Thus, f.o.b. price will be high and delivered price low when U is small, whereas f.o.b. price will be low and delivered price high when U is large. As U goes to zero, sales go to zero and profit therefore goes to $-A$. At the maximum point on each curve p is of course greater than marginal cost. At that point delivered price is at the level that just chokes off demand at some point on the perimeter of the market area. For the circle, demand is just zero at every point on the perimeter for the profit-maximizing U. As U increases beyond its profit-maximizing value, demand at the perimeter becomes negative since, as shown above, delivered price increases with U. We can summarize by saying that the non-negativity conditions are satisfied for all positive values of U to the left of the maximum and for no value of U to the right of the maximum for each curve. The second minimum occurs at the point at which p equals marginal cost and profit is thus again equal to $-A$ (just as at $U = 0$), although the non-negativity conditions are not satisfied at this point.

FREE ENTRY

The basic notion to be employed in this section is that firms will continue to enter the industry as long as there exists some pattern of market areas that will permit more firms per square mile with all firms making at least zero profits.[5] For any of the four market-area

---

5. It should be emphasized that we consider only static industry equilibriums in this paper. We do not consider adjustment processes, and we make no attempt to ascertain whether any adjustment process will converge to industry equilibrium from any

forms shown in Figure 1 (or for any other regular polygon whose graph is not shown), the smallest market area within which the firm can break even is determined by the smallest positive root of the quartic for the market-area form. Thus, we want to ask which of the four smallest positive roots is such as to maximize the number of firms per square mile.

A simple observation demonstrates that, contrary to Lösch's claim, the answer is not necessarily the hexagon. It follows from the results in the last section that changing A (or D or the c's) moves the horizontal axis up or down in Figure 1, but does not otherwise change the graphs. Clearly it is possible for the horizontal axis to be above the maximum point on the graph for the hexagon but below the maximum point on the graph for the circle. Then, no firm could break even with a hexagonal market area, but it could with a circular area. This disproves Lösch's contention. The basic notion in this demonstration is simply that, if the circle is the most profitable market area, then it must be possible for the industry to be sufficiently unprofitable for the most profitable market area to be the only one in which firms can break even. We have thus shown that free entry need not result in space-filling market areas. Rather, it is possible that even when the industry is in long run equilibrium, there will be interstices in which families do without the product in question.

The above paragraph would be no more than a minor exception to Lösch's result if it were true that free entry could result in circular market areas only when there was no possibility of a firm breaking even with a hexagonal market area. However, that is not the case. As between circular and hexagonal market areas, values of U are ranked inversely to the maximum number of firms per square mile. Thus, if, and only if, the smallest positive root of $Y_H(U)$ is smaller than the smallest positive root of $Y_C(U)$ will free entry result in hexagonal market areas. An equivalent condition is that the graph of $Y_H(U)$ should first cut the horizontal axis to the left of the point at which it first cuts the graph of $Y_C(U)$. It follows from the table of points of intersection presented under (c) before that $Y_H(U)$ and $Y_C(U)$ intersect to the left of the maximum of either function. Therefore, which market form results from free entry will depend on the precise relationship among all the parameters. In particular, for given values of all other parameters, it is always possible to find some values of A such that hexagonal areas will result and other values, even though both shapes permit positive profits.

The foregoing analysis suggests that it may even be possible for

---

particular arbitrary initial arrangement of firms and market areas. One way to envisage the adjustment is to assume a *tâtonnement* process in which no plants are actually built until equilibrium is reached.

free entry to result in triangular or square market areas, but that turns out not to be the case. The reason is that, for a given value of U, a triangular area permits fewer firms per square mile than a square area, and a square area permits fewer firms per square mile than a hexagonal area. In fact, a firm with a hexagonal market area and a parameter U_H has the same size market area as a firm with a square market area and a parameter $0.9306\ U_H$, and the same size market area as a firm with a triangular market area and a parameter $0.8165\ U_H$. It can be shown that, although triangular or square market areas may result in smaller U's than does a hexagonal market area, those U's cannot be sufficiently smaller to permit more firms in the industry.[6]

So far we have restricted our attention to space-filling polygons and to circles. The fact that free entry may result in circular market areas suggests that some polygons with more than six sides may also be possibilities even though they are not space-filling. The general case is complicated by the need to consider both the area served per firm and the maximum "density" (ratio of area covered to total area) in the case of non-space-filling polygons. In spite of a search through the extensive mathematical literature on the packing of convex bodies into various kinds of space, we are unable to present an analysis of the general case.[7] We can, however, demonstrate that a number of polygons with more than six sides are possible market areas under free entry.

Consider a set of circles packed to give maximum density as shown in Figure 2. Then each circle will have exactly six points of contact with other circles. Now circumscribe a dodecagon (12-sided regular polygon) around each circle so that at each point of contact between circles there are two parallel, touching sides of adjoining dodecagons. This arrangement is the densest packing for the dode-cagons as well as for the circles. The circles and the dodecagons have the same U and the same maximum number of figures per square mile. (The dodecagons have the greater density.) It follows that more circles than dodecagons can be packed per square mile if and only if the circles have a smaller U than the dodecagons have. Now it was

---

6. The proof consists in showing that $Y_H(U) - Y_S(0.9306U) \geqslant 0$ and $Y_H(U) - Y_T(0.8165U) \geqslant 0$ for all admissible values of U. The former inequality, for example, holds for all values of U in the interval $0 \leqslant U \leqslant -1.4260c_3/c_4$. This interval includes all values of U such that (a) the firm with a square market area takes up no more room than the firm with a hexagonal market area, and (b) the firm with a square market area makes at least as much profit as the firm with a hexagonal market area. Similar statements hold for the triangular and hexagonal areas.

7. The most complete reference we have found in this literature is *Lagerungen in der Ebene auf der Kugel und im Raum*, by L. Fejes Tóth (Berlin, 1953). This monograph contains a large number of further references to the literature.

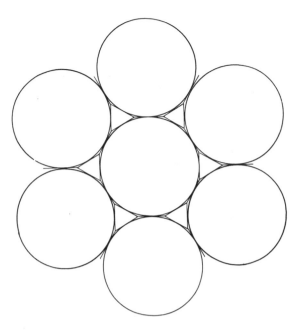

FIGURE 2

stated in (c) of the preceding section that the quartics for polygons like those shown in Figure 1 approach the quartic for the circle as the number of sides of the polygon approaches infinity. The properties of these quartics show that, for any set of values of the other coefficients, there must exist some A such that the smallest (zero-profit) U for an s-sided polygon will be smaller than the smallest U for an $(s+i)$-sided polygon $(i > 0)$. It follows that, for such an A, dodecagon-shaped market areas maximize the number of firms per square mile and are therefore industry-equilibrium market-area forms.

The above argument holds for any s-sided polygon that can be circumscribed around densely packed circles without overlapping. This set includes all values of s which are integer multiples of six. Therefore any polygon with a number of sides that is evenly divisible by six is a possible market-area form. Of course, as s becomes large, the difference between an s-sided polygon and its inscribed circle becomes negligible. What about s-sided polygons when s is not an integer multiple of six? We are unable to tell whether any of them are candidates or not because we have been unable to find good inequalities for their maximum densities. We conjecture the result that the only possible market areas are circles and regular polygons with a number of sides that is an integer multiple of six.

WELFARE CONSIDERATIONS

The model presented in this paper bears a family resemblance to models of monopolistic competition.[8] In particular, free entry results in the familiar tangency condition between the negatively sloped demand curve and the average cost curve, and therefore f.o.b. price equals average cost. The f.o.b. price thus exceeds marginal production cost, and delivered price exceeds marginal production plus transportation cost. Therefore, in any welfare model that requires the equality of marginal cost and price for a social optimum, our firms misallocate resources.

Thus, our model indicates misallocation in the standard sense that monopolistic firms produce too little for a social optimum. This is an inevitable consequence of the zero-profit condition and declining average cost. There is, however, another sense in which misallocation is conceivable in our model, and it is worthwhile to ask whether it actually occurs. That is, we might ask whether there is any way of producing and distributing more cheaply the amount that our firms actually produce. In other words, we might ask whether the firms in our model produce their output with a minimum cost combination of production and transportation resources. If not, we can conclude that free entry has induced firms not only to produce the wrong output, but also to produce the output they have chosen in a socially inefficient way.

The possibility of the second kind of inefficiency arises from the fact that a given quantity of output can be produced either by a small number of large firms, each of which has low average production cost but high transportation costs, or by a large number of small firms, each of which has high average production costs but low transportation costs. Therefore, it is worth asking whether firms of the size and shape that result from profit maximization and free entry use a socially efficient combination of production and transportation costs.

The question that we want to ask is how total production and transportation costs vary as a given industry output is produced by a small number of large firms or by a large number of small firms. We do not, however, want to require that the consumption of each family should remain constant as firm sizes change. The consumption of a given family will depend, for a given f.o.b. price, on whether it is supplied by a small nearby firm or by a large distant firm. Instead, it seems sensible to ask how total production and transportation costs

---

8. On p. 109, Lösch points out this resemblance and refers to location as one form of product differentiation.

would vary if, as firm sizes changed, f.o.b. price were varied in such a way as to keep the average demand per family constant.

It follows from equation (10) that, if f.o.b. price is varied in this way, the dispersion of demand among families will be greater, the larger are the firms. For example, compare the following two situations:

1. Firms are small. Production per family is ten units; 90 per cent of the families consume between nine and eleven units.

2. Firms are large. Production per family is ten units; 50 per cent of the families consume between nine and eleven units.

Many plausible social welfare functions would not indicate social indifference between situations (1) and (2). The justification for our comparison of costs between situations like these is that no welfare significance attaches to the particular amount of demand dispersion that results from free entry. We have no reason to think that a small increase or decrease in the variance of demand per family (for a given average) either increases or decreases social welfare. Therefore, it is worthwhile to ask what would happen to costs if we moved from situation (1) to situation (2). The comparison can be made as follows .

Quantity sold per family is proportional to quantity sold per square mile. Quantity sold per square mile is firms per square mile times quantity sold per firm. We will restrict the analysis to hexagonal market areas because the calculations are easier for space-filling figures. However, similar conclusions hold for circles. For the hexagon, area per firm is $3.464U^2$ and therefore firms per area are $1/3.464U^2$. From equation (4a), we get quantity sold per firm. Integrating equation (4a) for $s = 6$ and collecting terms, we get

$$\text{quantity sold per sq. mile} = D(a - bp - 0.7020\, btU). \qquad (9)$$

Thus, the quantity sold per family will remain constant as U varies if p also varies so as to keep the terms in parentheses constant in equation (9). This requires.

$$p = \text{constant} - 0.7020 tU. \qquad (10)$$

Now total cost per square mile (that is, per family) is firms per square mile times cost per firm, or cost per square mile $= (1/3.464U^2)$ $(kx + A)$

$$= \frac{1}{3.464U^2}\left[12kD\left(\frac{aU^2}{2\sqrt{3}} - \frac{bpU^2}{2\sqrt{3}} - 0.2026btU^3\right) + A\right], \qquad (11)$$

again using equation (4a) to eliminate x. If price is set by equation (10), we get

$$\text{cost per sq. mile} = \text{constant} + \frac{A}{3.464U^2}. \qquad (12)$$

Equation (12) is a paradoxical result. It says that the larger the firms are, the smaller the cost of production and transportation will be for the industry as a whole, provided firms vary price in such a way as to keep the average demand per family constant. Going from equation (11) to equation (12), all the terms that contain t drop out. The reason for this is that, as U increases and p decreases, the extra transportation cost of supplying more distant customers is just offset by the decrease in transportation cost that results from the fact that customers close to the firm buy more, and customers far from the firm buy less, the larger is U. Therefore, the only effect as U grows is that there are fewer firms per square mile each producing proportionately more output at lower unit cost.

We have therefore shown that the average output per family that results from free entry could be produced and distributed more cheaply if firms were larger. Thus, in the restricted sense in which we have used the term, an efficient allocation of resources is not provided by free entry in our model.

We cannot conclude from equation (12) that it would be most efficient for a single firm to supply the entire infinite market. It follows from equation (10) that, as U increases, delivered price rises at the perimeter of the market area. Therefore, a value of U will eventually be reached at which demand is zero at the edge of the market area. The firm's market area cannot increase beyond that size without changing the average amount demanded per family.

The above analysis has shown that there exist a price level and market size that, in our sense, would make more efficient use of resources than occurs as a result of free entry. This more efficient situation is not, of course, a profit-maximizing situation. We cannot, therefore, conclude that consumers would benefit from a policy that simply restricted entry into the industry in order to increase firm size. In fact, the reverse is true. If firms set the profit-maximizing price, consumption per family will increase as U decreases. For the hexagon, this can be seen by comparing equation (7H) with equation (10). As U shrinks, the profit-maximizing f.o.b. price falls off more rapdily than the rate that would keep demand per family constant. Therefore, as U shrinks, average demand per family rises if firms vary p so as to maximize profit.

PART IV LOCATIONAL EQUILIBRIUM ANALYSIS

13

Equilibrium of the Household

INTRODUCTION

An individual who arrives in a city and wishes to buy some land to live upon will be faced with the double decision of how large a lot he should purchase and how close to the center of the city he should settle. In reality he would also consider the apparent character and racial composition of the neighborhood, the quality of the schools in the vicinity, how far away he would be from any relatives he might have in the city, and a thousand other factors. However, the individual in question is an "economic man," defined and simplified in a way such that we can handle the analysis of his decision-making.[1] He merely wishes to maximize his satisfaction by owning and consuming the goods he likes and avoiding those he dislikes. Moreover, an individual is in reality a family which may contain several members. Their decisions may be reached in a family council or be the responsibility of a single member. We are not concerned with how these tastes are formed, but simply with what they are. Given these tastes, this simplified family will spend whatever money it has available in maximizing its satisfaction.

The city in which the individual arrives is a simplified city. It lies on a featureless plain, and transportation is possible in all directions. All employment and all goods and services are available only at the center of the city. Land is bought and sold by free contract, without any institutional restraints and without having its character fixed by any structures existing upon the ground. Municipal services and tax rates are uniform throughout the city. The individual knows the price of land at every location, and, from his point of view, this is a given fact, not affected by his decisions.

In this chapter we shall find how much land and where such an individual would buy in such a city. Finding these things constitutes

1. Purposeful simplification for analysis is so much the rule and its advantages and disadvantages have been discussed so thoroughly that further discussion of it here is unnecessary. However, on the particular issue of residential location and urban structure, an interesting polemic was started by Walter Firey (*Land Uses in Central Boston*, chap 1), who attacked the simplifications of human ecologists. A reply from this group may be found in Amos Hawley, *Human Ecology*, pp. 179–180, 286.

the equilibrium solution for the individual. It will be found in this chapter by means of classical consumer equilibrium theory, though the unusual nature of the problem will call forth unexpected turns from the theory. However, though classical theory is satisfactory for the description of individual equilibrium, it does not enable us in this case to aggregate individuals to arrive at a market solution without a radical reformulation. In order to understand this reformulation, the classical solution must be thoroughly grasped. It will be explored in detail in the following pages, first diagrammatically, and later mathematically . . . .

DIAGRAMMATIC SOLUTION OF INDIVIDUAL EQUILIBRIUM

To describe individual equilibrium diagrammatically, we must represent graphically both all of the alternatives open to the individual and his pattern of preferences. By joining these two diagrams, we can observe which of the opportunities open to the individual he will choose.

Opportunities open to the individual

The individual has at his disposal a certain income which he may spend as he wishes. Out of this income he must pay for his land costs, his commuting costs and for all other goods and services (including savings). We wish to describe diagrammatically all of the choices open to the consumer, subject to the restriction of his budget. This restriction may be expressed thus:

Individual's income = land costs + commuting costs + all other
expenditures

First let us examine his expenditures for all goods and services excepting land and commuting costs. The individual may buy greater or smaller quantities of a wide variety of goods. We may denominate the quantity of each good he purchases by $z_1, z_2, \ldots, z_n$, for each of n goods. If the prices of these n goods are $p_1, p_2, \ldots, p_n$, then the expenditure by the individual for any good z_i will be equal to the price of that good times the quantity of the good purchases: $p_i z_i$. His total expenditure for the goods and services in this category will be:

$$p_1 z_1 + p_2 z_2 + \ldots + p_n z_n.$$

However, for the sake of simplicity we shall group all these various goods and services into one composite good, z. The price of this composite good will be a price index, p_z. The expenditure on all goods and services other than land or commuting costs will be $p_z z$.

This simplification will not affect the logic of the subsequent analysis. As an alternative, z may be considered to be money, and p_z may be regarded as unity.

Second, let us examine the individual's expenditures on land. From the point of view of the individual, a price structure is given which specifies a price for land at every location. This price structure is represented by curve $P(t)$ in Figure 1. Price of land, P, varies with distance from the center of the city, t.[2] By expressing the price structure in this manner, it is clear that when a location is chosen, a given price of land is implied.

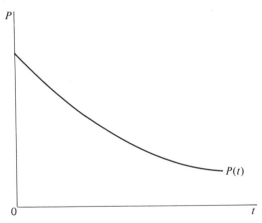

FIGURE 1   Diagrammatic structure of land prices.

However, in purchasing land the consumer not only chooses a location but must also decide upon the quantity of land he will acquire. We shall represent this quantity by the letter q. The expenditure on land will be equal to the price of land times the quantity purchased: $P(t)q$.

Thirdly, we wish to consider commuting costs. These will increase with increasing distance from the center of the city. We shall represent these costs by the function $k(t)$ where t corresponds to the same location as in $P(t)$.

We can now write the budget equation that will contain all of the choices open to a person of income y:

$$y = p_z z + P(t)q + k(t) \tag{1}$$

2. It will be assumed here that the price of land decreases with increasing distance from the center of the city. It will be seen that this is a requirement for the existence of both individual and market equilibrium as well as essentially true for most cities.

where y: income;
         P_z: price of the composite good;
         z: quantity of the composite good;
         $P(t)$: price of land at distance t from the center of the city;
         q: quantity of land;
         $k(t)$: commuting costs to distance t;
         t: distance from the center of the city.

Equation (1) contains within it all the possible alternative ways in which the individual may spend his money. We shall now diagram this function. This can be done in a 3-dimensional set of co-ordinates in terms of the variables z, q, and t. These three variables are the determining ones since income (y) and the price of the composite good (p_z) are given, and the price of land, $P(t)$, and commuting costs, $k(t)$, are functions in terms of t. We shall obtain a 3-dimensional surface that will represent all of the alternatives open to the consumer, and this surface will be called the *locus of opportunities*. Every point on the surface is a possible alternative open to the consumer; every point not on the surface is not a possible alternative.[3] To describe the locus of opportunities surface we shall consider sections through it by holding each of the three variables constant in succession and observing the variations of the other two.

First, let us fix t at any distance $t = t_0$. The individual can now choose between varying quantities of land, q, and the composite good, z, while distance is for the moment fixed at t_0. Distance being fixed, so are price of land, at $P(t_0)$, and commuting costs, at $k(t_0)$. Equation (1) becomes

$$y = p_z z + P(t_0)q + k(t_0),$$

which may be rewritten as

$$q = \frac{y - k(t_0)}{P(t_0)} - \frac{P_z}{P(t_0)} z.$$

This is a linear equation, with a slope equal to the negative of the ratio of the prices of the two goods. Its intercepts are $q = 0$, $z = [y - k(t_0)]/P_z$, and $z = 0$, $q = [y - k(t_0)]/P(t_0)$. It is shown in Figure 2.

3. The locus of opportunities is a generalization of the budget or price line of the usual case. Both describe all of the choices available given a certain income. However, while the budget line considers choices among goods at definite prices, in this case the locus of opportunities considers a good, q, of varying price, $P(t)$, and a good, t, which has no price but determines the price of good q and commuting costs, $k(t)$. Though the budget line is therefore a special case of the locus of opportunities, they both serve the same analytical function.

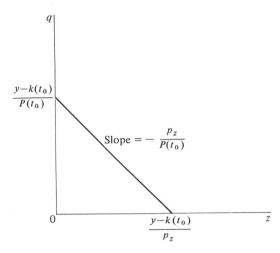

FIGURE 2   Locus of opportunities between q and z, when t is constant at t_0.

Now let us hold the composite good constant at $z = z_0$, and allow q and t to vary. Equation (1) becomes

$$y = p_z z_0 + P(t)q + k(t),$$

which may be rewritten as

$$q = \frac{y - p_z z_0 - k(t)}{P(t)}.$$

This is not a simple linear equation. The price of land, $P(t)$, in the denominator, decreases with increasing distance from the center of the city. Therefore the quantity of land that may be bought, q, increases with distance, since land is becoming cheaper. On the other hand, distance enters into the numerator in the form of commuting costs, $k(t)$. As distance increases, so do commuting costs, and consequently the amount of land that may be purchased decreases. Thus, distance acts in opposing directions upon the quantity of land. The resulting curve is shown in Figure 3. The curve of q on t rises up to the point at which marginal increases in commuting costs are equal to the savings realized from the decreasing price of land. Therefore, the amount of land that may be bought with increasing distance decreases. . . .

And lastly, let us hold q constant at q_0 and allow t and z to vary. Equation (1) becomes

$$y = p_z z + P(t)q_0 + k(t),$$

207

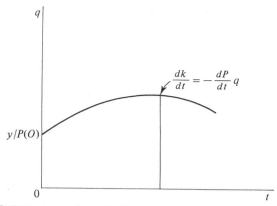

FIGURE 3   Locus of opportunities between q and t, when z is constant at z_0.

which may be rewritten as

$$z = \frac{y - P(t)q_0 - k(t)}{p_z}.$$

The denominator of the fraction is a constant, p_z. The numerator, on the other hand, contains two expressions in terms of t. The first, $P(t)q_0$, will cause z to increase with t since $P(t)$ will be decreasing and the expression is preceded by a negative sign. The second, $k(t)$, also preceded by a minus sign, increases with t and therefore causes z to decrease. The resulting curve is shown in Figure 4. These two opposing effects of distance will cause the amount of the composite good to increase as long as the savings resulting from cheaper land exceed the increases in commuting costs, and the amount of the composite good will decrease when increases in commuting costs exceed the savings resulting from cheaper land. . . .

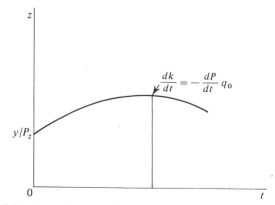

FIGURE 4   Locus of opportunities between z and t, when q is constant at q_0.

Now that we have three sections through the locus of opportunities surface, we may draw it in three dimensions. This has been done in Figure 5. A section parallel to the q–z plane would yield a curve corresponding to that of Figure 2. A section parallel to the q–t plane would yield a curve corresponding to Figure 3. And a section parallel to the z–t plane will yield a curve corresponding to that of Figure 4.[4] The shell-like surface contains all of the combinations of land (q), the composite good (z), and distance (t) open to the consumer, and his equilibrium solution must be a point on this surface.[5] It should be noted that a higher income would have yielded a locus of opportunities surface of the same shape but above

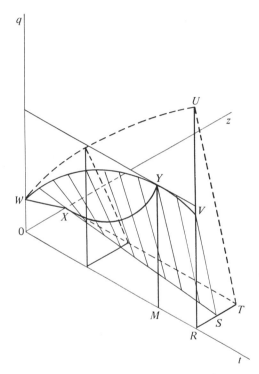

FIGURE 5   Locus of opportunities surface.

4. At $q = 0$, such a section would show z decreasing monotonically with increases in t. This, of course is a special·case of the typical humped curve, where the high point of the curve occurs at $t = 0$.

5. The surface bounded by dashed lines corresponds to the locus of opportunities that would obtain if there were no commuting costs. It is, of course, higher than the surface for the case with costs of commuting, since these costs are equivalent to reductions in income or reduced purchasing power. As one instance, the quantity of land $q = RV$ bought where there are commuting costs (and no z is purchased) will be $[y - k(r)]/P(R)$, while the quantity of land $q = RV$ that would be bought if there were no commuting costs would be $y/P(R)$. The quantity of land lost to commuting expenses is $k(R)/P(R)$.

the one in Figure 5, while a lower income would have yielded one below it.

Preference of the Individual

We now wish to map the individual's preferences. When the mapping of preferences is joined with the mapping of opportunities, individual equilibrium will correspond to that opportunity which yields the individual greatest satisfaction.

Preferences will be mapped through *indifference surfaces*. In this case an indifference surface will be a set of combinations of quantities of land and and the composite good and distance, such that the individual will be equally satisfied by any of these combinations. Hence, he may be said to be indifferent among all of the combinations represented by the indifference surface. However, the usual shape of indifference surfaces is that of a bowl propped up against the corner of a box. In this case, the strange nature of the good distance will result in an unusually shaped indifference surface. We shall arrive at the shape of the surface by examining sections through it.

Let us begin by holding the composite good, z, constant, and allowing the quantity of land, q, and distance, t, to vary. Land q is a good of the ordinary type. All other things being equal, the individual will prefer to have more than less of it; that is to say, he will prefer to have ample living space and not to be crowded. Distance, t, on the other hand, is unusual. We assume that, all other things being equal, a rational individual will prefer a more accessible location to a less accessible one. Since t represents the distance from the center of the city, and thus the distance the individual must commute to the principal place of shopping, amusement, and employment, we may say that accessibility decreases as t increases. In other words, the individual would prefer t to be smaller rather than larger, so that t may be thought of as a good with negative utility (that is, satisfaction). Increases in t produce dissatisfaction.

Given these two goods, then, how will they vary while maintaining a constant level of satisfaction? Given any combination of land and distance, a small increase in distance will produce dissatisfaction, and will have to be compensated for by a small increase in the quantity of land for satisfaction to remain the same. The indifference curve, between land and distance, therefore, will be a rising curve, q increasing with t, as in Figure 6. Had we plotted accessibility rather than distance against land, we would have obtained a downward sloping indifference curve of the usual shape. However, since distance can be measured directly, while accessibility implies some subjective

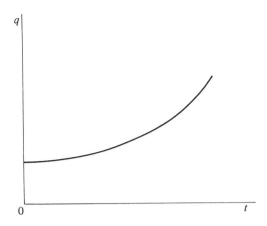

FIGURE 6   Indifference between q and t, for a constant z_0.

pattern of preference (or nuisance value of distance) which may vary from one individual to another, it is better for our purposes to use distance as the variable and to let the shape of the indifference curves take care of the relation between distance and accessibility.

In spite of the direction of the slope of this indifference curve, it remains true, as in the usual case, that lower curves will represent less satisfaction (less land at the same distance, or more distance for the same quantity of land) and higher curves greater satisfaction. It also remains true that curves of this family will not cross.

Now let us hold distance constant at $t = t_0$ and observe the variations between land and the composite good. Given any combination of q and z, a small decrease in one will have to be compensated by a small increase of the other for satisfaction to remain constant. This is the usual type of indifference curve, as in Figure 7. The curve will

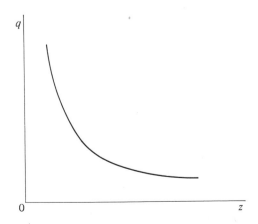

FIGURE 7   Indifference curve between q and z, for a constant t_0.

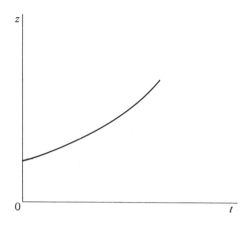

FIGURE 8   Indifference curve between z and t, for a constant q_0.

not only slope downward to the right, but it will also be convex toward the origin, by reason of the diminishing marginal utility of the goods.

Finally, let us hold the quantity of land constant at $q = q_0$ and allow distance and the composite good to vary. A small increase in distance increases the nuisance of commuting, and requires a small increase in the quantity of the composite good for satisfaction to remain constant. There will result a curve as in Figure 8, sloping upward to the right.

We can now draw an indifference surface in these three dimensions, z, q, and t, by combining these three sections. Figure 9 shows such a surface. Figure 10 shows the same surface; the trace XY on

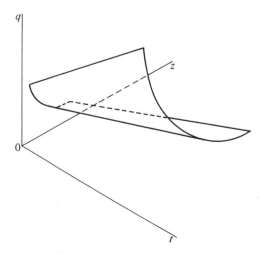

FIGURE 9   An indifference surface.

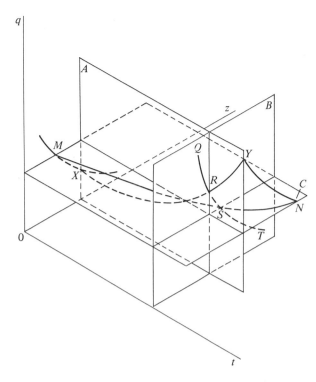

FIGURE 10   Sections through an indifference surface.

plane A corresponds to Figure 6 above, where q and t vary and z is held constant; trace $QRST$ on plane B corresponds to Figure 7, where q and z vary and t is held constant; and trace MN on plane C corresponds to Figure 8, where z and t vary, q being held constant.

The indifference surface shown in Figure 9 represents all of the combinations of the three goods, z, q, and t, which yield the same level of satisfaction to the individual. Combinations of these goods yielding different levels of satisfaction would be represented by similarly shaped surfaces, higher ones for more satisfaction and lower ones for less.

Equilibrium of the Individual

We now have a description of the individual's preferences in the indifference surfaces mapping, and a description of all of the opportunities open to the individual in the locus of opportunities surface. If we join the two mappings, we can see which of the available opportunities the individual will prefer. This will be the combination of goods represented by the point at which the locus of opportunities surface touches the highest (that is, most satisfactory) of the indifference surfaces with which it comes in contact. If the point be z_i, q_i, t_i, the individual will purchase quantity z_i of the composite good at price p_z, he will occupy q_i land at distance t_i from the center of the city, for which he pays a price $P(t_i)$, and he will spend $k(t_i)$ on commuting costs.

By examining carefully the shape of the indifference and of the locus of opportunities surfaces, it becomes clear that the point of equilibrium must lie within the portion of the locus of opportunities (Figure 5) bounded by the curves WX, XY, and YW. At the equilibrium point, the locus of opportunities and the indifference surface must be tangent to each other, since both are smooth surfaces touching at a point. Therefore the two surfaces must be parallel at that point. The indifference surface (see Figure 9) is shaped like a trough, and it moves up and away from the t-axis. The locus of opportunities, however, moves up and away from the t-axis only over the portion WXY. Therefore tangency between the curves and individual equilibrium are possible only in this section.

MATHEMATICAL SOLUTION OF INDIVIDUAL EQUILIBRIUM

The mathematical solution of individual equilibrium parallels the diagrammatic solution but is at once more general and more compact. We may start with the proposition that the individual has a given income, y, which he may spend as he pleases between z and q, after he pays the commuting costs $k(t)$ attendant to his location. This proposition is expressed in the *budget balance* equation

$$y = p_z z + P(t)q + k(t). \tag{1}$$

As before, we assume that we are given the price of the composite good p_z and the functions of the cost of land with distance, $P(t)$, and of commuting costs with distance, $k(t)$. The problem consists of finding the possible set of z, q, and t which both satisfies the budget balance equation (which corresponds to the locus of opportunities surface) and yields the individual the greatest satisfaction.

The satisfaction of the individual is given in the function

$$u = u(z, q, t), \tag{2}$$

called the utility function. Given a set of values z_0, q_0, t_0, we find u_0 by means of this function. For another set z_i, q_i, t_i, we would find u_i.

Then, if u_i is greater than u_0, we may say that the set z_i, q_i, t_i is preferable to the set z_0, q_0, t_0.[6]

The individual will try to maximize his satisfaction within the restraints of his income. In other words, the problem is to discover which combination z_i, q_i, t_i that satisfies the budget balance equation (1) yields the highest value for u in equation (2). This is done by differential calculus. Differentiating the utility function (2) we obtain

$$du = u_z dz + u_q dq + u_t dt.[7] \tag{3}$$

At the point at which satisfaction, u, is maximized, $du = 0$, so that

$$du = 0 = u_z dz + u_q dq + u_t dt. \tag{4}$$

According to the conditions of maximization for multivariable functions, we can hold all variables but two constant, and the sum of the partials times the differentials of the remaining two will still equal zero. Thus, if we hold t constant so that $dt = 0$, equation (4) becomes

$$du = 0 = u_z dz + u_q dq + 0. \tag{5}$$

Equation (5) may be rewritten as

$$-dz/dq = u_q/u_z. \tag{6}$$

If we hold q constant, so that $dq = 0$, from equation (4) we obtain

$$du = 0 = u_z dz + 0 + u_t dt. \tag{7}$$

Equation (7) may be rewritten as

$$-dz/dt = u_t/u_z. \tag{8}$$

Now we return to the budget balance equation (1). Differentiating we have

$$dy = y_z dz + y_q dq + y_P dP + y_k dk. \tag{9}$$

---

6. The reader is reminded that the values of u have only ordinal properties, and that they are equivalent to the naming (in some sequence) of the indifference surfaces.

7. For convenience in notation, as is frequently done, we shall denote the partial derivative of a function with respect to a variable by the name (letter) of that function with the variable as a subscript. Thus,

$$u_z = \partial u/\partial z; \quad u_q = \partial u/\partial q; \quad u_t = \partial u/\partial t.$$

But y is a given constant, so that $dy = 0$. As we have an explicit statement of the equation (1), we can find the partial derivatives. These are:

$$y_z = p_z; \ y_q = P(t); \ y_P = q; \ y_k = 1.$$

Substituting these into equation (9), we obtain

$$0 = p_z dz + P(t)q + q dP + dk. \tag{10}$$

We can solve for dP and dk in terms of dt by the differentials of $P(t)$ and $k(t)$, so that

$$dP = (dP/dt)dt \text{ and } dk = (dk/dt)dt.$$

Substituting these into equation (10), we have

$$0 = p_z dz + P(t)dq + q(dP/dt)dt + (dk/dt)dt,$$

which may be rewritten as

$$0 = p_z dz + P(t)dq + dt(q dP/dt + dk/dt). \tag{11}$$

Equation (11) is, of course, merely a rewriting of equation (9).

The rule that we may hold all variables but two constant applies to constants as well as maxima. Since y is a constant, from equation (11), holding first t and then a constant, we may say that

$$0 = p_z dz + P(t)q + 0,$$

and

$$0 = p_z dz + 0 + dt (q dP/dt + dk/dt).$$

These may be rewritten as

$$-dz/dq = P(t)/p_z, \tag{12}$$

$$-dz/dt = (q dP/dt + dk/dt)/P_z. \tag{13}$$

Combining equations (6) and (8) with equations (12) and (13), we obtain

$$u_q/u_z = P(t)/P_z \tag{14}$$

and

$$u_t/u_z = (q \, dP/dt + dk/dt)/P_z. \tag{15}$$

Equations (14) and (15), together with the budget balance equation (1), are three equations which, when solved simultaneously yield the individual's optimal combinations of the three unknowns, z, q, and t.[8] Finding these unknowns constitutes the solution of the individual's equilibrium.

Interpretation of the Mathematical Solution

The interpretation of the mathematical solution is the same as that of the diagrammatic solution, though it permits greater precision. The budget balance equation (1) requires no explanation, since we constructed it by definition. It corresponds to the locus of opportunities of the diagrammatic solution. However, equations (14) and (15) should be examined closely.

First, let us look at the relation between the utility function and the indifference surface. The indifference surface is the locus of all combinations of goods z, q, and t which yield the same satisfaction to the individual. In terms of the utility function this means that all these combinations of z, q, and t will yield the same value for u. The marginal rates of substitution between goods (the rate at which the individual is willing to exchange small quantities of one good for small quantities of another) are represented in the diagrammatic solution by the slope of the indifference surface. The slope is measured parallel to the plane defined by the axes of the two goods. In the mathematical solution, this slope (that is, the marginal rate of substitution) is represented by the ratio of the marginal utilities of the two goods. The marginal utility of a good is the partial derivative of utility, u, with respect to that good.

Returning now to equations (14) and (15), we note that the left-hand sides of the equations are marginal rates of substitution. The right-hand sides of the equations make statements about costs. As in the usual case in this type of analysis, these equations state that, at equilibrium, the marginal rate of substitution between two goods is equal to the ratio of their marginal costs. If they were not, the individual would not be at equilibrium since he could increase his satisfaction by acquiring more of the relatively cheaper good.

Equation (24) is very simple. It states that, at equilibrium, the marginal rate of substitution (u_q/u_z) between land (q) and all other

---

8. Strictly speaking, we do not have just three equations and three unknowns. We have seven unknowns: z, q, t, $P(t)$, dP/dt, $k(t)$, and dk/dt. The additional four equations are given by the stated functions $P(t)$ and $k(t)$ and their derivatives. This proliferation of unknowns and equations occurs if we regard the four additional unknowns as requiring numerical solution. If we view P, k, dP/dt, and dk/dt as functions in terms of t, then the three original equations are sufficient since we then have only three unknowns. The whole matter of the number of equations between three and seven depends on whether we count unknowns and equations before or after we have effected the substitutions for $P(t)$, $k(t)$, dP/dt, and dk/dt.

goods (z) is equal to the ratio of their prices, that is, their marginal costs.

Equation (15) is somewhat more complicated. It states that, at equilibrium, the marginal rate of substitution (u_t/u_z) between distance (t) and the composite good (z), is equal to $(q\,dP/dt + dk/dt)/p_z$. In the denominator we recognize p_z, the price and marginal cost of z. The numerator represents the marginal cost of spatial movement. It is the change in the price of land dP/dt (as it changes with distance) times the quantity of land, q, plus the change in commuting costs, dk/dt. Thus, once again the marginal rate of substitution is equal to the ratio of the marginal costs.

We had assumed that a near location was preferred to a distant one, since commuting is generally regarded as a nuisance. This means that u_t is a marginal disutility, and has negative utility; in short, that $u_t < 0$. But we had also assumed that increases in good z had a positive utility ($u_z < 0$), and implicitly, that $p_z > 0$. It follows, therefore, that the expression $q\,dP/dt + dk/dt$ must be smaller than zero for equation (15) to hold.

Let us examine this expression. We can expect that $dk/dt > 0$, since commuting costs increase with the distance traveled. The value of q, the quantity of land, can certainly be no less than zero. We must conclude that dP/dt is negative, for otherwise the expression would be positive. That is to say, the individual cannot arrive at equilibrium except on a negative stretch of the curve $P(t)$. If $P(t)$ were positively inclined — price of land increasing with distance from the center of the city — the individual would move toward the center, where he would get cheaper land and do less commuting.

There is a further conclusion. Since, for equilibrium, it is necessary that $(q\,dP/dt + dk/dt) < 0$, the individual will never settle where $-(q\,dP/dt) < dk/dt$. This is the same conclusion we arrived at diagrammatically, when we stated that the individual will only settle where the savings derived from cheaper land exceed increased commuting costs. This is the portion WXY of the locus of opportunities surface in Figure 5.

14

Integrating the Leading Theories of Plant Location

I

The theory of plant location has developed along two lines.[1] The first approach, which is largely Germanic in orgin,[2] emphasizes the search for the least-cost site by abstracting from demand. It assumes competitive pricing, different costs among locations, and a given buying center. In conformance with its purely competitive frame-work, an unlimited demand for the output of any firm exists at the prevailing price, and all sellers have access to the buying center.[3]

The second approach is an outgrowth of monopolistic competition analysis. In this theory, buyers are conceived to be scattered over an area rather than confined to a given consuming point. The cost of procuring and processing raw materials is assumed to be the same everywhere, and each seller charges an identical net-mill price leaving delivered price to vary with the distance between consumers and suppliers. Sellers, by dispersing, thus gain control over buyers situated near their plants. In this analysis, demand for the output of a firm is accepted as a variable factor governed by the location of competitors. The market area approach differs from the least-cost theory

1. A third type of theory may be contrasted with the two theories to be presented herein. This third approach would include the psychic income motive, as compared with the maximum pecuniary profit theories that are to be integrated herein. See Melvin L. Greenhut, "Observation of Motives to Plant Location," *Southern Economic Journal*, XVIII, pp. 225–228.
2. See Johann Heinrich von Thünen, *Der Isolierte Staat in Beziehung auf Landwirtschaft und Nationalökonomie*, 3rd ed., 1875; Alfred Weber, *Über den Standort des Industrien*, Part I, Reine Theorie des Standorts, 1909.
3. See Laurent Dechesnes, *La Localization des Diversés Productions*, 1945, p. 11. Dechesnes though indicating dissatisfaction with Weber's theoretical and mathematical presentation praises the fact that Weber pointed out the two fundamental factors in plant location: production cost and transportation cost.

But see August Lösch, *Die räumliche Ordnung der Wirtschaft*, 1944, who repeatedly criticizes Weber for disregarding the effects of location on demand and for assuming that each firm could sell its entire output at the given price. See pp. 11, 17, 18, 185.

The author wishes to acknowledge his indebtedness to the Research Foundation of the Alabama Poltytechnic Institute for a grant and encouragement.

Reprinted from the Southern Economic Journal, *18 (July 1951–April 1952), pp. 526–38, by permission of the publishers and the author.*

because it emphasizes the control over specific buyers that is offered by locations in a space economy.[4]

The present paper correlates these two approaches. It presents an integrated exposition whereby both cost and demand influences are revealed as co-determinants of location. The objective is sought first by briefly examining the Weberian framework. The purpose of this investigation is to ascertain whether Weber's system excludes spatial inter-relations or whether it is fully adaptable to a cost and locational monopoly pattern. Second, the analysis proceeds within a market area type of exposition. This study points out the inadequacy of a special or particular approach by illustrating the fallacy of a one-sided location theory; further, it shows how the Weber locational framework can be included within a model normally used for market area analysis.

II

It is manifest that Weber's system excludes monopolistic locational advantages only under his given price (purely competitive) assumption; without it, Weber's framework can be made to include some monopolistic aspects. Thus, with price a variable, the entrepreneur at the least-cost site can undersell his rivals and drive them out of the market; his location thereby offers monopolistic advantages. It is, however, equally manifest that this broader Weberian framework (each firm influences and controls price to some extent) is inadequate: (1) There is no reason for locating at other than the least-cost location;[5] the seller at this site can undersell his rivals and force them out,[6] same where the market demand is so much greater than the possible supply of this firm as to offer profitable entry for additional competitors. (2) It does not show the locational monopolistic gains where the market demand for the output of a firm is so much in excess of plant capacity (managerial capabilities) as to offer profitable entry for other firms. This shortcoming is the result of Weber's assumption of a point-formed buying center, an hypothesis which fails to reflect the fact that each seller is a locational monopolist to some degree, regardless of numbers and homogeneity of products. Weber's presupposition of a given buying center rather than a market area necessitates this result, for the firm which is at *the* least-cost site monopolizes all

4. See Arthur F. Smithies, "Optimum Location in Spatial Competition," *Journal of Political Economy*, XLIX, 1941, pp. 423–439 [Selection 7 of this volume], for a leading article on the monopolistic aspects of plant location.

5. As will be shown later, a high-cost location may offer greatest profits.

6. The duopolist and oligopolist can become monopolists; the monopolistic competitor adds to his monopoly controls.

buyers, *if* other firms are forced to locate at higher cost sites, and *if* managerial limitations and diseconomies are not so pronounced as to permit competition from rivals. Reversing this last assumption suggests an opening for other competitors and thus a return to Weber's purely competitive assumptions. Such reversal points to an unlimited market for each firm, and it indicates a temporary situation where the firm at the least-cost site gains more by raising price than by lowering it.[7] (3) The broader Weberian framework is exclusive of locational inter-relationships. For, if the seller at the least-cost site is unable to satisfy the demand, future sellers would seek the next available least-cost site; their choice of location would be independent of the presence of rivals. Because, in the real world, a firm generally sells, at least to some extent, over a market area; a framework that is completely limited to a single buying point must be deficient. Market area models have the advantage of displaying spatial interdependence as well as of being able to suggest probable locations where majority sales are made to one buying center, with some sales extending over an area,[8] and vice versa.[9]

III

Assume the following conditions:

1. Buyers scattered equally between P and O' (Figure 1).

2. Freight rates proportional to distance.[10]

7. The above discussion of open entry suggests the case where rivals may enter a market because of differentiation of products rather than because of managerial limitations and/or diseconomies of scale. In this event, the firm at the least-cost site acquires locational monopolistic advantages through its ability to undersell rivals; it reaps a gain from lower cost and high cross-elasticities in demand; and accordingly, its location offers control over some buyers. Weber's system meets the test of "monopolistic gains through location" when open entry is due to heterogeneity.

8. There are some market situations in which firms sell almost entirely to one buying center. In these cases either the broader or purely competitive Weberian framework may be quite adaptable. But just as the weight of present day opinion appears ready to discard marginal utility analysis, so too, the Weberian locational triangles should be dropped if a broader type of model is available which may include them as well as other situations.

9. It is significant to note that the market area-interdependence system suffers a minor deficiency; it requires an assumption of standardized products. To admit product differentiation weakens the generality of the theory, for such fact permits overlapping in market areas. This shortcoming does not irreparably damage the market area-interdependence system; it merely modifies the precise conclusions deduced from this theory.

10. In order to achieve complete realism, the arms of the Y (which illustrate the freight rate in market area diagrams) should be made jagged and/or curved. But this type of pictorial representation is quite unnecessary. There is no reason why the general conclusions arising from an assumption of rates proportional to distance should not

3. The freight rate on the raw material and/or the finished product is fixed; it does not vary with the quantity transported. (This assumption is maintained throughout the article.)

4. Freight cost on procuring each unit of raw material exceeds the cost of distributing each unit of final product.

5. The cost of the raw material is constant; it does not vary with the amount of materials purchased. (This assumption is maintained throughout the article.)

6. Marginal and average costs of processing the raw material are zero.[11]

7. Demand is the same for all buyers. The demand curve is of the straight line variety, which decreases in elasticity as price is lowered. (This assumption is maintained throughout the article).

8. Sales are f.o.b. mill and are non-discriminatory. (This assumption is maintained throughout the article.)

9. The source of the materials is linearly west of the market; it is found at point O (Figure 1).

10. Sales advantages are cost advantages; there are no special gains derived by locating proximate to the consumer.

In Figure 1 the dotted line XZ represents cost of shipping the raw material. The stright lines CD and BE are the costs of transporting the finished product from sites A and A'. A location east of A, for example A', is less profitable than the site at A. The firm will locate at or near the source of materials depending upon availability of sites.

If now the fortuitous assumptions of zero marginal and average costs of production are relaxed, it may be hypothesized in their stead that such costs are constant and positive at any location. Let it be further assumed that these production costs vary at the different locations, decreasing generally as distance from the material source increases. More specifically, any point on the ST curve (Figure 2) represents the level of marginal and average costs existing at the particular location represented by that point. This level of costs is applicable for all outputs. (See RQ, $R'Q'$ and $M'Q''$, Figure 2). AR

---

apply to a more complicated world. Accordingly, this unrealistic assumption (freight rates proportional to distance), being methodologically cleaner, will be maintained throughout the article.

11. The cost of the raw materials is included in the cost of producing the material in the first model (see OXZ, Figure 1).

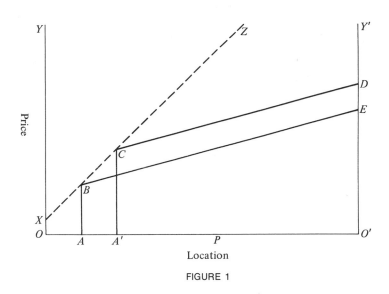

Location

FIGURE 1

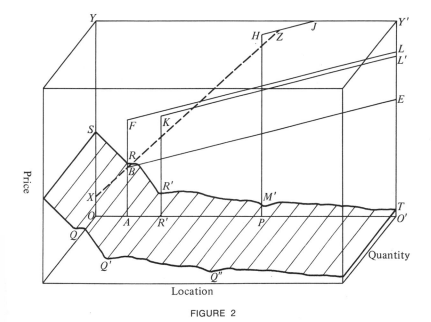

Location

FIGURE 2

is therefore the marginal cost of production at A.[12] BE, as in Figure 1, represents the slope of the distribution cost, while XZ is the freight rate on the raw material; FL is then the composite sum of the procurement; distribution, and marginal costs per unit of product for a plant located at A, while KL' and HJ represent the same summations at A' and P, respectively. Again, the pull of materials is dominant, though modified somewhat by the difference in the costs of the variable agents of production at the alternative sites.

If now the cost of the material and its procurement is included in marginal cost, and the single seller charges the monopoly price less freight absorption on the finished product, Figure 2 can be transposed into Figure 3.[13]

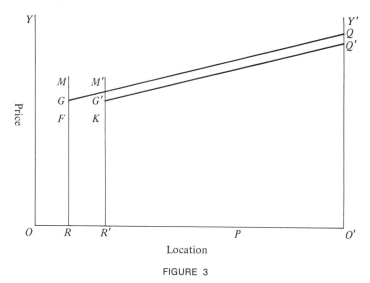

FIGURE 3

Let AF represent the marginal cost at A; and $A'K$ the same cost at A'.[14] AG is the price at A, while AM is the monopoly price that

12. Marginal and average costs, as used in this model, do not include cost of raw material, but consist only of labor and other variable costs; the cost of raw materials is included in the cost of procuring these materials, which is shown separately (see OXZ). Fixed costs are assumed to be zero everywhere, and this assumption will not be relaxed in later models. Though rents, taxes, *etc.*, differ generally in a real world, such variations are unnecessary complications for the principles sought in this article.

13. The costs of location P and the third dimension used in Figure 2 are dropped in Figure 3.

14. Including the delivered cost of materials with other variable costs does not affect the constant nature of the marginal costs at A and A'; but it does affect the height of these costs. Now they are greater at A' than at A (cf. AR and $A'R'$, Figure 2, with $A'K$, Figure 3). This reversal is due to the cheaper cost of obtaining the material at A, a fact which obscures the greater "inefficiencies" of production at this location.

would have been charged in the absence of freight cost on the final product. Correspondingly, $A'M'$ is the monopoly price at A', and $A'G'$ the monopoly price less freight absorption. GQ and $G'Q'$ are the respective f.o.b. mill prices plus transport costs to the different buyers. As in the prior model, the delivered prices from A' are less than those from A; sales are therefore greater at each point in the market and profits enhanced.

In traditional economic theory, average cost is regarded as the summation of the average variable and average fixed cost. But to the buyer of merchandise, who is located at a distance from the seller, average cost of production is supplemented by the delivery charges on the finished goods. In the final analysis, the sum of the procurement, processing, and distribution costs determine the plant location, *ceteris paribus*.

Weber's assumption that the demand for the product of a firm is formed at a point and that it is independent of the seller's location fulfills the *ceteris paribus* condition mentioned above. In effect, it enables the same type of abstraction from space as has marked the general economic theory. Both the least-cost theory of plant location and the classical economic theory of value consider the market (buyers) as if it (they) were concentrated at a single point. Realistically, however, sales are made over an area which varies in size as rivals enter or leave. It follows that the spatial concept of the least-cost location must include the demand curve, the magnitude of which varies among locations; otherwise expressed, the number of buyers and/or dollar value of sales potential increase or decrease as location is changed. These factors are variables in spatial analysis; which, by considering sales receipts, offers in the place of Weber's least-cost location, the maximum-profit or *real* least-cost location.

The maximum-profit location (*real* least-cost location) is that site at which the spread between total receipts and total costs is the greatest. This location is not necessarily at the place where the commodity can be produced at the lowest possible cost, inclusive of freight on the finished product to a given point m miles from the seller's factory. In fact, considering all practical size plants, the minimum point on the average cost curve (including freight on the final product over m distance) at the maximum-profit location may be in excess of the lowest cost of producing (and shipping) the product elsewhere. The significant comparison lies in the fact that the sales output which maximizes profits at the most profitable site cannot be duplicated elsewhere, except at higher total cost (including freight on the final product). By definition the maximum-profit location (*real* least-cost location) is that site from which a given number of buyers (whose purchases are required for the greatest possible profits) can be served at the lowest total cost.[15] This concept, which may include spatial implications, is indeed a broad inclusion. It is shown diagrammatically in Figure 4.

The abscissa, in this figure, represents distance from any factory "to a given number of buyers and/or sales receipts." The delivered

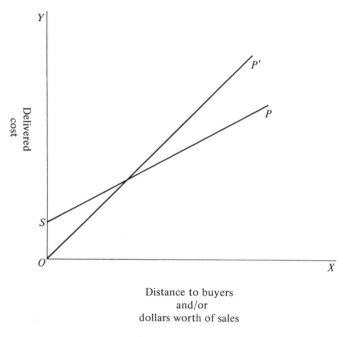

Distance to buyers
and/or
dollars worth of sales

FIGURE 4

15. While Weber's least-cost location fits the above definition, it completely fails to convey spatial implications. (See Section II.) For example, the minimum point on the average cost curve of the firm at Weber's least-cost location may be in excess of the least-cost combination elsewhere. But, (1) the greater amount of sales obtained by the firm at Weber's optimum location (which quantity makes it the most profitable location and hence the least-cost location at this output) is due to the equation between marginal cost and average revenue; the greater amount of sales obtained by the firm at the maximum-profit location may be due to a more profitable average revenue curve, which is, itself, an expression of the larger market area served by the firm at the maximum-profit location. This firm equates marginal cost with marginal revenue; (2) Weber's least-cost location meets the definition of the maximum-profit location only under the assumption that one site suffers diseconomies of scale at such a very small output that another site may yield greater profits at a larger output, thus being the least-cost location at that output. And while Weber's agglomerating advantages (especially economies of scale) impart validity to this idea, his framework limits the unity between the least-cost location and the maximum-profit location to such types of factor advantage. The maximum-profit location is not limited in this regard; it may also offer savings in freight cost to *more distant* buyers. A precise definition of Weber's least-cost location must emphasize the cost of procuring, processing, and distributing goods to a *given* buying point.

cost from the factory is shown on the ordinate. *SP* represents the delivered cost from a factory at the maximum-profit location; *OP′* is the delivered cost to buyers from a factory not so favorably situated.[16] Broadly speaking, the maximum-profit location may be the one where the total cost to buyers, who are located *m* distance from the factory, exceeds the like cost from another location, but which cost, for example, per thousand buyers and/or per thousand dollars worth of sales, is less than that offered by other locations. Shipments by eastern manufacturers to west coast buyers via Panama canal, as compared with the all rail transport to these buyers from mid-western sites, illustrates the idea.

This definition of least cost is all inclusive. Not only are the transfer charges on final goods considered, but also, the presence of competitors is inherently included. This fact may be clearly seen by the following thought.

In the absence of competitors, more buyers may be serviced within a given distance from the factory than if there were competing rivals seeking sales to the same buyers. It follows that if B locates subsequent to A and does so at the same place as A, more (sufficient) sales at lower costs are generally expected. Any other location is less favorable. Should B, on the other hand, locate elsewhere, the antithesis to the above expectation is generally the case. From the standpoint of the locating firm, minimum cost of production is not the objective; nor for that matter is lowest total cost including transport charges to a point *m* miles from the factory; rather, minimum total cost, as compared to sales, is the desired end. The maximum-profit (*real* least-cost) location fulfills this objective.

IV

Following in the line of tradition set by von Thünen and Weber, the least-cost approach has stressed such problems as the respective pulls of the material and market, the influence of labor, taxes, *etc.*, on the plant location. Under the influence of Hotelling, other writers have emphasized the demand and competitive side of plant location. In a sense, the least-cost school has been concerned predominantly with the location of any concern as governed by costs. The interdependence school of thought takes up from that point; it seeks to

16. The delivered cost includes the average cost of producing a unit of goods plus the freight cost on delivering this unit to the consumer. The increasing separation between *SP* and *OP′* (to the right of the intersection) may be explained as follows: (1) different modes of transport, or (2) different freight rate systems, and/or (3) different numbers of buyers.

explain the conditions under which firms, within a given region, will be mutually repulsed or attracted in their search for maximum demand. These divergent approaches, as commonly interpreted,[17] can be subjected to diagrammatic analyses. Figure 5 illustrates the lack of correlation between these two approaches.

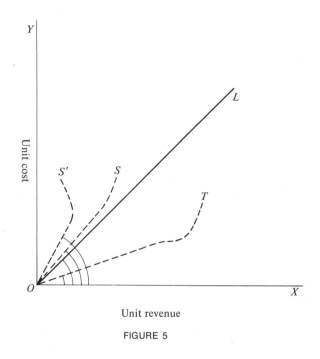

FIGURE 5

Let the OY axis represent unit cost of production and distribution at different locations. As used here, unit cost is the average cost of transporting a unit of raw material and manufactured goods m miles,[18] plus the average cost of processing the material. It is further assumed

17. See S. Weintraub, *Price Theory*, 1949, p. 287. Professor Weintraub expresses the view that Hoover's *Location of Economic Activity* narrows the gap between the literature on spatial competition and the theory of industrial location. The only way of interpreting this remark is to presume that the writer accepts the Weber type of analysis on plant locations as a simple least-cost presentation, while Hoover's presentation is regarded as a *real* least-cost theory. In other words, Weintraub considers Weber's least-cost location to be the site from which goods may be delivered to the given buying center at the lowest cost. But Hoover's least-cost location is apparently regarded in the same sense as my definition of the maximum-profit (*real* least-cost) location. This interpretation follows naturally the difference between Weber's assumption of buyers located at a point and Hoover's discussion of market areas.

18. It is assumed that there is one source of supply and one consuming center, both of which are situated at different points in a linear market. See Stephen Enke, "Space and Value," *Journal of Political Economy*, XLVI (1942), pp. 627–637, 629–630, wherein he describes the case of consumers situated at a given point.

that there are no economies or diseconomies of scale, and, in fact, that regardless of location, only a given output can be produced and sold.[19] It follows that any movement upward from the origin indicates an increase in unit cost of production plus unit cost of procurement and distribution. Under the "simple" approach to least-cost locations, such movement away from zero indicates a failure to locate in accordance with material, market, labor pulls, and other cost factors. Seemingly, it would be non-economic.

The abscissa is termed the unit revenue. Any movement to the right from the origin signifies an increase in unit receipts, or, in other words, a higher net-mill price.[20] The ordinate is in accord with the simple concept of the least-cost location; the abscissa, in turn, suggests locational interdependence.[21]

The OL curve in Figure 5 is drawn at a 45 degree angle, ($\ominus$). It is the line of indifference. Any movement along this line increases unit revenue and unit cost by the same amount.

The OT curve is positive in slopes; its angle $\varnothing$ is less than angle $\ominus$. Unit revenue increases more than unit cost at many locations[22] on this curve.[23] It follows that the curve OT represents a series of locations where gains can be reaped at higher-cost sites. The unit cost of producing the commodity and of procuring and distributing it m miles is greater at sites to the right of O than at O; nevertheless, profits are enhanced.[24]

This illustration represents the special case where a firm could have located at a point of lower costs, with respect to customers at a given distance away from the seller's plant, but in considering the aggregate demands, profitably moved elsewhere. The location

---

19. Demand is thus conceived to be infinitely inelastic.

20. In order to make location and price fully comparable, it is assumed that the mill which charges a higher net price delivers at a higher total price to the same group of buyers as the mill which quotes the lower net price. The higher net-mill price is the result of contact advantages, such as speed of service; the buyers' demand for the product of a firm strengthens or weakens as the seller shifts his location.

21. A full representation of location interdependence requires more than a mere display of contact advantages. It would have to show a demand curve which shifts to the left or right with a change in the seller's location. Under this broad representation, the simplifying assumption of given production and sales, as well as the hypothesis of point forming supply and consumption centers, would have to be discarded. In turn, a more complicated analytical device, framed in a total cost and total revenue pattern, would be required. See Enke, *op. cit.*, p. 630, wherein he discusses the case of spatial separation of buyers (several consuming points), and see Lösch, *op. cit.*, p. 14, wherein he states that sales (quantity taken times unit price) may vary with location, and, therefore, cost is not the sole determinant.

22. Indicated by any point on this curve.

23. The site of greatest profit is the point of least slope on the OT curve.

24. The OS and OS' curves, in Figure 5, represent the cases where the only feasible location is the one of least cost.

decision as ultimately viewed therefore involves a balance between access to buyers and net-mill cost.[25]

The definition of the maximum-profit location may be further illustrated by the pictorial device used earlier in this article. This type of representation (Figure 6) shows locational interdependence.

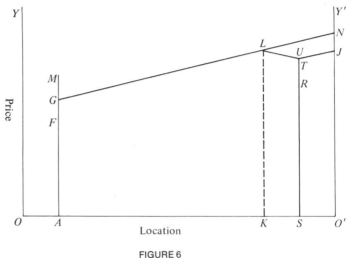

FIGURE 6

It assumes that there are several sellers at the least-cost site, and that the buying market extends from A to O'. AF represents the marginal cost of the several sellers at A; AG is the price charged by each of these sellers; and AM is the price that would have existed if all buyers were located at A. The demand curve at the buyer's factory is a straight line decreasing in elasticity. The demand of the buyer, as it appears to

25. It might be observed that the difficulty in the use of the term least cost is a typical illustration of the effect of spatial concepts in the oftentimes non-spatial world of economic theory. In the absence of freight, least cost refers to the lowest average cost of production. But as soon as freight cost becomes an element of price, the least-cost location changes its meaning; it then refers to the place from which total delivered-to-customers cost is least, given equal sales receipts for all firms.

Besides causing terminological difficulties, the concept of space requires different assumptions than those used in non-spatial economics. For example, the cost theory of location requires an abstraction from demand. This need is met by assuming a constant demand at point-formed consuming centers; an assumption which is, itself, an abstraction from space. The interdependence theory, on the other hand, emphasizes the factor (demand) assumed away by writers who are primarily interested in other location determinants. (See H. Hotelling, "Stability in Competition," *Economic Journal*, XXXIX (1929), pp. 41–57 [Selection 6 of this volume], A. P. Lerner and H. W. Singer, "Some Notes on Duopoly and Spatial Competition," *Journal of Political Economy*, XLV, pp. 145–186; A. Smithies, *op. cit.*; M. Copeland, "Competing Products and Monopolistic Competition," *Quarterly Journal of Economics*, LV (1940–41), pp. 1–35. Each of these writers assumes a different type of demand curve; each derives a different location for a firm seeking maximum profits.)

the seller under an f.o.b. mill delivery, is the same demand curve reduced in size by freight cost. Each seller has divided the market equally.[26]

GN (Figure 6) represents cost of transporting the finished product from A. Assume further that at location S, marginal costs are equal to SR, price is ST, and price in the absence of freight would have been SU. Delivered price is TJ, TL. The location at S may prove more profitable than a location at A.

It is worthy of note that this type of pictorial representation may include Weber's special case of plant location. Thus, if the market were assumed to be formed at a point, for example at O' in Figure 6, the Weber least-cost site would be at S. This figure also has the advantage of admitting locational interdependence into the conceptual picture. For, if it is assumed that two rivals are considering a location in the K-O' region, it can be shown that one may locate slightly east of S and the other at a somewhat greater distance to the west of S.[27]

26. In Figure F-1, two sellers have anticipated the entire market demand to be YD. As divided equally, each one regards YB as the demand for his product. Subtracting

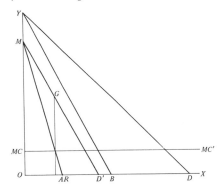

FIGURE F-1

average transport costs over half the length of the buying market (AO', Figure 6) leaves the net demand for each seller's product. Thus the average revenue curve at the seller's factory is equal to MD'. Marginal revenue for each seller is shown by MR; AG is the price which maximizes profits.

See Weintraub, *op. cit.*, pp. 161, 162, where in discussing and diagramming Cournot's duopoly, it is stated that the relevant demand curve for the second firm is derived by subtracting laterally the influence of the first from the total market demand curve.

Under monopolistic assumptions (as in the present model) this procedure cannot be followed; the height of the ordinate must remain the same. The only way of showing the presence of a competitor in this type of case is by a westerly movement along the abscissa.

27. Under the assumptions of (1) an identical straight line demand curve of negative slope for all buyers, (2) non-discriminatory f.o.b. mill pricing, (3) equal freight rates at all locations, (4) equal and constant marginal costs of production at all locations, and (5) perfect knowledge, two firms would seek the first and third quartile locations in respect to the K-O' market. (See Smithies, *op. cit.*, pp. 429–432).

Site-selection of firms depends largely upon freight rates, the shape of the marginal cost curves, the competitive history of the firms, the elasticity of demand for the product, and the respective conjectures on cost at alternative locations.

V

The analysis presented in this paper leads to the conclusion that the theories of the least-cost location and the interdependent location are, despite their differences, quite similar; both emphasize the search for the site which offers the greatest spread between total costs and total revenues. It is really the assumptions that differ.[28] Though Weber explicitly ignores spatial inter-relationships of demand, it is nevertheless the case that this factor is *inherent* to his system. Any producer, in deriving his least-cost location, must choose first among buying centers.[29] The determination of the best consumption point (area) involves the concept of demand, or otherwise expressed, it is the location of competitors which predetermines price and sales at any buying point for any firm. In this sense, both schools are concerned with a given dollar volume of sales at least cost. Location in the backyard of rivals is therefore self explained; more customers, or the same number of customers (assuming all buyers have identical demands), can be served at price P and cost X than is possible from any other location. From this standpoint, the finding of the least-cost theory matches the conclusion of the interdependence theory of location. They both may over-exaggerate the importance of the site offering greatest profit potential. Considerations other than maximum profit potential guide some plant locations.[36]

28. The concept of the market area is the force which leads the Hotelling school into the problem of demand and spatial interdependence. The assumptions of given price and buyers concentrated at a point enable the Weberian disregard of sales and interdependence as location factors.

29. It should be pointed out at this time that the buying center which promises greatest profits is not always the one selected. See M. Greenhut, *op. cit.*, pp. 226–227, case study five, where the principle of the minimax, as related to psychic income, guided the selection of the market area.

30. See Greenhut, *loc. cit.*, for empirical findings supporting this view; and see von Neumann and Morgenstern, *The Theory of Games and Economic Behavior*, 1947, pp. 94, 95; Jacob Marschak, "Rational Behavior, Uncertain Prospects, and Measurable Utility," *Econometrica*, XVIII (1950), pp. 111–141, 139; A. Alchian, "Uncertainty, Evolution, and Economic Theory," *Journal of Political Economy*, LVIII (1950), pp. 211–221, 213, for theoretical discussions which emphasize the importance of considerations other than maximum profits.

15

The Equilibrium of Land-Use Patterns in Agriculture

Starting with Thünen, a number of writers have presented systems for describing the spatial equilibrium of agricultural production. All of these schemes have been deficient or incomplete in one respect or another. The purpose of this article is to integrate and extend the disparate elements of such a location theory.

An effort will be made to define an explicit distance-rent function. Using this function, location will be pictured as a result of the ration maximization process. In the conventional statement of the firm equilibrium profit is maximized. In the equilibrium statement that follows, it is rent arising from the advantage of position that is maximized. The solution is worked out in a multiple-product economy and, in the process, the conditions that give rise to zonal production and the conditions for entry are made explicit. The whole space system is enlarged at the end with the consideration of demand and the mutually interdependent price system. There follows an attempt to illustrate and summarize the nature of the space-price equilibrium under simplified conditions and by means of simple equations. No effort is made to introduce modifying and complicating factors into the analysis.

DEFINITION OF TERMS

The lead of Thünen is followed by recognizing that the controlling factor in the determination of land-use is land rent. That form of land-use which provides the greatest rent will make the highest bid for the land and hence displace all others. The following formula expresses as a function of distance the additions to total land rent made by each new unit of the land devoted to the cultivation of a single commodity as the distance from the market is increased.[1]

$$R = E(p-a) - Efk \qquad (1)$$

1. If the previous theorists in the field of agricultural location have been guilty of a common weakness it is their failure to develop an explicit distance function.

Reprinted from the Southern Economic Journal, 21 (July 1954–April 1955), pp. 173–87, by permission of the publishers and the author.

The variables are classified as follows:

Dependent Variable
    R = rent per unit of land

Independent Variable
    k = distance

Constants or Parameters
    E = yield per unit of land
    p = market price per unit of commodity[2]
    a = production cost per unit of commodity
    f = transport rate per unit of distance for each commodity.

This explicit statement of a distance-rent function brings several points to our attention. The present analysis conceives of the *industry*[3] as the maximizing unit.[4] This does not mean that the traditional firm equilibrium is unimportant. It merely means that it is subordinated in order to simplify the statement and highlight the essential characteristics of the space-price equilibrium. Nor does it mean that rent maximization conceived and described on an industry level is inconsistent with profit maximization on the firm level. It is the effort of competing firms to maximize profits that establishes the level of rent for any given land use.

In order to subordinate the substitution problems characteristic of the firm equilibrium, it is necessary to make certain simplifying assumptions. (1) *We assume perfect mobility and divisibility of all factors other than land (i.e., returns to scale are constant).* (2) *We assume undifferentiated resources over space so that yield (E) is everywhere the same.* (3) *The supply of factors is adequate for all production and is available at constant prices.* These three assumptions make it possible to assume that the cost of production per unit (a) is constant at any distance from the market. We recognize, of course, that E, a and f typically bear some functional relationship to distance in a realistic case. To analyse the character of this relationship necessitates a detailed analysis of the

2. Under conditions of competition p will naturally be considered as a parameter by the groups of firms that make up each industry.

3. In this paper the term *industry* is used primarily to designate a level of aggregation that abstracts from the substitution problems of the firm. More specifically, it is a group of firms (or farms) producing a single farm product, or, later, a group of firms producing a similar combination of farm products by a similar process.

4. In so far as there has been developed for agriculture an articulate theory of location, it has been almost exclusively on an industry level of analysis as distinct from the theory of the firm. This may be due in part to the fact that this level of analysis shows some promise for handling a range of problems that is considered significant for social policy. Attention is instinctively focused upon the competition of production systems for the use of the land. More important is the fact that this amount of aggregation of the variables offers an attractive degree of theoretical simplification. At the outset we intend to maintain this convention.

theory of the firm. Thus it is simpler at the outset to consider them as parameters. The essential character of the spatial orientation of products on an industry level is not significantly modified by this simplification.

It is worth emphasizing that in the statement that follows the hypothetical production unit (the industry) is concerned with maximizing rent and not profits. It is because of this factor that the present system considers space or distance explicitly. The production problem is not one of adjusting output to a marginal revenue line, but one of adjusting the spatial location of production to a marginal rent line. Rent in this case cannot be stated as a function of output. Rather it must be expressed as a function of distance from the market. Hence the explicit consideration of space.

With the marginal rent function written in the form of equation (1) and with the assumptions implicit in the designation of the parameters, it becomes plain that the formula describes a linear functional relationship between the two variables, distance and rent. This is graphically presented in Figure 1.

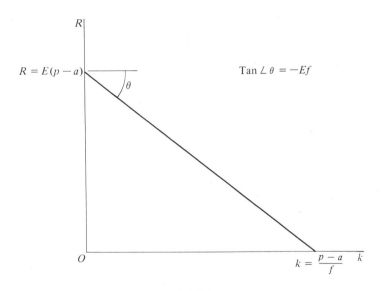

FIGURE 1

The R-intercept tells us that a unit of land producing at the market will derive a rent equal to the yield times the net receipts per unit. The slope reveals that, as we leave the market the maximum addition to total land rent per unit of land, $E(p-a)$, is diminished for each unit of distance at a rate equal to the product of the yield and freight rate. The rent is entirely absorbed at the k-intercept where $k = (p-a)/f$.

LOCATION AS A RESULT OF THE RATIONAL MAXIMIZATION PROCESS

The motive force which lies behind the determination of production location in agriculture is the same as that which lies behind the equilibrium of all economic forces—namely, the maximization of economic return. In the equilibrium statement that follows rent arising from the advantage of position is maximized.

Maximization Solution for One Product

Consider the mechanics of the solution portrayed in Figure 1. We see that the sloping rent line which has been plotted may be interpreted as a marginal rent line for an industry producing this product. For any value of k it tells the rent that will be derived from the infinitesimal unit of land at that distance from the market. Thus, as the industry expands its production by placing into cultivation more distant land (i.e., as we increase the value of k), this line tells us the amount that will be added to total rent by each successive unit of land—in short, the marginal increment.[5] In this case the variable plotted along the horizontal axis is distance, not output, and we ignore for the moment the influence of the correlated output upon price. Since rent is expressed net of production costs, we recognize the horizontal base line (Ok, Figure 1) to be the marginal cost line. The solution that maximizes economic gain is where marginal rent equals marginal cost [i.e., where $k = (p - a)/f$].

Maximization Solution for Two Products

Equilibrium Conditions Extend the same kind of solution to the case where there are two industries producing two products. Such a case is presented in Figure 2.

Consider first the maximization problem of industry I.

The marginal rent of this industry is represented by AB. However,

5. An acute observer might point out that the formula given for marginal rent is the derivative of the area under the curve in Figure 1. Since production will be extended in every direction away from the market, the *total* rent derived from the production of any crop must equal, not the area under the curve but the volume of a solid cone of revolution. The true marginal, rent, therefore, will be the derivative of this volume and not of the aforementioned area. The first derivative of this function, however, corresponds to equation I multiplied by a factor of proportionality, $2\pi k$. Since this factor makes the marginal rent function a quadratic and since it is always divided out in the important operations like determining product boundaries and equilibrium conditions, we have chosen to use the simpler form. It can be demonstrated mathematically to give the same results.

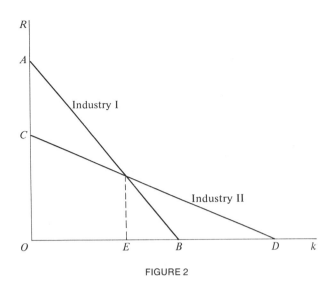

FIGURE 2

industry II can produce over the same region at a marginal rent represented by *CD*. Since the increment of rent for each unit of land for industry I is greater than for industry II near the market, industry I will produce near the market. However, the rent yielding potential of industry II over the same area represents an alternative use of the land. This alternative can be thought of as an opportunity cost for industry I. Thus, we see that *CD* is a new constraint for industry I (in contrast to $R = 0$ in the one-product case). Industry I will consequently extend its production spatially until its marginal rent equals marginal (opportunity) cost, both expressed as a function of distance. This determines the spatial limit of product I at *E* in Figure 2.

The equilibrium solution for industry II presents a new problem. Since industry II has been outbid for the use of the land near the market, it has two margins to consider. Spatial location in our scheme is measured in terms of radial distance from the market. There is in this case, therefore, both an inner and outer limit to establish. In Figure 2 both industry I and industry II can produce with profit over the area *OB*. (We speak of areas because we are really concerned with the entire ring determined by these radial distances.) Over part of this area industry II yields the larger return. It will extend its production toward the market until its marginal rent, *CD*, equals *AB* — which now represents marginal cost for industry II. The limit of this extension is *E* and this establishes the inner limit of production of product II. The outer limit for industry II duplicates the equilibrium for the one-product case. It is established where marginal rent, *CD*, equals marginal cost — i.e., the base line *Ok*.

Conditions for Ring Formation Before we consider more than two products or industries, let us examine the conditions that are necessary for rings to be established in the two-product case. Since these marginal rent lines are, under the present assumptions, linear distance functions, an examination of these functions should give us some information.

If we examine Figure 3a we can readily make one generalization. In order for ring formation to develop, the marginal rent functions must cross. One way of expressing this condition is to say that one industry must have a steeper negative slope $(-E_1f_1 < -E_2f_2)$ at the same time that its R-intercept is greater than the R-intercept of the second industry $[E_1(p_1 - a_1) > E_2(p_2 - a_2)]$.[6] By the same token, Figure 3b reveals that if an industry has a smaller negative slope when its R-intercept is greater, or has a larger negative slope when its R-intercept is smaller, no ring formation will result. In the former case the industry will be dominant, and in the latter case the industry will be excluded. In short, the rent functions must cross in the positive quadrant.

3a.   3b.

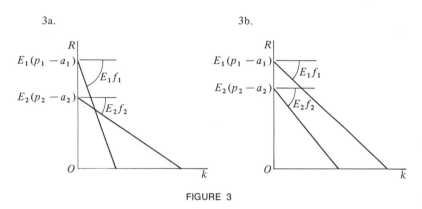

FIGURE 3

These conditions for ring formation reveal the logic of crop transition in its simplest form. At the market one industry (industry I in Figure 3a) will yield a greater rent return than the other and will be produced there to the exclusion of the other. However, the superiority of product I is lost with distance because the freight charges (E_1f_1) reduce this superior rent yield more rapidly per unit distance than is the case for product II. If this does not happen (as in Figure 3b) then product I dominates the entire area.

Summary statements about the logic of crop transition seem to

---

6. Or, conversely, one industry must have a smaller negative slope at the same time that its R-intercept is smaller than the R-intercept of the second industry. This amounts to the same thing since it depends on the order in which the industries are numbered.

have been the favorite sport of earlier writers in the field. For example, it is an often cited Thünen generalization that products whose transport costs are high relative to value will be produced closest to the market.[7] Even if we assume that transport rates are identical so that transport costs are proportional to weight and volume, it does not follow that the product for which the transport cost forms the largest percentage of value will be located closest to the market. Examine Figure 3a. It cannot be established that the transport cost should form a larger percentage of the net value at the market for product I than for product II. Further, when one takes into account the change in transport costs over distance we see that they may form varying percentages of the net market value depending upon the distance from the market.

Again, Brinkman and Lösch both claim that products with the highest yield per acre would be produced closest to the market.[8] It is plain from the previous exposition that a product with high market price and transport rate might occupy the favored market position even though its yield in terms of transport units was less than some other product.

Multiple Product Solution

Equilibrium Conditions   Consider next the equilibrium solution for any number of products or industries. The technical conditions of production and the state of our knowledge establish a large number of products or agricultural industries that are technically, if not economically, feasible. These we shall designate I_1, $I_2, \ldots I_n$. Each of these industries has a marginal rent function of the type we have been discussing, $R_1, R_2, \ldots R_n$. We number these industries in the order of decreasing slopes of their marginal rent functions.

It is a simple matter to make a generalized statement about the spatial equilibrium for any industry. Take I_3 in Figure 4 to represent any industry, I_r. This industry will extend its production toward the market as long as it has an advantage over the best alternative (in this case I_2). This establishes the inner boundary which we designate as k_{ri} (rth industry, inner limit). At the same time it extends its production

7. Johann Heinrich von Thünen, *Recherches sur l'influence que le prix des grains la richesse du sol et les impots excerent sur les systems de culture*, translated from German by M. Jules Laverriere (Paris: Guillaumin et Cie, Libraries, 1851), p. 2.

8. Theodor Brinkman, *Economics of the Farm Business*, English edition translated by Elisabeth Benedict (Berkeley: University of California Press, 1935), p. 89. August Lösch, *Die raumliche Ordnung der Wirtschaft* (second edition, Jena: Verlag Gustav Fisher, 1944), p. 29.

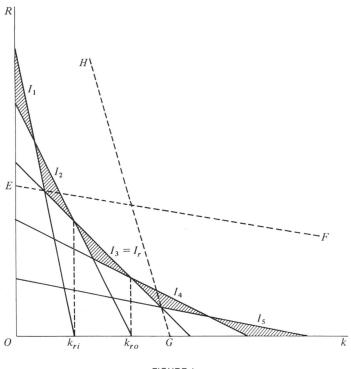

FIGURE 4

away from the market as long as its marginal rent is higher than marginal opportunity cost (in this case I_4). This establishes the outer limit, k_{ro}. On the strength of this we can make a summary statement. The spatial equilibrium of an industry is established when

$$R_r = R_{r-1} \text{ (establishes } k_{ri}) \qquad (2)$$

$$R_r = R_{r+1} \text{ (establishes } k_{ro})$$

This includes all possible cases, for when $R_r = R_1$, $k_{ri} = 0$. Also when $R_r = R_n$, $R_{r+1} = 0$ and k_{ro} is readily established.

Conditions for Entry   The above conditions, however, describe the equilibrium process only for an industry that finds it profitable to produce. There are certain additional conditions that must be fulfilled before any industry, I_r, can establish its existence in competition with the rest.

In the two-product case we do not describe the conditions necessary for either industry to be assured of its existence. The reason is obvious. When the conditions for ring formation are met, the production of both industries is assured. We need two conditions to establish ring formation; one to assure that the marginal rent functions will cross, and another to assure that the intersection will occur in the positive quadrant. Once we consider a multiple-product case we practically guarantee the existence of ring formations.[9] However, to establish the existence of ring formation in the multiple-product case does not assure that any one industry can establish its existence in competition with the rest. It is necessary for us to develop additional conditions that will, if satisfied, assure that a particular industry will produce.

An investigation reveals that two conditions are necessary. First, the value of k for $R_r = R_{r-1}$ must be smaller than the value of k for an intersection of R_r with any of the industries with a smaller slope. This condition assures that I_r will not be excluded by the competition of any of the industries that come after it in the order of diminishing slopes. Second, the value of k for $R_r = R_{r+1}$ must be greater than the value of k for the intersection of R_r with any of the industries with a greater slope. This condition assures that I_r will not be excluded by the competition of any of the industries that come before it in the order of diminishing slopes.

CONSIDERATION OF DEMAND AND THE MUTUALLY INTERDEPENDENT PRICE SYSTEM

Market Equilibrium in the One-Product Case

The maximization procedure we have been discussing for the industry shows that the spatial extent of production is inevitably determined by the process of maximizing rent. We can explain the essential elements by considering the simple one-product case depicted in Figure 1. In this case both the radial extent of production $[(p-a)/f]$ and the total area of cultivation $[\pi(p-a/f)^2]$ are explicitly determined. Also the total supplied to the market at a given price is determinate and equals $[E\pi(p-a/f)^2]$.

All of this is based on the assumption (as has all of the discussion up to this point) that the price (p) is a given and constant quantity. Once we take into account the influence of demand upon the space

9. Out of n possible cases any two may not fulfill the conditions above, but it is highly improbable that there will not be some combination among these that will satisfy these conditions. Lösch classifies the values of the variables that will result in ring formation in the two-product case. He concludes that zonal production arrangements will be a special case. In so doing he overlooks precisely the point made in this note. Lösch, *op. cit.*, ch. 5.

equilibrium, however, such a simplification is no longer admissible. Even though the industry considers price as a parameter in the maximization of rent, price is certainly variable in the market. Once price is considered to be variable we see that as the price (p) increases so does the spatial extent of production [i.e., $(p-a)/f$] which gives the greatest return, and with it the area of production and supply. Thus, we have a positively sloping curve for the commodity, and with each supply is a determinate spatial location of production. If we face this with a negatively sloping demand curve in the central market, there must be an equilibrium price for which the spatial location of production is consistent. This reveals the essential character of the space-price equilibrium.

Market Equilibrium in Multiple-Product Case

The space-price equilibrium works itself out in a similar manner for the multiple-product case. Consider any industry (I_r) depicted by the marginal rent line AB in Figure 5. In this case as in the one-product case the total area producing product r is explicitly determined but is now the area of a ring instead of a circle. Thus,

$$A = \pi(k_{ro}^2 - k_{ri}^2).$$

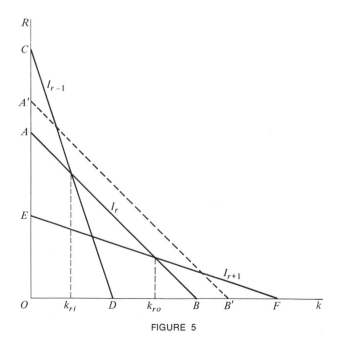

FIGURE 5

By the same token at a given price the total amount of the product supplied to the market is determined and equal to $E\pi(k_{ro}{}^2 - k_{ri}{}^2)$. Again, if the price ($p_r$) increases, so does the spatial extent of production which gives the greatest return and with it the area of production and supply. We see this graphically portrayed in Figure 5 in terms of the shift from AB to $A'B'$. The increase in p_r does not change the slope of the marginal rent line ($-Ef$) but serves to increase the R-intercept $E_r(p_r - a_r)$ and thus produce a vertical shift. The boundaries for I_r are seen to be farther apart. This establishes once again a positive slope for the supply curve. When faced with the negative market demand for the product of I_r, an equilibrium price is established.

However, the derivation of a supply curve for I_r as a function of p_r takes place in a different setting from that described in the simple case. In the general case, when the price of r increases the boundaries (k_{ri} and k_{ro}) are moved farther apart. The production area (and hence supply) of both I_{r-1} and I_{r+1} is immediately diminished. This is true because the inner boundary of I_r is the same as the outer boundary for I_{r-1} and the outer boundary of I_r is the same as the inner boundary for I_{r+1} and the outer boundary of I_r is the same as the inner boundary of I_{r+k}. If the supplies of both I_{r-1} and I_{r+1} are in equilibrium with their prices before the increase in p_r, this equilibrium will be destroyed. Since the demand for the products of these two industries will be large relative to the reduced supply, their prices will rise. This will cause vertical shifts in CD and EF (Figure 5) similar to that depicted by $A'B'$. This will serve to increase the supply of the products of I_{r-1} and I_{r+1} until equilibrium has been reestablished for these two industries. However, the values of k_{ri} and k_{ro} are changed once again, and the production of I_r is restricted. We can go on in this fashion but this is sufficient to establish the most important point. The spatial orientation of any agricultural industry, and hence its supply, is determined not only by its own equilibrium price, but by the equilibrium price of all other industries as well. There is no simple way, therefore, of describing this spatial equilibrium for any one industry. The orientation of them all must be simultaneously determined, and the only way to handle the solution is by means of a system of equations.

SUMMARY: GENERAL EQUILIBRIUM STATEMENT OF THE SPACE ECONOMY FOR AGRICULTURE

There seems to be a serious question in the minds of many concerning the utility of mathematical formulae in describing the complicated relationship of pricing. I am convinced that they can serve a useful function in giving a "birds-eye view" of the complicated interrelated nature of the space-price equilibrium. There follows an attempt to illustrate and summarize the nature of the space-price equilibrium under simplified conditions and by means of simple equations. No effort is made to introduce modifying and complicating factors into the analysis.

There are two conditions of equilibrium. (1) All individuals and industries in the economic society base their maximum positions upon equilibrium price. In short, they regard prices as constant parameters independent of their influence. (2) The equilibrium prices are determined by the condition that the demand for each commodity must equal its supply. Lange calls the first of these conditions the *subjective* condition of equilibrium and the latter the *objective* condition.[10]

Subjective Conditions of Equilibrium

The subjective condition of equilibrium is carried out in part by the actions of individual consumers attempting to maximize their utility. The equilibrium process for the consumer is so well known that there is no need to elaborate upon it here. Suffice it to say that the consumers maximize the total utility derived from their income by spending it so that the marginal utility of a unit of income is equal for all commodities. This involves the usual assumptions about the possibility of ordering consumer utilities and the independence of consumer choice. Through this process, with incomes and prices given, the demand for consumer goods is determined. This part of the equilibrium process can be represented by equations(3).

$$D_1 = F_1(Y_1, Y_2, \ldots Y_s; p_1, p_2, \ldots p_n) \tag{3}$$

$$
\begin{array}{cccc}
\cdot & \cdot & \cdot & \cdot \\
\cdot & \cdot & \cdot & \cdot \\
\cdot & \cdot & \cdot & \cdot
\end{array}
$$

$$D_n = F_n(Y_1, Y_2, \ldots Y_s; p_1, p_2 \ldots p_n)$$

$Y_1, Y_2, \ldots Y_s$ represent the income of the s individuals in the economic system. $D_1, D_2 \ldots D_n$, and $p_1, p_2, \ldots p_n$ represent the aggregate demand and the prices of the n commodities it is possible to produce. This system of equations states that the demand for each good is a function of consumer incomes and the prices of all goods. Implicit in this

10. Oskar Lange and F. M. Taylor, *On the Economic Theory of Socialism*, edited by B. E. Lippencott (Minneapolis: University of Minnesota Press, 1938), p. 65.

system of functional equations is the entire equilibrium process of the household. The presentation of this set of equations forces us to point out two additional simplifying assumptions.[11] Since we are concerned with the spatial equilibrium for agriculture alone, (4) *we include in our system only agricultural commodities.* In short, we assume the economy to be completely agrarian. The inconsistencies that result from this assumption are obvious, but it facilitates a brief exposition of the equilibrium process. (5) *We assume* Y_1, Y_2, ... Y_s *to be known constants.* No attempt is made in this analysis to describe the relationship between income and the ownership of and the demand for productive factors.

The effort of each producing industry to maximize revenue represents the second aspect of the subjective condition for equilibrium. It is at this point that the general equilibrium statement of the space economy for agriculture differs markedly from the typical general equilibrium statement. This distinction was made in some detail in the definition of terms.

The details of the production (i.e., spatial) equilibrium for each industry have been carefully worked out earlier in the paper. We content ourselves here to recall that each industry maximizes its rent by expanding in both directions (i.e., both toward and away from the market) until its marginal rent equals its marginal opportunity costs. This process establishes the spatial limits of production for the industry, k_{ri} and k_{ro}. We recall further that these limits are determined by the marginal rent function of the industry in question and the marginal rent functions of those industries restricting its extension on either side. The two latter functions serve as opportunity cost restraints for the industry in question. We also see that, when we allow for the influence of demand and variable market price, the k_{ri}'s and k_{ro}'s are, in reality, determined by the marginal rent functions of all industries. This part of the equilibrium process, therefore, can be represented by the equations (4).

$$k_{1o} = \varphi_1(E_1, a_1, f_1, p_1; E_2, a_2, f_2, p_2; \ldots E_n, a_n, f_n, p_n) \qquad (4)$$

$$\cdot \qquad \cdot \qquad \cdot \qquad \cdot \qquad \cdot$$
$$\cdot \qquad \cdot \qquad \cdot \qquad \cdot \qquad \cdot$$
$$\cdot \qquad \cdot \qquad \cdot \qquad \cdot \qquad \cdot$$

$$k_{no} = \varphi_n(E_1, a_1, f_1, p_1; E_2, a_2, f_2, p_2; \ldots E_n, a_n, f_n, p_n)$$

This set of equations expresses the outer limit of each industry (k_{ro}) as a function of the marginal rent functions *for all industries.* We can also set up a similar set of equations for the inner limits for each

---

11. The first three assumptions were made explicit in the definition of terms.

industry. However, this would be redundant for the inner boundary of one industry is the same as the outer boundary of the one which joins it nearest the market. Thus, once all the outer boundaries are determined, we know all of the inner boundaries.

E, a, and f in the above equations are all constants. This makes explicit the sixth simplifying assumption. (6) *The transport rate is constant over time and space.* It should also be pointed out that in order for equations (4) to be valid *we must assume* (7) *that the industries are ordered around a single market.*

Earlier in the paper we pointed out that the supply of a product is determined once the spatial boundaries for that product are determined. Equations (5) express their relationship.

$$S_1 = E_1 \pi (k_{1o}^2 - k_{1i}^2) \tag{5}$$

$$S_n = E_n \pi (k_{no}^2 - k_{ni}^2)$$

In order for this relationship to be expressed in so simple a form, *it is necessary to assume* (8) *that we have an undifferentiated transport network* so that the marginal rent function of each industry is the same in all directions away from the market.

Objective Conditions   We come at last to the objective conditions of equilibrium. It is necessary for the supply of a commodity to equal the demand. This is the market equilibrium condition. Thus,

$$D_1 = S_1, D_2 = S_2, \ldots D_n = S_n. \tag{6}$$

Solution of the System   The four sets of equations (3-6) form a complete system. A careful inspection of these equations show that there are 4_n unknown variables in the system. These are shown in Table 1.

TABLE 1

VARIABLES	NUMBER OF UNKNOWNS
prices $(p_1 \ldots p_n)$	n
demand $(D_1 \ldots D_n)$	n
boundary $(k_{1o} \ldots k_{1n})$	n
supply $(S_1 \ldots S_n)$	n
	$4n$

There are n equations in each of the four sets giving $4n$ equations. When solved simultaneously this system, given the present assumptions, will yield a unique solution. This solution will provide the price of every commodity, the quantity of each commodity that will be produced and consumed, and *at the same time* will explicitly determine the spatial orientation of production.[12]

One thing further needs to be pointed out. Conceptually we have included in the *n* products all products that are technically feasible, given the state of the arts. We know that all of these need not establish their existence in competition with the rest. However, this presents no problem. If any one industry or product does not fulfill the conditions for entry outlined previously, this in effect removes four unknowns and four equations from the system. They exert no influence upon the equilibrium solution. However, these possibilities always remain. If at any time the character of demand and/or technology changes, it is possible for these industries to enter the system.

This, then, is the general equilibrium statement of the space economy for agriculture. It is highly simplified, but it is adequate to illustrate that the location of agriculture is a part of the equilibrium process resulting from the exercise of the rational economic motive. We hope that it has served to synthesize and extend the elements of a location theory for agriculture.

In our exposition of the general equilibrium system there are listed eight limiting assumptions. (There are really more, not emphasized, that are common to all economic equilibrium systems — spatial or otherwise.) It is the removal of these limiting assumptions that will raise legitimate questions about the generality and utility

12. The solution presented is similar to that made familiar by Hicks and others (following Walras). Since the demand and supply functions are homogeneous in the prices, the solution is homogeneous of the zero degree. Hence, there is one less than $4n$ independent functions. (If the values of all but one of the functions are known, the value of that one follows.) In the usual procedure, therefore, one of the n goods is taken as a *numeraire*, as Walras calls it. The prices of all other goods are expressed in terms of the price of the *numeraire*. The solution is in terms of $4n-1$ ratios, the relative prices.

It should be pointed out, however, that the conventional solution is not mathematically correct. We became involved in the attempt to find a common solution for two sets of incompatible equations. The assumption of fixed incomes in the demand equations is incompatible with the assumption of the maximization of rent revenue in the supply equations. (These variable rents represent incomes for consumers.)

Two approaches can be taken in removing this incompatibility. We can introduce a new set of equations that will specify how the social product is distributed. A second alternative is available that allows us to avoid complicating the analysis further. We can assume that the government owns all productive factors and produces according to our maximization criteria. It takes all of the social product and pays to individuals money incomes that are specified in amount. If we make this assumption we can make our system of functions consistent and retain them without alteration. Since, in effect, the *numeraire* is now extraneous to the system, the demand functions become homogeneous in both incomes and prices. There are now $4n$ independent functions, and each solution will give absolute money prices for all n commodities.

I am indebted to Dr. Cecil Phipps of the Mathematics Department at the University of Florida for this bit of enlightenment relative to the mathematics of the solution.

of the concept of rings or zones and about the reality of a unique solution.

We regret that space will not allow a discussion of the modifying influence of taking some of these factors into account—such things as differentiated resources and transport systems, the reality of curvilinear and discontinuous distance-rent functions, and the results of considering the firm equilibrium.[13] This is out of the question. However, we would like to suggest the consequences for location analysis of considering the joint-cost character of farm production on the level of the firm.[14]

When this is done one realizes that it is an unnecessary simplification to assume that an agricultural ring or zone is engaged in the production of a single product. Any one ring or zone of agricultural production may be devoted to any number of products in combination. Further, the same crop may appear in several successive zones. This fact has been a source of confusion. It has led many to conclude that, in a realistic situation, the Thünen rings do not exist. This is not true. For example, one cost interrelationship may call for the production of A, B and C jointly. An alternative cost interrelationship may result in the joint production of A, B and D. The production of A, B, and C will yield one marginal rent line on an industry level, and the production of A, B, and D will yield another. As the distance from the market increases a point is reached where the rent line for ABC falls below the rent line for ABD. When this takes place ABD as a system replaces ABC. Throughout the area encompassed by these two zones both A and B will be produced, sometimes with C and sometimes with D. To the uninitiated it may appear that there is nothing left of the zonal pattern of arrangement attributed to Thünen. However, the analysis is not altered in any essential respect. When the combination of products which forms any one system is altered by the addition of a new product or the replacement of an old, a new ring or zone is established.[15] Once we recognize that farming takes place in systems, the analysis is complicated in two ways: (1) the rent

13. If the reader is interested in a detailed account of the consequences of these factors for the location of agricultural production, see Edgar S. Dunn, Jr., *The Equilibrium of Land-Use Patterns in Agriculture* (Gainsville: University of Florida Press, 1954).

14. We would like to emphasize that to dip into the theory of the firm to consider the reality of multiple-product production is not intended at this point to unleash all of the variability over space of yield (E) and cost of production (a). We are considering the modifications of one aspect of the firm equilibrium alone—namely, joint-cost and multiple-products.

15. Many interesting results may be identified with irregular transformation functions of various types. Large changes in local prices may bring about very little change if the transformation function is sharply curved. A wavy transformation function may bring about abrupt and discontinuous change in the product mix with a small change in local prices. In another case we might find recurrence of a production system at different distances from the market.

yield and the marginal distance rent lines are based upon the total operation and not the production of one product; (2) the total number of possible rings or zones is greatly increased. The number of rings is no longer limited to the number of feasible products but to the number of possible combinations of these products in systems. These are important differences and they change the whole complexion of the location analysis for agriculture. However, the basic principles that describe the equilibrium of the space economy remain unaltered.

Two closing comments are in order. This kind of descriptive analysis is certainly not an operational model. An exercise of this sort must find its utility as a framework of reference in identifying important variables and important interrelationships in tackling any specific research problem. It may particularly serve the latter. Research in the field of farm economics and regional analysis needs sorely to take account of these interrelationships. As a single example, in developing a prognosis for the citrus industry in Florida, how important it is to be aware of the competition for the use of the land it faces from a growing cattle industry.

Lastly, this descriptive system is particularly lacking in that it does not take into account industrial production and its interrelationship with agriculture, nor does it take into account the influence of multiple markets. Isard has a recent article in which he develops a mathematical analysis that is completely general in the sense that it handles all forms of production and considers market areas and supply areas as well. His unifying principle implies the various existing location theories and must be considered a core element of a general theory of location.[16]

16. Walter Isard, "A General Location Principle of an Optimum Space Economy," *Econometrica*, 20, 3 (July 1952), pp. 406–430. [Selection 16 of this volume].

A General Location Principle of an Optimum Space-Economy

Elsewhere the author has: (*a*) pointed to the relative neglect of the space factor by economic theorists [*14*], (*b*) emphasized that any economy is in fact a space-economy and that as a consequence for certain problems spatial analysis is essential [*14, 17,* and *23*, pp. 695–722, 799–809], and (*c*) developed certain concepts for spatial analysis which at the same time permit the fusion of modern production theory and much of Weberian location dogma [*15*]. It is the purpose of this paper: (*a*) to formulate mathematically with the use of these concepts a basic principle of an optimum space-economy[1] and (*b*) to demonstrate how this principle implies various existing location theories and must be considered a core element of a general theory of location.

WEBERIAN THEORY RESTATED AND GENERALIZED

Imagine a general spatial transformation function as

$$\phi(y_1, y_2, \ldots, y_k; \; m_A s_A, m_B s_B, \ldots, m_L s_L; \; x_{k+1}, x_{k+2}, \ldots, x_n) = 0 \qquad (1)$$

1. The space-economy will be assumed to operate under a set of conditions of which many are customarily postulated by economists. To the same extent that the postulates are unacceptable to the reader, the ensuing analysis will be devoid of significance. For a dissent from the profit maximization (or cost minimization) principle typical of human ecologists and economists of similar inclinations, see Boulding [*5*].

Also, it is recognized that the term *optimum* can be interpreted in several different ways. The analysis that follows will be concerned with an optimum space-economy, primarily from a location standpoint with emphasis on transportation costs. Further, we approach the problem only in terms of an existing economy with given transport facilities and rate structure. Equally important, however, is an approach which attempts to determine the transport network and rate structure simultaneously with the location of economic activities. Excellent analyses of an optimum transportation system given the geographic distribution of economic activities are to be found in Koopmans [*18*], Koopmans and Reiter [*19*], Dantzig [*6*], and Beckman[*2*].

It seems very likely that the analysis developed in the framework of this paper will also prove valid for an optimum space-economy where the character of the transport net and rate structure is also viewed as variable and to be determined.

The author is greatly indebted to John Kimber for help in formulating mathematically the various location theories and to Paul A. Samuelson for valuable suggestions. The author alone is responsible for the shortcomings of the analysis.

Reprinted from Econometrica, 20 (July 1952), 406–30, *by permission of the Econometric Society and the author.*

where the variables $y_1, y_2, \ldots, y_k$ represent quantities of various inputs other than distance inputs; $m_A s_A, m_B s_B, \ldots, m_L s_L$ represent quantities of various distance inputs, and $x_{k+1}, x_{k+2}, \ldots, x_n$ represent quantities of various outputs. In this formulation, $m_A, m_B, \ldots, m_L$ represent the weights of various raw materials and finished products subject to shipment, and $s_A, s_B, \ldots, s_L$ represent the distances the respective raw materials and products are moved. By definition, $m_I s_I$ represents distance inputs (say, ton-miles of transportation) involved in the shipment of the raw material I from its source(s) to the site of production, or the product I from this site to the consumption point(s).

Distance inputs are explicitly set apart in this function, for a study of their variation is basic to an understanding of the operation of the very simple level and assume the Weberian problem of transport orientation (see Friedrich [11, Chapter 3]).

Given the locational triangle IJC in Figure 1, where points I and J each represent a unique source of a raw material and C the market point, and find in this enclosed area the location for the point of

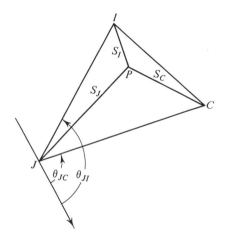

FIGURE 1

production that minimizes total transportation costs per unit of output. This problem is subject to the postulate that prices and the required amounts per unit of output of all inputs (including raw materials) except distance inputs are invariant with the site of production. The only variables are the three distance inputs $m_I s_I$, $m_J s_J$, and $m_C s_C$; since m_I and m_J are fixed and m_C is taken as unity, distance inputs vary simply because distances vary.

Since total revenue and costs on all inputs (except distance inputs) are thus fixed, the firm's customary problem of maximizing profits

$$V = -p_1 y_1 - p_2 y_2 - \cdots - p_k y_k - r_A m_A s_A - r_B m_B s_B - \cdots - r_L m_L s_L \\ + p_{k+1} x_{k+1} + p_{k+2} x_{k+2} + \cdots + p_n x_n, \tag{2}$$

where $p_1, p_2, \ldots, p_n$ are prices, and $r_A, r_B, \ldots, r_L$ are transport rates, is reduced to the problem of minimizing transport costs,

$$K = r_I m_I s_I + r_J m_J s_J + r_C m_C s_C. \tag{3}$$

Either in maximizing profits or minimizing transport costs, the firm is restrained by the spatial transformation function of equation (1) which in the latter case becomes simply

$$f(s_I, s_J, s_C) = 0, \tag{4}$$

and implies that the firm must choose quantities of distance inputs consistent with measuring the three distances s_I, s_J, and s_C from a common point P within the locational triangle (see Figure 1).

A necessary and sufficient condition that within the locational triangle P be a stationary point of K is that

$$dK = d(r_I m_I s_I) + d(r_J m_J s_J) + d(r_C m_C s_C) = 0 \tag{5}$$

or that

$$\frac{r_I}{r_J} = -\frac{d(m_J s_J)}{d(m_I s_I)}\bigg|(m_C s_C) = \text{const.}$$

$$\frac{r_I}{r_C} = -\frac{d(m_C s_C)}{d(m_I s_I)}\bigg|(m_J s_J) = \text{const.} \tag{6}$$

$$\frac{r_J}{r_C} = -\frac{d(m_C s_C)}{d(m_J s_J)}\bigg|(m_I s_I) = \text{const.}$$

Equations (6) obtain since

$$d(r_i m_i s_i) = r_i d(m_i s_i) \qquad (i = I, J, C), \tag{7}$$

for, by definition, r_i is fixed. The right-hand terms in equations (6) represent the marginal rate of substitution between the respective distance inputs. Of equations (6), any two conditions are necessary and sufficient, since with equation (4) any two imply the third.[2] We thus have three equations to determine the three unknowns.

2. For, since all directional derivatives of the transport cost function are continuous, the vanishing of the derivative of the function in two directions at point P (in our case, let us say, along the two arcs where s_C and s_J in turn are constant) implies that the derivative vanishes in all directions (for example, along the arc where s_I is constant).

For the stationary value to be a minimum; i.e., a point of minimum transport cost, it is sufficient that the second derivative be positive along any arbitrary straight line through P.[3] Since along any

$$\frac{d^2 s_i}{du^2} \geqslant 0 \qquad (i = I, J, C),$$

such line where u is the arc length on an arbitrary line along which the derivative is evaluated and where the equality cannot hold for all values of i in this Weberian problem of fixed m_i and r_i,

$$\frac{d^2 K}{du^2} = \sum m_i r_i \frac{d^2 s_i}{du^2} > 0 \qquad (i = I, J, C). \tag{9}$$

The transport cost surface is everywhere convex downward and of necessity there is only one minimum point.

In terms of the space-economy, equations (6) state the important condition that *at the point of minimum transport cost, the marginal rate of substitution between any two distance inputs, the other held constant, must equal the reciprocal of the ratio of their prices, namely, the corresponding transport rates.*

The above condition, it must be emphasized, holds when the minimum transport cost point is not at one of the vertices of the triangle, i.e., when

$$(r_i m_i)^2 < (r_j m_j \cos \theta_{ij} + r_k m_k \cos \theta_{ik})^2$$

$$+ (r_j m_j \sin \theta_{ij} + r_k m_k \sin \theta_{ik})^2 \quad (i \neq j \neq k; i,j,k = I, J, C), \tag{10}$$

where θ_{ij} and θ_{ik} are angles cut off by an arbitrary straight line through i and directions i to j and i to k, respectively.[4]

In words, if we conceive the problem as one of the equilibrium of forces, [*11*, pp. 227–232], the magnitude of the resultant of the forces (locational pulls) acting from any two corners on the third corner is greater than the magnitude of the force (locational pull) acting from the third.[5]

---

3. If such is the case, it follows that in a neighborhood of P, total cost increases with any arbitrary movement away from P. Therefore P must be a minimum point.

4. In Figure 1, we illustrate for $i = J, j = C$, and $k = I$.

5. When any one of the inequalities (10) does not hold, and this can be true of only one of the three which compose the set, three types of cases may be distinguished: (a) when $m_i r_i > m_j r_j + m_k r_k$. This corresponds to the Weberian category where one raw material or the product is dominant; (b) when one of the inequalities (10) becomes an equality. Here, in the direction of the resultant force, the slope of the transport cost surface vanishes as point i is reached from within the triangle. However, in all other directions, the directional derivative $\neq 0$ as i is approached; (c) when one of the

The fact that any one of the inequalities (10) does not hold is necessary and sufficient that the point corresponding to i be the minimum transport cost point. In a movement away from i the marginal rate of substitution between distance inputs associated with i and distance inputs associated with any other corner j is then given by:

$$\frac{r_i}{r_j} \geqslant -\frac{d(m_j s_j)}{d(m_i s_i)}\bigg|\ m_k s_k = \text{const.} \tag{11}$$

Economically speaking, this means that any small movement away from the transport optimum point along a path for which distance inputs to or from k is constant involves savings of transport cost on one set of distance inputs which are smaller than (or in an extreme case, equal to)[6] the additional outlays on the other set of distance inputs.

We now extend the problem and consider the shipment of many raw materials to a production point and of product(s) to many consuming points (l variable distances).

The transport cost equation with l terms

$$K = r_A m_A s_A + r_B m_B s_B + \cdots + r_L m_L s_L \tag{12}$$

is subject to $(l-2)$ restraints

$$\phi_i(s_A, s_B, \ldots, s_L) = 0 \qquad (i = 1, \ldots, l-2), \tag{13}$$

since the determination of the values for any two of the distance variables necessarily determines the values of all the others. There are only two independent variables.

As in the case of three distance variables, a necessary and sufficient condition that a point P, not coinciding with any raw material or consumption site, be a stationary point is that

$$\frac{r_i}{r_j} = -\frac{d(m_j s_j)}{d(m_i s_i)}\bigg|\ \sum_{k=A}^{L} r_k m_k s_k = \text{const.} \quad (j \neq k \neq i)\,(i,j = A, \ldots, L). \tag{14}$$

inequalities (10) is reversed but type (a) does not obtain. Here, as in type (a), all directional derivatives $\neq 0$ as i is approached.

As Dean has neatly pointed out, in cases of type (a) Weber's emphasis on weight loss, purity, and addition of ubiquities is correctly placed; however, in cases of type (b) and (c) "the only pertinent concerns are relative gross weight and relative distance" [7, p. 19]. This is clear from inequalities (10). Weber and others who have employed his concepts have "... seriously overestimated the determinate influence upon location of weight-losing materials, when they are not dominant, and underestimated the attractiveness of pure materials, which are never dominant" [7, p. 19].

6. This extreme case occurs when one of the inequalities (10) becomes an equality and when the movement is at the same time along the path of the resultant acting on corner i.

Of these equations, any two imply the rest.[7] These two together with the $l-2$ restraints determine the l unknowns.

For the stationary point to be a minimum it is sufficient that the second derivative be positive along any arbitrary straight line through P, which is the case as shown above.

However, the above conditions exist only when P does not coincide with any raw material or consumption site. The sufficient and necessary conditions that P does coincide with any such site are exactly analogous to those stated above for three distance variables except that there are $(l-1)$ terms in each of the parentheses of inequalities (10). In a movement away from corner i the marginal rate of substitution between any two distance inputs is then given by:

$$\frac{r_i}{r_j} \geqslant -\frac{d(m_j s_j)}{d(m_i s_i)}\bigg|\ \sum_{k=A}^{L} r_k m_k s_k = \text{const.} \tag{15}$$

In words, equations (14) state that at a point of minimum transport cost, which does not coincide with a raw material or consumption site, the marginal rate of substitution between any two distance inputs, total transport cost on all other distance inputs held constant, must equal the reciprocal of the ratio of their prices, namely, the corresponding transport rates.

INCLUSION OF MARKET AND SUPPLY AREAS AS VARIABLES

In the previous section the market points to be served are stipulated beforehand. To the extent that there are many, and particularly if there is an infinite number in an area of approximately continuous density, the above location analysis may be said in a sense to embrace market area theory. But in a major respect such a statement would be invalid. Market area analysis has as its essential core the problem of demarcating boundaries and consumers to be served. The problems of determining transport relations and sites of production are also vital, but only in a framework where the area itself is a variable (see [20, 10, 9, 24, 12, 22, and 13]). The analysis, hitherto developed, posits a fixed market area and is thereby inapplicable.

However, it is not difficult to extend the analysis to encompass the market area (and later, the supply area) as a variable. The initial

---

7. Except in the extreme case where the curve (defined by $\Sigma_{k=A}^{L} r_k m_k s_k = \text{const.}$; $j \neq k \neq i$) along which the first of the derivatives is taken is tangent at P to the other curve along which the second of the derivatives is taken. In such a case the two equations are not independent, and a second independent equation must be introduced.

step is to state the condition of indifference that defines the market boundary, which we take to be:

$$r^*s^* + \sum_{i=A}^{F} b_i r_i s_i = T, \tag{16}$$

where r^* represents transport rate (with regard to the unit of product) to the boundary line, being invariant with direction;[8] s^* represents radius of circle defining boundary line; $A, \ldots, F$ denote the various raw materials required; b_i represents a constant coefficient indicating the number of units of raw material i used per unit of product; r_i represents transport rate on a unit of raw material i; and T represents the difference between the maximum price p_0 the consumer is willing to pay and the unit costs of production π (excluding transport costs) which are held constant throughout this section of the analysis. Equation (16) states that at the market boundary the sum of the transport costs on the unit product and on the raw materials required to yield the unit product is just equal to the difference between unit costs of production and the maximum price the consumer is willing to pay.

For the moment it is useful to consider the simplified case where each consumer purchases one and only one unit of product, for which he is willing to pay a maximum price p_0, $(p_0 = T + \pi)$, but for which he actually pays a delivered cost price (i.e., π plus transport costs on raw materials and the unit of product he purchases). The resulting total (consumer or social) surplus is:

$$Tm - K = Tm - \sum_{i=A}^{F} m_i r_i s_i - \int rsd\psi(s) \tag{17}$$

where m represents number of units produced (consumed), r represents transport rate (with regard to the unit of product), s represents distance from P to the consumer, $\psi(s)$ represents the quantity consumed inside circle with radius s and center at P, and the Stieltjes integral is evaluated over an area with P as center and s^* as radius.

Since, by definition,

$$m = \int d\psi(s) \tag{18}$$

we rewrite equation (17):

$$Tm - K = Tm - \sum_{i=A}^{F} m_i r_i s_i - m\overline{rs} \tag{19}$$

8. When r^* is not invariant with direction, the resulting market area is noncircular. The ensuing analysis, however, is not altered save that visual conception becomes more difficult.

where $\bar{rs}$ represents the average unit cost of transporting the product from P to all consumers.

To maximize surplus,[9] we set:

$$d(Tm-K) = d(Tm) - \sum_{i=A}^{F} r_i d(m_i s_i) - d(m\bar{rs}) = ($$ (20)

which with equation (16) is subject to $(f-2)$ restraints expressing as before the fact that only two of the s_i can be independent. Equation (20) implies:

$$\frac{r_i}{r_j} = -\frac{d(m_j s_j)}{d(m_i s_i)}\bigg|_{Tm} - \sum_{k=A}^{F} r_k m_k s_k - m\bar{rs} = \text{const.}$$ (21)

$$(j \neq k \neq i)(i,j = A, \ldots, F),$$

$$\frac{r}{r_j} = -\frac{d(m_j s_j)}{d(m\bar{s})}\bigg|_{Tm} - \sum_{k=A}^{F} r_k m_k s_k = \text{const.}$$

$$(j \neq k)(j = A, \ldots, F).$$

Of equations (21) any two independent ones imply all the rest.[10] These two in addition to equation (16) and the $(f-2)$ restraints on the variation of the s_i determine the f unknown distances and s^*. Equations (21), however, are only necessary and not sufficient conditions for a maximum point except where the density of consumption is constant throughout the region,[11] and perhaps certain other special cases. It is easily seen, for example, that variation in consumer density over a region may lead to relative maxima at points tending to be central with respect to districts of heavy density and to relative minima in sparsely populated districts in between. As before, second-order conditions can be stated to distinguish between stationary points and the best of the maxima can only be determined by direct computation.

Equations (21) state that at the point of maximum surplus the marginal rate of substitution between any two distance inputs (distance inputs on the product being equal to the sum of distance inputs

9. The problem is not to minimize total transport cost subject to equation (16) and the $(f-2)$ restraints. For in such a problem P would *tend* to be a center in a market area containing as sparse a population as the restraints permit. Clearly, this is not optimum from a social standpoint.

10. Equations (20) and (21) and others to follow which are based upon equation (17) and others which employ the Stieltjes integral are valid only when the Stieltjes integral $\int rsd\psi(s)$ is differentiable in the relevant region. The Stieltjes integral rather than the Riemann is employed since the Riemann is a special case of the Stieltjes and since the Riemann cannot be used as the Stieltjes can for cases where discrete consumption points exist at finite distances from the boundary line within a market (or supply) area.

11. When such is the case, the point of minimum transport cost on raw materials is the point of maximum surplus P. Any movement away from P increases average cost (K/m) and decreases m, and thereby decreases surplus $(Tm-K)$. Thus P is a maximum.

involved in delivering each individual unit from P) is equal to the reciprocal of the ratio of their transport rates, the difference between T_m and total transport costs on all other distance inputs held constant.[12] Also, it logically follows that the point of maximum surplus is the point of minimum total transport cost for serving the market area defined with P as center.[13]

The simplification that each consumer purchase one and only one unit can now be relaxed. Without specifying the nature of each consumer's demand function, we can conceive of: (*a*) a firm, located at one site only, levying a fixed profit α per unit; or (*b*) each consumer, except when he is on the boundary, obtaining per unit product purchases a surplus β measured, let us say, by the difference between some given price and the lower delivered price (π plus costs of transportation); or (*c*) society attributing a value γ (in addition to the delivered price the consumer pays) to the consumption of each unit.[14] In each of these cases and a multitude of others that the reader may wish to construct, the form of the necessary conditions for equilibrium is not altered though their content is.

In the first case we maximize

$$\alpha m = \int (\alpha + p + \pi) \, d\psi(s) - K = (\alpha + \bar{p} - \pi) m - K \qquad (22)$$

12. Any movement away from P resulting from the substitution of a distance input on one raw material for a distance input on a second raw material may involve a shrinking or expansion of the circular market area and change in m as well as change in the other distance variables. The market area itself can of course encompass raw material sites.

13. Suppose the m consumers, contained in the circle with P as center and s^* as radius, could be served with lower total transport costs from P', necessarily not forming a circular area around P'. P' would then yield greater surplus. But since a circular area with center at a production site will, by our equations, always yield greater surplus than a noncircular area around the same point, a circular area around P' must then yield still greater surplus than that around P. But this contradicts the fact that P is the point of maximum surplus. Thus P must be the point of minimum transport cost for the m consumers.

It also follows that at P average transport cost (K/m) for the given market is at a minimum which, since

$$d\left(\frac{K}{m}\right) = d \sum_{i=A}^{F} b_i r_i s_i + d(\bar{r}s) = 0$$

yields to the relations,

$$\frac{r_i}{r_j} = -\frac{d(b_j s_j)}{d(b_i s_i)} \Bigg| \sum_{k=A}^{F} b_k r_k s_k + \bar{r}s = \text{const.} \qquad (j \neq k \neq i)\,(i,j = A, \ldots, F).$$

These relations which are implied by, but do not imply equations (21), may facilitate testing the stationary character of points.

14. We fully appreciate the unreality of these conceptions. However, since economics has not yet reached the stage where the welfare of a group of consumers can be quantitatively evaluated, and since the validity of the relations emphasized in this paper is independent of the nature of any welfare functions, these simple conceptions suffice for the immediate purpose.

where p represents the delivered price (excluding the profit charge) to consumers, s represents the distance from P, and $\bar{p}$ represents an average delivered price (excluding profit charge) over all units sold. In effect, equation (22) resembles equation (19) except that $(\alpha + \bar{p} - \pi)$ has been substituted for T. The form of the necessary conditions for a maximum in this problem resemble those expressed in equations (20) and (21) for the previous problem, save that $(\alpha + \bar{p} - \pi)$ is always substituted for T.[15] However, the path along which substitution of distance inputs on raw material i for distance inputs on raw material j can take place is totally different. In such a substitution, the market area tends to shift, expand, or contract; each consumer tends to alter the number of units he purchases; and thus p' and m tend to change. To determine a path of substitution becomes more difficult.

In the case of (b) or (c) above, we merely substitute β or γ for α in all the equations. The form of the necessary equilibrium conditions remains the same, although again the content differs.[16]

Heretofore, we have posited that each raw material originates at a single point. The analysis can now be extended to embrace raw material supply areas, each composed of any number of originating sites. To do so with respect to any raw material i requires the substitution of $\int r_i s_i d\psi\ (s_i)$ or $m_i \overline{r_i s_i}$ for the term $m_i r_i s_i$ in the above equations where $\psi_i(s_i)$ is the quantity of raw material i supplied within a circle of radius s_i and P as center. With the introduction of a supply (or purchasing) area for any raw material the problem is changed in a way exactly analogous to the way it was changed with the introduction of a market area. The reader will find, if he cares to reformulate the problem mathematically, that the fundamental form of the substitution relations remain unchanged, though these relations bear upon different paths and have different content.[17]

THE PRINCIPLE EXTENDED TO THE CASE OF MANY PRODUCERS

Having generalized the analysis to embrace a market area, variation in consumption patterns over space, and a supply area for

---

15. Also, α must be subtracted from T in equation (16).

16. Where no raw materials are required in production, equations (16) and (20) become $r^*s^* = T$ and $d(Tm - K) = d(Tm) - d(mr's') = 0$. The radius s^* is thus invariant with production site. However, if we wish to express equilibrium conditions in terms of distance inputs and not in terms of the vanishing of the partial derivatives in the x and y directions, we can divide distance inputs on the product into three or more subdivisions of distance inputs, each corresponding to a set of consumers asymmetrically located. The analysis would proceed as above where there are several distance inputs to consider.

17. Of course, substitution can now involve change in one raw material supply area vis-á-vis change in another raw material supply area, or in the market area, and so forth.

each raw material where such areas overlap so that a point may be both a market site and a site at which several raw materials originate, we now proceed to allow more than one production site. In doing this we could maintain the postulate of constant unit production cost (excluding transportation). We would then obtain a statement implying geographic patterns such as those depicted in Palander and Hoover [24, Chapter VI; 12, pp. 53–55] where, for example, we may have at one and the same time production: (a) at raw material sites, each serving a district of consumers, (b) at each point along a closed elliptical shaped curve, each point serving the consumers in the hinterland along its pole line only, and (c) at each consumption site contained in the elliptical shaped curve, each such site meeting its own needs only.

However, we need not dwell upon such an unrealistic situation that can be considered a special case of the more general type which allows variation in the unit cost of production (as Lösch does). A region may be conceived as divided up into several market areas, each served from a production site and bounded on all sides. As before, any boundary line, not a boundary line between two producers, is defined by a condition corresponding to equation (16), namely,

$$\sigma_\mu + r_\mu^* s_\mu^* + \sum_{i=A}^{F} b_i r_i s_{i\mu} = p_0, \qquad (\mu = 1, \ldots, \eta), \tag{23}$$

where σ_μ represents the marginal production costs (excluding transportation) at site P_μ, and $s_{i\mu}$ represents the distance between P_μ and the site of raw material i.[18]

Our problem is to maximize, let us say, *social* surplus:

$$\gamma m = m(\gamma + \bar{p} - \bar{\pi}) - K \tag{24}$$
$$= m(\gamma + \bar{p} - \bar{\pi}) - \sum_{i=A}^{F} \sum_{\mu=1}^{\eta} m_{i\mu} r_i s_{i\mu} - \sum_{\mu=1}^{\eta} m_\mu \bar{r} \bar{s}_\mu,$$

where $\bar{p}$ represents the average delivered price on all units produced (consumed); $\bar{\pi}$ represents the average unit production costs on all

18. We have defined the boundary in terms of marginal production cost plus unit transport cost rather than average unit production cost plus unit transport cost. This insures an optimum spatial arrangement for society as a whole, but involves a net loss for each producer when he is producing on the falling section of his average cost curve and when delivered price is based on marginal cost at P_μ. The reader may substitute π_μ (average unit production cost) for σ_μ in equations (23) and in subsequent equations which define boundary conditions among producers. This, however, would not be consistent with an optimum space-economy, though of course it would be consistent with an optimum space-economy subject to the restraint that delivered prices be based on average unit production cost. This problem which lies outside the scope of this paper has been treated at length in the literature on welfare economics. Refer, for example, to Bergson [4] and the literature cited therein.

units; $m_{i\mu}$ represents the total weight of raw material i used by producer μ; m_μ represents the total units (weight) of product consumed in market area served by producer μ, and $rs_\mu = (1/m_\mu) \int rs_\mu d\psi_\mu(s_\mu)$ represents the average transport cost per unit of product in shipping the product from P_μ to customers in the corresponding market area.

First, it should be noted that since there is an infinity of market sites (consumers) in our wholly or partially continuous areas, one may treat an infinity of variables, the distance from any consumer to a corresponding producer being a variable. However, it is immediately possible to reduce the infinity of variables to a finite number by considering each market area as a whole and by introducing boundary conditions between the market areas of any two producers. Imagine that any two producers shift their common boundary within any small element of area without affecting the market areas and outputs of other producers. Let the first obtain dm_ρ new sales from this element while the second lose dm_ρ $(= - dm_\nu)$ sales. If γm is a maximum, such a shift should not reduce total costs when through some pricing arrangement the intensity pattern of consumption of all other elements in the two market areas is held unchanged, as it can be. For, if this were not so, the resulting decrease in total costs would make possible an increase in m, and thus γm. Therefore, with such a shift, for $d(\gamma m) = 0$, we must have:

$$d(\pi_\rho m_\rho) + d(r_\rho m_\rho \bar{s}_\rho) + d\left(m_\rho \sum_{i=A}^{F} b_i r_i s_{i\rho} \right)$$

$$= - d(\pi_\nu m_\nu) - d(r_\nu m_\nu s_\nu) - d\left(m_\nu \sum_{i=A}^{F} b_i r_i s_{i\nu} \right) . \quad (25)$$

where π_ρ and π_ν represents the average unit production costs (excluding transportation) of producers at sites P_ρ and P_ν, respectively. Since

$$d(\pi_\rho m_\rho) = \sigma_\rho dm_\rho,$$
$$d(\pi_\nu m_\nu) = \sigma_\nu dm_\nu = -\sigma_\nu dm_\rho, \quad (26)$$

and since

$$d(m_\rho \bar{s}_\rho) = s_\rho{}^0 dm_\rho,$$
$$d(m_\nu \bar{s}_\nu) = s_\nu{}^0 dm_\nu = -s_\nu{}^0 dm_\rho, \quad (27)$$

where s_ρ^0 and s_ν^0 represent the distances from P_ρ and P_ν, respectively, to any point on their common boundary line, equation (25) becomes, after cancelling dm_ρ,

$$\sigma_\rho + r_\rho s_\rho{}^0 + \sum_{i=A}^{F} b_i r_i s_{i\rho} = \sigma_\nu + r_\nu s_\nu{}^0 + \sum_{i=A}^{F} b_i r_i s_{i\nu}$$

$$(\rho \neq \nu)(\rho, \nu = 1, \ldots, \eta). \quad (28)$$

Equations (28) furnish the boundary (indifference) conditions dividing a market domain between any two producers, each boundary representing a locus of points of equal delivered prices.

The problem is now reduced to one involving a finite number of variables, namely, to that of maximizing γm [where the η market areas are defined by equations (23) and (28)], subject to $\eta(f-2)$ restraints on the variation of the distances, which express for each producer the fact that in choosing his production site only two of his f distance variables can be independent. Thus γm can be considered as a function of independent coordinates in 2η dimensional space.

In this new framework, setting $d(\gamma m) = 0$, we obtain:

$$\frac{r_i}{r_j} = -\frac{d(m_{j\rho}s_{j\rho})}{d(m_{i\nu}s_{i\nu})} \qquad (29)$$

evaluated along the path

$$m(\gamma + \bar{p} - \bar{\pi}) - \sum_{k=A}^{F} \sum_{\mu=1}^{\eta} m_{k\mu}r_k s_{k\mu} - \sum_{\mu=1}^{\eta} m_\mu \bar{r}s_\mu = \text{const.}$$
$$(j\rho \neq k\mu \neq i\nu).$$

Of relations (29),[19] each of which holds in $2\eta - 1$ independent directions, and yields $2\eta - 1$ independent equations, any two together holding in 2η and only 2η independent directions are required to provide necessary and sufficient conditions for a stationary point. These provide the equations for determining the 2η independent unknowns. Again, complex second-order conditions are required to distinguish among maxima and other stationary points, and only direct computation will yield the best of the maxima points.

Economically speaking, relations (29) state that in a small variation of any production site from its corresponding position in a geographic pattern of production sites which yields maximum surplus, the marginal rate of substitution of one distance input for another must be equal to the reciprocal of the ratio of their transport rates, *social* surplus plus total revenue less total production costs and less total transport cost on all other distance inputs being held constant. It should be emphasized that variation of any production site tends to entail variation in all production sites, as well as market areas, and so forth.

In order to avoid further complications in detailing the above relations, it has been postulated that each raw material originated from one fixed site only. However, just as we have treated many producers serving a spatially extended market, we can treat many

19. Analogous to the second of the equations (21) the ratios in relations (29) should be viewed as involving distance inputs on product [e.g. $d(m_\mu \bar{s}_\mu)$ vis-à-vis $d(m_{i\nu}s_{i\nu})$ or vis-à-vis $d(m_\nu s_\nu)$] as well as distance inputs on raw materials.

producers procuring their supplies of each raw material from a spatially extended supply area. New unknown boundary equations are introduced, but so are new conditions to determine them. The reader can easily develop analysis in this direction.

One further salient point must be noted. The derived boundary (isotant) equations (28) contain market area theory, developed by Launhardt, Fetter, Palander, Hyson, and others [20, 10, 9, 24, 12, 22, and 13]. In the usual case, only two producers, each at a particular site, are considered, and transport costs on raw materials are neglected or assumed to be zero or already accounted for in the price which each producer charges. Where marginal cost is the basis for determining the price at the factory[20] then equations (28) are relevant and they will yield (a) straight line boundaries, when $\sigma_\rho = \sigma_\nu$ and $r_\rho = r_\nu$, (b) hyperbolic boundaries when $\sigma_\rho \neq \sigma_\nu$ and $r_\rho = r_\nu$, (c) circular boundaries when $\sigma_\rho = \sigma_\nu$ and $r_\rho \neq r_\nu$, and (d) Descartes ovals or hypercircles as boundaries when $\sigma_\rho \neq \sigma_\nu$ and $r_\rho \neq r_\nu$.[21]

AGRICULTURE LOCATION THEORY EMBRACED AND GENERALIZED

Another major branch of location theory, stemming from the work of von Thünen [25], and developed by Aereboe [1] and Brinkmann [3], and most recently by Dunn [8], has as its object the explanation of the geographic pattern of agricultural activities. Immediately, it is seen that, since the von Thünen problem concerns itself with the formation of zones, each devoted to the cultivation of a particular crop or combination of crops, the general location statement hitherto developed must be extended to treat more than one commodity if it is to encompass agricultural location theory.

As in the previous analysis, we shall abstract from price changes, prices being determined and fixed beforehand. However, this position is much less tenable in the case of agricultural location theory. Since several commodities vie for the purchasing potential of the city market, and since significant changes in the outputs of the various agricultural commodities may be involved in spatial (zonal) shifts, it is only by price changes, direct and indirect, and their

20. Where another method of pricing is employed, the process of maximizing *social* surplus γm will be constrained by such a method and will yield boundary equations similar to (28) except that the factory price charged the peripheral consumer by each producer will substitute for marginal cost. The boundaries yielded by these new equations will still be of the same type as those derived by traditional market area analysis.

21. Where the transport rate is a function of distance, then the hyperbolic, circular and hypercircular boundaries become distorted and need to be described by more complex functions.

resultant effects upon the several outputs that appropriate and complete adjustments can be made to locational shifts. To account for repercussions through price changes, as a truly general equilibrium system would, is however beyond the scope of this paper.[22] Since agricultural location theorists have traditionally omitted price changes from their formulations of concrete equilibrium conditions, there is no inconsistency in demonstrating how their analysis is implied by our general principle.

We shall proceed from the simple to the more complex. Imagine a single city, surrounded by land of uniform quality, consuming commodities $k+1, \ldots, n$ whose prices $(p_{k+1}, \ldots, p_n)$ are set. Our problem is to determine the location and the quantities, $(m_{k+1}, \ldots, m_n)$, of the agricultural commodities which will be produced, given the freight rate $(r_{k+1}, \ldots, r_n)$, and cost function for each commodity, $\pi_{k+1}, \ldots, \pi_n$ and $\sigma_{k+1}, \ldots, \sigma_n$ representing their average unit and marginal costs, respectively.

Discarding the assumptions of constant yield of a given crop per acre, regardless of distance from the city, and of constant average unit cost — assumptions which have characterized the algebraic statements of Brinkmann, Lösch, and Dunn[23] — we have for the given commodity a unique marginal rent function, which traces out the amount of rent which would be yielded by each unit circumferential band of land as we proceed radially outward. Each marginal rent function declines continuously since local price (net of transport cost) falls off with distance from the city market and since, too, as a result intensity per unit of land falls off given uniform fertility of land and hence a production function invariant with distance.[24] However, since only one commodity (or one combination of commodities that is fixed proportionally and thus can be viewed as a single commodity) can be cultivated on any given piece of land, it is necessary to think in terms of stretches of land devoted to the cultivation of one and only one commodity.

Consider total rent for society

$$R = \sum_{\tau=k+1}^{n} \left[\int_{\tau} \Gamma_{\tau}(p_{\tau} - \pi_{\tau}) \, dW - \int_{\tau} \Gamma_{\tau} r_{\tau} s \, dW \right] \tag{30}$$

22. The reader may refer to the nonoperational general equilibrium statements, involving the simultaneous determination of price and spatial structure, in Lösch, [22, 1st ed., 1940, pp. 57–63] and Dunn, [8, Chapter 6].

23. It should be noted that Dunn has pushed the analysis on to the individual firm level, and has shown the inconsistency of these assumptions for firm analysis. Thereby, he has been able to sketch graphically the approximate character of the necessary modifications of analysis on the industry level. A revision of his mathematical statement, however, was not made.

24. Under the usual assumption that the farmer is not incurring loss, and thus is operating at a point on the rising section of his marginal cost curve.

under the simplification that no transportation costs are incurred on raw materials, labor, and other inputs[25] and where the Riemann integral $\int_r$ is taken over the area devoted to the production of the τth commodity, Γ_r representing the intensity of production of τ associated with the element of area dW.[26] Setting $dR = 0$, we obtain

$$\frac{r_i}{r_j} = -\frac{d \int_j \Gamma_j s \, dW}{d \int_i \Gamma_i s \, dW} \tag{31}$$

evaluated along the path

$$\sum_{\tau=k+1}^{n} \int_\tau \Gamma_\tau (p_\tau - \pi_\tau) \, dW - \sum_{\substack{\tau=k+1 \\ j \neq \tau \neq i}}^{n} \int_\tau \Gamma_\tau \, r_\tau \, s \, dW = \text{const.}$$

$$(i, j = k+1, \ldots, n).$$

Immediately, it is seen that these relations imply a concentric circular zone (in the extreme case approaching a line) pattern of cultivation. First, zones, whatever their shape, must be contiguous to each other and to the city market. Otherwise, there would be empty spaces which would then permit a shifting of some zone closer to the city market thereby reducing transport costs on one commodity without affecting transport costs on any other commodity. But this is inconsistent with equations (31). Secondly, since the transport rate is independent of direction, the contiguous zones must also be concentric and circular because equations (31) also imply pattern symmetry.[27]

25. The simplification is made merely to facilitate presentation. As will be shown later, another term representing transport costs on raw materials and on labor can be brought into the brackets of equation (30); the analytical technique remains unaffected. It should be noted that von Thünen and Brinkmann would insist upon two additional terms, a *negative* one for transport costs on industrially produced goods used as inputs and shipped from the city market, and a *positive* one for transport costs of the agriculturally produced inputs from any element of area to the city market. The latter, positive term represents the differential price advantage any element of area has over the city market in procuring agricultural raw materials (including food for labor), since the difference between the price at the city market and the local price at the element of area for any such raw material is the cost of shipping that raw material from the element of area to the market.

26. We employ the Riemann integral throughout this section since intensity of production of any element of area (farm) is a critical issue in agricultural location theory. The use of Stieltjes integral would conceal the intensity variable. Also, since agricultural production tends to assume a continuous character, the Stieltjes integral would in any case tend to reduce to a Riemann integral. However, in the latter part of this section where a continuous market area is considered, the use of the Stieltjes integral would have definite advantage in an extension of the analysis to include cities as discrete consumption points within the market area, provided the integral is differentiable in the relevant region.

27. Thus the analysis in its more vital aspects can be reduced to the problem of examining relations along any straight line through the point representing the city market.

Of equations (31), only $n–k$ are independent, and they determine the $n–k$ variable boundaries separating the zones in which the $n–k$ commodities are produced. These equations are only necessary conditions for maximum rent. Elaborate second-order conditions are required to distinguish a maximum from other stationary points. With marginal rent functions for all commodities plotted on a single graph, (marginal rent measured along the ordinate), the absolute maximum obtains when the commodity produced on any given unit of land corresponds to the marginal rent function having the highest ordinate for that unit of land.[28]

Economically speaking, equations (31) state that for maximum rent the marginal rate of substitution between any two distance inputs, each on a particular crop, must equal the reciprocal of the ratio of their transport rates, the sum of rent on all other commodities plus the total difference between sales value and production costs for the two crops held constant. It must be borne in mind that the path along which the sum is held constant may involve shifts of the zonal boundaries of other crops as well as of the two explicitly considered and may call for changes in the intensity of cultivation and in unit production costs of other crops as well as of these two. Thus the path may be quite complex.

Despite this complexity, equations (31) imply relatively simple boundary determining equations. Imagine only two boundaries shift, namely, those s_ρ and s_μ distances from the city, representing respectively the outer boundaries of the zones producing crops ρ and μ. Further, let at least one other zone intervene, ρ being nearer the city. From equations (31) where $i = \rho$ and $j = \mu$ we would have with a small change of s_ρ and corresponding change of s_μ:

$$r_\rho \Gamma_\rho s_\rho{}^2 ds_\rho = -r_\mu \Gamma_\mu s_\mu{}^2 ds_\mu \tag{32}$$

where $2\pi s\, ds$ substitutes for dW and 2π is cancelled. Also from the restraint of equation (31) defining the path, we have, after cancelling 2π,[29]

$$\Gamma_\rho(p_\rho - \pi_\rho)s_\rho\, ds_\rho - \Gamma_{\rho+1}(p_{\rho+1} - \pi_{\rho+1})s_\rho\, ds_\rho + \Gamma_\mu(p_\mu - \pi_\mu)s_\mu\, ds_\mu$$
$$-\Gamma_{\mu+1}(p_{\mu+1} - \pi_{\mu+1})s_\mu\, ds_\mu + r_{\rho+1}\Gamma_{\rho+1}s_\rho^2\, ds_\rho + r_{\mu+1}\Gamma_{\mu+1}s_\mu^2\, ds_\mu = 0 \tag{33}$$

28. With this graphic picture in mind, it is seen that there can be no relative maxima if we allow any particular crop to be produced in more than one zone, however wide these zones may be. For, given any position other than the absolute maximum already described, there is always at least one way in which a small substitution of distance inputs on one commodity for distance inputs on another can increase rent. This may involve a shift of some element of area from the cultivation of one crop to the other, and the formation of new, or deletion of old, zones, and a corresponding increase or decrease in the number of boundary variables.

29. In equation (33) are contained all the elements which change in the restraint governing the path, namely, the sales revenue and production costs associated with

where $\Gamma_{\rho+1}$ and $\pi_{\rho+1}$ are evaluated at s_ρ, and $\Gamma_{\mu+1}$ and $\pi_{\mu+1}$ at s_μ. Similarly two equations of like form are obtained when in equations (31) we let $i = \rho$ and $j = \mu + 1$, and where as before distances s^ρ and s_μ only are varied. These latter two equations, with equations (32) and (33) yield algebraically:[30]

$$r_\mu s_\mu \Gamma_\mu - r_{\mu+1} s_\mu \Gamma_{\mu+1} = \Gamma_\mu (p_\mu - \pi_\mu) - \Gamma_{\mu+1}(p_{\mu+1} - \pi_{\mu+1}). \qquad (34)$$

Equations of the type (34) represent another way of expressing necessary conditions for maximum rent.[31] Each such equation states that with a small shift of the boundary line between any two zones, the change in overall transport costs for the two crops is equal to the change in the sum of the difference between sales value and production costs for each of the two crops. Or, if in each of equations (34) the first term on the left side is carried over to the right and the last term on the right to the left, the necessary conditions for maximum rent are that with any infinitesimal shift of the boundary between two zones, marginal rent on the one crop must equal marginal rent on the other. In graphic terms, the marginal rent functions of the two crops must intersect or, be tangent at the boundary line.[32]

These boundary conditions, implied by equations (31), are identical with those obtained by Lösch, [22, pp. 28–32], and Dunn, [8, Chapter 6] except that Γ_i and π_i are constants in Lösch's and Dunn's schema while they are variables in our formulation. Treating intensity and unit production costs as variables not only is realistic but has the distinct advantage, as Dunn noted, of facilitating the unification of theory for the industry and for the individual farm unit.[33] Postulating Γ_i and π_i as constants throughout a zone precludes any such thing as a firm adjustment to a lower or higher local (net) price for product and rent payment for land, and thus in essence is inconsistent with customary firm analysis. However, with Γ_i and π_i as variables, we derive that since a farmer will produce on the rising section of his marginal cost curve up to the point where his marginal costs (σ_i) just equals the local (net) price $(p_i - r_i s_i)$, $d\sigma_i/ds_i = -r_i$; and therefore, $d\Gamma_i/ds_i = -r_i d\Gamma_i/d\sigma_i$. As $d\Gamma_i/d\sigma_i$ is positive on the rising section of the marginal cost curve, $d\Gamma_i/ds_i$ is negative. Thus intensity of cultivation

---

crops ρ, $\rho + 1$, μ, and $\mu + 1$, and transport costs associated with crops $\rho + 1$ and $\mu + 1$. Since the path defines a constant sum, the total of these changes must be zero.

30. By eliminating the three unknowns ds, ds_μ, and s_ρ.

31. These equations are also obtainable when more than two boundaries are shifted.

32. This condition also characterizes stationary points other than the absolute maximum, including relative maxima when each crop is restricted to production within one zone only.

33. Though, of course, when there is no definite bunchings of firms with respect to similarity of product or output mix, there may not be any justification or meaning in the distinction between firm and industry.

falls off in any zone from land unit to land unit, or farm unit to farm unit with increase of distance from the market.[34] And thus we have an adjustment to the fall in local price appropriate to both firm and industry analysis.

When within any zone it is desirable to consider each firm by itself, because outputs or output combinations for various firms are too heterogeneous or for other reasons, each firm can be considered an industry. More boundary variables are introduced but so are more equations to determine the boundaries. Boundary equations (34) come to hold between firms whether or not they produce a homogeneous output as well as between groups of firms (industries), each corresponding to a zone. Thus firm and industry analysis are mutually consistent in this spatial framework, and in the extreme case, may be considered as one and the same thing.

Hitherto, we have excluded consideration of transport costs on raw materials. Such can easily be introduced explicitly into the analysis by inserting into the brackets of equation (30) the term

$$- \int_\tau \sum_{i=1}^{k} \Gamma_\tau b_{i\tau} r_s s_i \, dW,$$

where s_i is the distance of the source of raw material i from the element dW. With this term inserted, marginal rates of substitution between distance inputs on raw materials, and between distance inputs on a raw material and distance inputs on a product, are obtainable from the required revision of equations (31). It should be noted that in general the zonal boundaries will no longer be concentric circles because pattern symmetry will have been lost.[35]

If, however, raw material i is supplied not from a single point source, but from an area, s_i becomes a variable for any given element dW, representing the distance from dW of the element of the raw material supply area, dU, which furnishes the i required by dW. As a result additional equations of the order of (31) result which relate, for example, distance inputs on raw material i used by crop τ,[36]

$$\int_{U_\tau} \Gamma_i s_{i\tau} \, dU,$$

34. However, because of differences in production cost functions, transport rates, and market prices, intensity per land unit, however measured, need not fall off from zone to zone or from a farm unit in one zone to a contiguous farm unit in the next zone.

35. Hence, it becomes necessary to think in terms of a boundary defined by an equation rather than by a radial distance alone. Analysis along a straight line is in general no longer valid.

36. This is, of course, equivalent to

$$\int_\tau \Gamma_\tau b_{i\tau} s_i \, dW.$$

and distance inputs on raw material i used by crop $\tau + 1$,

$$\int_{U_{\tau+1}} \Gamma_i s_{i_{\tau+1}} dU.$$

These determine the boundary lines cutting off the portion of the supply area of raw material i which serves each crop.[37]

A still more general framework, encompassing more than one city market, can be handled. Consider first a relatively small number of city markets close enough to compete for the potential crops of at least some land. Here an industry (agricultural activity) and its corresponding zone of cultivation must be defined not only in terms of the crop produced but also the city market served. The number of industries is thus multiplied but so also is the number of equations (31) to determine boundary lines.[38]

Where the number of city markets becomes large and attains the approximate continuity of a market area we reach the most general type of framework, that is, many markets each consuming many products, many producers of any given product, many raw materials used by each producer, and many sources (a supply area) of each raw material. An alternative approach to this most general framework follows from the analysis of Section III. There we considered many producers of a single commodity demanded by a population spread over an area and requiring many raw materials, each furnished from a supply area. By introducing many commodities in this framework we reach the same problem as when we inject the market area into the Thünen type framework. It seems, however, more desirable to generalize from the Thünen type framework. In this framework prices are explicitly assumed as given and we avoid the problem, which thus far has not been satisfactorily handled, of relating social surpluses, or consumer utilities, or satisfactions derivable from several commodities.[39] This problem would confront us if we were to proceed from the analysis of Section III.

37. Also, $dR = 0$ implies equations guaranteeing the appropriate pairing off of elements of area in any portion with the elements in the crop zone which the portion serves.

38. In the case of only two cities, in which the ruling market prices are different, there will tend to be two hinterlands, one corresponding to each city. In each hinterland, zonal pattern symmetry will exist with respect to the cultivation of any given crop when no raw materials are employed. However, on the two sides of any small stretch of the border separating the two hinterlands, in general different types of crops will be cultivated at different intensities per unit of land, though marginal rent is the same.

39. In essence, the Thünen type framework assumes away this subjective evaluation problem. It treats only objective, measurable elements, and on the basis of these latter alone yields a spatial pattern of economic activity and land use.

Generalizing the Thünen type analysis we have for total rent:

$$R = \sum_{\tau=k+1}^{n} \left[\int_H \Gamma_{H\tau}(p_\tau - \pi_\tau)\, dH \right.$$

$$\left. - \int_H \Gamma_{H\tau} r_\tau s_\tau\, dH - \int_\tau \sum_{i=1}^{k} \Gamma_\tau b_{i\tau} r_i s_i\, dW \right], \qquad (35).$$

where $\Gamma_{H\tau}$ represents the intensity of the effective demand for product τ in the element dH of the consumption market area at the price p_τ, p_τ being fixed for each element but varying from element to element, π_τ represents the average production cost of τ at the element dW, where an element dW may serve more or less than one element dH, and s_τ represents the distance from the element dH of the element dW producing the τ which is demanded at element dH.

Setting $dR = 0$ yields again equations of the order of (31), though more complex. These, nonetheless, can be easily set down by the reader. A whole new set of substitution relations, however, is embraced. For example, there may be substitution between distance inputs on the product τ going to city A, $\int_{\tau A} \Gamma_\tau s_{\tau A}\, dW$,[40] and distance inputs on the product τ going to city B, $\int_{\tau B} \Gamma_\tau s_{\tau B}\, dW$, or on the product $\tau+1$ going to city B, etc. More generally, the consumption market area may be divided up into any two or more meaningful parts and distance inputs on product τ going to any α part can be considered vis-à-vis distance inputs on any other product going to any area or meaningful part of an area, or on any raw material going to any production area or meaningful part of a production area of any good[41] and so forth. In this way, within the hypothesized framework of the space-economy, one can make the most comprehensive statements concerning equilibrium conditions and substitution relations among distance inputs. This the reader can easily do by setting down equations of the order of (31) that, however, correspond to total rent as defined in equation (35).

---

40. Equivalent to $\int_H \Gamma_{H\tau} s_\tau\, dH$ where the integral $\int_H$ is evaluated over the area of city A.

41. As a consequence, if attention is paid to a given crop alone, without regard to destination or market, multiple zones of cultivation will appear, each in general asymmetrical with respect to any selected focal point. Where a given good is produced at a finite number of plants, as in the analysis of Section III, the cultivation zone or production area of that good has in effect been reduced to a finite number of points, the intensity of cultivation or production at other points being zero. Any one point may still be a potential source of all raw materials, and a potential market for all goods.

CONCLUDING REMARKS

We have treated what may be called a continuous space-economy, continuous transportationwise, and continuous to some extent at least with respect to market and supply areas. This stands in strong contrast to the highly discontinuous realistic one. Although analysis in terms of geographic shifts in the large, from focal point to focal point, is highly desirable and should be the subject of future study, such has been beyond the scope of this paper.

We have attempted to demonstrate the usefulness of the concept distance inputs in deriving conditions for the efficient operation of a space-economy. A basic principle—in a sense an intuitively obvious one—has emerged, namely, that the marginal rate of substitution between any two distance inputs or groups of distance inputs, however the distance inputs or groups of distance inputs may be defined, must equal the reciprocal of the ratio of their transport rates, social surplus (however defined) less transport costs on all other distance inputs held constant. This principle implies a large part of existing location theory. Weberian transport orientation is embodied in such a principle and with this principle we can take transport orientation out of the narrow geometric framework in which it has hitherto been confined, and determine the optimal transport point for the more generalized case when many raw material and market points are involved. The principle, too, encompasses all market (and purchasing) area theory, implying the customary boundary conditions which separate the market areas of producers (and hinterlands of focal points). Likewise, the von Thünen type of agricultural location theory is embraced and can be generalized to harbor a much broader range and a more realistic set of situations.[42]

More important, this general principle fuses the separate partial location theories. It thus can serve as a basic core of a general location theory, from which for the most part, existing location theories are derived as special cases of the most general situation, embracing many market points, each consuming many commodities, each of which is produced by many producers, each of whom uses many raw materials and inputs, each of which is furnished by a supply area.[43]

Perhaps most important is that this principle allows existing location theory to be stated in a form comparable to that of modern production theory. By incorporating distance inputs into the trans-

42. The proof that the hexagonal spatial designs of Lösch are also implied is being developed in other manuscript.

43. For example, one can derive Weber's theory of transport orientation by assuming one market point, consuming one unit of one commodity, produced by a single producer, using two raw materials, each obtainable at a single source.

formation function, and thereby yielding a spatial transformation function, we can extend existing production theory so that to a large extent it embodies the location factor explicitly. At the same time location theory can now consider change in a number of parameters. For example, the relation between economies of scale and the number and geographic distribution of plants can be examined through substitution between distance inputs and all other inputs as a whole; or the relation between the spatial extent and capital intensity (time extent) of production, through substitution between distance inputs and capital inputs.

Finally, with the concept of distance inputs and this principle we are in a better position to incorporate location analysis into operational, empirical economic models and thus increase their utility. For instance, the interregional and regional input-output models [21, 16] posit that the spatial extent of any line of production with respect to its inputs is fixed, and thus many types of locational shifts are precluded with change in final demand (bill of goods). Expressing locational shifts in terms of distance inputs and inserting where possible appropriate relations into the structural matrix promises to overcome at least partially this limitation. Especially would this be so if at the same time theoretical and empirical research is pursued on the discontinuities within the space-economy and on the conditions governing geographic shifts from focal point to focal point.

REFERENCES

1. AEREBOE, F., *Allgemeine landwirtschaftsliche Betriebslehre*, Berlin: P. Parey, 1923, 697 pp.
2. BECKMANN, M., "A Formal Approach to Localization Theory" and "A Continuous Model of Transportation," Cowles Commission Discussion Papers: Economics Nos. 293 and 2022, respectively.
3. BENEDICT, E. T., H. STIPPLER, and M. R. BENEDICT, *Theodor Brinkmann's Economics of the Farm Business*, Berkeley: University of California Press, 1935, 172 pp.
4. BERGSON, A., "Socialist Economics" in *A Survey of Contemporary Economics*, H. S. Ellis, ed., Philadelphia: The Blakiston Co., 1948, pp. 424–428.
5. BOULDING, K. E., *A Reconstruction of Economics*, New York: John Wiley and Sons, 1950, 311 pp.
6. DANTZIG, G. B., "Application of the Simplex Method to a Transportation Problem," Chapter XXIII in *Activity Analysis of Production and Allocation*, Cowles Commission Monograph 13, T. C. Koopmans, ed., New York: John Wiley and Sons, 1951, pp. 359–373.
7. DEAN, W. H., JR., *The Theory of the Geographic Location of Economic Activities*, selections from the doctoral dissertation, Cambridge, Mass.: Harvard University Press, 1938, 46 pp.

8. DUNN, E. S., *The Equilibrium of Land-Use Patterns in Agriculture*, doctoral dissertation, Harvard University Library, 1952, 348 pp.
9. ENGLÄNDER, O., *Theorie des Güterverkehrs und der Frachtsätze*, Jena; G. Fischer, 1924.
10. FETTER, F. A., "The Economic Law of Market Areas," *Quarterly Journal of Economics*, Vol. 38, May, 1924, p. 525.
11. FRIEDRICH, C. J., *Alfred Weber's Theory of Location of Industries*, Chicago: University of Chicago Press, 1929, 256 pp.
12. HOOVER, E., *Location Theory and the Shoe and Leather Industry*, Cambridge, Mass.: Harvard University Press, 1937, 323 pp.
13. HYSON, C. D., AND W. P. HYSON, "The Economic Law of Market Areas," *Quarterly Journal of Economics*, Vol. 64, May, 1950, pp. 319–327 [Selection 10 of this volume].
14. ISARD, W., "The General Theory of Location and Space-Economy," *Quarterly Journal of Economics*, Vol. 62, November, 1949, pp. 476–506.
15. ———, "Distance Inputs and the Space-Economy; Part I; The Conceptual Framework and Part II: The Locational Equilibrium of the Firm," *Quarterly Journal of Economics* Vol. 65, May and August 1951, pp. 181–198 and 373–399, respectively [Part II reprinted as Selection 3 of this volume].
16. ———, "Interregional and Regional Input-Output Analysis: A Model of a Space-Economy," *Review of Economics and Statistics*, Vol. 33, November, 1951, pp. 318–328.
17. ISARD, W., AND G. FREUTEL, "Regional and National Product Projections and Their Interrelations," *Conference on Research in Income and Wealth*, New York: National Bureau of Economic Research, forthcoming.
18. KOOPMANS, T. C., "Optimum Utilization of the Transportation System," ECONOMETRICA, Vol. 17, July 1949, Supplement, pp. 136–46.
19. KOOPMANS, T. C., AND S. REITER, "A Model of Transportation," Chapter XIV in *Activity Analysis of Production and Allocation*, Cowles Commission Monograph 13, T. C. Koopmans, ed., New York: John Wiley and Sons 1951, pp. 222–259.
20. LAUNHARDT, W., *Mathematische Begründung der Volkwirtschaftslehre*, Leipzig: W. Englemann, 1885, 216 pp.
21. LEONTIEF, W., AND W. ISARD, "The Extension of Input-Output Techniques to Interregional Analysis," Part II in *Studies in the Structure of the American Economy*, New York: Oxford University Press, 1952, forthcoming.
22. LÖSCH, A., *Die räumliche Ordnung der Wirtschaft*, Jena: G. Fischer, 1944, 380 pp.
23. NOYES, C. R., *Economic Man in Relation to his Natural Environment*, New York: The Columbia University Press, 1948, Vol. II, pp. 695–1443.
24. PALANDER, T., *Beiträge zur Standortstheorie*, Uppsala: Almqvist and Wiksells, 1935, 258 pp.
25. THÜNEN, J. H. VON, *Der isolierte Staat in Beziehung auf Landwirtschaft und Nationalökomie*, Berlin: Hempel and Parey, 1895.

PART V

V

GENERAL EQUILIBRIUM THEORY

17

Equilibrium Among Spatially Separated Markets: Solution by Electric Analog

Economists—especially in the lecture hall—have long resorted to physical analogs to aid their exposition. An obvious next step is to use physical analogs of economic models to solve certain economic problems. The growing number of analog computers that economists are becoming familiar with suggests that this next step will hereafter be taken with increasing frequency.[1]

One class of problems in economics that has long resisted attack concerns the effect of transportation costs upon local price and commodity movements when traders are located at many different points.[2] Value theory has always tended to assume one of several very special locational patterns when there are numerous buyers and numerous sellers, each one of whom is influenced by several other buyers or sellers. In the case of pure competition theory it has been *necessary* to assume that: (1) all buyers and sellers are similarly located, (2) all buyers are at one location or all sellers are at some other location, or (3) buyers and sellers are scattered but all traded units pass through some *node* or market.[3] The situation has not been very satisfactory in the case of monopolistic competition theory either.[4]

A more general case, within the class relating to a homogeneous good, is where there are several variously located trading units. Each trading unit may be a seller at some relatively high price and a

1. The work done by N. F. Morehouse, R. H. Strotz, and S. J. Horwitz ("An Electro-Analog Method for Investigating Problems in Economic Dynamics: Inventory Oscillations," *Econometrica*, 18 (October 1950), pp. 313–328) is an interesting and recent example.

2. It was not by accident that Alfred Marshall, even though his famous *Principles* contained an entire book on value theory and a mathematical appendix besides, always analyzed the simplest kinds of buyer and seller location.

3. Some of the reasons why no other location assumption would be logically possible have been set forth by the author elsewhere ("Space and Value," *Quarterly Journal of Economics*, 56 (August 1942), pp. 627–637).

4. Monopolistic competition theory, at the present time, cannot readily handle a hypothetical situation in which there are numerous sellers located at different points because different sets of these will be interdependent in the sense that a price change by any one will shift the demand schedules of others. The theory at present concentrates on one seller at a time and adopts a *ceteris paribus* approach. Mutual interdependence is not explicitly incorporated into the analysis.

Reprinted from Econometrica, *19 (January 1951), 40–47, by permission of the Econometric Society and the author.*

buyer at some other relatively low price. These trading units are so located that shipment between any paired points occasions some transportation expense but not so great a cost as to insulate any one trading unit from all others. These trading units might be households or firms but they can perhaps more readily be conceived as towns or regions.

If there are only three such regions, and the importing and exporting propensities of each region as a function of the local net price are known, together with the intervening freight costs per unit, the equilibrium prices and quantities can be determined without undue difficulty. If there are more than three trading regions the problem is mathematically soluble, in the sense that there are enough equations to match the unknowns, but except by iteration the proper method of solution has not been apparent to those mathematicians who were consulted. However, and especially if the trading function of each region is approximately linear, a solution can readily be obtained from the simple electric analog described below. The purpose of this note is to set down a solution for the three-region case and to explain the solution of multiple-region cases by this analog. A few comments will finally be made regarding the possibility of solving more complicated problems and the comparative utility of analog and digital computers in solving these problems.

THE THREE-REGION CASE

There are three regions trading a homogeneous good. Each region constitutes a single and distinct market. The regions of each possible pair of regions are separated — but not isolated — by a transportation cost per physical unit which is independent of volume. There are no legal restrictions to limit the actions of the profit-seeking traders in each region. For each region the functions which relate local production and local use to local price are known, and consequently the magnitude of the difference which will be exported or imported at each local price is also known. Given these trade functions and transportation costs, we wish to ascertain:

1. The net price in each region,

2. The quantity of exports or imports for each region,

3. Which regions export, import, or do neither,

4. The aggregate trade in the commodity,

5. The volume and direction of trade between each possible pair o regions.

Actually, of course, in ascertaining the first *or* second, one obtains answers to all the other questions except the fifth.

For each region (R), at each several local price (P), the quantity exported (E) is equal to local production minus local use at that price. Imports are viewed as negative exports. The price in region I at which local use equals local production will be A_1. If trading functions are linear, $E_1 = b_1(P_1 - A_1)$, $E_2 = b_2(P_2 - A_2)$, etc. The transportation cost per unit from R_1 to R_2, which is assumed independent of volume, is symbolized by T_{12}, and in the reverse direction by T_{21}. The conditions for general equilibrium are that total exports equal zero (when imports are negative exports) and that the price in each importing region be equal to the price in each region that exports to it plus the freight cost per unit from the exporting to the importing region.

The essential difficulty is that one cannot tell, simply from a knowledge of A and T values, which regions will export, import, or not trade at all. For instance, suppose $A_1 < A_2 < A_3$; we can be sure that R_1 either exports or does not trade and that R_3 either imports or does not trade. But it is not obvious whether R_1 will export to R_2, whether R_3 will import from R_2, or whether R_2 exports or imports or is isolated, even if we make the simplifying assumption that the cost of transport per unit between any pair of ports is the same in both directions. To be more specific, even if $(A_3 - A_1) > T_{13}$, there may be a flow of trade from R_2 to R_3 which reduces P_3 sufficiently below A_3 that trade from R_1 to R_3 may not be profitable. The point is that R_1 will export only when $(P_i - A_1) > T_{1i}$ and will import only when $(A_1 - P_i) > T_{i1}$. Unfortunately, all we know about P_i is that, for each trading nation, it will differ from A_i.

Assuming all areas trade, we know that $P_1 > A_1$ and that $P_3 < A_3$, and that $P_3 = P_1 + T_{13}$. The real question is then whether R_2, having an A_2 value between those of A_1 and A_3, will be a net importer or a net exporter. One way to determine the trading role of R_2 is first to ascertain what the values of P_1 and P_3 would be if only R_1 and R_3 are considered together. Then, when $E_1 + E_3 = 0$ and $P_3 = P_1 + T_{13}$, R_2 will import if $A_2 > (P_1 + T_{12})$ and will export if $P_3 > (A_2 + T_{33})$. If neither condition is satisfied, always assuming transport cost per unit between two regions is always the same in both directions, R_2 will not trade.[5]

A numerical example may clarify some of these ideas. Let us suppose $A_1 = \$6$, $A_2 = \$11$, and $A_3 = \$14$. Let us suppose $T_{13} = \$4$, $T_{12} = \$3$, and $T_{23} = \$2$. R_1 must export to R_3 and P_3 must be 4 higher than P_1. P_2 must *either* be $\$3$ greater than P_1 *or* $\$2$ less than P_3; it cannot be *both* because $P_3 - P_1 = \$4$. If it is possible to extract very large exports from R_1 at a $\$7$ or $\$8$ price, while R_3 will absorb only small import quantities at a $\$13$ or $\$12$ price, P_1 will rise less above $\$6$

than P_3 will fall below \$14. Hence R_2 will become an importer and P_2 will be \$3 higher than P_1 but less than \$2 below P_3, so that R_2 and R_3 will not trade with one another.

Once the role of R_2 is known, the three-region case can be reduced to a two-region case for solution. If R_2 is an importer, R_2 and R_3 can be combined, and "brought to R_1," as it were, by restating their trading functions in terms of R_1 net prices. Thus, instead of P_2 we can always write $P_1 + T_{12}$, and also substitute $P_1 + T_{13}$ for P_3. The equation $E_1 = -(E_2 + E_3)$ can then be restated as

$$b_1(P_1 - A_1) = -[b_2(P_1 + T_{12} - A_2) + b_3(P_1 + T_{13} - A_3)],$$

and this gives us

$$P_1 = \frac{b_1 A_1 + b_2(A_2 - T_{12}) + b_3(A_3 - T_{13})}{b_1 + b_2 + b_3}.$$

Obtaining numerical values for P_2, P_3, E_1, E_2, and E_3 is now a straightforward affair.[6]

One special characteristic of the three-region case, as compared with situations in which *more* than three regions trade, is that the volume of trade between each pair of regions can be quickly computed once E_1, E_2, and E_3 are derived from P_1, P_2, and P_3. Two of the quantities E_1, E_2, and E_3 will be either both positive or both negative, and this will show how the trade of the third region is allocated; for instance, if E_2 and E_3 are both negative, E_{12} must equal $-E_2$ and E_{13} must equal $-E_3$, because we know that a region cannot simultaneously be an exporter and importer, and hence there can be no trade between R_2 and R_3.

To summarize, the important first step in determining the equilibrium solution is to ascertain the trading role of the region having an intermediate value for A. If, when this region is removed from the system, the prices in the other two regions which result are too *high* for this region to remain neutral, it will be an exporter [e.g., if, excluding R_2, $(P_3 - T_{23}) > A_2$]; conversely, it will be an importer if the prices of the other two regions are too low for it to remain neutral [e.g., if excluding R_2, $(P_1 + T_{12}) < A_2$]. The region with the highest A value

5. If $T_{12} + T_{23} = T_{13}$, R_1 will ship to R_3 through R_2.

6. Had R_2 been an exporter rather than an importer, we would know, in equilibrium, that $P_3 = P_2 + T_{23} = P_1 + T_{13}$ and that $E_1 + E_2 = -E_3$. The value of P_1 would then be obtained by solving the equation

$$P_3 = \frac{b_3 A_3 + b_1(T_{13} + A_1) + b_2(T_{23} + A_2)}{b_1 + b_2 + b_3}.$$

The rest follows readily enough.

is always an importer, if it trades; and the region with the lowest A value is always an exporter, if it trades.

If one considers a large trading system in a single commodity for which there is a regional or national market in a great many areas, it becomes extremely difficult to obtain answers, through mathematical procedures, to the five questions asked above. A solution is theoretically possible. But the procedure is not apparent unless an iterative method is adopted. Accordingly, it seems desirable to seek some physical analog; fortunately, providing export supply schedules can be viewed as linear, there does exist a simple analogy in electricity.[7]

One might represent the various A, P, and T values, which are all expressed in money per unit, by voltages. The physical commodity flows (E's) might be represented by amperages. However, it is necessary to reverse the usual but artificial electrical convention that current flows from high to low voltages so as to accord with the economic fact that commodities flow from low to high prices.

Let us suppose that the money to voltage ratio is 1¢ to 1 volt and that the quantity to amperage ratio is about 1,000 bushels to 1 amp. Suppose recent experience results in the belief that a change in P_1 of 1¢ usually causes a change of 200 bushels in the quantity exported or imported by R_1. Suppose also that the present situation entails exports of 10,000 bushels at a price of \$1. If we can assume a linear trading function for this region we have a hypothetical A_1 value of 50¢ or 50 volts. The value of b_1, which in economics is 200 bushels for each 1¢, in electricity is 0.2 amps for each volt. Hence, to represent b_1 in an electric circuit, we must employ a 5-ohms resistor to represent b_1.[8]

If we know A_i, b_i, and T_{1i} and T_{i1}, we can obtain answers to our questions, with the aid of the electric circuit depicted in Figure 2. This diagram is for four regions. The A's are represented by voltages; e.g., a voltage reading across BA_1 will represent the price in cents per bushel at which R_1 will neither import nor export. The b's are represented by resistances of different ohms ratings. The more responsive a region's exports or imports are to local net price changes, the lower will be the resistance inserted between the A and P points. The ohms rating of the resistor between A_1 and P_1 should be equal to the reciprocal of the number of thousands of bushels change in exports per 1¢ change in price of R_1. Transportation costs are represented by

---

7. This alternative was originally suggested by Dr. H. H. Germond, at the RAND Corporation, one of the mathematicians originally consulted.

8. For those who have forgotten their electrical theory, the current amperage (i) through part of a circuit is equal to the voltage drop ($v_1 - v_2$) over this circuit divided by the resistance in ohms (r) of that part of the circuit. Hence, while we have $E_1 = b_1(P_1 - A_1)$ in economics, we have $i = (1/r)(v_1 - v_2)$ in electricity; in bushels and cents we have 10,000 bushels = 200 bushels per 1¢ (100c − 50¢); and in amps and volts we have 10 amps = 1/5 ohms (100 volts − 50 volts).

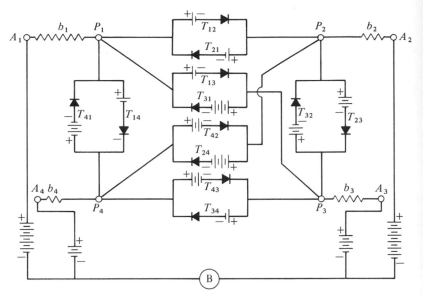

FIGURE 1   Electric circuit for determining prices and exports of a homogeneous good in spatially distinct markets.

opposed voltages; for instance, T_{12} is represented by the reversed battery at the top center of the diagram. The voltage of this reversed battery which represents T_{12} should be equal to the cost in cents of transporting one bushel from R_1 to R_2.

It will be noticed that, between each pair of P points, there is a unit comprising two reverse batteries and two rectifiers. The rectifiers act like flap valves; they will let current through only in the direction indicated by the arrowhead. If T_{12} differs from T_{21}, as well it might, the counter voltages must be adjusted accordingly. There is one of these units for each pair of nations and two rectifiers for each unit; for n regions we will need $n(n-1)$ rectifiers.

When this circuit is connected, the whole system will immediately move into stable equilibrium. A voltmeter reading between B and P_1 will indicate the local price in cents in R_1; prices prevailing in the other regions can be found in a similar way. The volume and direction of trade moving between R_1 and R_2 can be read from an ammeter connected between P_1 and P_2; however, a positive current flow from a high voltage to a low voltage must be interpreted as a commodity flow from the lower price area to the higher price area. The volume of trade between *each* pair of regions can be discovered in the same way. The sum of all these individual movements is the total volume of trade.[9]

9. If there is a change in demand or supply in any region, and we have some idea of how this may raise or lower the region's whole schedule of imports or exports, we

Circuits such as this could facilitate the analysis of many spatial trade structures. There are numerous commodities for which there are different market centers separated but not isolated by transportation costs. Examples, within the United States, are butter, apples, cotton, and petroleum, to mention only a few. Unfortunately, because each commodity usually has three or more trading centers, most of these cases have in the past been too difficult to handle analytically. The economic theory of spatially interdependent markets, as regards application as well as presentation, has consequently tended to be limited to two-region cases. In practice this has been a serious handicap because two-region cases are rather rare in the real world.

ALTERNATIVE MECHANICAL AIDS

If one so desired, a more complex analog could be constructed that would not be limited to simulating linear trading functions. Instead of a fixed resistor a servo-actuated rheostat might be substituted that would have the effect of varying the effective b_1 with P_1, etc. However, in view of the difficulties attached to estimating actual trading functions, the practical objections to assuming linear trading functions in the neighborhood of equilibrium prices are perhaps not very great.[10]

Instead of the relatively simple electric circuit shown in the figure, it might be supposed that a solution could better have been obtained by employing one of the digital computers or electronic differential analyzers now available.

Digital computers could eventually solve the multiple-region problem, and with greater accuracy if enough significant figures were included in enough reruns. However, the necessary computations would be laborious to program and long to complete. An initial value for, say, P_1 or E_1 would have to be assumed and then the P and E values for all other regions would have to be derived therefrom. However, the algebraic sum of all E values would be zero on the first run only by accident. The solution would then have to be approximated by iteration, with a lower P_1 value being next assumed if the algebraic sum of all E values were positive, and vice versa. The greater accuracy that could eventually be obtained with a digital computer would

can adjust the A voltage accordingly, and then, with voltmeter and ammeter, perhaps read off the new equilibrium. Alternatively, a change in transportation costs between a pair of regions could be taken into account by altering the appropriate counter voltage.

10. It may be of interest to point out that more elaborate analog computers can handle this sort of problem in a dynamic setting by employing inductances and observing the time paths of the variables on an oscilloscope (see Morehouse *et al.*, *op. cit.*).

hardly justify the time and effort in view of the imperfect reliability of estimated trading functions.

Differential analyzers are, of course, an implicit type of analog computer because their various units perform the mathematical operations specified by the equations of the system being studied. They handle nonlinear relations almost as readily as linear ones. An electronic differential analyzer could solve the multiple-region case outlined above in short order. However, such a machine is vastly more expensive to construct than the electrical circuit suggested here.

CONCLUSIONS

A relatively simple electric circuit can be used to determine equilibrium prices and commodity movements when a number of buyers and sellers trade a homogeneous good. A special simplifying requirement is that freight cost per unit be independent of traffic volume; however, unit freight costs need not be the same in both directions between paired traders. Another simplification is obtained if the trading functions can be approximated by linear equations; however, the circuit can be modified to handle nonlinear cases at the cost of simplicity and money. Also, the circuit can be modified, by eliminating one rectifier between each pair of traders, so as to handle the special case in which each trading unit is either always a seller or always a buyer if it trades at all. Digital computers could laboriously approximate solutions through iterative methods. Electronic computers of the differential analyzer type could handle nonlinear cases with ease, but it would probably be wasteful to use such expensive equipment for this job. Given the necessary data and the relatively simple circuit illustrated here, the resultant equilibrium prices and quantities can be measured with fair accuracy by voltmeters and ammeters in the manner described. *Gloria in excelsis Deo.*

18

Spatial Price Equilibrium and Linear Programming

INTRODUCTION

Increasingly, modern economic theorists are going beyond the formulation of equilibrium in terms of such marginal equalities as marginal revenue equal to marginal costs or wage rate equal to marginal value product. Instead they are reverting to an earlier and more fundamental aspect of a maximum position: namely, that from the top of a hill, whether or not it is locally flat, all movements are downward. Therefore, the real import of marginalism is embodied in the following type of statement: for any produced units of output, extra revenues exceed extra costs; but for any further producible units, extra revenue would fall short of extra costs. These marginal inequalities—which need not apply to small local movements alone—do, in well-behaved cases with smooth slopes, imply the usual marginal equalities. But they are more general, in that from them we can derive most of what is potentially useful in marginal analysis, a point which has been missed by both the defenders and attackers of "marginalism." And more than that, the marginal inequalities can apply to cases (like simple comparative advantage) where the marginal equalities fail.

In recent years economists have begun to hear about a new type of theory called *linear programming*. Developed by such mathematicians as G. B. Dantzig, J. v. Neumann, A. W. Tucker, and G. W. Brown, and by such economists as R. Dorfman, T. C. Koopmans, W. Leontief, and others, this field admirably illustrates the failure of marginal equalization as a rule for defining equilibrium. A number of books and articles on this subject are beginning to appear. It is the modest purpose of the following discussion to present a classical economics problem which illustrates many of the characteristics of linear programming. However, the problem is of economic interest for its own sake and because of its ancient heritage.

The first explicit statement that competitive market price is determined by the intersection of supply and demand functions

The author is professor of economics at the Massachusetts Institute of Technology and consultant to the Rand Corporation, whose help in this research is acknowledged.

Reprinted from the American Economic Review, *42 (June 1952), 283–303, by permission of the American Economic Association and the author.*

285

seems to have been given by A. A. Cournot in 1838 in connection, curiously enough, with the more complicated problem of price relations between two spatially separate markets—such as Liverpool and New York.[1] The latter problem, that of "communication of markets," has itself a long history, involving many of the great names of theoretical economics.[2] Dr. Stephen Enke in a recent interesting paper generalized the problem of interspatial markets and gave it an elegant solution.[3]

Proceeding from the Enke formulation, I propose in this paper (1) to show how this purely descriptive problem in non-normative economics can be cast mathematically into a *maximum* problem; and (2) to relate the Enke problem to a standard problem in linear programming, the so-called Koopmans-Hitchcock minimum-transport-cost problem.[4]

Spatial problems have been so neglected in economic theory that the field is of interest for its own sake. In addition, this provides a reasonably easy-to-understand example in the new field of linear programming. But, most important, insight into the fundamental nature of economic pricing is provided by the present discussion.

FORMULATION OF THE TWO PROBLEMS

In the Cournot-Enke problem, we are given at each of two or more localities a domestic demand and supply curve for a given product (*e.g.*, wheat) in terms of its market price at that locality. We are also given constant transport costs (shipping, insurance, duties, etc.) for carrying one unit of the product between any two of the specified localities. What then will be the final competitive equilibrium of prices in all the markets, of amounts supplied and demanded at each place, and of exports and imports?

From the description of the above problem, an economist would

1. A. A. Cournot, *Mathematical Principles of the Theory of Wealth* (1838), Chap. X.
2. J. Viner, *Studies in International Trade*, New York, 1937, pp. 589–91 gives references to Cunyngham (1904), Barone (1908), Pigou (1904), and H. Schultz (1935); for a non-graphic literary exposition, see F. W. Taussig, *Some Aspects of the Tariff Question*, Cambridge, Mass. (1915 and 1931), Chap. I.
3. S. Enke, "Equilibrium Among Spatially Separated Markets: solution by Electric Analogue," *Econometrica*, 19 (Jan. 1951), pp. 40–47 [Selection 17 of this volume].
4. See T. Koopmans, *Activity Analysis of Production and Allocation* (Monograph 13 of the Cowles Commission, published by John Wiley, 1951) for references. The special transport problem itself is dealt with in Chapters XIV and XXIII and independently deals with a problem considered in 1941 by F. L. Hitchcock and in 1942 by a Russian mathematician, L. Kantorovitch. For a readable account, see T. C. Koopmans, "Optimum Utilization of the Transportation System" *Econometrica*, 17, Suppl. (July 1949), pp. 136–46.

be tempted to guess that it includes inside it the following Koopmans problem, which I slightly reword to bring out the similarity: A specified total number of (empty or ballast) ships is to be sent out from each of a number of ports. They are to be allocated among a number of other receiving ports, with the total sent in to each such port being specified. If we are given the unit costs of shipment between every two ports, how can we minimize the total costs of the program?

Note that total shipments in or out of any one place are an unknown in the first problem, whereas they are given in the second. In this sense the first problem is the more general one and includes the second inside itself. Note, too, that, as it stands, the first problem is one of decentralized price-mechanics: innumerable atomistic competitors operate in the background, pursuing their private interests and taking no account of any centralized magnitude that is to be maximized. Yet, even without Adam Smith's "as-if" principle of the Invisible Hand, our teleological faith in the pricing mechanism is such that we should be surprised if the resulting allocations resulted in costly cross-haulages: we instinctively feel that arbitragers could make money getting rid of any such inefficiencies.

A final hint suggests that the first problem, which is definitely not a maximum problem to begin with, might be convertible into a maximum problem. Enke provides a simple ingenious electric circuit for its solution in the case of linear market functions. At least since the work of Clerk Maxwell and Kirchhoff a century ago it has been realized that the equilibrium of simple passive electric networks can be described in terms of an extremum principle — the minimization of "total power-loss."[5]

It is not surprising, therefore, that the Enke problem can be artificially converted into a maximum problem from which we may hope for the following specific advantages: (1) This viewpoint might aid in the choice of convergent numerical iterations to a solution. (2) From the extensive theory of maxima, it enables us immediately to evaluate the sign of various comparative-statics changes. (*E.g.*, an increase in net supply at any point can never in a stable system *decrease* the region's exports.) (3) By establishing an equivalence between

---

5. In its simplest form, such a minimum problem is of conventional interior differentiable ("Weierstrassian") type, and it does not involve the quasi-linear boundaries, inequalities, and vertexes encountered in linear programming. Nonetheless, A. W. Tucker in an unpublished Office of Naval Research memorandum "Analogues of Kirchhoff's Laws" (Stanford, 1950) noted the similarity of the Kirchhoff-Maxwell problem to the linear programming problem of the Koopmans type. Moreover, I gathered from personal conversation with Professor Tjalling Koopmans that when he first solved the transportation problem years ago, before linear programming had been explicitly formulated, the analog with the network problem readily occurred to him and helped guide his explorations toward a solution. See *Activity Analysis, op. cit.* pp. 258–59.

the Enke problem and a maximum problem, we may be able to use the known electric devices for solving the former to solve still other maximum problems, and perhaps some of the linear programming type. (4) The maximum problem under consideration is of interest because of its unusual type: it involves in an essential way such non-analytic functions as absolute value of X, which has a discontinuous derivative and a *corner*; this makes it different from the conventionally studied types and somewhat similar to the inequality problems met with in linear programming. (5) Finally, there is general methodological and mathematical interest in the question of the conditions under which a given equilibrium problem can be significantly related to a maximum or minimum principle.

THE TWO-LOCALITY CASE GRAPHICALLY TREATED

The two-variable case provides a convenient introduction to the principles involved. The general n variable case then follows without much difficulty. Figure 1 shows the usual textbook back-to-back diagram determining the equilibrium flow of exports from market I to

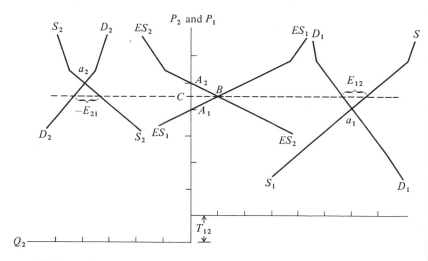

FIGURE 1   Equilibrium is at B where exports of I match imports of II at the differential between P_2 and P_1 equal to transport costs, T_{12}. Note shift in lower axis of II.

II. Before trade, equilibrium would be at $P_1 = A_1$ where supply and demand in the first market just meet; or what is the same thing, where the excess-supply function ES_1 to ES_1, which is equal to the demand subtracted laterally at every price from the supply curve, is at its zero point. Likewise, $P_2 = A_2$ if no trade is possible.

But now suppose that goods can move from I to II for T_{12} dollars per unit, and from II to I for T_{21} dollars per unit. Since the pre — trade price is lower in I than II, trade will obviously never flow from II to I and so only the T_{12} figure is relevant. Because the initial differential in prices exceeds the transport costs, there will be a positive flow of exports from I to II, and P_2 will come to exceed P_1 by exactly T_{12}. For this reason the axes of market I have been displaced relative to those of market II by the distance T_{12}.

The new equilibrium is shown at B where the excess supply or exports of market I exactly equal the algebraically negative excess supply or imports of market II. The bracketed distances E_{12}, and $-E_{21}$, and CB are all exactly equivalent depictions of these flows.

Of course, if A_1 and A_2 had been closer together than T_{12} (or T_{21}), then the markets would have split-up and separate equilibria would be at (A_1, A_2). Had A_2 been less than A_1 by more than T_{21}, then the flow of exports would have automatically reversed directions so that E_{21} would be positive and E_{12} negative. What makes the problem interesting is its complicated non-linear equilibrium conditions:

$$\text{If } P_2 = P_1 + T_{12}, \tag{1a}$$

any non-negative E_{12} may flow; $E_{12} > 0$ implies $P_2 = P_1 + T_{12}$.

$$\text{If } \quad P_2 < P_1 + T_{12} \quad \text{and if} \quad P_1 < P_2 + T_{21}, \tag{1b}$$

then $E_{12} = 0$ and $E_{21} = 0$.

$$\text{If } \quad P_1 = P_2 + T_{21}, \tag{1c}$$

then $E_{21} \gtreqless 0$, depending upon total world supply and demand, etc.; $E_{21} > 0$ implies $P_1 = P_2 + T_{21}$.

Figure 2 provides a new graphical restatement of what is shown in Figure 1. The same excess-supply curves are shown but this time the prices in the two countries are measured *from the same level* rather than with one axis shifted by the amount of transportation cost. However, the transport costs do enter into the problem. Look first at the two upper curves of the figure only. Now the final equilibrium is determined at JK where the two excess-supply curves differ vertically by T_{12}, as shown by the bracket.

This same equilibrium determination of exports and imports (E_{12} and $-E_{21}$) is shown in the lower part of the figure by the heavy NN curve which represents the *vertical* difference between the two excess supply curves. The final equilibrium is at F where the net excess-supply curve hits the curve of discontinuous transport costs $WXYZ$.

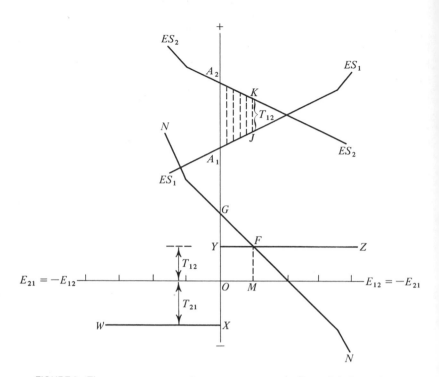

FIGURE 2   The same excess-supply curves appear as in figure 1, but now lower axes are evenly aligned. Transport costs enter through the discontinuous curve *WXYZ*. Equilibrium is where the *net* excess-supply curve for the two markets — *NN* = vertical subtraction of ES_1 from ES_2 — intersects *WXYZ* at *F*. (Alternatively, equilibrium is where *JK* vertical distance equals T_{12}.)

Figure 2 has the merit of suggesting how a shift in one or both of the excess supply curves would cause the equilibrium intersection to be shifted over to the *WX* interval, with II exporting to I as in equation (1c). It also suggests how the intersection *might* be on the *XY* interval, with exports and imports zero, and with prices related as in (1b).

DEFINING SOCIAL PAY-OFF

Figure 2 paves the way toward a maximum or minimum formulation of the problem. An economist looking at these figures would naturally think of some kind of consumers surplus concept. The area A_1JKA_2, and *OMFG*, its equivalent, cry out to be compared with the area under the transport curve, *OMFY*. However, the name consumers surplus has all kinds of strange connotations in economics. To avoid these and to underline the completely artificial nature of my procedure, I shall simply define a "net social pay-off" function, with three components:[6] NSP = Social Pay-off in I + Social Pay-off in II − Transport Cost.

The social pay-off of any region is defined as the algebraic area under its excess-*demand* curve. This is equal in magnitude to the area under its excess-supply curve but opposite in algebraic sign. However, since the second market has been put back-to-back to the first, the area under the second market's excess-supply curve in Figure 2 does measure the second market's pay-off; and from it we must *subtract* the area under the first country's excess-supply curve. *Hence, the area under the net curve NN in Figure 2 does perfectly measure the combined social pay-off of both markets.*

In Figure 3 the curve *NON* indicates how the combined payoff of the two markets varies with algebraic exports from 1 to 2. From this we subtract the curve of total transport cost *UOU*. Total transport cost

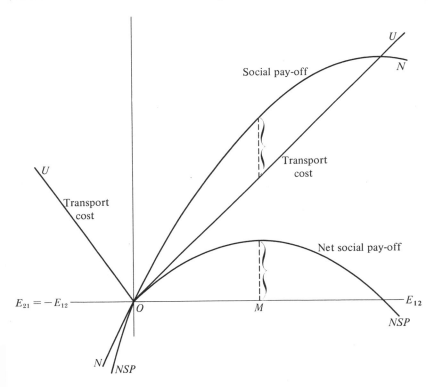

FIGURE 3   Same equilibrium as in previous figures is shown as the maximum of net social pay-off or maximum vertical difference between upper two curves.

6. This magnitude is artificial in the sense that no competitor in the market will be aware of or concerned with it. It is artificial in the sense that after an Invisible Hand has led us to its maximization, we need not necessarily attach any social welfare significance to the result.

has a corner at the origin because of the discontinuity between T_{12} and T_{21} as shown in *WXYZ* of Figure 2; the algebraic integral of this discontinuous function leads to the V-shaped total function *UOU*.[7] We find our equilibrium where the vertical distance between the two upper curves is at a maximum. This same optimal level of exports (E_{12}) or imports ($-E_{21}$) is also shown at the maximum point of the net social pay-off curve, the third curve which measured the vertical distance between the upper two.

This completes the two-variable case. Figure 4 illustrates that three possible cases could have emerged, corresponding to equations (1).

In Figure 4a, region I exports to II so that the maximum point is smooth; the corner in the curve, due to the discontinuity in the rate

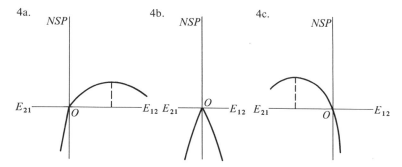

FIGURE 4   Types of maxima for net social pay-off. Because of transport costs, each curve of net social pay-off has a corner at the origin. In (4b) price differentials are too little to surmount transport costs, so trade is zero.

of transport cost, is on the vertical axis and does not affect the maximum. Similarly Figure 4c shows a normally smooth maximum without corners; II is then exporting to I. Figure 4b shows the intermediate case where the maximum point is a cusp with a corner; the transport cost discontinuity is obviously to blame.

The final point to emphasize is this: Once the separate pay-off functions are set up as areas or integrals of the excess-supply curves and once transport-cost functions are known, a clerk could be given the task of experimentally varying exports so as to achieve a net maxi-

7. The mathematical symbolism for this function can be written in many equivalent ways:
e.g.
$$t_{12}(E_{12}) = T_{12}E_{12} \text{ for } E_{12} \geqq 0$$
$$= T_{21}(-E_{12}) \text{ for } E_{12} \leqq 0$$

and still other equivalent symbolisms (involving absolute values of E_{12}, etc.) can be found.

mum. He could proceed by trial and error, always moving in a direction that increased the net pay-off, and he would ultimately arrive at the correct equilibrium. The existence of pathological corners would not impair convergence; rather it might accelerate convergence.[8]

THE GENERAL CASE OF ANY NUMBER OF REGIONS

Instead of two regions suppose we have $i = 1, 2, \ldots, n$ regions. The algebraic amount of exports from i to j we can write as E_{ij} and it will of course be the same thing as the algebraic imports of j from i, $-E_{ji}$. Table 1 shows the two-way table relating these interregion exports to the total algebraic exports of any region, E_i. (Note that about half the numbers in the table will be negative.) Suppose too that we are given T_{ij}, the transport cost per unit of product moved from region i to region j. These transport costs could also have been arranged in a two-way table. Finally suppose that for each region we

TABLE I

REGION	1	2	...	j	...	n	TOTAL EXPORTS (ALGEBRAIC)
1		$E_{12} = -E_{21}$		E_{1j}	...	$E_{1n} = -E_{n1}$	$E_1 = \sum E_{1j}$
2	E_{21}	..		.			$E_2 = \sum_j E_{2j}$
.							
.							.
.							
i	E_{i1}	.		$E_{ij} = -E_{ji}$		E_{in}	$E_i = \sum_i E_{ij}$
.							.
n	E_{n1}	.		E_{nj}			$E_n = \sum_j E_{nj}$
TOTAL IMPORTS (ALGEBRAIC)	$-E_1 = \sum E_{i1}$	$-E_2 = \sum_i E_{i2}$	...	$-E_i = \sum_i E_{ij}$	...	$-E_n = \sum_i E_{in}$	$0 = \sum_i \sum_i E_{ij}$ = TOTAL NET EXPORTS

8. Mathematically, calling the excess-supply functions $s_i(E_i)$,

$$NSP = -\int_0^{E_{12}} s_i(x)\,dx - \int_0^{-E_{12}} s_2(x)\,dX - t_{12}(E_{12}).$$

By setting $dN/dE_{12} = 0$, we arrive at conditions equivalent to equations (1):

$$-T_{21} \leq s_2(E_{21}) - s_1(E_{12}) \leq T_{12}, \qquad E_{12} + E_{21} = 0 \tag{1}$$

and with $E_{12} \neq 0$ implying that one of the equality signs holds. A gradient method of making dE_{12}/dt proportional to dN/dE_{12} would always converge for positive sloping s_1 functions.

have an excess supply function $s_i(E_i) = P_i$, which is calculated by taking the lateral difference between local supply and demand functions.

As in the two-variable case, we can define a social pay-off for every region in terms of the area under the excess-demand or excess-supply function. This will depend only upon the total exports of the region and can be written

$$S_i(E_i) = \text{area under the excess-demand curve} = -\int_0^{E_i} s_i(x)\,dx. \quad (2)$$

The transport costs can be written as a function of exports between any two regions; or as $t_{ij}(E_{ij}) = $ a V-shaped curve like that shown in Figure 3.[9]

Now we can form a final net social pay-off for all the regions as the sum of the n separate pay-offs minus the total transport costs of all the shipments:

$$NSP = \sum_1^n S_i(E_i) - \sum_{i<j}\sum t_{ij}(E_{ij}). \quad (3)$$

Because $E_i = E_{i1} + \cdots + E_{in}$, this is a function of all the E_{ij}'s and when we have found its maximum we have arrived at the final unique equilibrium trade pattern.[10]

Providing that all domestic supply curves cut demand curves from below (as price rises), which is the so-called case of normal or stable intersection, the excess-supply curves will never be falling curves; and it will necessarily follow that the maximum position will exist and be unique. At the maximum point, we will find

$$-T_{ij} \leqq s_i(E_i) - s_j(E_j) \leqq T_{ji} \qquad (\text{for all } i, j = 1, \ldots, n) \quad (4)$$

with both inequalities holding only if $E_{ij} = 0 = E_{ji}$; if $E_{ij} > 0$, then the right-hand equality must hold; and if $E_{ji} < 0$, the left-hand equality must hold. Recalling that the s_i's and P's are the same thing, we obviously end up with the proper n-region generalization of equations (1) that were derived for the two-region case.

Our task has now been successfully completed. The problem in

9. Mathematically, this function has a corner at the zero export point, and will equal $T_{ij}E_{ij}$ if i exports to j and $T_{ji}E_{ji}$ if j exports to i. Note T_{ij} need not equal T_{ji} but it can be shown by definition $t_{ij}(E_{ij}) = t_{ji}(E_{ji})$.

10. Since we know that the imports of one region are the exports of another, we do not have to specify all the $n^2 E_{ij}$'s in Table 1. Instead we can work with all those that are above the hollow diagonals of the Table, inferring those below by using the identity $E_{ij} = -E_{ji}$. Thus, we may adopt the convention of having $i < j$, and may work with $n(n-1)/2$ unknown E_{ij}'s. Incidentally, most of the E_{ij}'s will turn out to be zero: *i.e.*, a typical export region will export to only a few other regions and a typical importer will import from only one or a few regions. More exactly, it is a theorem of linear programming that the number of positive exports need not exceed $n-1$. It will also be true that if T_{ij} and E_i are all integers, the E_{ij}'s will all be integers.

descriptive price behavior has been artificially converted into a maximum problem. This maximum problem can be solved by trial and error or by a systematic procedure of varying shipments in the direction of increasing social pay-off.[11]

Once the exports are determined between any two places, it is obvious that the total exports of any and every place are also determined. Some of the n-regions will end up as positive net exporters; some will end up as net importers (negative net exporters); some may even end up in perfect balance, with zero imports and exports. Reflection will show that we are free to omit all such balanced regions from our further discussion, since so long as they remain in balance they need not export or import from any locality.[12]

It follows that we can divide our n-regions up into $i = 1, \ldots, m$ export regions and $i = m+1, \ldots, n$ import regions. Reflection will show that a net import region will never export to any region. (Why send exports out if you have to expensively ship in imports to replace them? Instead ship directly.) Reflection also shows that a net export region will never import from any region. Thus, the only non-zero E_{ij}'s are from an export region i to an import region j.

What does this mean for Table 1? It means that we can label our regions so as to give the first m numbers to our export regions and the last $n-m$ numbers to the import regions. Table 1 will then divide itself up into four major blocks: positive numbers will then be in only the upper right-hand block relating the exporting countries to the importing countries; the two blocks relating exporters to exporters and importers to importers will necessarily be full of zeros, and can be neglected. The block relating importers to exporters will consist of negative numbers only and will simply duplicate our positive numbers.

11. Even if this were not a market problem, we could set up pretended competitive markets whose supply and demand relations might be used to help compute the correct mathematical solutions. Computing clerks could be instructed to act like brokers and arbitragers, etc. Or we could dispense with all markets, and instead watch how NSP is changing as we change each E_{ij}, continuing to move always in the direction of increasing NSP. Doing this long enough will carry us to the top of the hill. For the case where the excess-supply curves are straight lines Enke has given a simple electric circuit, consisting of resistances, rectifiers, and batteries, which will give the final solution as a measurement of currents and voltages. See Enke, *op. cit.*, Figure 1, p. 45 and the next section below.

12. That is $E_i = 0$ implies $E_{ij} = 0 = E_{ji}$ for all j. Note that I am adopting the convention of not treating cargo shipped *through* a port as at all part of its exports or imports. Thus, cargo going from London to San Francisco is not to be treated as both an import and export of Panama. A similar philosophy tells me that T_{ij} data have already been adjusted so that it is no longer cheaper to send cargo from i to j via a third port k: such an "indirect" route would already have been defined to be the cheapest direct route and by our convention the port k would not be explicitly involved. Such preliminary adjustments of the definition of T_{ij} have made it satisfy the "Pythagorean" relations $T_{ij} \leq T_{ik} + T_{kj}$, etc.

Table 2 shows the relevant configuration. Note that all the numbers shown by symbol are positive: Thus $(-E_n)$ represents positive imports because algebraic exports E_n are negative for an importing

TABLE 2

REGIONS	$1 \cdots m$	$m+1,$	$m+2$	$\cdots n$	TOTAL EXPORTS
exporters					
1		$E_{1,m+1}$	$E_{1,m+2}$	$\cdots E_{1,n}$	(E_1)
2		$E_{2,m+1}$	$E_{2,m+2}$	$E_{2,n}$	(E_2)
.	zeros				
.		.			
.		.			
m		$E_{m,m+1}$	$E_{m,m+2}$	E_{mn}	(E_m)
importers					
$m+1$					
.	redundant				
.	negative		zeros		
.	numbers				
n					
TOTAL IMPORTS		$(-E_{m+1})$	$(-E_{m+2})$	$\cdots(-E_n)$	

country. Note that a table of T_{ij}'s is definable for *all* countries and all blocks; but with the given positive exports and imports shown in the margins of the table within parentheses, we would be interested only in the T_{ij}'s in the upper right-hand corner.

RELATION TO THE KOOPMANS LINEAR PROGRAMMING PROBLEM

In this and the next section, I shall try to relate the results of our international trade problem to the newly developed theory of linear programming (defined austerely by the mathematician as "the maximization of a linear expression subject to linear inequalities"). For the theorist these are important sections, and to an economist who has heard about this new field and would like to get an idea of what it is all about, these will serve to indicate its general flavor. Though I have tried to use only the most elementary tools, these two sections are not summer-hammock reading; and for this reason, the remaining sections have been arranged so that a reader can go directly on to them, skipping the more technical material.

Imagine now that the positive totals in parentheses $(E_1, \ldots, E_m)$ and $(-E_{m+1}, \ldots, -E_n)$ were given to us by Enke while at the same time he concealed from us the entries $E_{i,m+j}$ giving the detailed breakdowns. Then for us to find the missing numbers so as to minimize total transport cost would be precisely the Koopmans-Hitchcock problem in linear programming.[13]

How do we know that Enke's solution for E_{ij}'s does truly minimize transport cost? Since I have shown that Enke does maximize net social pay-off, and since the expressions $\Sigma_1{}^n S_i(E_i)$ in NSP of equation (3) depend only on the regional totals of exports $(E_1, \ldots, E_n)$, it follows that maximizing NSP would be impossible unless the E_{ij}'s were optimal for minimizing transport cost. Thus the Cournot-Enke problem does have inside it the Koopmans problem.[14]

Despite its likeness to the Kirchhoff-Maxwell quadratic maximum property of electric networks, the Koopmans problem cannot be solved by simple Kirchhoff networks unless entirely new laws of resistance can be inserted into such a network.[15] However, we can utilize the Enke network, which uses standard resistances and rectifiers, to solve any Koopmans problem. But we must work backwards: we must experimentally vary Enke's A_i's, which he puts into his network as prescribed voltages, until we achieve the requisite n totals $(E_1, \ldots, E_m, -E_{m+1}, \ldots, -E_n)$.[16] We can read off the required interregional exports as electric currents from the resulting Enke analog network.

The above method is of interest because it suggests that any linear programming problem may be solvable as an unconstrained extremum problem provided we can imbed it in a suitably generalized problem.[17] Since the Air Forces and Bureau of Standards have set up their electronic calculators so as to solve transportation problems in

13. We minimize

$$\sum_{i=1}^{m} \sum_{j=m+1}^{n} T_{ij} E_{ij}$$

subject to

$$\sum_{j=m+1}^{n} E_{ij} = E_i \qquad (i = 1, \ldots, m)$$

and

$$\sum_{i=1}^{m} E_{ij} = (-E_j) \qquad (j = m+1, \ldots, n) \qquad E_{i,m+j} \geq 0.$$

14. A close analogy is the Yntema-Robinson problem of determining best outputs for a monopolist discriminating among independent markets. This includes inside it the problem of best allocating a given total output among markets.

15. See *Activity Analysis*, p. 259.

16. This can always be done. The theory of the "dual problem" in linear programming assures us that there exists a set of parallel shifts of the excess-supply curves that will bring about any prescribed E_i configuration. The slopes of the excess-supply curves, Enke's b's can be arbitrary positive numbers. The procedure here described has the drawback of involving in effect a need to solve a set of simultaneous equations between the A's and E's. This might be mechanized by servomechanisms. (Query: does the "dual network" to Enke's solve the "dual problem" of linear programming?)

17. Thus, if we use ordinary matrix notation and are given m arbitrary c's and

relatively short time, there is no need to pursue the computational advantage of analog networks any farther here.

EQUILIBRIUM PRICES AND THE DUAL PROBLEM

The equilibrium prices as given by equations (4) arise naturally in the Enke problem but are completely absent from the initial formulation of the transport problem. However, as an economist, Koopmans sought to introduce some kind of price mechanism into the calculation and he did succeed in defining a set of prices or potentials that correspond to our s_i's and P_i's. In doing this he was guided by economic and electric analogies and he was able to anticipate the mathematicians' theories of what is called the "dual problem" in linear programming. Mathematical theory assures us that every minimum problem in linear programming can be, so to speak, turned on its side and can be converted into a related maximum problem. The answer to this maximum problem also gives the correct answer for the quantity that was to be minimized.

For sake of brevity I shall simply refer the reader to the theory of linear programming for interpretations and proofs of the following remarks: (1) The P's or s's of equation (4) are the dual variables to the E_{ij}'s of the transport problem;[18] (2) $P_i - P_j$ can be interpreted in

---

$m(\geqq n)$ arbitrary x's, suppose we seek to maximize $Z = b'x$ subject to $Ax = c$ and $x \geqq 0$. Then for any $n \times n$ positive definite matrix B, there exists an n-vector v such that

$$Z^* = c'Bc - v'c + b'x = x'A'BAx - v'Ax + b'x$$

will be at a maximum for $x \geqq 0$ only if $Ax = c$. Having somehow found such unknown v's, we can solve Z by solving Z^*, an unconstrained extremum problem. For special A's and B's this can be converted into a simple analog network problem. In every case we can solve the dual problem by taking proper combinations of the optimal derivatives of Z^*. Actually Z^* need not be quadratic but can be more general. A natural generalization of the Koopmans problem would be to have the flow of shipments vary directly with the marginal costs of transport $T_{ij} + P_i - P_j$. This would differ from the Enke problem in that E_i would then be a function of all P's and not of P_i alone. Dr. Martin Beckmann has written a number of interesting Cowles Commission Memoranda dealing with the case of continuous markets located everywhere in the plane. The partial differential equations of equilibrium correspond very closely to those of the Koopmans problem and a potential function plays a similar rôle. For the continuous case too, we can imbed the problem into a more general situation in which there is an excess-supply function at every point.

18. Defining the profitability of any export from i to j as $\pi_{ij} = P_j - P_i - T_{ij}$, then for all $\pi_{ij} \leqq 0 \leqq P_k$, the maximum of $Z = -\Sigma P_k E_k$ will equal the minimum achievable transport costs. For any $\pi_{ij} < 0$, $E_{ij} = 0$, and for any $E_{ij} < 0$, $\pi_{ij} = 0$. Z can be rewritten $\Sigma\Sigma E_{ij}(P_j - P_i)$ so that we can think of the problem as that of finding the price differentials that will maximize the total *gain* in value of amounts shipped, subject to nonpositive profitabilities on each shipment. It may be mentioned that only price differences are determinate and that the "dual variables" corresponding to export regions are related to their prices.

the Koopmans problem as an element of indirect marginal cost to be added to direct marginal cost T_{ij}—this term takes into account the money advantages of having an empty ship at j rather than at i; (3) If we change some E_i's, then the resulting increase in total transport cost is related to the P's; (4) Pricing in a competitive market could conceivably keep a system in the proper optimal configuration.[19]

19. The present techniques, generalized in the manner indicated by cited work of Beckmann, can be used to throw light on many of the problems arising in connection with the basing point controversy. Oligopolists selling a homogeneous product want some pattern of pricing that will lead to a single *unambiguous price* at any geographical point. Usually, too, the pattern must be such as to lead to a not-too-obviously-wasteful flow of transport, and it must provide for a fairly stable and not-too-lopsided sharing of the market by the different producers. Historically, so long as most production is in fact concentrated in one advantageous place, such as Pittsburgh, a single basing pattern meets these criteria and is not too inefficient. Such a pattern of course encourages consumers to move toward the base; but to the extent that customers do not move, it encourages producers to move out toward them so as to receive in the form of higher net prices the transport costs saved or "phantom freight."

In any case, in a dynamic world any one locality will usually lose its dominant advantages in time and many plants will be operating away from the single basing point. Consequently, the system will lead increasingly to an inefficient pattern of transport and will become increasingly vulnerable to public criticism and to competition. A multiple basing point system may then come into effect and this will represent a compromise between FOB pricing and delivered pricing: within each region, the basing point pattern will prevail but at the shiftable boundaries of the regions there may be price competition between regions.

The requirements for the regional pattern of prices and flow of commodities is so strictly determined by perfect-competition assumptions that it is easy to show how basing point patterns deviate from the spirit and the letter of the competitive pattern: thus when producers all over the country respect a single basing point pattern, the contour lines of equal-delivered-price surround the basing point in a manner superficially similar to a perfect-competition pattern; but the flow of transports is *not* perpendicular to the contour lines of price and so we instantly detect the absence of perfect competition. For any given pattern of producer and consumer location and observed flow of product, linear programming permits us to calculate the optimal minimum cost of transport and to compare it with the actual.

The optimum pattern never permits of overlapping markets of differently located plants; so it is obvious that an omnipotent combine of oligopolists would never use the arbitrary pattern of price discrimination implied by basing points. Nonetheless, there is nothing at all surprising about the use of this pattern; for after all an omnipotent combine of oligopolists would not engage in competitive advertising and many other things which we expect actual imperfect competitors to engage in. Except in times of formal or informal price control, imperfect non-discrimination is only one out of an infinity of patterns, we should not be at all surprised by the existence of price discrimination. Moreover, contrary to some views in the literature, the pattern of price discrimination implied by adhering to basing point formulas is *not* particularly a strange or arbitrary one: it can be shown to presuppose that the elasticity of demand of customers for the delivered output of the basing point mills increases slightly with distance from the basing point, an assumption that no one would defend as exact but also an assumption that no assistant vice-president would be motivated to denounce strongly. Under oligopoly the most precious of all devices are those that lead to an informal consensus and the basing point system has the great virtue that within a region it reduces the whole pattern of pricing *to a single unknown*, around which sentiments can form and in terms of which mere price-competing is obviated.

ILLUSTRATIVE CASE STUDY

A numerical example may help to clarify the theoretical relations. Unless there are at least four regions, no problem of optimizing the pattern of exports can arise. So consider regions I, II, III, IV characterized by the following transport costs (in $ per unit of shipment), as shown in Table A.

TABLE A

$$
\begin{bmatrix}
\cdot & T_{12} & \cdot & T_{13} & T_{14} \\
T_{21} & \cdot & \cdot & T_{23} & T_{24} \\
\cdot & \cdot & \cdot & \cdot & \cdot \\
T_{31} & T_{32} & \cdot & \cdot & T_{34} \\
T_{41} & T_{42} & \cdot & T_{43} & \cdot
\end{bmatrix}
=
\begin{bmatrix}
\cdot & 9 & \cdot & 8 & 7 \\
4 & \cdot & \cdot & 4 & 1 \\
\cdot & \cdot & \cdot & \cdot & \cdot \\
5 & 1 & \cdot & \cdot & 5 \\
6 & 2 & \cdot & 6 & \cdot
\end{bmatrix}
$$

Let us suppose that initial local conditions of demand and supply are such as to make Regions I and II exporters and III and IV importers. Suppose further that I initially exports only to III while II exports to both III and IV. In that case the data in the upper right-hand block of the transport cost array are alone relevant. The resulting export shipments are perhaps as shown in Table B.

TABLE B

REGIONS	III	IV	EXPORTS	LOCAL PRICE
I	38	0	(38)	($10)
II	2	50	(52)	$14
Imports	(40)	(50)	90	
Local price	$18	$15		

If only the data in parentheses in Table B were given, we could from the cost data in Table A deduce the remaining numbers in B. To do so we would have to solve the Koopmans problem and its so-called dual problem; however, in solving the more general Enke problem, all P's would already have been determined by supply and demand conditions, as would have all the unknowns of the problem.

To understand the necessary pattern of price, Figure 5a is useful. It represents what the mathematical topologist calls a "tree," and it shows the flow of exports by means of arrows. Note that all four markets are connected and that competition will freeze all P's as soon as any one P in the tree is known.

Now let us suppose that there is an increase in domestic supply and a decrease in domestic demand in I, so that I's excess supply function increases. It will be shown in the next section that this must depress P_1. At first, therefore, the *qualitative* pattern of trade will be

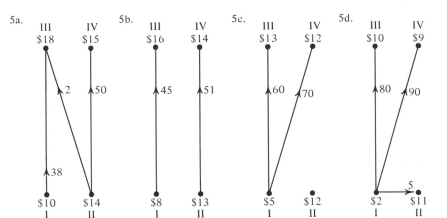

FIGURE 5   Four-region trade equilibria. The changing network of trade as excess-demand at I increases. (Arrows show direction of trade while nearby numbers show its magnitude. Dollar figures refer to regional prices.)

unchanged; and hence, all P's must decrease by exactly the same amount as P_1 decreases. (Incidentally, algebraic exports of *all* other regions must at first go down if their markets are to be cleared.)

However, if the excess-supply function at I increases enough, region II's export market to III may be completely captured by I. This case is shown in Figure 5b. Our tree has now split off into two trees, or what the mathematician calls a "forest." Now P_2 and P_4 are interconnected but they are independent of P_1 and P_3. This is called the case of "degeneracy" in the theory of linear programming, and its theory is well understood.[20] From this point on further increases in excess-supply at I will depress P_1 and P_3 equally but will leave P_2 and P_4 unchanged, and will not affect exports or consumption in those regions.

But if excess-supply in I increases by still more, it will finally so depress P_1 as to permit I to capture II's remaining export market in IV. II is now isolated as in Figure 4c, which shows a lopsided forest.

20. This "degeneracy" is not quite the same thing as the following phenomenon: there may for some E's be more than one optimal trade pattern, with choice between the different optima being a matter of indifference. Thus, Koopmans, *op. cit.* p. 253, has called attention to the following kind of a situation: shipments from London to San Francisco meet shipments from New York to Honolulu in Panama; provided we are dealing with homogeneous shipments of wheat or empty vessels, it is obviously *indifferent* whether we reroute some of the London-Frisco shipments to Honolulu — provided an equal and opposite rerouting of New York cargo is simultaneously made. The cost data of Table A provide such an example when III is exporting say 15, IV exporting 30, I importing 25 and II importing 20. It then becomes a matter of indifference as to how III's exports are divided between I and II, provided that IV's shipments compensate. Professor Robert Solow points out to me that creating a fictitious set of two intermediate ports — V' which receives 45 and V''' which exports 45 — will get rid of the indeterminacy.

In this region P_1, P_3, and P_4 all fall equally, and imports of III and IV gradually increase. P_2 and II's consumption remain unchanged, with her export remaining zero.

In the ultimate stage shown by Figure 5d, excess-supply increases so much in I that we again have a tree. I has become an exporter to everybody; all prices are from now on locked together and go down equally.

To clinch his understanding of the principles here shown, the reader should draw the diagrams that would precede Figure 5 as the excess-supply function in I is *reduced*. He can show how all P's rise together until I ceases to export and becomes isolated; how all other P's then remain unchanged, until finally I becomes an importer from II and a tree is formed; still further increases in P_1 will finally cause III and IV to become exporters to I rather than importers, finally putting I in the ultimate importer stage. The reader may also experiment with *ceteris paribus* shifts in excess-supply in some other region. If he rigorously specifies a local excess-supply curve at each point, he can rigorously work out the equilibrium solution at each stage; however, it will be a sufficient test of his understanding if he can correctly infer the qualitative direction in which P's and E's must shift.

COMPARATIVE STATICS

We can now cash in on our success in converting the spatial equilibrium system into a maximum problem: for such systems it is easy to make rigorous predictions as to the qualitative direction in which the variables of the system will change when some change is made in the data of the problem.

Let me begin with a simple case. Suppose the transport cost rises between i and j. What effect will this alone tend to have on the trade pattern? I think anyone will guess that, however other variables may change, exports from i to j must certainly decrease or at worst remain the same; such exports can certainly not increase.[21] This happens to be a correct conclusion. But how can we be sure that our intuition is correct in a system that may involve hundreds of unknowns? The analytic theory of maximum systems worked out in my *Foundations of Economic Analysis* provides us with just such assurance.

And as a matter of fact, if we try to discover why our intuition suggested the answer it did, we will discover, I believe, that we have

21. In the Enke formulation of the problem, the total E_i's are not held constant: they are changing as they must to restore the equilibrium. Of course, a similar theorem can be stated in the Koopmans case: an increase in T_{ij}, with all E_i's constant, can never increase E_{ij}.

consciously or unconsciously been already identifying the system with a maximum and we have been heuristically inputing teleology and wisdom into the system. Again, this happens to be a rigorously correct procedure once the system has been rigorously identified as a maximum one. Indeed, in the physical sciences, the somewhat mystical principle of Le Chatelier, which says that a system tends to react to a stress so as to minimize and counter its effects, is just such a heuristic teleological principle and derives its validity from the maximum conditions underlying thermodynamic equilibrium.

A more interesting application of the above kind of analysis is provided by the problem of a shift in the excess-supply function at one place alone, say at region I. Our intuition tells us that an increase in excess-supply at I should cause total exports from that region, E_1, to grow.

There is no loss in generality in assuming that the shift in the excess-supply function at I is a parallel vertical shift, so that we simply subtract a constant a_1 from the $s_1(E_1)$ expression in order to give the excess-supply curve the desired rightward and downward shift, with more being supplied at every price. Previously our net social pay-off could be written as a function of E_1 and other variables. This is still true, but now in the expression for *NSP* there will be an additional term $+a_1E_1$. The interested reader may be referred to Chapter 3 of *Foundations of Economic Analysis* for a full statement of the reasoning. It is enough to state here that the algebraic sign of the change in E_1 with respect to a change in a_1 must then be positive, or at worst zero. This rigorously confirms the conjecture that an increase in excess-supply at any point tends to increase the algebraic exports of a region and decrease its algebraic imports.

(1) How will such an increase in excess-supply affect price at I? (2) How will it affect prices everywhere else? (3) How will it affect algebraic exports, E_i, everywhere else? Our intuition does not respond so easily to these further questions. But anyone who has worked through the numerical example of the previous section will be able to make some fairly shrewd conjectures.

First, we would guess that an increase in excess-supply at I will depress P_1. Surprisingly, this turns out to be quite difficult to prove. For the result does not depend upon what happens at I alone, and no amount of graphical shifting of the curves in the I market can be relied upon for valid inferences. If region I were self-contained, an increase in its positively sloping excess-supply curve would certainly have to depress its price in order to get the market cleared. But in the previous paragraph, we have already seen that the net exports out of I have gone up, which by itself tends to relieve the redundancy of local supply and to increase rather than depress the local price. Which effect will be larger — the direct depressing effect on P_1 or the indirect upward effect on P_1 of the increased exports?[22]

The correct answer tells us that the final effect on P_1 of enhanced excess-supply at I *must* be downward. But how do we know that this is the correct answer? Not, I think, by simple maximum reasoning alone. The following considerations are more rewarding: (1) How does region I "force" an increase in its exports on the rest of the world if its price does not actually fall? Surely P_1 must decline or we shall have a contradiction to the rigorously proved result that I's exports do go up. (2) As to the change of all other P's, how does the rest of the world absorb extra algebraic imports unless prices there have "on the whole" fallen?

Actually, our previous numerical example and the theory of the dual problem in linear programming show us that very stringent conditions must be satisfied by the network of prices in spatial equilibrium. Consequently, a much stronger result can be asserted:

> An increase in excess-supply at I must have a downward effect on every single price, or at worst leave it unchanged. The downward effect on other prices cannot exceed the downward effect on its own price: for all regions that stay continuously connected by direct or indirect trade with I, the changes in P_i must exactly equal the drop in P_1; but any regions that at any time remain disconnected from I (as in Figure 5b) the change in P's will be less than the drop in P_1. And so long as we assume "normal" positive sloping excess-supply curves everywhere, we can confidently assert that an increase of excess-supply in region I must decrease algebraic exports everywhere else, or at worst leave some of them unchanged.

The proof of these statements can be supplied in a straightforward fashion by anyone who has mastered the reasoning of the previous numerical example relating to spatial price equilibrium. One of the remarkable features of the present model is the fact that economic intuition will lead to correct inferences in a system involving complex interdependence between any number of variables.[23]

---

22. Mathematically, $P_1 = -a_1 + s_1(E_1)$ so that $dP_1/da_1 = -1 + s_1'(dE_1/da_1)$. These last two terms are of opposite sign so the final sign is in doubt.

23. Perhaps some theoretical economists will feel that the answer to the effect on P's of an increase in I's excess-supply should have been immediately deducible from the J. R. Hicks stability conditions of *Value and Capital* (Oxford, 1946), Chaps. 5 and 8 and their appendixes. As far as the effect on P_1 itself is concerned, we must beware that we are not simply rewording the problem: "imperfect stability" is a definition and we must answer and not beg the question of whether the concrete specified Enke-Cournot system does or does not enjoy the property of being at least imperfectly stable. The problem is not quite so hopeless as this may sound, in view of the recognition in the 1946 edition of *Value and Capital* of the sufficiency of a maximum position to guarantee perfect and imperfect stability in a wide variety of cases. The present example is *not*

GENERALIZED RECIPROCITY RELATIONS

One last relation concerning reciprocity may be mentioned. Consider the effect on E_j of a unit change in the excess-supply curve at i. And let us compare it with the effect on E_i of a unit change in the excess-supply function at j. Qualitatively, these two effects have been shown to be of the same sign: increased excess-supply at any one point tends to decrease algebraic exports at any other point. We may, however, state a much more astonishing truth: a change in i's excess-supply function has *exactly the same quantitative effect* on E_j that a change in j's excess-supply function would have on E_i.

This reciprocity condition follows immediately from the maximum nature of the problem. Similar relations are known to hold in the field of physics due to the work of Maxwell, Rayleigh, and others. In the economic theory of consumer's behavior similar "integrability conditions" play an important rôle, as has been recognized by Slutsky, Hotelling, H. Schultz, Wold, Houthakker, and others.

I do not imagine that many people would be able to have derived such quantitative relations by intuitive reasoning. Nonetheless, these should not be regarded simply as some rather amusing and paradoxical relations turned up by mathematical reasoning. From a deeper methodological viewpoint, the way that we may test whether a given set of observations has arisen from a maximizing or economizing problem is in terms of such reciprocity relations.[24] To me, one of the most interesting of the present problems is the fact that the fundamental reciprocity relations implied by a maximum problem turn out to transcend the case where partial derivatives exist.[25]

---

directly one such case but it should be possible to make the necessary extensions to the theory so that it would be able to handle cases like the present. Among other things, the present example has the interesting feature of involving functions with corners where no derivatives can be uniquely defined and yet the important logical relations of a maximum position still prevail.

In connection with answering the question of the effect on prices other than P_1, problems of "complementarity" rather than stability are involved. The fact that all P's change in the same direction is related to the Mosak theorem concerning systems in which all goods are substitutes. J. L. Mosak, *General-Equilibrium Theory in International Trade Theory* (Bloomington, 1944) pp. 44, 49–51. Similar matrices have been studied by Leontief, Machlup and Metzler, Frobenius, Minkowski, Hawkins-Simon, Woodbury, Markoff, *et al.*, as discussed in a forthcoming paper by Robert Solow.

24. See Henry Schultz, *The Theory and Measurement of Demand*, Chicago, 1938, Chaps. I, XVIII, XVIX.

25. A more general theory shows that even at corners, where partial derivatives are not uniquely defined, we can extend the definition of a derivative to include all the admissible slopes of "supporting lines or planes" and then generalized reciprocity relations of the following type still hold. Plot E_j against a_i and also plot E_i against a_j. The former curve may at some points have a corner so that its generalized partial derivative is anything between, say, -0.33 and -5.92. It will then turn out that the second curve

CONCLUSION

The problem of interconnected competitive regional markets is one of the rare cases where a reasonably simple and self-contained theoretical treatment is possible. It is a good case to demonstrate the powers of the theory of linear programming since it enables us to give rigorous proofs to plausible conjectures. It so happens that much of the literary discussion of the effects of tariffs and of exchange depreciations is, in the first instance at least, couched in terms of just this model. Thus when a journalist or economist tells you that depreciation of the pound will tend to increase U.K. exports to the United States, to decrease U.K. imports, and to raise pound prices on both categories of goods while depressing dollar prices on them, he is either repeating from memory what someone has worked out from a Cournot-type model or he is himself thinking in terms of such a model.[26] Needless to say, the partial equilibrium assumptions involved in the domestic demand schedules and the neglect of aggregative relations constitute a serious defect of such a model except as a rough first approximation to the answers in especially favorable cases. Good economic theory will recognize these limitations rather than be predisposed to neglect them.

---

must also have a corner at the point corresponding to the corner of the first, and its range of indeterminacy of slope must also be between -0.33 and -5.92. Analogous relations hold in many variables. Thus, within the field of linear programming there exist quite a number of natural generalizations of the relationships that hold for regular differentiable functions.

26. For elaborations and criticisms see G. Haberler, "The Market for Foreign Exchange and the Stability of the Balance of Payments," *Kyklos*, Vol. III (1949), pp. 193–218; J. Viner, *Studies*, Chicago, 1938, pp. 590–91. Mention should also be made of work by Yntema, Joan Robinson, J. J. Polak, and others.

19

Equilibrium Among
Spatially Separated Markets:
A Reformulation

INTRODUCTION

In a 1951 article in *Econometrica*[4; Selection 17 of this volume], Stephen Enke formulated the problem concerning competitive equilibrium among spatially separated markets and suggested how a solution in the case of linear market functions might be obtained by electric analog. Proceeding from the Enke formulation, Samuelson, in an article appearing in 1952[10; Selection 18 of this volume], shows how this purely descriptive problem in non-normative economics can be cast mathematically into a maximum problem and relates the Enke specification to a standard problem in linear programming, the so-called Koopmans-Hitchcock [7, pp. 222–259 and 359–373] minimum-transport-cost problem. Samuelson then suggests that, after the problem in descriptive price behavior has been artificially converted into a maximum problem, it can be solved by trial and error or by a systematic procedure of varying shipments in the direction of increasing social payoff.

Within the framework of interconnected competitive markets the purpose of this article is to show that by postulating appropriate *linear* dependencies between regional supply, demand, and price it is possible to convert the Samuelson-Enke formulation into a quadratic programming problem. Given this quadratic programming formulation a computational algorithm is specified to obtain directly and efficiently the competitive optimum solution for regional prices and quantities and interregional flows. The existence, uniqueness, and regularity of the optimum solution are discussed and an example is given to indicate the structure of the problem and the corresponding programming tableau.

In the presentation, the Samuelson partial-equilibrium (one commodity) formulation will be restated. In this specification the interdependencies with other commodities will be disregarded and attention will be concentrated on the interdependencies that exist

Reprinted from Econometrica, *32 (October 1964), 510–24, by permission of the Econometric Society and the authors.*

between the different markets or regions in the production, pricing, and use of the one commodity. The formulation will then be extended to consider the case of multiple-commodity competitive equilibrium among spatially separated markets. Again attention will be directed to the interdependencies between markets and commodities in spatial pricing and allocation, and the interdependencies with "other" commodities (commodities other than the set considered) and the effects of changed income resulting from trade will be disregarded.

In the models to be put forth we assume the existence of aggregate linear regional demand and supply relations instead of deriving them from individual utility functions and from transformation or production functions.

DEFINITIONS AND NOTATION

In order to simplify the presentation, definitions and notation to be employed in the following sections will now be given.

Let

i, j denote the regional demand and supply points, where $i, j = 1, 2, \ldots, n$.

h, k denote the products demanded and supplied, where $h, k = 1, 2, \ldots, m$. h, k are elements of the total commodity set.

$P_4{}^k = (p_1{}^k, p_2{}^k, \ldots, p_n{}^k)'$ denote the regional prices at the demand points for the kth product.

$D^k = (d_1{}^k, d_2{}^k, \ldots, d_n{}^k)'$ denote the linear regional demand relations for the kth product. The $(d_i{}^k)$ are linear functions of the regional prices $(p_i{}^k)$ such that

$$d_i{}^k = \alpha_i{}^k - \sum_{h=1}^{m} \beta_i{}^{hk} p_i{}^h, \tag{1}$$

where $\alpha_i{}^k > 0$, $\beta_i{}^{hk} \geqslant 0$ for $h = k$, $\beta_i{}^{hk} \gtreqless 0$ for $h \neq k$ for $i = 1, 2, \ldots, n$ and $h, k = 1, 2, \ldots, m$. Alternatively the inverse of (1) is

$$p_i{}^k = \lambda_i{}^k - \sum_h \omega_i{}^{hk} \sum_j x_{ij}^h. \tag{1a}$$

$P^k = (p^{1k}, p^{2k}, \ldots, p^{nk})'$ denote the regional supply prices for the kth products.

$S^k = (s_1{}^k, s_2{}^k, \ldots, s_n{}^k)'$ denote the linear regional supply relations for the kth product. The $(s_j{}^k)$ are linear functions of the regional prices (p^{jk}) such that

$$s_j{}^k = \theta_j{}^k + \sum_{h=1}^{m} \gamma_j{}^{hk} p^{jh}, \tag{2}$$

where $\theta_j{}^k = 0$, $\gamma_j^{hk} \geqslant 0$ for $h = k$, $\gamma_j^{hk}0 \gtreqless$ for $h \neq k$ for $j = 1, 2, \ldots, n$ and $h, k = 1, 2, \ldots, m$. Alternatively the inverse of (2) is

$$p^{jk} = \mu_j{}^k + \sum_h \eta_j^{hk} \sum_i x_{ij}^k. \tag{2a}$$

$P = (P_d{}^k, P^{sk}|k = 1, 2, \ldots, m) = (p_1{}^1, p_2{}^1, \ldots, p_n{}^1, p^{11}, p^{21}, \ldots, p^{n1}, p_1{}^2,$
$p_2{}^2, \ldots, p_n{}^2, p^{12}, p^{22}, \ldots, p^{n2}, \ldots, p_1{}^m, p_2{}^m, \ldots, p_n{}^m, p^{1m}, p^{2m}, \ldots, p^{nm})'$
denote the vector of nonnegative prices at the i, j demand and supply points.
$X = (x_{ij}^k|k = 1, 2, \ldots, m; i, j = 1, 2, \ldots, n) = (x_{11}^1, x_{12}^1, \ldots, x_{1n}^1, \ldots, x_{n1}^1,$
$x_{n2}^1, \ldots, x_{nn}^1, \ldots, x_{11}^m, x_{12}^m, \ldots, x_{1n}^m, \ldots, x_{n1}^m, x_{n2}^m, \ldots, x_{nn}^m)'$ denote the non-negative flows of commodities from region i to region j.
$T = (t_{ij}^k|k = 1, 2, \ldots, m; i, j = 1, 2, \ldots, n) = (t_{11}^1, t_{12}^1, \ldots, t_{1n}^1, \ldots, t_{n1}^1,$
$t_{n2}^1, \ldots, t_{nn}^1, \ldots, t_{11}^m, t_{12}^m, \ldots, t_{1n}^m, \ldots, t_{n1}^m, t_{n2}^m, \ldots, t_{nn}^m)'$ denote the unit transportation cost for shipping the commodities from region i to region j.
$C = (C^k|k = 1, 2, \ldots, m) = (\alpha_1{}^1, \alpha_2{}^1, \ldots, \alpha_n{}^1, -\theta^{11}, -\theta^{21}, \ldots, -\theta^{n1}, \ldots,$
$\alpha_m{}^1, \alpha_m{}^2, \ldots, \alpha_m{}^n, -\theta^{1m}, -\theta^{2m}, \ldots, -\theta^{nm})'$ denote the vector of demand and supply equation intercept values.

A RESTATEMENT OF THE SAMUELSON FORMULATION

In the Samuelson partial equilibrium (one commodity) formulation the problem of descriptive price behavior is *artificially* converted to a maximum problem which is concerned with maximizing net social payoff (*NSP*). Social payoff in any region is defined as the albegraic area under the excess demand curve [10, pp. 287–292]. Net social payoff for all regions is defined by Samuelson as the sum of the n separate payoffs minus the total transport costs of all shipments.[1]

In mathematical form under Samuelson's formulation, for the n-region one-product case, the net social payoff may be written in definite integral form as:

$$NSP(X^k) = \sum_i \int_0^{\sum x_{ij}^k} p_i{}^k d\xi_i{}^k - \sum_j \int_0^{\sum x_{ij}^k} p^{jk} d\xi^{jk} - \sum_i a_i{}^k - \sum_i \sum_j t_{ij}^k x_{ij}^k$$

$$= \sum_i \lambda_i{}^k \sum_j x_{ij}^k - \tfrac{1}{2} \sum_i \omega_i{}^k \left(\sum_j x_{ij}^k \right)^2 - \sum_j \mu_j{}^k \sum_i x_{ij}^k$$

$$- \tfrac{1}{2} \sum_j \eta_j{}^k \left(\sum_i x_{ij}^k \right)^2 - \sum_i a_i{}^k - \sum_i \sum_j t_{ij}^k x_{ij}^k,$$

1. As noted by Samuelson [10, p. 288], "This magnitude is artificial in the sense that no competitor in the market will be aware of or concerned with it. It is artificial in

where $a_i{}^k$ is the sum of producer's and consumer's surplus for the kth product in the ith region under pre-trade equilibrium.

In order to derive the necessary conditions for the maximum of $NSP(X^k)$, subject to nonnegative x_{ij}^k, we form the following Lagrangean

$$\phi(X^k, W^k) = NSP(X^k) + W^{k\prime}X^k, \qquad (4)$$

for $W^k \geqslant 0$ and $X^k \geqslant 0$.

The Kuhn-Tucker [8] conditions for the maximum of $\phi(X^k, W^k)$ are[2]

$$\partial\phi/\partial x_{ij}^k = p_j{}^k - p^{ik} - t_{ij}^k + w_{ij}^k \leqslant 0 \ \text{ and } \ (\partial\phi/\partial x_{ij}^k)\cdot x_{ij}^k = 0. \qquad (5)$$

$$\partial\phi/\partial w_{ij}^k = x_{ij}^k \geqslant 0 \quad \text{and} \quad (\partial\phi/\partial w_{ij}^k)w_{ij}^k = x_{ij}^k \cdot w_{ij}^k = 0. \qquad (6)$$

If the domain of the integral is converted from X^k to P^k the following equivalent programming problem results:

Maximize

$$f(P^k) = \sum_i \int_0^{p_i{}^k} d_i{}^k dp_i{}^k - \sum_i \int_0^{p_i{}^k} d_i{}^k dp_i{}^k - \sum_j \int_0^{p_i{}^k} s_j{}^k dp^{jk} + \sum_j \int_0^{p_i{}^k} s_j{}^k dp^{jk}$$

$$= \sum_i \alpha_i{}^k p_i{}^k - \tfrac{1}{2}\sum_i \beta_i{}^k (p_i{}^k)^2 - \sum_j \theta_j{}^k p^{jk} - \tfrac{1}{2}\sum_j \gamma_j{}^k (p^{jk})^2 - \sum_i b_i{}^k, \qquad (7)$$

subject to

$$p_i{}^k - p^{jk} \leqslant t_{ij}^k \quad \text{and} \quad p_i{}^k, p^{jk} \geqslant 0, \qquad (8)$$

where $\hat{p}_i$ and $\hat{p}^{jk}$ are the equilibrium regional prices for the kth commodity under pre-trade equilibrium, and $b_i{}^k$ is the integral constant for the product in the ith region that results from evaluating

---

the sense that after an Invisible Hand has led us to its maximization, we need not necessarily attach any social welfare significance to the result." In a recent article Smith [12] has shown that the concept of minimizing economic rent may be employed to deduce the conditions of spatial price equilibrium and that the rent minimization problem is the dual of a maximum problem which differs only by a constant from Samuelson's problem. Thus if one considers the rent minimization specification to have more intuitive economic appeal or, in the words of Smith[12, p. 133], "make the Invisible Hand distinctly more visible and more teleological," this paper could be reformulated using this concept.

2. The economic interpretation of these equilibrium conditions is that the difference in prices between any two regions can differ at most by the unit cost of transportation (otherwise arbitrage would be profitable), and in equilibrium for those regions between which flows take place $p_j{}^k - p^{ik} = t_{ij}^k$. For the regions where $p_j{}^k - p^{ik} < t_{ij}^k$ no flows take place, i.e., $x_{ij}^k = 0$. These price conditions are recognized as being consistent with those resulting from competitive behavior and the uncoordinated efforts of the n suppliers to sell their outputs at the maximum possible prices.

the integrals whose upper bounds are the pre-trade equilibrium prices.

MULTIPLE COMMODITY FORMULATION

Given this single commodity formulation let us now extend our model to handle the m commodity n region case. Proceeding as before, the net social payoff function for the multiple commodity case in the domain of X is:

$$NSP(X) = \sum_k \sum_i \lambda_i^k \sum_j x_i^k - \tfrac{1}{2} \sum_k \sum_i \left(\sum_h \omega_i^{hk} \sum_j x_{ij}^h \right) \sum_j x_{ij}^k \qquad (9)$$

$$- \sum_k \sum_i \mu_i^k \sum_j x_{ij}^k - \tfrac{1}{2} \sum_k \sum_i \left(\sum_h \eta_i^{hk} \sum_j x_{ij}^h \right) \sum_j x_{ij}^k$$

$$- \sum_i \sum_j \sum_k t_{ij}^k x_{ij}^k - \sum_k \sum_i a_i^k.$$

The necessary conditions for the maximum of $NSP(X)$, subject to nonnegative X, are the same as (5) and (6) for $k = 1, 2, \ldots, m$. By then converting the domain from X to P we arrive at the following programming problem:
Maximize

$$f(P) = \sum_i \sum_k \alpha_i^k p_i^k - \tfrac{1}{2} \sum_i \sum_h \sum_k \beta_i^{hk} p_i^k p_i^h - \sum_j \sum_k \theta_j^k p^{jk} \qquad (10)$$

$$- \tfrac{1}{2} \sum_j \sum_h \sum_k \gamma_j^{hk} p^{jk} p^{jh} - \sum_i \sum_k b_i^k$$

subject to (8) for all $i, j,$ and k

Again b_i^k is the integral constant for the kth product in the ith region that results from evaluating the integrals whose upper bound are the pre-trade equilibrium prices. Since this quantity is a constant it can be dropped from the objective function without loss of any necessary information. Ignoring the integral constant, (10) may be written compactly as:
Maximize

$$f(P) = P'C - \tfrac{1}{2} P'QP, \qquad (11)$$

subject to

$$G'P \leq T, \qquad (12)$$

$$P \geq 0, \qquad (13)$$

where Q is a symmetric positive semi-definite quadratic matrix [5] composed of the demand and supply behavior coefficients. The matrix is of order $2mn \times 2mn$ and is structured as follows:

$$Q = \begin{bmatrix} \beta_i^{11} & & \beta_i^{21} & & \cdots & \beta_i^{m1} & \\ & \gamma_i^{11} & & \gamma_i^{21} & \cdots & & \gamma_i^{m1} \\ \beta_i^{12} & & \beta_i^{22} & & \cdots & \beta_i^{m2} & \\ \cdot & \gamma_i^{12} & \cdot & \gamma_i^{22} & \cdots & \cdot & \gamma_i^{m2} \\ & & & & & & \\ \cdot & \cdot & \cdot & \cdot & \cdot & \cdot & \cdot \\ \cdot & \cdot & \cdot & \cdot & \cdot & \cdot & \cdot \\ \beta_i^{1m} & \cdot & \beta_i^{2m} & \cdot & \cdots & \beta_i^{mm} & \cdot \\ & \gamma_i^{1m} & & \gamma_i^{2m} & \cdots & & \gamma_i^{mm} \end{bmatrix}, 2mn \times 2mn, \quad (14)$$

where

$$\beta_i^{hk} = \begin{bmatrix} \beta_1^{hk} & & & & \\ & \beta_2^{hk} & & & \\ & & \cdot & & \\ & & & \cdot & \\ & & & & \beta_n^{hk} \end{bmatrix}, n \times n; \quad (15)$$

$$\gamma_i^{hk} = \begin{bmatrix} \gamma_1^{hk} & & & & \\ & \gamma_2^{hk} & & & \\ & & \cdot & & \\ & & & \cdot & \\ & & & & \gamma_n^{hk} \end{bmatrix}, n \times n. \quad (16)$$

The matrix G is of the following block diagonal form:

$$G = \begin{bmatrix} G^1 & & & & \\ & G^2 & & & \\ & & \cdot & & \\ & & & \cdot & \\ & & & & G^m \end{bmatrix}, 2mn \times mn^2, \quad (17)$$

and

$$
G^k = \begin{bmatrix}
1 & & 1 & & \cdots & & 1 & \\
& 1 & & 1 & & & & 1 \\
& & \cdot & & & \cdot & & \cdot \\
& & & \cdot & & \cdot & \cdots & & \cdot \\
& & \cdot & & \cdot & & & \cdot \\
& & 1 & & 1 & & \cdots & & 1 \\
-1 -1 \cdots -1 & & & & & & & \\
& & -1 -1 \cdots -1 & & & & & \\
& & & & \cdots & & & \\
& & & & \cdots & & & \\
& & & & & \cdots & & \\
& & & & -1 -1 \cdots -1 & &
\end{bmatrix}, \; 2n \times n^2. \quad (18)
$$

THE PRIMAL-DUAL PROGRAMMING FORMULATION AND ALGORITHM

Given the quadratic programming problem, (11), (12), and (13), in the domain of P, our task is now to show that this problem is equivalent to the initial problem (to maximize (9) subject to X non-negative) and that both problems can be solved in an efficient manner. In developing the argument for this formulation let us first note that in order to obtain an economically feasible solution for (9) the following constraint set

$$
H = \{(P, X) \mid G'P \leqslant T, C - QP = GX, P \geqslant 0, X \geqslant 0\} \quad (19)
$$

must be non-vacuous.

Further let us define a set R as follows:

$$
R = \{P \mid G'P \leqslant T \quad \text{and} \quad P \geqslant 0\}. \quad (20)
$$

In order to reduce the quadratic programming problem (11), (12), and (13) to a more operationally feasible form, use is made of two theorems. The first theorem is concerned with the reducibility of non-linear programming problems to linear programming formulations, and the second is the duality theorem of linear programming. For our problem the theorem concerning reducibility is as follows:

If the above quadratic programming problem has an optimum

solution at $\bar{P} \in R$ then the linear programming problem of maximizing

$$[C - Q\bar{P}]'P \tag{21}$$

subject to (12) and (13) has a solution at $P = \bar{P} \in R$.[3]

Given the primal linear programming problem (21), (12), and (13), the dual may be formulated as:

Minimize

$$T'X \tag{22}$$

subject to

$$GX \geq C - Q\bar{P} \quad \text{and} \quad X \geq 0. \tag{23}$$

Now define a set X^* as follows:

$$X^* = \{X \mid GX \geq C - Q\bar{P} \quad \text{and} \quad X \geq 0 \quad \text{for} \quad \bar{P} \geq 0\}. \tag{24}$$

---

3. The proof of this theorem is as follows:
For any $P \in R$ and $\bar{P} \in R$

$$[(1-t)\bar{P} + tP] \in R; \quad 0 \leq t \leq 1.$$

By the assumption that $\bar{P}$ maximizes $f(P)$ or $f(\bar{P}) \geq f(P)$ subject to constraints (12) and (13), we have

$$f[\bar{P} + t(P - \bar{P})] - f(\bar{P}) \leq 0; \quad 0 \leq t \leq 1. \tag{3.2}$$

Thus

$$\frac{1}{t}[f(\bar{P} + t(P - \bar{P})) - f(\bar{P})] \leq 0; \quad 0 < t \leq 1. \tag{3.3}$$

As $f(P)$ is quadratic, by Taylor expansion we get

$$\frac{1}{t}\left[t(P - \bar{P})\frac{\partial f(P)}{\partial \bar{P}} + \frac{t^2(P - \bar{P})^2}{2}\frac{\partial^2 f(P)}{\partial \bar{P}^2}\right] \leq 0. \tag{3.4}$$

Taking the limit of (3.4) for $0 < t \leq 1$, we obtain

$$\lim_{t \to 0}\frac{1}{t}\left[t(P - \bar{P})\frac{\partial f(P)}{\partial \bar{P}} + \frac{t^2(P - \bar{P})^2}{2}\frac{\partial^2 f(P)}{\partial \bar{P}^2}\right] \tag{3.5}$$

$$= \lim_{t \to 0}\left[(P - \bar{P})\frac{\partial f(P)}{\partial \bar{P}} + \frac{t(P - \bar{P})^2}{2}\frac{\partial^2 f(P)}{\partial \bar{P}^2}\right]$$

$$= (P - \bar{P})\frac{\partial f(P)}{\partial \bar{P}} \leq 0.$$

Thus

$$P\frac{\partial f(P)}{\partial \bar{P}} \leq \bar{P}\frac{\partial f(P)}{\partial \bar{P}}. \tag{3.6}$$

Since

$$C - Q\bar{P} = \frac{\partial f(P)}{\partial \bar{P}}, \tag{3.7}$$

the theorem is proved.

Next we want to make use of the results of the duality theorem of linear programming[3, 9] stated in the following form:

If R and X^* are non-vacuous, then

$$[C - Q\bar{P}]'P \leq T'X \text{ for any } P \in R \text{ and } X \in X^*, \tag{25}$$

and

$$[C - Q\bar{P}]'\bar{P} = T'\bar{X} \text{ for some } \bar{P} \in R \text{ and } X \in X^*. \tag{26}$$

By combining the primal and dual problems we may then form the primal-dual programming problem:

Maximize

$$[C - Q\bar{P}]'P - T'X \leq 0 \tag{27}$$

subject to (12), (13), and (23).

By setting $\bar{P} = P \in R$, and using the same argument as before we have the following formulation:

Maximize

$$g(P, X = [C + QP]'P - T'X \leq 0 \tag{28}$$

subjected to

$$G'P \leq T \quad \text{or} \quad G'P + V = T, \tag{29}$$

$$G'X + QP \geq C \quad \text{or} \quad G'X + QP - Y = C, \tag{30}$$

and

$$P \geq 0, \quad X \geq 0, \quad V \geq 0, \quad Y \geq 0, \tag{31}$$

where

$$V = \begin{bmatrix} V^1 \\ V^2 \\ \vdots \\ V^m \end{bmatrix} \tag{32}$$

with

$$V^k = (v_{11}^k, v_{12}^k, \ldots, v_{1n}^k, v_{n2}^k, \ldots, v_{nn}^k)' \tag{33}$$

and

$$Y = \begin{bmatrix} Y^1 \\ Y^2 \\ \vdots \\ Y^m \end{bmatrix} \tag{34}$$

with

$$Y^k = (y_1{}^k, y_2{}^k, \ldots, y_n{}^k, y^{1k}, y^{2k}, \ldots, y^{nk})'. \tag{35}$$

It is now necessary to investigate the relation between the feasibility set H of our original problem and the feasibility set $A = \{(P, X) | G'P \leqslant T, \; GX \geqslant C - QP, \; X \geqslant 0, \; P \geqslant 0\}$ in the above programming problem. If there are no P and X common to the two, our problem is infeasible. Let us proceed by defining a set B such that

$$B = H \cap A$$
$$= \{(P, X) | G'P \leqslant T, GX = C - QP, GX \geqslant C - QP, X \geqslant 0, P \geqslant 0\}$$
$$= \{(P, X) | G'P \leqslant T, GX = C - QP, X \geqslant 0, P \geqslant 0\} = H. \tag{36}$$

Therefore, B is the nonnegative set of P and X satisfying the exact demand and supply relations (1) and (2), and (12). Thus the second constraint set is reduced to

$$GX + QP = C, \tag{37}$$

$$P \geqslant 0 \quad \text{and} \quad X \geqslant 0. \tag{38}$$

This then leads to the following primal-dual programming problem:
Maximize

$$g(X, P, V) = [C - QP]'P - T'X = [GX]'P - [G'P + V]'X$$
$$= -V'X \leqslant 0, \tag{39}$$
subject to
$$G'P + V = T, \tag{40}$$

$$GX + QP = C, \tag{41}$$

$$P, X, V \geqslant 0. \tag{42}$$

Equivalence of the primal-dual programming problem (thus the programming problem, (11), (12), and (13)) to the original problem defined in the domain of X can be shown as follows: (19) is the same as (41), the first half of (5) is the same as (40), and (39) at its optimum is the same as the second half of (5) and (6). Thus, if the primal-dual programming problem above is solved, then the solution vectors are the optimal solution vectors for the original problem.

Formulation (42) through (45) leads to the Wolfe[16] and Barankin-Dorfman[2] algorithm for quadratic programming. The algorithm was modified for this problem by making use of the necessary equilibrium relations (5), (6), (and footnote 2) among regional prices, transportation cost, and regional commodity flows. The primal-dual formulation of quadratic programming makes use of these relations in selecting incoming variables. The tableau given as Table I shows the characteristics of the algorithm for our problem.

TABLE 1   Spatial Equilibrium Simplex Tableau

		c	0	0	0
		P_0	$X \geq 0$	$P \geq 0$	$V \geq 0$
$-M$	z_1	T		G'	I
$-M$	z_2	C	G	Q	

In Table I, I is an $mn^2 \times mn^2$ identity matrix, z_1 and z_2 are mn^2 and $2mn$ artificial variables used as initial basic variables, and M is any positive real number attached to all artificial variables.

Excess demand or supply functions play an important role in the paper by Samuelson[10] and in many of the papers concerned with existence, stability, etc. of general equilibrium prices and quantities [1]. Likewise our programming problem can be formulated using linear excess demand and supply functions.

If, however, we use linear excess demand or supply functions in our formulation, nonnegativity restrictions are not specified for the x_{ii}^k. Thus solutions may result which are not economically meaningful.

EXISTENCE, UNIQUENESS, AND REGULARITY

In view of the nature of the problem specified let us restate the constraints and the results of the primal-dual problem as follows:

$$G'P \leq T; P \geq 0, \tag{43}$$

$$GX = C - QP; X \geq 0 \quad \text{and} \quad P \geq 0, \tag{44}$$

and

$$[C - Q\bar{P}]'\bar{P} = T'\bar{X}. \tag{45}$$

The existence theorem [7, p. 323, and 14] for this problem may be stated as:

If both of the sets (43) and (44) are non-vacuous, then $B = H$ contain some $\bar{X}$ and $\bar{P}$ satisfying (45).

The existence of an optimum solution $(\bar{P}, \bar{X})$ thus depends on the existence of non-empty sets R and B.

We have previously assumed the concavity of $f(P)$[4] and the convexity of the constraint sets (43) and (44), and therefore the assumptions of Lemma 2 of the Kuhn-Tucker article[8] are satisfied.

4. Concavity of $f(P)$ is defined here not in the form of (10) but in the form when $P_i^k = P^{ik}$.

Further, by the fact that the saddle point $(\bar{P}, \bar{X})$ implies the optimality of $\bar{P}$, as proved by Uzawa[15], the solution, if it exists in B $(= H)$, is the regular maximum solution. If $(\bar{P}, \bar{X}) \notin H$ then this implies $y_i^k > 0$ for some i and k. This type of solution· is defined as "irregular." If $(\bar{P}, \bar{X}) \in H$, this implies $y = 0$. This type of solution is defined as "regular."

Strict concavity of $f(P)$ may not be assured when substitution and complementarity terms appear in (1) and (2). In order to insure strict concavity of the quadratic function $f(P)$ it is necessary and sufficient that all principal minors of Q are positive. For concavity to hold it is necessary and sufficient that they are nonnegative.

COROLLARIES OF THE MODEL

The formulation can be amended to handle the case of either fixed regional demand or supplies. Alternatively this formulation provides a basis for the analysis of interregional activity analysis models when the regional demands for final commodities are represented by well behaved linear functions and output is limited by the geographical distribution of resources, processing facilities, etc.

The formulations thus far presented have considered solutions over the space dimension. As noted by Samuelson[11], economic relations in time have many of the properties of economic relations in space. Therefore the model could also, by reformulation, be used to obtain solutions over the time dimension. In this reformulation time periods would substitute for regions, storage costs or carrying charges would substitute for transport costs, and flow activities would be between time periods. The model could, of course, be generalized to handle both the time and space demensions simultaneously. Adding the time dimension to the model generates a method for handling many difficult problems that are concerned with price adjustment and allocation over time.

Also, competitive behavior has been assumed for the participants throughout the presentation. The model, however, could be reformulated to handle other types of market configurations[6]. Thus, for example, the interpretation could be that of a monopolist who attempts to maximize his total revenue when faced with linear regional demand functions and when his output is determined by a short run linear supply or cost functions.

AN EXAMPLE

An illustrative problem will now be given for a three-region one-commodity case. Let the linear demand and supply functions for each region be as follows:

Region 1	Region 2	Region 3
$d_1 = \alpha_1 - \beta_1 p_1$	$d_2 = \alpha_2 - \beta_2 p_2$	$d_3 = \alpha_3 - \beta_3 p_3$
$s^1 = \theta_1 + \gamma_1 p^1$	$s^2 = \theta_2 + \gamma_2 p^2$	$s^3 = \theta_3 + \gamma_3 p^3.$

Given unit transport costs t_{ij} between each pair of regions, the model and the programming problem can be formulated as follows:
Maximize

$$f(P) = P'C - \tfrac{1}{2}P'QP = \begin{bmatrix} p_1 \\ p_2 \\ p_3 \\ p^1 \\ p^2 \\ p^3 \end{bmatrix}' \begin{bmatrix} \alpha_1 \\ \alpha_2 \\ \alpha_3 \\ -\theta_1 \\ -\theta_2 \\ -\theta_3 \end{bmatrix} - \tfrac{1}{2} \begin{bmatrix} p_1 \\ p_2 \\ p_3 \\ p^1 \\ p^2 \\ p^3 \end{bmatrix}' \begin{bmatrix} \beta_1 & & & & & \\ & \beta_2 & & & & \\ & & \beta_3 & & & \\ & & & \gamma_1 & & \\ & & & & \gamma_2 & \\ & & & & & \gamma_3 \end{bmatrix} \begin{bmatrix} p_1 \\ p_2 \\ p_3 \\ p^1 \\ p^2 \\ p^3 \end{bmatrix}$$

subject to

$$G'P \le T; \begin{bmatrix} 1 & & & -1 & & \\ & 1 & & & -1 & \\ & & 1 & & & -1 \\ 1 & & & & -1 & \\ & 1 & & & & -1 \\ & & 1 & & & -1 \\ 1 & & & & & -1 \\ & 1 & & & & -1 \\ & & 1 & & & -1 \end{bmatrix} \begin{bmatrix} p_1 \\ p_2 \\ p_3 \\ p^1 \\ p^2 \\ p^3 \end{bmatrix} \le \begin{bmatrix} t_{11} \\ t_{12} \\ t_{13} \\ t_{21} \\ t_{22} \\ t_{23} \\ t_{31} \\ t_{32} \\ t_{33} \end{bmatrix}$$

$$GX + \begin{pmatrix} \beta & 0 \\ 0 & \gamma \end{pmatrix} P = \begin{pmatrix} \alpha \\ -\theta \end{pmatrix};$$

$$\begin{bmatrix} 1 & & & 1 & & & 1 & & \\ & 1 & & & 1 & & & 1 & \\ & & 1 & & & 1 & & & 1 \\ -1 & -1 & -1 & & & & & & \\ & & & -1 & -1 & -1 & & & \\ & & & & & & -1 & -1 & -1 \end{bmatrix} \begin{bmatrix} x_{11} \\ x_{12} \\ x_{13} \\ x_{21} \\ x_{22} \\ x_{23} \\ x_{31} \\ x_{32} \\ x_{33} \end{bmatrix} + \begin{bmatrix} \beta_1 & & & & & \\ & \beta_2 & & & & \\ & & \beta_3 & & & \\ & & & \gamma_1 & & \\ & & & & \gamma_2 & \\ & & & & & \gamma_3 \end{bmatrix} \begin{bmatrix} p_1 \\ p_2 \\ p_3 \\ p^1 \\ p^2 \\ p^3 \end{bmatrix} \begin{bmatrix} \alpha_1 \\ \alpha_2 \\ \alpha_3 \\ -\theta_1 \\ -\theta_2 \\ -\theta_3 \end{bmatrix}$$

and

$$p_i, p^j, x_{ij} \ge 0 \qquad (i, j = 1, 2, 3).$$

The simplex tableau consistent with this formulation is shown as Table 2.

In obtaining solutions for problems of this nature a linear programming deck for the IBM 7094 was modified.[5] Several example problems were solved and the time required to obtain solutions of problems the size of the one given above was approximately 0.2 of a minute.

SUMMARY

In this paper we have attempted to indicate how spatial equilibrium formulations in the case of linear well-behaved regional demand and supply functions can be converted to a quadratic programming problem. An algorithm was specified which could be used to obtain the competitive price and flow solution. The existence, uniqueness, and convergence properties of the model were investigated and the conditions for obtaining optimum solutions are noted. The potential uses of this formulation are discussed and an illustrative example is given.

One of the major purposes of this paper has been to specify a spatial formulation that could be empirically implemented. Consistent with this objective the algorithms presented are efficient for obtaining a solution and can be used with only a slight modification of available linear programming routines. The formulation put forward is perhaps most valuable in the partial equilibrium one-commodity case considered by Enke and Samuelson or in the situation when a few commodities are considered jointly. As the number of commodities jointly considered is extended, the assumption, for example, that the effect of changed income resulting from trade can be ignored may become quite tenuous, and the application of the formulation becomes somewhat doubtful. There should, however, be many practical multi-commodity spatial problems where the assumptions inherent in the model would not be violated to a significant degree.

REFERENCES

1. ARROW, K. J., D. BLOCK, AND L. HURWICZ: "On the Stability of the Competitive Equilibrium, II," *Econometrica*, 27 (1959), pp. 82–109.

5. The program was modified relative to the choice of an incoming activity. The rules for the modification are as follows: (1) If x_{ij}^k is in the basis, do not introduce v_{ij}^k, and if v_{ij}^k is in the basis, do not introduce x_{ij}^k; (2) if the previous procedure terminates with one or more initial slack variables, z_i's, still in the basis and every counterpart variable of the variables with $z_j - c_j < 0$ in the basis, then put a large minus c_j on the counterpart variable in the basis and test if other variables can be brought in. Continue (if possible) the procedure until (a) the normal termination or (b) no finite solution is reached.

TABLE 2 Spatial equilibrium simplex tableau with regional demand and supplies represented by linear functions

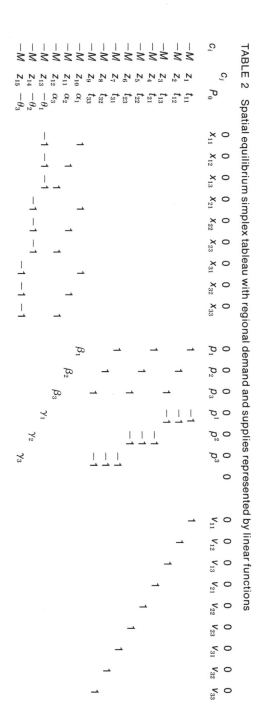

c_i		P_0	x_{11}	x_{12}	x_{13}	x_{21}	x_{22}	x_{23}	x_{31}	x_{32}	x_{33}	ρ_1	ρ_2	ρ_3	ρ^1	ρ^2	ρ^3	v_{11}	v_{12}	v_{13}	v_{21}	v_{22}	v_{23}	v_{31}	v_{32}	v_{33}
c_j	P_0		0	0	0	0	0	0	0	0	0	0	0	0	0	0	0	0	0	0	0	0	0	0	0	0
$-M$	z_1	t_{11}										1			-1			1								
$-M$	z_2	t_{12}											1		-1				1							
$-M$	z_3	t_{13}												1	-1					1						
$-M$	z_4	t_{21}										1				-1					1					
$-M$	z_5	t_{22}											1			-1						1				
$-M$	z_6	t_{23}												1		-1							1			
$-M$	z_7	t_{31}										1					-1							1		
$-M$	z_8	t_{32}											1				-1								1	
$-M$	z_9	t_{33}												1			-1									1
$-M$	z_{10}	α_1	1	1	1										γ_1											
$-M$	z_{11}	α_2				1	1	1								γ_2										
$-M$	z_{12}	α_3							1	1	1						γ_3									
$-M$	z_{13}	$-\theta_1$	-1			-1			-1			β_1														
$-M$	z_{14}	$-\theta_2$		-1			-1			-1			β_2													
$-M$	z_{15}	$-\theta_3$			-1			-1			-1			β_3												

2. Barankin, E. W., and R. Dorfman: *On Quadratic Programming*, University of California Publications in Statistics, 1958.

3. Dantzig, G. B., and A. Orden: "Duality Theorems," RAND Report R.M.—1265, The RAND Corporation, Santa Monica, California. October, 1953.

4. Enke, S.: "Equilibrium Among Spatially Separated Markets: Solution by Electric Analogue," *Econometrica*, 19 (1951), pp. 40–47 [Selection 17 of this volume].

5. Hicks, J. R.: *Value and Capital*, London: University of Oxford Press, 1948, pp. 310–311.

6. Houthakker, H. S.: "The Capacity Method of Quadratic Programming," *Econometrica*, 28 (1960), pp. 62–87.

7. Koopmans, T. (Ed.): *Activity Analysis of Production and Allocation*, New York: John Wiley and Sons, 1951.

8. Kuhn, H. W., and A. W. Tucker: "Non-Linear Programming," in *Proceedings of the Second Symposium on Mathematical Statistics and Probability*, edited by J. Neyman, University of California Press, 1951, pp. 481–492.

9. ——— (Eds.): *Linear Inequalities and Related Systems*, Princeton: Princeton University Press, 1956.

10. Samuelson, P. A.: "Spatial Price Equilibrium and Linear Programming," *The American Economic Review*, 42 (1952) [Selection 18 of this volume].

11. ———: "Intertemporal Price Equilibrium: A Prologue to the Theory of Speculation," *Weltwirtschaftliches Archiv*, Band 79 (1957), pp. 181–221.

12. Smith, V. L.: "Minimization of Economic Rent in Spatial Price Equilibrium," *The Review of Economic Studies*, 30 (1963), pp. 24–31.

13. ———: "An Experimental Study of Competitive Market Behavior," *The Journal of Political Economy*, 80 (1962), pp. 111–137.

14. Tucker, A. W.: "Linear and Non-Linear Programming," Symposium on Modern Techniques for Extremum Problems, *Journal of Operations Research*, p. 251.

16. Uzawa, H.: "The Kuhn-Tucker Theorem in Concave Programming," in *Studies in Linear and Non-linear Programming*, edited by K. Arrow, R. Hurwicz, and H. Uzawa, Stanford University Press, 1958, pp. 32–37.

17. Wolfe, P.: "The Simplex Method for Quadratic Programming," *Econometrica*, XXVII (1959), pp. 382–398.

CONCLUSION

EDWIN VON BÖVENTER

Towards a United Theory of Spatial Economic Structure

INTRODUCTION

The aim of the present paper is to discuss the most important economic principles which determine the spatial structure of an economy and to show the way in which the various economic factors are interrelated. Simple models of economic structure will be discussed; a general framework for the theoretical analysis of spatial structures will be developed; and it will be demonstrated that all the existing models of spatial economic structure e.g. Thünen, Christaller and Lösch are special cases of such a framework.

By spatial structure I mean the spatial distribution of producers of various goods and services (including retail services) and of consumers in cities and towns of various sizes as well as the spatial layout of these centers. A structure is, of course, largely the result of the uneven distribution of the natural resources of the earth (including natural transport routes and climate). The purely economic factors that determine the spatial differentiation of an economy can be grouped as follows: (1) external and internal economies or indivisibilities, (2) the demand for land inputs and (3) transport costs. The first of these factors tends to encourage a spatial *concentration* of economic activities; the second factor, a spatial *dispersion*; and the resulting centrifugal and centripetal forces interplay via the level of transport costs. For a particular industry, the net force of these factors depends to a very large extent on the spatial distribution of the demand facing the industry; and this differs very much as between industries. Alternative assumptions about the relative strength of these three factors can lead to many different spatial structures. One extreme is the total geographic concentration of production when agglomeration economies dominate. A second is a complete dispersion of all production on a homogeneous plain when linear

The author is associated with the University of Münster, Germany. He expresses his gratitude to the Rockefeller Foundation for enabling him to do this research in Philadelphia and in Cambridge, Mass., U.S.A., and to the members of the Department of Regional Science at the University of Pennsylvania for many valuable discussions and suggestions.

Reprinted from Papers and Proceedings of the Regional Science Association, *Zurich Congress, Vol. 10 (1962), 163–80, by permission of the regional Science Association.*

homogeneous production functions obtain for all economic activities.

In this paper I shall (1) discuss how assumptions about these factors have been combined in the current theories of spatial structure, (2) indicate the important factors which should be taken into account, (3) formulate a general framework for analysis, and (4) on the basis of this general framework derive more specific applications. It will be seen that all of them represent combinations of *basic* elements of Thünen, Christaller and Lösch models and their extensions.[1]

First, let me briefly indicate how these attempts to derive models of a spatial economic structure can be related to other parts of current location theory, which can be classified into four groups:

1. Agricultural and industrial location theories were developed separately. While Thünen's model of agricultural location embodies most of the relevant economic factors and thus really represented an application of general economic theory, the industrial location theory as represented by Weber's models and location triangles was first *formulated* in terms more reminiscent of physical science than of economics and thus stood quite apart from general economic theory. It was Predöhl who first emphasized the applicability of a general economic principle, the substitution principle, to industrial location decisions. Isard later tried to formulate a general model and to show explicitly how the same principle underlies existing location theories. In 1958 Moses demonstrated explicitly how within an extended Weber-Launhardt model, the quantities produced and the input coefficients are to be determined simultaneously.

2. Another approach from the very beginning tried to apply the general equilibrium conditions to location decisions. As example, for this kind of theory we may list the models by Beckmann, Lefeber, and Isard; also the interregional programming models by Stevens should be noted in this connection.[2] All these can easily be reduced to the classical models without a spatial dimension by setting all transportation costs equal to zero.[3]

3. We might list here the models of *spatial competition* such as those developed by Hotelling and Singer. These models focus on certain important aspects of competition that arose when the con-

1. While in a previous paper I have tried to combine the Thünen, Christaller, and Lösch models by applying them to different parts of the economy, in the present article I try to integrate the three systems in a more fundamental way. See: E. von Böventer, "Die Struktur der Landschaft; Versuch einer Synthese und Weiterentwicklung der Modelle J. H. von Thünens, W. Christallers und A. Löschs," *Schriften des Vereins für Socialpolitik, N.F.*, 27, pp. 77–133, Berlin, 1962.

2. A general equilibrium type of approach has also been chosen by this author in his recent book *Theorie des räumlichen Gleichgewichts*, Tübingen, Mohr (Siebeck), 1962.

3. We thus have the same kind of correspondence principle as holds for static theory and dynamic economic theory when all time subscripts are dropped.

sumers and a *limited* number of competitors are separated by transport costs.

4. Finally, we have the attempts to derive *regional structures* on the basis of purely economic factors: as illustrated by models of Christaller and Lösch. A general equilibrium system from which to derive such a structure was not available. Therefore, Christaller and Lösch — just as Thünen had done before them — used the tools of *partial* analysis and obtained quite significant results even for the *whole* space-economy.

Thus, today quite different bodies of location theory are tied together in principle but vary in their approaches.

The main difficulty in location theory is that in order for a general equilibrium model to have an optimal solution which the market or theoretical solution process necessarily approaches and which fulfils the usual welfare conditions of production, it is necessary to assume linear homogeneous production functions. Indivisibilities and agglomeration economies, which are basic for locational analyses, in particular for urban analysis can not be incorporated in such a model. If they are included, the substitution principle, *if it is applied at the margin only*, loses much of its force and becomes useless in finding the optimal spatial structure. For this reason, the marginal principles have to be supplemented by the *total conditions* of equilibrium.

The aim of this paper is to indicate a way how, in spite of the above mentioned difficulties, to arrive at certain general statements within a unifying location framework (if not a general equilibrium model). The specific theories of spatial structure will be shown to be contained in this framework as special cases arising out of specific quantitative assumptions about the various economic factors which have to be taken into account.

AGRICULTURAL AND URBAN LOCATION THEORY

The aim of current as well as Thünen's agricultural location theory, is to determine the most profitable use to which a given piece of land can be put, as a function of its distance from the market. Though the optimum size of the *firm* is also considered, the starting point of the analysis has always been the *industry* level. Prices at the market, freight rates, and possibly prices of inputs other than land are given, and the economic problem is the allocation of resources which maximizes the value of output subject to usual restrictions on all inputs including land. The solution to this problem yields the familiar Thünen rings with crops having the steepest rent surfaces cultivated closest to the center. In the ring structure, size of the farm, and output per acre and per farm are determined. Shifts in market prices and other parameters can be incorporated in a more general equilibrium model[4]. Such modifications do not affect the basic nature of the adjustment processes and of the ring formation. Summarizing, we have:

Givens: 1. The commodity prices at the center (as well as all input prices),

2. Transportation rates to the center;

Variables: 1. The distance from the center,

2. The size of the farm,

3. The outputs per acre, or, via (2), per farm, and

4. The input coefficients.

We now turn to a related formulation of Urban Location Theory. As Alonso has noted, "urban and agricultural theory will form a unified theory of land uses and land values."[5] Thus, for the location of a commercial establishment serving the Center (the *market* in agricultural location theory), the analogy is easy to see. To determine the size of the farm and the output per acre (and hence also the output per farm), or the size of the commercial lot and the total output of the establishment, involves the same principle. The other variables, namely, the distance from the Center and the input coefficients, correspond to those in agricultural location theory. Prices and freight rates are also given, and assumptions about population movements and input prices can be treated in the same way as in agricultural location theory. The conditions which would hold at the boundary for different agricultural uses or for different commercial uses must in equilibrium also be fulfilled at the boundary line between these two types of land uses (commercial and agricultural).

The same analogy can also be applied to residential use of land within a city. Terms relating to the production sphere are simply replaced by counterpart terms in the consumer household sphere (i.e., "outputs" become "inputs" and vice versa).

In the study of residential use we have, by analogy to agricultural use:

Givens: 1. The factor prices at the Center which are offered for the potential services of the household,

2. Transportation rates to the Center;

4. For an extension of this kind, see: Edgar S. Dunn, *The Location of Agricultural Production*, Gainesville, Fla., University of Florida Press, 1954. Dunn also extends the analysis on the *firm* level.

5. William Alonso, *A Model of the Urban Land Market*, Ph. D. Dissertation, University of Pennsylvania, 1960.

Variables: 1. The distance from the Center,

2. The size of the lot,

3. The factor supplies sold at the Center per household ("outputs" of the household), or, via (2), per acre,

4. All consumer goods bought ("inputs" of the household).

The important characteristics and similarities of the two types of theories discussed so far can be summarized under the following headings:

i. All activities are entirely center-oriented. Economic relationships between and among commercial establishments or residential households *outside the Center* are not allowed: joint or interrelated activities are counted as one activity. Thus each quantitatively different combination of the outputs of various (agricultural) commodities is to be counted as *one* particular production process yielding a special bid rent function.[6]

ii. Though the transportation surface may, as a starting point, be assumed to be homogeneous, the consideration of transportation networks or of differential freight rates in different directions from the Center can be treated. As Thünen pointed out, this means only that the rings will be stretched in the directions where transportation is cheaper.

iii. There are no urbanization and localization economies. It is only the internal (scale) economies or indivisibilities which, together with all the market prices and on the basis of all the factors of production available, determine the size of the farm, of the commercial establishment, or of the residential lot. Urbanization economies can be introduced into a Thünen system, where they would lead to the formation of villages; and later on we shall also consider agglomeration economies within the context of urban location theory.

iv. Purely theoretical difficulties arise, in connection with the determination of the *shape* of the lot. (Again Alonso has been one of the first students to struggle with this problem.) The usual derivations about rent surfaces hold in a straightforward way only for the case where each buyer of land obtains a whole ring of land around the center, however thin this ring may be. Special problems arise because the utility or the productivity of every square inch of land depends not only on *how many* other square inches of land are available to the producing unit or household but also on *where* they are located. Unless

6. The bid rent function is a function which for each particular use shows (on the basis of given profit or utility levels) what rents the producers or consumers would be willing to pay for a unit of land, as function of the distance from the Center. This concept has been introduced by Alonso, *op. cit.*

the individual lots are very small the result may be that price of a marginal square foot of land *between* two producers may differ very much from the actual *average price* paid for the other square feet of land. Thus there may be certain discontinuities in the rent surface. It is interesting to note that in the case of lots which are not ring shaped but more compact even the quite simple concept of the distance from the Center becomes problematical. A particular spot on the lot from which it must be measured has to be determined. However, the more we approach a state of perfect competition the less important this problem becomes. It also becomes less important the more distant a ring is from the Center, because with increasing diameters a larger number of households can be accomodated on a ring of a given width. (This is a theoretical, but not a practical, problem.)

v. An important result that both agricultural and urban location theory obtain is declining intensity of land use with increasing distance from the Center. This result can be derived in quite a simple and straightforward way. With identical factor supplies at all points of the plain, the marginal revenue products rise towards the Center. Since, as can be shown, this implies also a rise in *real* factor income towards the Center, movements of all mobile factors towards the Center are induced. Consequently, the ratios of land to labor and to capital fall. The intensity of land use thus rises towards the Center, even if only one commodity is produced. This well-known result is stressed because it will turn out to be very useful in extending models of industrial spatial structure. The fact that extensive land uses with low transportation costs per unit of land, are to be found far from the Center, has its parallel in urban location theory. When there is a large amount of land occupied by a residence unit, in comparison with the costs incurred by a *large* demand for land, the commuting costs per unit of land are relatively small, i.e., in comparison with the total cost of the land, and it pays to move far out from the Center; whereas a residence unit occupying a small amount of land has *relatively* high transportation costs and hence saves relatively much by locating closer to the Center. Such a unit, like an intensive crop, is transportation-oriented, whereas both households and crops with extensive land uses, are price-oriented. Historical factors will be brought in below.

Because of the changing ratios of other factor inputs to the land inputs with growing distance from the Center, the marginal product of the land, or the rent function, falls less steeply than it would with constant factor proportions. Thus even with only one activity and with transportation cost proportional to distance, the shape of the rent function (as a function of distance from the Center) is concave away from the origin. Through the consideration of a great number of *different* commodities[7] or households it becomes even more concave. However, if the marginal transportation costs or marginal disutility of commuting over large distances rise at certain points, it is not impossible that over certain ranges the rent function becomes convex.

vi. A last characteristic shared by urban and agricultural location theories is that factor movements and the balance of payments mechanism are usually not explicitly considered.

BASIC CHARACTERISTICS OF THE MODELS OF SPATIAL STRUCTURE BY W. CHRISTALLER AND A. LÖSCH

Both Christaller and Lösch start their analysis of the structure of the landscape with a homogeneous plain. At each point of this plain, the amount and quality of the natural resources, the production functions, the population density, the consumer preferences and all other economic and non-economic factors are identical. On this plain, any number of commodities may be produced. Production functions, transportation costs and demand functions are generally different for each commodity, and therefore lead to different optimum output quantities per plant and to different optimal sales areas. Thus there are internal economies which for given transportation costs and given consumer demand conditions determine an optimum sales area for each commodity on this homogeneous plain. Lösch states his five equilibrium conditions (which are implicit in Christaller) as follows: (1) the location for an individual must be as advantageous as possible; (2) the locations must be so numerous that the whole space is occupied; (3) abnormal profits must disappear; (4) areas of supply, production, and sales must be as small as possible; and (5) at the boundaries of economic areas it must be a matter of indifference to which of two neighboring locations they belong. (Furthermore, price discrimination and collusion between the producers are not considered).[8]

For each individual commodity, the well-known hexagonal distribution of production sites is generated over the entire plain; and the problem becomes the identification of the optimal spatial distribution of plants for different commodities whose sales areas are different. *So far*, there is no difference between the Christaller and Lösch

---

7. Note that a *combination* of certain processes or of agricultural crops can only be justified by input economies arising out of this combination or by advantages of a crop rotation. It would never pay, unless heavy imperfections of the markets were present, to combine *independent* activities.

8. See: August Lösch, *The Economics of Location*, New Haven, Yale University Press, 1954, pp. 94–97.

models: both conduct a *partial analysis for individual goods on a homogeneous plain* with a perfectly even distribution of demands; *each producer produces only one good* (or several commodities with identical market areas); *there are no intermediate goods; labor and other inputs are drawn only out of the own market area; and there are no urbanization and localization economies which lead to changes in the input coefficient or cost functions.* Note that just as in agricultural and urban location theory, there are *internal,* but no *external economies of production.*

The basic difference between Lösch and Christaller arise out of the different procedures employed in combining the market networks of the individual goods. While Lösch considers first the commodity with the smallest market area and then introduces other commodities with successively larger market areas, Christaller starts, *in effect,* with the largest market area and then turns to commodities with ever smaller market areas. Thus, Christaller constructs his system from the top to the bottom, while Lösch builds his starting from the bottom. Since the system of both Christaller and Lösch are known, we present here only a listing of some of the characteristics of Christaller's system, and a list of some of the main differences between Christaller and Lösch. The key characteristics of the Christaller hierarchy of central places are as follows:

1. Each higher order central place produces, or supplies, also all commodities which are offered by *all* lower order central places. (This is the effect of starting "at the top" of the system.)

2. The resulting spatial distribution within the system is not optimal, because the actual market area sizes can only be multiplied or divided by multiples of three. Therefore an optimum, without excess profits can only be obtained for commodities whose market areas are equal to that of the market of the initial "B-Places" or equal to 3, 9, 27 (etc.) times that size, or one-third, one-ninth (etc.) that size.[9]

3. Producers have *preferences* for the production centers already in existence, but there are no real external economies or diseconomies *which have any impact on the cost or the demand functions.* Furthermore, even though there are agglomerations of different economic activities particularly in the higher-order central places, prices or land values or rents are in no way affected by this. This also holds for Lösch.

4. Population movements and demand changes caused by the establishment of the production centers are not considered. This point, in connection with the statement under (3), is the main reason

---

9. See: Brian J. L. Berry and Allen Pred, *Central Place Studies,* Philadelphia, Regional Science Research Institute, 1961; and Walter Isard, *Location and Space-Economy,* New York, John Wiley, 1956, for more detailed summary of Christaller and Lösch.

why the model is a *partial* equilibrium system and thus, *as a whole*, it is partly inconsistent.

5. On the basis of the assumptions made so far, no statements about the sizes of the central places are possible — other than the weak statement that each higher-order central place is *at least* as great as all lower order central places. Christaller's derivations about the size of the cities are based on additional empirical information.

In contrast to Christaller's analytical procedure, Lösch in his basic model in *The Economics of Location* starts with the smallest units, with farm settlements which, as Christaller's "B–Places," are situated in the centers of regular hexagons. Lösch then considers commodities with larger market areas — commodities which it does not pay to produce in each of the smallest units. It is important to note that, similar to Christaller's assumptions, the only possible production sites are the centers of the smallest hexagons. Now, for commodities whose (optimal) sales area is greater than the smallest hexagons, the possible production sites are, as seen from any given place such as *C* in Figure 1, the second closest, the third closest, fourth, fifth, sixth (etc.)

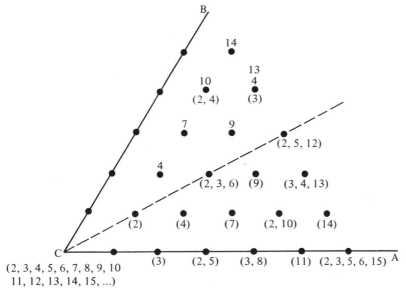

FIGURE 1   Part of a Lösch System.

closest sites, and the corresponding sales areas are 3, 4, 7, 9, 12 (etc.) times as large as the smallest hexagons. At first, Lösch considers the possible market nets for the individual commodities, and then he varies the sites until as many production centers as possible coincide, with *each* commodity being produced at the Center of the System, *C*.

In Figure 1, only part of a 60 degree sector of the system (BCA) has been pictured, because all six sectors of the system are symmetrical. In Figure 1, the numbers in the parentheses indicate the commodities produced at the respective places. While in Christaller's model the spatial arrangement of the system is determined once the sites of the "B–Places" are known, the Lösch system has exactly one degree of freedom left after the spatial determination of the Center and of the smallest hexagonal network. That is to say, though all the sites for the commodities with the second and the third largest sales areas are uniquely determined by the location of the Center, for commodity No. 4 there are two alternatives: we *assume* point (4) has been chosen, but the point denoted by 4 could have been taken just as well (here, the 4 is not included in a parenthesis, which indicates that this good is *not* actually produced there), site 4 being located symmetrically to site (4) with respect to line CD. The locations for commodities No. 5 and 6 are again uniquely determined, but the case for commodity No. 7 (and also for Nos. 9 and 13, etc.) is the same as for No. 4: again there are two alternative sites, (7) and 7. For commodities with alternative sites, Lösch now applies the rule about the agglomeration preferences mentioned above: all producers always locate as near as possible to other producers. As far as the distances to existing production sites are concerned, there is only one difference between points (7) and 7; i.e., (7) is closer to (4) than 7 is. Had 4 been chosen by the producers of commodity No. 4, point 7 would have been selected now. Similar considerations apply to the locational choices for commodities No. 9, No. 13, No. 14, etc.

The main differences between the Lösch system and the Christaller hierarchy of central places are as follows:

1. The deviations from the optimal spatial layout for the individual commodities are much smaller in a Löschian than in a Christaller system because of the greater number of possible sizes for the individual market areas. Setting the smallest market area equal to unity, the possible sizes are 1, 3, 4, 7, 9, 12, 13, 16, 19, 21, 25, 27, ... in a Lösch system but only 1, 3, 9, 27, ... in a Christaller system.

2. An extremely important result is the partial specialization of production as between different centers. Smaller cities may, as in reality, supply big cities with commodities which these do not produce themselves. (It is a definite theoretical drawback, however, that the overall center produces *everything*.)

3. Without further assumptions almost no statements about the sizes of the centers are possible; it is only certain that the overall center is larger than all other cities. But (either in terms of output or employment) nothing can be said about the relative sizes of the following sets of centers: (a) (2), (3), (4), (7), (9), (11), (14) and (b) (7), (3; 8), (9), (2; 10),

(11), (2; 5; 12), (2; 4; 13), (14), (2; 3; 5; 6; 15). Two extremely simplified assumptions would be to make the size of the centers either a function of the number of establishments or a function of the number of local markets supplied.

We can now summarize the essential features of the two spatial structures in the following way:

A. Both systems have in common the hexagonal arrangement of the production sites and the sales areas of a particular commodity.

B. The procedures by which all networks of markets are constructed are different, however, and can in a way be considered as two possible extremes: Christaller starts with the "most national" commodity; Lösch, by contrast, with the "most local" commodity. In economic-historical terms, Christaller's method of deriving his system may be thought of as describing the population growth in an area which at the beginning is very thinly populated. Lösch's system would appear to be a more adequate description of a landscape in which a certain *dense* ground structure exists, with, in the beginning, entirely self-sufficient small spatial units (if new commodities with ever-increasing internal economies of production are introduced). It is solely this difference in the derivation of the systems which has the effect that Lösch's system becomes much more complicated than Christaller's.

C. In both Lösch and Christaller, entire systems of networks are derived for an indefinite number of commodities on the basis of purely partial analysis for the individual goods. Because of the ensuing population movements and the different degrees of spatial concentration of production,[10] this leads to certain inconsistencies—unless the following assumptions are made which rule out all changes in the spatial demand function. (i) There must be no population movements; all employees are commuters. (ii) All employees of enterprises must be drawn *evenly* out of the market area served by the enterprise, because only in this way can it be guaranteed that the commuting costs for all enterprises of the same industry are equal everywhere (this means that the supply elasticity of all kinds of labor with regard to changes in the industrial wage structure is zero). (iii) No employee is allowed to do any shopping on his way to work, because otherwise the original assumption of the even spatial distribution of demand becomes invalid. On each trip made by a household member only *one* purchase must be made, and if firms deliver their goods, then only *one* household can be serviced at a time. This is an essential part of what, within the two systems, is implied by the statement that there

---

10. The most important factors in this connection are discussed by Isard, *op. cit.*, pp. 269 ff.

are no external economies; there must be no external economies in shopping. If there are population movements, then the resulting spatial structure depends partly on whether the optimum size of a plant is determined mainly by economic or by technological factors: in the first case it could even happen that large plants at the big centers coexist with small firms in more rural areas and that the latter have (even geographically) smaller market areas than the former.

D. For reasons similar to those just mentioned, there are no intermediate goods which are exchanged on the market. The only exchange that takes place is the purchase of agricultural goods and of labor inputs by the industrial firms in return for their own industrial goods (final commodities).

E. Strictly speaking, there can be no Thünen ring formation within either of the systems, because of the assumption of the even spatial distribution of demands.

F. Industrial production must not consume any space, because otherwise land values and hence cost functions would be different for two firms of the same industry in different size cities.

G. Balance of payments considerations are neglected.[11]

H. Strictly speaking, the two systems can, with all the qualifications listed, be applied only to a space with a *dense* population distribution because otherwise economic transactions do not take place at all between the points considered in Figure 1, and statements about their market boundaries and prices become partly irrelevant. If the space between the smallest centers in a Lösch system is not densely populated, the Löschian optima are not the only ones. Otherwise, to give an example, a firm with an optimum output sufficient to satisfy the demand of *two* units would also be consistent with the Löschian conditions.

All these critical remarks and qualifications of the two systems are expounded here because it is only when the limitations of these systems are completely understood that one can try to extend them. This does not in any way belittle the great achievements which both systems represent: they should be judged as the first attempts to derive in exact terms a spatial differentiation of economic activity on a homogeneous plain on the basis of economic factors alone. Neglecting all the necessary qualifications listed above let me state as the most important positive results of the two models the following: (i) Lösch's system is realistic and capable of an extension in that *on a homogeneous plain a specialization of production in different centers an interregional or interurban exchange of industrial goods and a complicated network of markets*

11. On this point, see W. F. Stolper, "Standorttheorie und Theorie des internationalen Handles," *Zeitschrift fuer die gesamte Staatswissenschaft*, 112 (1956), 193–217.

is derived. (ii) In its final result, as far as the *overall system of a hierarchy of cities or central places* is concerned, *where the individual economic activities are neglected*, Christaller's system gives both a better description of reality—at least with regard to Southern Germany in the 'thirties—and has the advantage of being simpler, or more elegant, whereas the Lösch system is very difficult to test at all.[12]

Thus in a way the two systems can be thought of as supplementing each other: If modified substantially, Lösch's system can be taken to describe the spatial distribution in the secondary sector; Christaller's system may be applied to the tertiary sector, and, then, Thünen's system to the primary sector.[13]

THE CHOICE OF A SITE: GENERAL STATEMENT

The main intent of the previous discussion has been to show that the various branches of traditional location theory ask different questions, and use different assumptions and general frameworks of analysis. We may now summarize the most important characteristics of the separate theories in the following way:

1. In the agricultural and urban location theories, the most efficient use of a *given piece of land* is determined as a function of distance from a given point (Center) and of the (input and output) prices at this Center. Analysis is restricted in that this Center point is taken as given, but there are *real locational choices*. These are between alternative uses of the land, and the optimal locations of a number of crops or a number of different urban uses are simultaneously determined. Internal economies enter but play only a secondary role, and external economies may be brought into the picture much later.

2. In industrial location theory, the essential factors are the distances from a number of points—the input origins and the output destinations. Local cost differentials including land rents are given. Only one commodity is considered; and the optimal location on *alternative pieces* of land is to be determined. At least in the original formulation of the theory, internal economies, input substitution, alternative uses of the land play only a subordinate role but—as

---

12. The Christaller system can be tested for its *overall* validity with regard to the hierarchy of the central places, where the individual market nets are neglected and where, most important, they do not have to comply with the theory (as in general they do not, at least not for the industrial goods). But the Lösch system does not have such aggregative features; therefore a test of this system rests on the findings for individual commodities—unless one forgets completely about the important feature of specialization and concentrates only on spatial densities.

13. An extension along these lines has been attempted by the author in the paper "Die Struktur der Landschaft," *loc. cit.*

Hoover, Isard and Moses have shown — can all be considered more or less extensively; and external economies come in much later, just as in agricultural location theory. Within the framework of industrial location theory, *exact* statements on the marginal locational alternatives can be derived, but generalizations are very difficult.

3. In the models of spatial structure the focus by contrast is on *internal economies*. These, together with the input prices, transportation costs and the demand functions, determine the optimum output quantities per plant and the market areas. A kind of *external economy* is also important — though its introduction is partly inconsistent with the setup of the model. The question of the most efficient, or optimal use of a piece of land is not considered at all in the models of spatial structure. Thus there is no real choice between alternative uses of land, no choice to be based on economic considerations such as labor and other input costs, interindustry relations etc.

4. Starting with *foreign trade theory* models, some authors have redefined the national or regional units as *individual sites* and thus tried to determine the optimal specialization of production in the individual locations (and thus also justified the typical assumption of foreign trade theory that *intra*-regional transportation costs are zero).

All these are quite different analytical frameworks. To set them a wider perspective, I shall try to indicate all the important factors which in a more comprehensive theory would have to be taken into account. The models discussed above will then emerge as special cases within a more general framework.

Assuming each individual tries to maximize his utility, let us ask the question on which factors this utility depends and how these factors are related to locational decisions. In simple terms, let utility, U, be a function of:

i. Income or profits (and hence possible expenditures), Y,

ii. Leisure, L, and

iii. Other non-monetary advantages, A, where A_p and A_b refer to private and business non-monetary advantages.

Thus:
$$U = U(Y, L, A_p, A_b).$$

The non-monetary business advantages (A_b) depend on such factors as independence as an operator, the degree of power and prestige, and the market share. Since these are not necessarily of any direct or clear-cut locational significance, they shall be ignored in the following. The most important other determinants of U are:

for A_p: 1. physical aspects of the environment;

2. Social aspects of the environment; e.g. proximity to friends (H_F), distance from undesirable social areas (H_U);

for L: 3. Distance to work, either plants (P) or tertiary establishments (T);

4. Distance to shopping centers and other tertiary establishments (T);

5. Distance to cultural and social activities centers;

for Y: 6. Characteristics of the production function: indivisibilities, internal and external economies;

7. Location of natural resources, including climate (R_N);

8. Quantities, kinds, and locations of existing capital equipment and consumer durables (other resources, R_0);

9. Total population and its spatial distribution (households, H);

10. Distances from suppliers of inputs (P_S);

11. Distance from purchasers (who demand the products of unit considered, either producers, P_D, or tertiary establishments, T_C);

12. Distances from competitors (producers, P_C or retailers, T_C); and

13. Distances from *other* producers or sellers (with whom no direct economic relationships exist: producers, P_N, or retailers, T_N).

There is, however, no clear-cut dividing line between the entries under A_P and L; the distances listed under L affect not only the non-monetary factors but also have monetary consequences. Also note that prices are not mentioned here since they are determined within the system by the production functions, and demand functions, and the available resources and their spatial distribution.

What general statements can now be made about the resulting spatial pattern?

i. The more uneven the distribution of the factors given by nature, the more irregular will be the spatial structure of the economy (*ceteris paribus*).

ii. The greater the indivisibilities and the importance of agglomeration and juxtaposition economies, the greater will be the spatial concentration of production.

iii. There is always an incentive to minimize, *ceteris paribus*, the relevant distances under (3), (4), (5), (7), (8), (9), and, in particular, those under (10) and (11), i.e., all the distances over which either inputs or outputs have to be transported.

iv. With regard to the distances under (12) and (13), no generalization is possible. In the absence of all external economies one would *ceteris paribus*, *maximize* them because the other establishments are competitors for labor and land and/or for customers (this holds for the Christaller and Lösch models). However, where *strong* agglomeration or juxtaposition economies might arise (as where customers combine several purchases) there is incentive to *minimize*, within certain limits, these distances (and industrial agglomerations or shopping centers develop).

At this point let us see how in the various branches of traditional location theory the approach has been limited as compared with the general statement presented above.

a. *Agricultural location theory.* For obvious economic reasons which do not have to be elaborated here, the relative weights to be attached to the (H–P) and the (H–R) distances are so great for agriculture that in the optimum these distances are zero: For all practical purposes h (the individual household) and p (the individual production site) and r (the soil resources used by the particular farmer) coincide in space for each individual farmer. As long as external economies are neglected, the essential variable to be determined for a given crop and its producer is the distance (p–T) to the respective purchasing center's traders. (p–T) is established via the interactions with all other producers P_N (producers of other crops at other distances from this center), i.e. via the simultaneous determination of the land rents. With external economies, which lead to the formation of villages, the distances to competitors (albeit on a more or less perfect market) play a role [p–P. (12)] and *some* of them are minimized.

b. In *urban location theory*, we have, quite analogously, the problem of determining h–P or h–T [(3) and (4)]; also h–H_F has to be considered.

c. In traditional *industrial location theory*, the most important distances, which, *ceteris paribus*, are to be minimized, are p–R_N (7) to raw material sites, p–P_S (10) to suppliers, and p–P_D or p–T (11) to the location of demand, where p–H (9), the distances to labor pools, and p–R_O (8), the distances to pools of capital, enter implicitly into the picture via wage and interest rate differentials. The distances p–P_C (12) and p–P_N (13) enter into the extensions and qualifications of the solutions.[14]

---

14. See: Edger M. Hoover, *Location Theory and the Shoe and Leather Industries*, Cambridge, Mass., Harvard University Press, 1937; and Isard, *op. cit.*

d. *Christaller's and Lösch's models.* In these two models of spatial structure, only one distance plays a vital role: $p-P_C$ (12) from any given producer to his closest competitors (this is determined by internal economies and the demand conditions). The distance $p-P_C$ is *maximized* and this *implies*, under the assumptions about the homogeneous plain, that the distances $p-H$ (9) to the consumer households and $p-R$ (7) to the natural resource inputs are minimized. Only *after* $p-P_C$ (12) has been maximized is the distance $p-P_N$ (13) to the producers of other products *minimized*. All other factors are neglected.

We are now ready to state general principles governing all branches of location theory.

a. For all producer's and consumer's households the marginal rates of substitution of all commodities or services bought and used must be, in comparison with a standard good which is also bought, equal to the (marginal) price or cost ratios. For commodities not bought the marginal rate of substitution is greater.

b. The costs of a transformation process must be greater than (for processes not employed), or equal to (for process actually used), the (marginal) *net value added by manufacture*, or *net value added by retailing*, or *net value added by transportation*.

c. For each economic unit, expenditures and receipts have to be adjusted to each other so as to exclude the necessity of *undesirable* capital movements (in the widest sense of the word). This ensures automatically a balance of payments equilibrium for any region, however defined.

d. For municipalities and state and national governments equivalent conditions hold which have to take all external effects and indivisibilities into account.

Difficulties are encountered however, because of the necessity to define in quantitative terms a social welfare function and because of the necessity to levy taxes and to pay subsidies which for each household adjust the private costs of production to the actual social costs.

If opportunity costs are also considered these conditions imply, among other things, that on each market demand is not greater than supply, that no producer can improve his lot by locational shifts or by factor substitution, that there are no excess profits within the system, that prices of alternative suppliers are identical at their market boundary, that the agricultural and urban land uses are optimal.[15]

For any individual firm we may also follow Isard's presentation[16] and explicitly mention three *sets* of factors which determine the result

15. See: Isard, *op. cit.*, ch. 10, for further details.
16. *Ibid*, p. 138.

of the spatial adjustment process: (i) transfer costs, (ii) differences in the cost functions at different locations (other than those due to agglomeration economies) and (iii) agglomeration economies. On the basis of these three sets of cost factors, the optimum has to be chosen by each individual firm—and this is, within the limits mentioned above, *partly* possible within a substitution principle framework.

THE CHOICE OF A SITE: MORE SPECIFIC STATEMENTS

The equilibrium conditions and adjustment factors listed above are of too general a nature to serve as a guide to our inquiry into the spatial structure that will emerge under given conditions. Those equilibrium conditions, even if qualified to take into account indivisibilities and agglomeration economies, would suffice only if all demand functions and production and supply functions (including, in particular, all the functions which are related to agglomeration and other external economies) were numerically known and could be solved within a general equilibrium framework. Since this is not our goal, we shall formulate the relevant adjustment processes and their results in more specific terms. This will allow us to take a more simplified, and also more qualitative, approach to the question of the spatial economic structure. In this way we hope to be able to derive results with more substance than a formal general equilibrium approach. We shall state a number of important principles of spatial orientation and later on shall try to combine them into a single, more comprehensive picture.

1. As a first useful principle, which is derived within the Thünen framework, we have the relationships between the distances from a demand location and input proportions which are optimal at the different points of production. If at the demand location there is more capital available (i.e. the interest rates are lower) than in the supply regions, the production processes of a *given* commodity are both more capital intensive and less land intensive around the demand center than elsewhere. This reflects, among other things, the differences in the intensity of the use of land. By the same token, commodities with high transportation costs, with a high capital input content and a low land input content are, *ceteris paribus*, preferably produced closer to the demand center than other goods, and vice versa. This principle can be applied not only to the agricultural but also to the industrial sector, as we shall do later. The principle just stated, which we will call the *Thünen criterion*, serves to determine factor intensities or differential factor input ratios on the basis of variable commodity price ratios, as determined by the absolute prices

minus the respective transportation costs. This kind of analysis proceeds usually on an aggregative level for individual commodities or for whole industries. Less attention is therefore given to the question of the optimum size of the producing unit and of the related question of internal economies of production. To these questions we now turn.

2. To attack the question of the optimal size of the individual firm in a spatial setting we shall start with the neat presentation by E. M. Hoover of the relationship between internal economies on the one hand and transportation and distribution costs on the other hand.[17] Up to a certain point at least, unit production costs decline with an increasing size of the firm; but this implies a greater geographical concentration of production and with a spatial distribution of demand leads to a rise in the transportation costs for the finished product. The criterion for the optimum size of the firm is that with a rising (declining) concentration of production, the decline (rise) in unit production costs would be more than offset (would not be offset any more) by higher (lower) transportation and distribution costs. In the following we shall refer to this criterion, which actually represents an application of the time-honored substitution principle, as the *Hoover criterion*. It might also be pointed out that a comparison of this kind actually underlies the optimum market areas as established for the individual commodities by Christaller and Lösch. What is important about this principle is the following. If over a significant range of the production function unit costs (exclusive of all transportation costs) decline, and if the demand densities are different as between various geographical parts of the economy, if transportation costs are not negligible, then the optimal concentration of production is a function of the density of demand. In densely populated areas the optimal size of the firm will be greater than in other parts of the economy.

3. We have to investigate the important question of the optimal geographical concentration of different firms in big centers—the question of the importance of localization and urbanization economies. On a limited scale, this problem was first formulated by Weber for a number of individual plants in the context of his *critical isodapanes*: (positive) agglomeration economies have to offset the (negative) effect of greater transportation distances for the individual firms. (This point has also been discussed by Palander.) A more thorough analysis is, again, to be found in Isard's *Location and Space-Economy* (ch. 8): to determine the optimal size of an agglomeration, one has to know the combined effects of such factors as trans-

17. See: Hoover, *op. cit.*, pp. 99–103.

portation economies, labor economies, power economies, education economies, etc. We shall not go into any more details here and instead refer to Isard's analysis, and in the following we shall for brevity's sake subsume the relevant factors which determine the optimal degree of concentration of economic activities under the term *agglomeration criterion*. It might be pointed out that the optimum value obtained depends again on the population density of the whole region and varies directly with it (*ceteris paribus*). Even if the agglomeration economies of *production* become negative at the margin and thus decline absolutely in total, this may still be offset by positive transportation and marketing economies—in particular for all so-called market oriented industries. Another negative factor would be a poor natural resources base, so that raw materials would have to be brought from other regions where raw material requirements are large. We also have to point out that declining agglomeration economies, and even more so *negative* marginal agglomeration economies, make a strong case for government intervention to limit the size of the respective center purely on economic grounds. If marginal social overhead costs are significantly above their own average and taxes are levied on the basis of this *average*, then the tax contribution of expanding firms is much smaller than are their marginal social overhead costs. In the interest of equalizing marginal private and social overhead costs, all firms should be taxed so as to raise their cost levels to their marginal social costs. The application of this principle would limit the expansion of centers with negative agglomeration economies and encourage the growth of centers with social overhead costs whose marginal values are below their respective averages; the latter case would call for subsidies out of the surpluses of other regions. In this case, welfare economies would thus strongly justify interregional transfer payments in this connection.

4. Before proceeding, let us reiterate that all the three criteria for the determination of the factor in input ratios, for the optimal size of the firm and for the optimal size of an agglomeration center are based on, or can be derived from the simple marginal productivity and marginal utility rules and the balance of payments conditions. The way they become effective in a spatial setting depends not only on production functions and the initial distributions and tastes of the population and on the natural resource bases of the various regions of economy, but also upon factor mobility. The equilibrium criterion for population movements has been stated by Lösch quite simply in the following way. Everybody moves until he has reached the location which yields him, not the maximum real income, but the maximum utility from income, leisure, and non-monetary advantages.

In an evolutionary economy this statement would have to be expanded, however, to take account of all expected future incomes (and their utility levels) at all alternative locations. We would compare, for different points, the discounted value all the utility levels reached during future periods at different points and add them up and compare them.[18] In doing this, the costs of moving would also be considered (these can be prohibitive). The above equilibrium statement can also be given more substance, in particular in a more aggregative setting, by considering Ohlin's criterion for population movements and for the locational shift of a given industry, in connection with all the transfer costs.[19] This *Ohlin criterion* implies that transfers of industries and workers make necessary the computation of differential transportation costs on the raw materials used by these industries and on the finished goods they produce but also on the food and food products consumed by workers. This leads to differential food prices as a result of differential production and transportation costs and is one of the reasons for wage differentials, which may thus be interpreted as a kind of transfer cost.[20]

5. The principles and criteria listed above are applicable to both a homogeneous plain and an irregular surface of the earth. It is also clear that, in principle, nothing is changed if road networks develop — either on a homogeneous or an irregular plain. Any system that has developed would be "stretched out" along the traffic routes, as has been shown already by Thünen for agricultural location, by Palander for industrial location, and recently by Alonso for an urban setting.

6. Before we attempt to apply these principles simultaneously to a whole regional structure, consider how the Löschian network would be affected if these factors are taken into account. We need to know (1) what kinds of population movements are induced by the establishment of the production centers; (2) to what extent the growth of the centers is encouraged by real agglomeration economies (not just preferences); (3) how the optimum size of the firms changes as between different regions and cities; (4) how the optimal input coefficients of firms of the same industry vary from one region to the next or even between the center and the fringe of an urban area; (5) how the whole system of markets is influenced by the building of roads; (6) to what extent market areas overlap because of product differentiation and personal preferences of the consumers; and the many other questions which would crop up — not to mention the

18. See: my *Theorie. . . .*, *op. cit.*, pp. 158–161.
19. See: Bertil G. Ohlin, *Interregional and International Trade*, Cambridge, Mass., Harvard University Press, 1933, pp. 212–220.
20. See also: Hoover, *op. cit.*, ch. IV.

additional complications which arise out of irregularities of the plain, out of historical factors, and out of decisions which, from an economic point of view, appear to be not rational. But even if the latter complications are left out of the picture, it is obvious that the original Lösch system has to be modified to such an extent that very little remains of its specific *material content*. Lösch's system was a great achievement in that even on a perfectly homogeneous plain a spatial differentiation and a complicated network of markets and roads could be derived. But as the upshot of our present discussion we are nevertheless forced to state that what remains intact of the system is essentially only the result that even on a homogeneous plain there would be a specialization of production as between different points or regions, and furthermore the derivation that the optimal road system is laid out in angles of 60 degrees, rather than as a rectangular system. The latter result is, of course, the same as that developed by Christaller.

APPLICATIONS TO SIMPLE SPATIAL STRUCTURES

In a comprehensive model of a spatial economic structure, the most important variables to be determined are, apart from the population distribution and the quantities consumed at each location, (i) the input coefficients for each enterprise in each industry (or the various production processes actually used in the optimal solution), (ii) the optimum size of the firms at different location, (iii) the number of firms in each industry at each location or in each region, and (iv) the optimal road network. What makes the determination of the latter two variables particularly difficult is the fact that there is no *simple* economic relationship between the number and the size of the firms at a particular location on the one hand, and the agglomeration economies or diseconomies on the other. The optimum size of an agglomeration center is not necessarily a positive function of the optimum size of the individual firms. In a model of spatial structure, one would have to allow for such factors as imperfections in competition and for indivisibilities, and this would make the solution of a fullfledged general equilibrium system extremely difficult even if all the relevant production functions and the individual and social welfare functions were numerically known. I shall not attempt to set up such a system here but merely sketch a framework in which the working and the adjustment processes of the most important factors can be described in a qualitative way.

Sketch of an Economic System on a Large Plain

The starting point of the analysis is a large plain with unevenly distributed resources but an initially even distribution of the population. To focus on the role of transportation costs, let us assume that the *interregional* mobility of the factors of production is zero while there is perfect mobility of all goods, i.e., the transportation costs on all commodities are zero. The regions are defined in such a way that they are *small* in comparison with the size of the whole plain; let us assume that the number of regions is of the same order of magnitude as the number of industries. Due to the lack of transportation costs, we would have an *n* region economy but nevertheless a *one-point model* with certain restrictions on the possibilities of the combination of factors or production. This would actually be one of the traditional foreign trade models. If the number of regions and the number of commodities were only two, if the internal spatial structure were homogeneous *within* each region and if there were no intermediate goods, the old comparative advantage model could be applied (within narrow limits and under certain additional linearity assumptions however). But given our assumptions, the solution can only be found within a general equilibrium model — either as an expanded Walrasian system or as a nonlinear program. In the programming formulation, each household in each region would maximize its utility subject to (i) its utility functions, (ii) the production functions, which in the case of possible external economies may depend on all the quantities of all commodities produced at all locations, (iii) the inputs available, (iv) the output prices, and (v) the condition that for each household, and hence also for each region, the balance of payments is in equilibrium. This would determine all factors quantities and for all commodities the amounts produced and consumed everywhere and also all input and output prices.

The essential features of the system are: (1) The need for a *balance of payments equilibrium* is stressed from the outset. (2) There is a *maximum amount of competition* (within the limits determined by the production functions) because less efficient firms would not be protected from their more efficient competitors by transportation costs. (3) A very high degree of *interregional specialization* because of *large* internal economies and/or localization economies. (4) Because of the differential factor endowments of the individual regions, the *input coefficients and the optimum size of the firms* of a given industry vary as between regions. (5) *Regions with particularly poor natural resources* specialize in the service trades. (6) The spatial pattern is irregular partly because distances play no role in it; therefore, there are no advantages in choosing sites of production near the center of the region rather than places near the periphery.

Let us now introduce positive transportation costs on commodities, and consider the tertiary and the secondary sectors in turn.

a. For the whole *tertiary sector* it pays now to locate closer to the geographical center of the plain, since in this way the distance to the customers can be reduced. The optimal location does not, of course, have to be the exact geographical center; as a matter of fact, this optimal point could be a considerable distance away from the geographical center in case either the *natural* transportation routes favor particular other points on the plain or if the natural resources are distributed in a very uneven way (but we rule out cases of Australian geography). Since retailers as well as other suppliers of tertiary services minimize the distances from households and from input suppliers as discussed above, the *largest* center for tertiary activities would develop somewhere near the geographical center of the plain. In such a place, transportation costs would be minimized, and therefore the establishments located there would be able to undercut the prices of other units which supply the same services at other locations. Even if no deliberate choice of such a place were made, it would have a much better chance of survival than other places, and hence would grow faster.

We can now generally apply the Hoover criterion to all these activities and obtain a *number* of optimal supply points for all activities for which the distribution costs can be lowered by an amount greater than the rise in production costs if additional locations supply these goods. If one works this out in detail, one can actually derive a kind of a Christaller hierarchy of supply places even within our less restrictive setting. This system of tertiary supply point would be regular on a homogeneous plain but stretched out, due to the declining population density toward the periphery, and it would be even more distorted under our assumptions. It has to be stressed, however, that there is not necessarily—in contrast to Christaller's original system—a clearcut dividing line between the hinterlands of the centers of a given size. We have to allow for personal preferences and, above all, for product differentiation. The normal case in our system would thus be that a center C^1 supplies a certain variant i^1 of the commodity i, while center C^2 supplies variant i^2. Also, if one allows for historical accidents and for differential population densities and for regional differences in demand in subregions, it is possible than in subregion S^1 only centers of size C but not centers of the (smaller) size E supply a certain commodity i, while in S^2 it is also supplied by places of size E. Thus there may not be a unique relationship between types of commodities and the sizes of their supply centers which holds for the whole plain or even for a whole region. For these reasons alone, there might not be strict dividing line between different *types* of centers—as far as the commodities they supply are concerned. Indeed, on theoretical grounds one should expect only gradual changes. Therefore central place investigations in which a high degree of aggregation is employed both as to commodities and as to towns may not shed much light on the question of whether there exists a clearcut dividing line between different types of goods as far as their respective supply centers are concerned.

If there were no interregional factor movements, the tertiary activities could expand in the central regions only at the cost of reducing the primary and secondary sectors. However, if interregional factor movements take place, there would be a *tendency* for all the factors employed in the tertiary sector to *move* towards the places whose locations are optimal for tertiary activities.

b. For the *industrial sector* we now consider the minimization of the sum of the production and the transportation costs. As an analytical framework we need therefore a combination of the comparative advantage-balance of payments approach and an *extended* Weberian-Hooverian approach, or rather an industrial complex analysis type of approach.

For any individual enterprise there is now, *ceteris paribus*, a much greater incentive to move closer to the tertiary activities center C in order to minimize the distances to the respective customers, even if there are no agglomeration economies of any kind. These movements to the Center depend very much on the population movements that take place within the system. With low population mobility, the rise in production costs (wages in particular) may more than offset the possible gains in terms of transportation costs. We assume, however, that labor mobility has increased sufficiently for the movement to the center to be profitable for a number of industries. This incentive to move towards the center is based on the fact that the population density and, even more so (in potential-terminology), the population and the demand *potentials* are greater at the Center than anywhere else. At the same time that industries move closer to the center in order to minimize the effect of transportation costs, other firms can start producing at places farther away from the Center just because they are protected from the competition at the Center by transportation costs. Because of the decline in demand as one moves away from the Center, the optimal size of the firm may also decrease considerably for transportation-sensitive industries, this optimum thus being much greater at the Center than elsewhere, *ceteris paribus*.

What applies to the Center of the whole system also holds for smaller centers, and these tendencies are strengthened by the population movements and by the existence of agglomeration economies. Note that for these movements the marginal conditions as underlying the substitution principle for spatial adjustment do not suffice and that, furthermore, from a welfare point of view, special taxes and subsidies may be called for, as discussed above. The agglomerating tendencies for the secondary and for the tertiary sectors now strengthen each other. Since the centers are favored by agglomeration and transportation economies, they are able to attract not only workers but also capital, and this also has an effect on the optimal factor proportions in the various regions. Capital intensive industries will *ceteris paribus* move to the Center, while the most land-intensive industries can produce most profitably at the periphery – unless low land costs are more than offset by rising transportation costs.

The introduction of a road network into this system can be expected to reinforce the tendencies observed so far, because the roads increase the accessibility of the big centers and thus enhance their competitive position vis-a-vis other parts of the economy.

To gain an overall picture of the space-economy which is likely to develop, one needs only to apply all the principles or criteria discussed above. The result is, for each individual household and for each enterprise, at least a six-way pull. (i) The Center attracts enterprises because of its high demand-potential and because of agglomeration economies; and it repels firms because of high rents and higher wages (partly due to the effects of the *Ohlin criterion*). (ii) The periphery of the entire landscape has the advantage of low rents but also the disadvantage of a low *demand-potential* and hence long transportation distances. Furthermore, we have, at a *given distance* from the Center, (iii) the pull of the agglomeration economies towards areas with great population density and towards lower-order agglomeration economies towards areas with great population density and towards lower-order agglomeration centers on the one hand, and (iv) the pull into areas with both lower land prices and lower wages but also smaller demand on the other hand. Finally, there is (v) the attraction of sites with convenient transportation networks and, last but not least, (vi) the attraction of the raw material sites and of the suppliers of inputs. It can be expected that the forces listed under (iii) and (vi) would pull in exactly the same direction, viz., agglomeration centers are built at points with easy transportation, *and* road networks are laid out between centers that have already developed. To all industries the *Ohlin criterion* would have to be applied, and the significant result is that for most industries in all three sectors of the economy there are *multiple optima* for the size of the firm and for factor proportions. Thus within the limits set by technology, *different processes* describe the optimum for different geographical areas. In elaborating this point, let us look at all three sectors of the economy in turn. Since the mining and quarrying industries depend on (usually) very localized raw materials, we shall exclude them from the primary sector and consider them with the secondary sector instead.

1. *The primary sector—agriculture.* As far as interregional differences of soil fertility are concerned, a kind of extended comparative advantage analysis would show the optimal interregional specialization of agricultural production—within a general equilibrium framework, and with due consideration given transportation costs. Apart from such differences in natural fertility and their effects on our system, two points can be made. (i) There is a *system of Thünen rings* which will develop around the population centers, the intensity of the cultivation of the land rising towards the respective centers. It should be noted that with linear homogeneous production functions the areas around the centers should produce a smaller number of agricultural commodities than areas farther away from the centers— as soon as the (domestic) *demand outside the centers* is also considered. Around the main Center only the most transportation-sensitive crops are raised. But at all other places these are *also* produced for home consumption even if only in small quantities. This holds always unless the internal savings out of specialized production are so great that in spite of the transportation costs and handling charges it is cheaper to buy such goods from high-rent zones than to produce them in small quantities. Thus, as we move away from the Center the *equilibrium input coefficients gradually change for all crops.* (ii) *Within the Thünen rings, there is an agglomeration of agricultural enterprises in villages,* the size of the villages being determined by the external economies which arise when neighbors and tertiary establishments are close by, in comparison with the transportation costs to the fields. As, *ceteris paribus* transportation costs to the fields rise per employee if the intensity of production declines, *the optimum size of the village rises as one moves towards the Center.* In areas with *extensive* cultivation the tendency towards *separated* farm units increases, *ceteris paribus.* Thus even on a homogeneous plain there would be a systematic differentiation of village sizes, even if all the other sectors of the economy were neglected. (iii) *The final result is a hexagonal layout of the villages* (in which each hexagon is however distorted towards the periphery because of the systematic variation in the intensity of cultivation) *and a hierarchy in the size of the villages.* Summarizing we can describe the system as a kind of combination of Thünen and Christaller systems—a hierarchy of villages within a ring formation for the commodities. This would hold for an agricultural sector supplying just one Center of the whole system. With a system of

towns, we have *hierarchies of agricultural villages within systems of interrelated Thünen rings*.

2. *The tertiary sector.* (i) As shown above, the tertiary sector is dependent on the secondary sector for its spatial orientation; though even quite by itself it would develop a hierarchy of the Christaller type. Actually there is a strong interrelationship between the secondary and the tertiary sectors. The spatial distribution of the industrial enterprises determines, together with the natural traffic routes and the population distribution, the size of the (main) Center and of all the smaller centers of various sizes, but the industrial centers themselves and the population distribution are also heavily dependent on "natural" sites of distribution and on "natural" traffic routes. But *quite apart from the development of the secondary sector, a system of market nets and a hierarchy of tertiary centers would come into existence on a homogeneous plain.* Even on a homogeneous plain, there would be a strong effect of the tertiary on the locations within the secondary sector — most strongly for market-oriented industries. (ii) For the whole tertiary sector, quite significant variations in the optimal factor proportions can be expected to arise in the various regions and even in the different parts of a city — as a result of differential land prices and differences in demand. Thus we have again a *combination of a hierarchic structure and a Thünen structure for the factor intensities and firm sizes* — the hierarchic aspect being much stronger in this case than for the agricultural sector.

3. *The secondary sector.* The dependence of the secondary sector on raw materials and communications conditions has already been stressed sufficiently. What we have to discuss here is only the final result if road networks and the balance of payments mechanism are considered. It can be shown that if one takes these factors into account, as well as price and wage differentials, a system tends to evolve which is much more regular as far as the city sizes and its over-all shape are concerned than the irregular distribution of resources might indicate. The balance of payments mechanism would guarantee that there are no *holes* in the network of centers of a given size: such holes in the network of economic activities would be filled via the balance of payments adjustment process by advantageous production conditions and by favorable demand conditions (at least as long as the population densities have not become very different as between regions). Distances from competing supply centers are greater than in other regions; therefore it pays for additional producers to move into the region. This would also seem to be a reason why Christaller was able to observe a fairly regular system of cities in Southern Germany even though his assumptions for the *individual* goods *and* for the surface of the earth, which underlie Christaller's general system,

certainly did not correspond to reality. This is the *one result* which one can derive for our system; that the *sum of the irregular individual market nets may produce a much more regular spatial layout for the whole system*. The *second characteristic* of the system is a *systematic overall variation in the optimal input coefficients and in the commodities produced at the various centers*. The Main Center area uses processes with high agglomeration economies and (relatively) low transportation costs for the products it exports. It produces goods with very high transportation costs for domestic consumption; and it imports both land intensive goods whose agglomeration economies are small and goods whose production sites are determined by raw material sites. But there is also an *interurban specialization and exchange of goods whose specific locations are determined by more or less arbitrary decisions or accidental events*, and such locations are strengthened if agglomeration economies arise. Finally, toward the periphery, agglomeration economies become smaller; for these regions, the export commodities are those whose *production processes* are *ceteris paribus*, much more land intensive and much less capital intensive and much less subject to agglomeration influences than processes used close to the Center.

All these derivations are of a quite general nature and need to be qualified in many ways. Nevertheless the conclusion emerges that as one moves away from a center the input coefficients change in qualitatively the same way as they do in a purely agricultural system which supplies a center. Thus we have again, as long as transportation costs are significant, *a type of a ring formation with a systematic variation in the input coefficients, within a kind of a Christaller hierarchy*. Or we may describe the results as a *system of rings within a system of city hierarchies*, with a high degree of specialization of the cities.

Some Remarks About an Urban Structure

With regard to the structure of an urban region, if all economic activities were taking place at the center of the city and if they would not take any space, then the *Thünen type* of analysis would indeed apply to the *residential sector*. Nothing additional would have to be considered as long as all capital goods are neglected.

Let us first *ignore all external economies* and examine what happens under the simplifying assumption that the surface of the earth is perfectly homogeneous. In this case, for the whole *tertiary sector* a whole *Lösch system* with hexagonal market areas would be the optimal spatial distribution. This Lösch system would be a distorted one however, because the individual lots would be greater at the outskirts of the urban region than close to the Center. Thus demand would not be distributed evenly, and this would have an effect on the optimal sales quantities and hence the optimal sales areas; these would vary somewhat as between the Center and parts of the city farther away. One further modification would be necessary. Since with all external economies ruled out, the individual market nets would be entirely independent of each other, and hence the incentive to locate at the exact center would not exist. As a matter of fact, the market nets would be laid out in such a way that the sites for different ones would *not* coincide, the reason being that all activity takes space, which it does not in the Lösch model. Also, adjustments would have to be made to allow for the effect of the road systems. For the *secondary sector* the optimizing process would be the same in the urban region as on the *entire plain* — except for those firms which buy raw material from out of town, so that distances and freight costs would be more or less the same for all parts of the city. For these, latter, a modified Löschian spatial layout would evolve, just as for the tertiary sector. For *residential uses of land*, a Thünen system of land rents would develop because there would be more shops near the center than everywhere else, and because everybody tries to minimize the distances from *all* stores *and* from his workplace. This would also have to be modified somewhat because at a given distance from the Center rents would be higher near stores and factories than in purely residential neighborhoods with no stores whatsoever.

As soon as *external economies are introduced* many of the features discussed so far change substantially. (i) These changes would affect most visibly the services sector of this urban economy. The outcome for the tertiary sector would be (a) a Central Business District which stretches out along the roads, (b) smaller (neighborhood) shopping centers spread out over the entire region, and (c) large shopping centers at the outskirts, the latter taking advantage of the lower land rents. Again, there would be a hierarchy of centers with systematic variations in the optimal size of the establishments and the optimal input coefficients. (ii) For the optimal locations in the secondary sector, harbor facilities, road connections and railway nets would play an important role. (iii) The residential sector, à la Alonso, would show significant variations in lot sizes and in the Thünen ring formations that would develop. A ring theory of urban residential location is, furthermore, supported by the existence of consumer capital goods in the form of houses. The lot size structure as it has developed historically is therefore in most cases very difficult to change. Even if there were no other economic reasons, this factor alone would have the effect that the largest lots would be found at the outskirts as demand for land rises and transportation costs decline. The introduction of agglomeration economies would have another important effect. People of a similar status would tend to reside in the same neighborhood or the same community within the urban region, and thus there would be a differentiation as between different geographical sectors of the city region. The larger the city, the greater would be the effect of this kind of agglomeration economies, and it is quite significant that the *sector theory of urban structure* is most strongly supported by the findings for big cities (with a minimum population of 500,000). Thus theoretical considerations easily lead to the result that neither the sector theory nor the ring theory of urban location contains the whole truth, but that the two have to be combined.

In conclusion, we have attempted to sketch how various economic factors are interrelated and yield a spatial structure of an economy. The framework of analysis that has been presented is more general than existing location theories, and includes each of these as special cases. . . .

INDEX

Index